The Prime of Life

The Prime of Life 🐦

A HISTORY OF MODERN ADULTHOOD

Steven Mintz

The Belknap Press of Harvard University Press

CAMBRIDGE, MASSACHUSETTS, AND LONDON, ENGLAND

· 2015

Printed in the United States of America

First printing

Library of Congress Cataloging-in-Publication Data

Mintz, Steven, 1953–
   The prime of life : a history of modern adulthood / Steven Mintz.
     pages cm
   Includes bibliographical references and index.
   ISBN 978-0-674-04767-9 (cloth : alkaline paper)
    1. Adulthood—United States—History.   2. Adulthood—Social aspects—
United States—History.   3. Life change events—United States—
History.   4. Life cycle, Human—Social aspects—United States—
History.   5. United States—Social conditions.   I. Title.

HQ799.95.M56 2015
305.240973—dc23   2014040715

Book design by Dean Bornstein

For Maria Elena Soliño,

who challenges me every day to open up and grow

Contents

It is perfectly true, as the philosophers say, that life must be understood backwards. But they forget the other proposition, that it must be lived forwards.

—Søren Kierkegaard

Preface

Each generation must write a history that speaks to the issues of its time. We live at a moment when the human life course is undergoing profound transformations. A definition of childhood as a time of innocence and wonder no longer conforms to a social reality in which kids are far more knowing, electronically connected, and enmeshed in consumer culture than their predecessors. Similarly, adolescence is undergoing far-reaching transformations as the age of sexual initiation declines, rigid gender norms break down, and close cross-sex friendships grow more common. Meanwhile, a new life stage of prolonged but active retirement has recently emerged.

The most far-reaching changes have occurred in adulthood. In recent years, the transition to adulthood has grown more protracted and problematic as acquisition of the traditional markers of adult identity—marriage, childbirth, and entry into a full-time career—are delayed into the late twenties or early thirties. Moreover, growing numbers of those at midlife refuse to act their age. Instead, they wear youthful fashions, eschew activities previously associated with middle age, and actively resist the aging process. At the same time, certain expectations—of an unbroken marriage, a steady career, and a stable group of friends living in geographic proximity—have crumpled. In the age of Future Shock, the settledness that many assumed characterized the mature years has broken down. Life's changes occur whether aging bones and ossifying minds are ready or not.

This book places the far-reaching changes taking place in contemporary adulthood into historical perspective. It corrects a series of misconceptions, such as the myth that the transition to adulthood was more seamless and smoother in the past, as well as the notion that the adult life course was more stable and predictable than it has become. Despite the sense that the transition to adulthood has grown longer and riskier, coming of age has never been easy. Nor has there ever been a time when a majority of Americans experienced what we might consider the model life script: a stable marriage and a long-term career working for a single employer.

Adulthood is the one stage of life that lacks a history. We know a great deal about childhood, adolescence, and old age in the past, but adulthood remains a historical black hole. It is time to fill this void by tracing the emergence of a "traditional" adulthood, which took shape in the nineteenth century and reached its culmination in the 1950s, its breakdown in the early 1960s, and its gradual replacement by more diverse and individualistic conceptions of adulthood.

In addition to tracing the changing contours of a life stage often viewed as fit only for self-help books or melodramas involving the domestic travails of the suburban middle class, this book has two broader goals. One is to demonstrate the relevance of history to the behavioral sciences of psychology and sociology in characterizing the life stages. History offers a dynamic, diachronic perspective that underscores the importance of social and cultural contexts to the adult life span. Development across the life course is shaped less by psychology and supposedly universal "tasks" or "passages" as conceived by Freud and his followers than by the distinctive cultural, social, and historical circumstances of any particular era.

The other goal is more audacious: It is to draw upon history to better understand how earlier generations defined adulthood and sought to achieve successful, satisfying adult lives, and then to explore how historical circumstances limited or expanded the opportunities to achieve a meaningful and fulfilling adulthood. At a time when older conceptions of the good life have been thrown into disarray, historical experiences might broaden our sense of the range of adulthood's possibilities then and now.

For all of their wonders and pleasures, childhood and adolescence are life's preparatory stages, which lay the groundwork for the more substantial roles and responsibilities of adulthood. As life's culmination and centerpiece, adulthood is consequential in ways that childhood and adolescence are not. The choices adults make and their responses to the experiences that they undergo constitute the very essence of a person's identity. Adulthood is the time of life when individuals achieve emotional and intellectual maturity and support themselves and others.

Once shaped by clearly delineated social roles and formal relationships, adulthood today lacks an obvious or widely shared definition. For most contemporary adults, it is characterized by a job and money-earning capability, childrearing, and, curiously, autonomy, including the freedom to enter or leave relationships as well as jobs and to redirect one's life trajectory. As we shall see, many of the stresses of contemporary adulthood grow out of the lack of a clear consensus in the definition of adulthood today. It is much harder to be an adult who determines her or his own path than to follow a culturally prescribed life course.

There are several overarching themes that emerge throughout this exploration of adulthood. A major one involves adulthood's shifting meaning. The word itself is of recent vintage, dating only to the 1860s and 1870s. Prior to the late nineteenth century, the stage of life we call "adulthood" represented a series of formal roles, relationships, and responsibilities. But beginning in the late nineteenth century, the term arose to denote a state of being and state of mind. Only after World War II, did a single definition of adulthood, involving maturity, settling down, and adherence to proscribed gender roles, become dominant. Adulthood represented a plateau, and the words used to describe this life stage reflected that view: "serious," "stolid," and "settled down." It is this notion that is now undergoing far-reaching challenges and radical redefinition.

Another key theme involves the devaluation of adulthood. Today, no one says that life begins at forty, at least not without irony. Adulthood, once regarded as life's pinnacle, has come to be seen by many as a time of stress, remorse, routine, stagnation, and dissatisfaction. Adults, we are repeatedly told, lead anxious lives of quiet desperation. The classic post–World War II novels of adulthood by Saul Bellow, Mary McCarthy, Philip Roth, and John Updike, among others, are tales of shattered dreams, unfulfilled ambitions, broken marriages, workplace alienation, and family estrangement. Where once bildungsromane, or novels of initiation and coming of age, equated adulthood with liberation from arbitrary paternal authority and encrusted custom, recent novels of adulthood tend to view this life stage in terms of loss: lost health, lost looks, and lost liberties. No longer do the young long to grow up. Instead, the goal is simply to grow.

Adulthood's diversity is yet another major theme, as adult status is shaped by the irreducible facts of class, ethnicity, gender, sexual identity, race, and historical era. African Americans, Asian Americans, Latinos and Latinas, gays and lesbians, among other groups, illustrate the spectrum of adult experience in the United States and the forces impinging on adult lives. This book, however, attaches a special significance to social and economic class as a key divider in adult lives—reflecting the contention that many patterns of behavior attributed to race and ethnicity in fact arise from socioeconomic class. It also pays attention to gender, and especially to young women, as the primary driver of attitudinal and behavioral change, and the principal force behind fundamental transformations in definitions of love, friendship, marriage, childrearing, and work.

Another overarching theme involves the changing nature of the pressures of adulthood. Although adulthood has always been challenging, most of the stresses in the past were imposed from outside the individual. Today, however, while many stressors such as illness, accident, or job loss still lie outside an individual's control, more pressures and anxieties are self-inflicted and less easy to remedy.

An additional defining feature of the contemporary life course is its segmented, episodic character. Contemporary adulthood involves a great deal of spatial movement, job shifts, and dislocation. Contributing to the fractured nature of adult life histories are high rates of physical mobility, the decline of close family ties and of enduring friendships based on geographic proximity, and a highly fluid economy in which persistence with a single employer is rare. Today's young Americans with two or more years of college can expect to change jobs eleven times over the next forty years and to alter their skill set three times. Discontinuity has become a defining characteristic of contemporary adult life. Rather than following a well-trodden life course, today's adults must splice together a series of episodes that do not necessarily add up to the kind of coherent sequence signified by the word "career." Whereas an earlier culture generally demanded stoicism, acceptance, and acquiescence, today's fragmented society requires individuals to be flexible, adaptable, and resilient, to be prepared to move on, and to pursue opportunities as they present themselves.

Sharp discontinuities in adult experience were widely experienced in the past, but with a crucial difference. It was possible to view these episodes as part of a typical and shared life trajectory. In recent years, the script of adulthood has lost this sense of conceptual unity. Instead, in an ever more individualistic culture, in which marriage and childrearing occupy a diminishing place in adult lives, adults themselves must give their life trajectory meaning and coherence.

During the early modern era, a profound shift took place in how people came to understand life's meaning. An older aristocratic ideal had attributed meaning to honor and martial valor, and a traditional religious ideal had emphasized faith and transcendence. These gradually gave way to an emerging bourgeois ideal, which found increasing meaning in the private realm of love, marriage, childrearing, and work. Consequently, this history is organized around those aspects of adulthood. Coming of age, achieving economic independence, establishing enduring intimate relationships, raising the next generation, finding rewarding work, and coping with loss — these challenges of adulthood are timeless and universal. But how individuals address these challenges varies widely across cultures and historical eras.

Today, the roles, values, and expectations that defined a middle-class adulthood for more than a century have eroded. Many lament their passing, decrying the decline of lifelong commitment and responsibility to one person and to one job. Some worry that our present hyper-individualism is incompatible with long-term social connections or obligations beyond the self. But nostalgia for a vanishing world does little good. We can no more hold back the rush of social and cultural change than King Canute could command the tides to recede. Rather, we need to understand the underlying reasons for shifting circumstances, expectations, and demands on the adult in contemporary society. We must make the best of an imperfect world that will never fully conform to our wishes. As a Johnny Cash song puts it, "(I Don't Like It but) I Guess Things Happen That Way." What constitutes maturity is a willingness to confront our realities with candor and determination, make the best of the cards fate has dealt, and fulfill the obligations we have acquired in a responsible manner. This book seeks to positively embrace adulthood, a life stage that isn't for quitters.

The Prime of Life is the third book I have written charting the history of private life. *Domestic Revolutions* was the first comprehensive history of the American family since the social scientist Arthur W. Calhoun published his *Social History of the American Family* in 1917. Underscoring ethnic, class, and temporal diversity in family life, it identified a series of disjunctive shifts in family structure and composition, roles and functions, and emotional and power dynamics over the past three and one-half centuries. *Huck's Raft* followed and was the first inclusive history of American childhood. It placed children at the center of the events that shaped the American past. Colonization, the American Revolution, slavery, the Civil War, westward migration, the Industrial Revolution, foreign immigration, the Great Depression, two world wars, and the civil rights movement take on fresh meaning when viewed through the voices and experiences of children. Young people can be seen as a cultural avant-garde that has played a pivotal role in the evolution of behavior patterns, values, and sensibilities. Following *The Prime of Life*, I hope to complete a fourth volume, which will examine the transition to old age, the experience of retirement, confrontations with illness and mortality, and the shifting ways that the elderly have dealt with growing dependence.

The earlier books had deep personal roots. *Domestic Revolutions* was written at a time when I was striving to create my own family in a period of upheaval in gender roles and in definitions of what constituted a family. *Huck's Raft*, in turn, was written during a most wrenching period in the life of a parent, when my children were leaving the nest and I was reduced to the role of spectator and cheerleader. This book on adulthood, too, has intensely personal motivations. I wanted to provide historical perspective upon certain unsettling realities of contemporary adult life—the prevalence of divorce, the fragility of adult friendships, the psychopathologies of the workplace, and the difficulties that a culture of control has in dealing with loss.

In the middle of my life's journey, I found myself in a dark wood. That experience taught me a great deal about the capriciousness, unpredictability, and unknowability of the human heart, but it also revealed the consolations of love and friendship. It was in that dark wood that I learned a most significant lesson: that true adulthood comes not with physical maturity, economic independence, marriage, childbirth, entry into a career, or having one's own home, but only from coping with life's vicissitudes and being strengthened by them.

Little did I imagine when I entered that shadowy forest that the succeeding years would bring so many radical changes to my life. I owe a lasting debt to those who helped me to find my way. Alongside Claude Steele, Paula S. Fass, and my blood brother Bengt Sandin, I had the chance to spend a year at the Center for Advanced Study in the Behavioral Sciences, where one can write in the spaces of those who came before: Erik Erikson, Eugene Genovese, Thomas Kuhn, and my mentor David Brion Davis. To Alan Brinkley, Eric Foner, Alice Kessler-Harris, and especially Kenneth Jackson, I owe particular thanks for making the Columbia University History Department an ever-welcoming home. I will always be grateful to Jan Allen, whose example I have tried to emulate as I entered the world of academic administration, and to Margaret Crocco, the ideal collaborator in our joint efforts to improve History and Social Studies education in New York City. I also treasure my Columbia partners in various crimes, Andrew Delbanco, David Helfand, Thomas James, and, above all, Janet Metcalfe. New York would not have been nearly as vibrant without Charles Sims, Richard Winkler, and Robert Moulthrop. I lack the words to adequately thank my fellow traveler in the field of family history, Stephanie Coontz. Erica Goode, friend and confidante, knew my future in ways I never anticipated. Francisco

Cigarroa and Pedro Reyes gave me an extraordinary opportunity to help shape the future of higher education, and in Marni Baker Stein, a true visionary, I had the ideal comrade-in-arms in addressing the issues of access, affordability, and student success. Thanks to Nancy Rosin for sharing her images from her extraordinary collection of handcrafted valentines and friendship albums. Joyce Seltzer, editor extraordinaire, has a magical ability to transform dross into something richer, higher, and more profound. To my mother, father, and sisters, I owe an enduring debt for their unbending support and uninterrupted love.

If we are fortunate, as we grow older, we continue to grow intellectually, emotionally, and socially, and for that I thank Maria Elena Soliño, who has shown me what it truly means to be an adult. Her willingness to put up with my missteps is something I can never adequately repay. To Maria Elena and to our sons, the joys of our life, Carlos, Felipe, Sean, and Seth, I thank you profusely for accompanying me on my convoluted, sometimes painful, but ultimately rewarding journey through adulthood.

The Prime of Life

Prologue: The Voyage of Life

In a series of allegorical paintings completed between 1839 and 1842 and entitled *The Voyage of Life,* Thomas Cole, the founder of the Hudson River School of landscape painting, depicted four stages in the human life course: childhood, youth, adulthood, and old age. The first canvas introduced the paintings' theme: that life is a journey that can be divided into distinct stages, each with its own distinctive characteristics. This canvas shows an infant in a boat sailing through a rock-strewn landscape. A huge stony crag towers above the small boat, but the child is secure, protected by a guardian angel. The second painting, *Youth,* depicts the boat sailing through a lush, green landscape, reflecting youth's possibilities. But the painting also shows menacing rocks and dangerous currents lurking ahead, which the youth fails to anticipate.[1]

The series' third painting, *Manhood,* portrays this stage of life as a time of trials and testing. "Trouble," Cole wrote, is its main characteristic. "In childhood, there is no cankering care: in youth, no despairing thought. It is only when experience has taught us the realities of the world, that we lift from our eyes the golden veil of early life; that we feel deep and abiding sorrow." Cole illustrated this theme with a series of ominous images. A frightened figure must navigate his way past frothing, turbulent waters and dangerous shoals in a small, rudderless boat. As torrential rains fall on gnarled, weather-beaten trees, a host of demons, who represent both temptations to sin and mortal threats, look downward.[2]

In the final canvas, *Old Age,* the water has calmed, and the boat is headed toward the open sea. The guardian angel points the figure in the boat, who is now old and gray-haired, toward heaven. "The chains of

· I

P.I. Thomas Cole, *The Voyage of Life: Manhood*, 1842.

corporeal existence are falling away," Cole explained; "and already the mind has glimpses of Immortal Life."[3]

In this series of paintings, Cole gave powerful visual expression to a centuries' long view: that people's lives pass through a series of clearly delineated stages, each with its own well-defined qualities. This notion, however, is profoundly misleading. Rather than being a sequence of fixed stages, human development is an ongoing process, one that is shaped by highly contingent historical and cultural circumstances. It is remarkable how slowly this alternate view, which emphasizes context and maturation across the life span, has arisen. It was only in the eighteenth century that human development began to be understood in terms of a process of maturation and only in the second half of the twentieth century that the significance of socioeconomic forces in shaping life trajectories and schedules became widely recognized.

For centuries, the human life course has been represented through metaphors: as a circle, a cycle, a pilgrimage, a journey, a mission, a game, or, more recently as a sequence of psychosocial stages or tasks, or a series of passages or critical junctures and transitions. The notion that human development passes through a succession of stages is rooted in antiquity. Classical Greek and Roman writers identified three to seven distinct "ages of man," proceeding from conception to death. The Greek poet Hesiod, for example, advanced a five-fold division of the ages of man into the golden, silver, bronze, heroic, and iron age, which he modeled on his stages of human history.[4]

During the medieval period, artists, writers, physicians, astronomers, mathematicians, and theologians divided the stages of human life into three-, four-, five-, six-, seven-, and twelve-part schemata. Several paradigms predominated. There was a biological model, emphasizing growth, stasis, and decline, and a medical one, based on the four humors. Among the most enduring and influential models was one constructed by the physician Constantine Africanus, who divided the life course into *pueritia* (childhood), *iuventus* (youth), *senectus* (of age) and *senium* (old age). During the Renaissance, a philosophical or astrological model divided the life course into seven ages, as in Shakespeare's *As You Like It*, for example, where these ages begin with "puking" infancy and end with "second childishness and mere oblivion, sans teeth, sans eyes, sans taste, sans everything." Other models drew analogies between the life course and the Trinity or the three Magi; the four elements and their four qualities of heat, moisture, cold, and dryness; the four directions; the four seasons; the six days of creation; the seven days of the week; the seven planets; and the seven canonical hours of the day.[5]

In each of these models, there is an assumption that the human life course is a microcosm of a larger design. In classical antiquity, the human life course reflected the natural order and the ages of the world. During the Middle Ages, the focus shifted to a variant on some divine scheme of a path to salvation. Such models conveyed powerful messages about the transience and vicissitudes of life. Curiously, however, many contemporary age sanctions—driving at sixteen, voting at eighteen, or drinking at twenty-one—have their roots planted partly in these earlier ideas.[6]

Certain conventions dominated artistic representations of the ages of man. Artists typically depicted a boy playing with a top; a youth clad in a doublet, with a falcon on his wrist; a man in the prime of life wearing armor and bearing a sword. Infants crawl, the young walk and run, and the old hobble. Childhood was frequently associated with moisture and warmth, youth with warmth, maturity with dryness and cold, old age with cold and moisture. Key artistic metaphors included steps on a stairway, the growth and withering of a tree, or a wheel. Artists of the Renaissance were especially likely to depict the ages of woman, using the same four, six, and seven stage schemes represented in the ages of man. In these Renaissance schema, adulthood was understood in opposition to other life stages. The seriousness of adulthood was contrasted with the levity and naiveté of childhood and the unsettled emotions of youth.[7]

The division of the life course into discrete ages, phases, or stages makes it clear that our ancestors did indeed recognize separate periods in the life course, each with its own distinctive traits and characteristics. Infancy and old age were associated with physical weakness, childhood with foolishness, and adolescence with rashness. The highest stage, *gravitas* or *inventus* or *senior* (in Latin) or *presbyter* (in Greek), was roughly synonymous with the modern category of adulthood. It was often presented as the Aristotelian golden mean. Today, when middle age is often associated in popular culture with stasis, physical, sexual, and mental compromise, and the loss of the joys and freedom of youth, it is striking to discover that our forebears viewed this stage as the "perfect age," as, in Aristotle's words, the "acme."[8]

The metaphors that artists and authors have used for the life course have reflected the preoccupations of particular historical eras. In the Middle Ages, the movement through life was likened to a pilgrimage or the wheel of fortune, and these images offered didactic reflections upon the vanity, brevity, and vicissitudes of worldly life. The Renaissance and the Age of Discovery associated the life course with a voyage or journey. During the eighteenth century, the life course was commonly presented as a ladder, reflecting the Enlightenment's preoccupation with progress. The nineteenth century saw the appearance of a new metaphor, life as a game. Indeed, one of the first board games created was called "The Checkered Game of Life," which was first released by Milton Bradley, the pioneering game maker, in 1860. Darwinian evolution gave rise to the notion of life divided into a series of sequential stages arrayed in an evolutionary or devolutionary sequence. After World War II, the life course was commonly viewed as a series of developmental tasks, resembling the supposed stages of economic growth advanced by the American economist Walt W. Rostow. Subsequently, Erik Erikson's famous eight-stage model of psychosocial development mapped a trajectory from the oral-sensory stage, in which an infant's interaction with parents leads to trust or mistrust, to late adulthood, in which the elderly reflect upon their lives and feel contentment and integrity or disappointment and despair. Today's highly individualistic, therapeutic culture tends to view the life course as chapters in a book that we ourselves author.[9]

It is noteworthy that passage through the life stages, whether treated as cyclical or linear, progressive or retrogressive, was regarded as discontinuous. To be sure, written accounts, from Augustine's *Confessions* onward, often treated the voyage of life as a story of redemption, a passage to salvation, or, beginning in the late eighteenth century, as a tale of emancipation from entrenched custom, outmoded tradition, and prescribed status. But this journey was not considered a product of a gradual and continuous process of maturation, a word that did not enter the English language until the seventeenth century and was not widely adopted until the late nineteenth. In addition, the ages of man metaphor focused primarily on shifts in social status, rather than on physiological changes like puberty, on psychological transformations in emotions or cognition, on mental or emotional growth, or on the notion of a life course—the socially and culturally defined events, roles, and transitions that constitute the trajectory of a person's life.

Today, social scientists use the term "life cycle" to refer to the division of individual lives into a series of sequential stages. Each stage is defined in terms of three distinct conceptual components: biological, psychological, and social. The contemporary notion of adolescence, for example, consists of a biological component involving pubertal physical changes, rapid physiological growth, and sexual maturation; a psychological component involving drastic mood swings, inner turmoil, generational conflict, and a quest for identity; and a social component, which involves the shifting social experience, institutional treatment, and cultural definition of adolescence.

Each conceptual component of a particular life stage is affected by a changing historical and cultural context. This is true even in the case of biology. The age of first menstruation and the age at which the young achieve full physical stature have declined since 1850. The age of menarche appears to have fallen from approximately fifteen or sixteen in 1850 to between twelve and thirteen toward the end of the twentieth century, while the age of puberty for boys seems to have declined from around sixteen to thirteen or fourteen. Similarly, the age at which young men achieve full growth appears to have fallen from about twenty-five in the early nineteenth century to around twenty in the late twentieth century.[10]

At the same time, the way that the life stages are conceived has undergone profound shifts over the course of American history. Seventeenth-century colonists identified four distinct stages of life: childhood, youth, middle age, and old age. These categories were vaguely defined and not rigidly linked to a specific age range. Over time, the number of stages expanded, and their definition grew more nuanced and more completely organized institutionally, while the transition between stages became more abrupt and disjunctive, such as when an adolescent graduates from high school and enters early adulthood.

A variety of factors contributed to a more precise formulation of the life stages, including scientific and medical discoveries that identified childhood, adolescence, and old age as biologically and psychologically distinct phases of life, with their own characteristics, as well as social and institutional developments such as the emergence of age-graded schools, enactment of laws prohibiting child labor, and adoption of old age pensions, which contributed to the segregation of age groups from one another.[11]

P.2. *The Life and age of woman, stages of woman's life from the cradle to the grave.*

P.3. *The Life and age of man, stages of man's life from the cradle to the grave.*

The complex process by which a particular life stage was culturally and institutionally constructed can be seen in the eighteenth- and nineteenth-century "discovery of childhood." To speak of the "discovery of childhood" is not, of course, to imply that childhood was unknown to earlier Americans; they defined it, however, quite differently than later Americans did. Seventeenth-century New Englanders, for example, did not isolate children from the adult world. Nor did these early colonists establish special institutions for young children or set aside special rooms in their homes for them, consider that children had a unique psychology or see early childhood as a critical period in which an individual's personality is shaped. Moreover, the colonists did not dress children in distinctive clothing or represent them in art as other than little adults.[12]

Beginning in the eighteenth century, a new view of children gradually appeared. During a bitter mid-eighteenth-century theological debate over the issue of infant depravity, which deeply divided New England churches, a new conception of childhood began to be articulated, which viewed children not as little adults but as special creatures requiring attention, love, and time to mature. Religious liberals rejected older notions of original sin in infants and upheld a new view of babies as malleable creatures who embodied virtue, innocence, wholeness, and purity at birth. The new focus on, and respect for, the child could be seen in the profusion of books and toys created specifically for the delight of children; in the supplanting of the stiffly posed portraits of children in the seventeenth and early eighteenth century by more romantic depictions of childhood playfulness and innocence; and in the appearance of furniture specifically designed for children, painted in pastel colors, and decorated with animals or figures from nursery rhymes.

Early nineteenth-century reformers and educators invoked the new images of childhood in the creation of special age-segregated environments such as orphanages, Sunday schools, public schools, and reform schools, where youthful innocence could be protected and nurtured. By the second half of the nineteenth century, a growing sensitivity to children's unique needs and problems led physicians to establish a new branch of medicine, pediatrics, specifically devoted to infant and childhood diseases. At this time, "child savers" were inspired to establish the first organizations in American history to protect children from neglect and abuse, while journalists launched the first specialized children's magazines.

The discovery of adolescence provides another revealing example of how life stages are constructed. The term, derived from the Latin *adolescere*, meaning to grow up, entered popular discourse in the late nineteenth century to denote the distinct age range that extended from puberty to the end of the teen years. In contrast to the earlier concept of youth, which referred to a much wider age span (usually between seven and thirty years of age), adolescence carried much more clearly defined characteristics and was separated much more distinctly from adult society. G. Stanley Hall, who received the first Ph.D. in psychology in the United States, helped to formulate and popularize the modern conception of adolescence as a period of "storm and stress" rooted in the physiological changes associated with puberty. Hall and numerous popularizers disseminated a conception of adolescence as a critical stage of life during which young people form their personal identity. Among the factors that contributed to a recognition of adolescents as a clearly defined age group were the systematization, bureaucratization, and prolongation of education; the classification of students by age; the increasing specialization of occupations, which undermined apprenticeship systems; and growing public concern over juvenile delinquency and child labor.

Adolescence as a distinct age group, with unique needs and problems, was institutionalized in the late nineteenth and early twentieth centuries. Educators, social workers, and other advocates of the young, convinced that adolescents needed time to develop the intellectual and emotional capacities to face the challenges of adult life, supported restrictions on child labor and compulsory education laws, raised the school leaving age, expanded the number of high schools, and created numerous adult-sponsored youth organizations, such as the Boy Scouts and the Girl Scouts. The separation of adolescence from adulthood was embodied in the establishment of a separate juvenile court system and the emergence of a distinct youth market for leisure, evident in the rapid growth of dance halls and young men's clubs.

During the late nineteenth century, old age, like adolescence, began to be perceived in a new way—as a clearly delineated stage of life when the individual is alienated from the rest of society. In colonial America, old age generally commanded authority and respect, but by the end of the nineteenth century, the status attached to age had declined, and old age was increasingly associated with dependency, physical disability, mental debility, and a host of character problems including depression, bitterness, hypochondria, and an inability to absorb new ideas. A number of factors contributed to this more negative perception of old age, including the mounting economic dependency of the elderly in an increasingly urban and industrial society; the increasing incidence of chronic degenerative conditions among the elderly as medical advances reduced the number of deaths caused by infections and epidemic diseases and extended life expectancy; and a cult of youth, which regarded the elderly as inflexible, unadaptable, and out of step with the times, and as inefficient and unproductive workers.[13]

Increasingly, social workers, government policymakers, and businessmen regarded old age as a social problem. Old age homes appeared at the end of the nineteenth century. The first public commission on aging was established in Massachusetts in 1909; the first federal old age pension bill was also introduced in 1909; the first survey of the economic conditions of the elderly was conducted in Massachusetts in 1910; and the first noncontributory old age pension system was enacted in Arizona in 1914. Retirement was institutionalized during the early and mid-twentieth century with the introduction of company pension plans, the enactment of mandatory retirement laws, and the adoption of the Social Security system.

In recent years, the notion of distinct life stages and their implications has given way to the notion of a life course. Instead of identifying discrete stages of development, the life-course perspective focuses on passages through major life-cycle transitions, such as schooling, marriage, and entry into and exit from the labor force. The life-course approach analyzes the way particular historical contexts, as well as class, gender, or ethnic status, shape the timing and sequencing of the most important life transitions. It helps bring into focus the way that large-scale social processes, such as a war or an economic depression, affect the life experiences of particular groups of individuals.

Between the early seventeenth century and the mid-twentieth century, the timing of major life-cycle transitions grew increasingly specific and uniform. During the seventeenth century, age was an imprecise category, and key life experiences were not tied to distinct ages. Marriage customarily took place after a young man had achieved economic independence, which usually occurred only after he had received an inheritance following his father's death. Women bore children from their early twenties until menopause, twenty years later. Consequently, the age range of children within families was much greater than it is now. In colonial New England, half of all children grew up in families with nine or more children, and as a result, the term "child" included a spectrum of ages stretching from newborns to people in their twenties. Meanwhile, men and women retired only when they were incapable of working.

Nor was death linked closely to old age. Before 1850, nearly 60 percent of all deaths occurred among people fifteen or younger; another 20 percent of deaths took place among those between the ages of fifteen and forty-five. Today, in contrast, only about 10 percent of deaths occur among those younger than forty-five. Even in law, there was no fixed age of majority prior to the nineteenth century. The age at which the young might gain control over an inheritance ranged between fifteen and twenty-five; the age at which an orphan was permitted to choose a guardian varied between thirteen and sixteen; and the age at which a person might receive the right to vote could be anywhere between twenty-one and forty.

Although chronological age was a less important organizing principle in colonial society than it has since become, it would be a mistake to assume that age had no social meaning. There were a number of social and cultural rituals that marked an individual's progression through the life course. Around the age of six, colonial children stopped wearing shapeless smocks and began to wear pants or skirts and petticoats. Between the ages of six and fourteen, many boys, and to a lesser extent girls, went to work in another household, as apprentices or servants. Full religious communion usually took place among individuals in their twenties or thirties.

Age norms and age consciousness were relatively weak but not nonexistent. Youths in colonial New England, for instance, developed a distinctive youth culture characterized by such recreations as frolicking, dancing, and group singing. Beginning in the early eighteenth century, youths set up their own religious and secular organizations.

Over the course of the nineteenth century, age consciousness grew, as is evident in the popularization of a number of age-specific religious rituals, such as Christian confirmation and the Jewish bar mitzvah; the increasingly regular celebration of birthdays; the appearance, beginning in the 1870s, of mass-produced birthday cards; and the first references to a "proper" age of marriage in late-nineteenth-century etiquette books. It was also apparent in the emergence of the late-nineteenth-century child study movement, which sought to identify the distinctive features of children's emotional, physiological, and psychological development at each age.[14]

One factor that contributed to increasing age consciousness during the nineteenth century was a profound shift in the demographic structure of society. Prior to 1800, as a result of a very high birthrate and a relatively low death rate, America had one of the youngest populations in world history, with a median age around sixteen. After 1800, the birthrate fell sharply, and the median age of the population began to rise, reaching 18.9 years in 1850 and 24.1 years in 1910. As the population aged, the middle-aged and the elderly made up a growing presence. The percentage of those over sixty increased from 4 to 6 percent of the population in the seventeenth century to 15 percent in the late twentieth century and nearly 20 percent in the early twenty-first century.

Changes in the organization of the workplace also contributed to the increasing significance of age. Between 1800 and the Civil War, apprenticeship declined, and many teenage workers left the labor force or saw their status drop as they assumed unskilled jobs for "boy's wages." At the same time, many older workers, who were increasingly regarded as less productive than the middle-aged, retired or were forced out of the labor market. In the twentieth century, participation in the work force was further segmented as child labor laws and the first mandatory retirement rules (which appeared around 1910) defined entry into and exit from the labor force. Age became part of the definition of worker.

As a result of these shifts in employment, schooling, and the age structure of the population, the nature of the individual life course changed. During the early twentieth century, the timing and sequencing of major life-course transitions such as the age of leaving school, leaving home, beginning adult work, marrying, and establishing one's own household became increasingly uniform and predictable; consequently, a growing number of individuals experienced these transitions at the same time as other people of their own age, which, in turn, fostered the notion of generational cohorts. An increase in the duration of schooling and in the age of entry into the work force caused child labor to drop sharply: Between 1910 and 1930, the proportion of employed fifteen-year-old boys fell from one in two to one in six; the proportion of employed fifteen-year-old girls declined from one in four to one in twelve. The decline in teenage employment was accompanied by a marked increase in the length of schooling: In 1870, just 2 percent of young people graduated from high school, but by 1930, the percentage had climbed to nearly 29 percent.

Starting in the 1980s and 1990s, the trend toward relatively uniform sequencing and timing of key life events eroded. The pattern of individuals progressing from schooling to work-force participation became less dominant as an increasing number of high school students took after-school jobs. Similarly, the pattern in which couples progressed from engagement to marriage and childbearing declined as increasing numbers of couples cohabited prior to marriage, a higher proportion of births occurred to unwed mothers, and more married couples waited several years before having children.

The trend away from rigid age norms was apparent in increasing variation in the age of first marriage and the timing of college attendance. At the same time, certain institutionalized age categories, such as a twenty-one-year-old voting age and mandatory retirement at sixty-five, broke down. The Twenty Sixth Amendment lowered the voting age in federal elections to eighteen. In 1986, Congress amended the Age Discrimination in Employment Act of 1967 to strike down most maximum age restrictions in the work force. The abolition of the peacetime military draft in 1973 significantly reduced the proportion of adolescents entering military service, as well as removing a major factor structuring the lives of young men.

The shifts here described—from a notion of a sequence of fixed life stages to a more dynamic, contingent conception of the life course, from life decisions dictated by family needs to choices made on the basis of personal preference, from notions of human development rooted in universal psychological processes to an emphasis on the importance of cultural, historical, and socioeconomic contexts—underscore the fact that development persists across the life span and that while each life stage is meaningful in itself, development is cumulative. This is, of course, what is meant by the concept of "maturation." Prior to the seventeenth century, neither theologians nor other writers used the language of maturation or of personal growth. Clerics spoke of rebirth or redemption. Although artists visualized distinct stages of life, and moralists described the roles and duties assigned to husbands and fathers, wives and mothers, and children, there were no references to the process of maturation or psychological growth. People were far more concerned with the contrast between children, youth, adults, and the elderly than they were with transitions between these categories.[15]

Nor did the common law treat maturation as a process. English common law had long taken the position that legal rights and responsibilities were tied to individuals' chronological age, as well as their gender. In general, in England, a young person in the 1760s had to reach the age of fourteen before being subject to capital punishment. Girls could consent or refuse to consent to marriage at age twelve; choose a guardian at fourteen; serve as an executrix at seventeen; and dispose of property at twenty-one. Boys could consent to marriage and choose a guardian at fourteen, and like girls, serve as an executor at seventeen and dispose of property at twenty-one. But there was no discussion during the seventeenth or eighteenth centuries of how legal responsibility increased over time. Not until the nineteenth century, and much more substantially in the twentieth century, did jurists begin to argue explicitly that maturation was a process deserving legal recognition.[16]

Three key occurrences played a particularly crucial role in the rise of developmentalist thinking. One was theological. Only after predestinarian thinking gave way to Arminianism—the notion that individuals could gain salvation through their own efforts—did a modern conception of maturation as a process begin to take shape during the eighteenth and early nineteenth centuries. The breakdown of a certain kind of binary thinking that divided individuals into the mature and the immature, superiors and inferiors, rulers and subjects, and masters and dependents also contributed to an emphasis on a developmental process. As patriarchal and hierarchical ideologies came under assault during the Age of Revolution, the dualistic view that placed individuals into rigid roles gave way to a Romantic and idealistic conception of all people having potential for growth and development. A third key contributor to developmentalist thought was post-Darwinian biology, especially Ernst Haeckel's notion that individual development recapitulates the development of species as a whole.[17]

The notion of discrete stages persisted, however, with pioneering psychologists including G. Stanley Hall and Arnold Gesell attributing distinctive psychological traits to specific life stages defined by age. But there was also a growing emphasis upon development over time and especially upon transitions, including the transition from young adulthood to middle age. The French philosopher Henri Bergson anticipated the growing stress on a developmental process when he wrote: "To exist is to change; to change is to mature; to mature is to create oneself endlessly."[18]

Initially, developmentalist concerns focused on young children, whom John Locke likened to balls of clay or wax that might be shaped in any direction for good or ill. Children, according to a view that emerged during the eighteenth century, needed to be raised, not simply taught or disciplined. But in a context of radical social transformation, apparent in the rapid growth of commercialization and the spread of urban and industrial patterns of life, there were growing worries about the maturation of those in their late teens and twenties. Beginning in the middle of the nineteenth century, concern with proper chronological development and with providing youth with a more sharply defined ladder into adulthood grew.

In the contemporary United States, statutes define legal adulthood in multiple ways. Indeed, some states have twenty-five or more separate legal definitions of the age of adulthood, setting separate ages for acquiring a driver's license, drinking alcoholic beverages, renting a car, reserving a hotel room, entering into a legal contract, managing an estate, suing or being sued, voting, avoiding curfews, being released from parental control, being on trial in an adult court, consenting to medical treatment, or joining the military. Yet, in recent years, developmentalist ideas have increasingly reshaped legal thought. The abolition of the juvenile death penalty, for example, was based in part on the notion that the capacity for impulse control and risk assessment are less developed in the young, who are also more susceptible to peer pressure, more prone to sensation seeking, and less future-oriented. But maturation does not end at eighteen or twenty-one. The developmental process proceeds throughout a person's life. Nor is the process linear, undeviating, or preordained.[19]

Over time, the notion of a cycle of life gradually gave way to the notion of a life course, which recasts the trajectory of life not as the recapitulation of certain universal, unchanging, or predictable stages or transitions, but as a process with crests and valleys and a structure and design that gives it meaning and coherence. At various times, this process has been likened to a pilgrimage in quest of redemption or salvation, an odyssey of discovery, a struggle for liberation, or, more recently, a route to recovery or healing or self-affirmation. For Aristotle, the goal was *eudemonia,* the fulfillment of a person's potential; hence, it meant to flourish, thrive, or, in contemporary parlance, self-actualize. The Puritans, in contrast, believed that each individual had a calling, a particular vocation that one was morally obligated to find and pursue in the service of God and the common good. This notion, expressed in the New Testament's Epistle to the Ephesians 4:1, is rooted in the belief that God has created each person with certain gifts and talents that must be developed and utilized for the community's welfare. A secular culture redefined the purpose of life as the pursuit of ambition or happiness, understood in terms of pleasure or prosperity or a sense of accomplishment or, more modestly, in terms of achieving fulfillment in the mundane aspects of private life — thus, in love, friendship, childrearing, and work.

For some, life peaks early, with high school or college viewed as the most passionate, thrills-filled years of life and the years that follow leave them feeling washed up. For others, the high point occurs during early adulthood, when they marry and raise children or launch a career. It is then that life appears to be at its most intense, leaving in its wake a pervasive sense of nostalgia, wistfulness, and melancholy. In recent years, with rates of divorce and remarriage rising, family configurations becoming more diverse and malleable, and career changes occurring more frequently, the life course has grown more disjunctive, and life's trajectory has grown less coherent. Fewer adults are able to look back on their lives and see a common thread, such as steadfastness, faithfulness, self-sacrifice, or commitment. But this has also has meant that contemporary life has more crests and troughs than in the past, as well as more opportunities for growth, development, and renewal.

The course of life is not predetermined by the so-called "critical" or "formative" years; nor is it wholly a product of individual agency. It is certainly not predictable. Far from being etched in stone, the life course is a historical artifact, a trajectory shaped by contingent, historically specific circumstances. Only an appreciation of these circumstances can allow us to truly understand the factors that shaped the arc of adult lives in the past and that are transforming the course of life today.

CHAPTER ONE

The Tangled Transition to Adulthood

Adulthood no longer begins at age eighteen or twenty-one. Compared to their counterparts in the 1950s and 1960s, the young today take far longer to complete their education, obtain a steady job, achieve financial independence, marry, or bear children. At present, fewer than 20 percent of Americans in their late twenties have completed school, acquired a full-time job, moved away from their parental home, married, and had children, and only a third of thirty-to-thirty-four-year-olds have achieved these markers of adult status. A prolonged transitional period has emerged in which the young are no longer adolescents, but have not yet attained the traditional emblems of full adult status.[1]

Nor does the sequence of events marking the transition to adulthood follow an orderly progression from school completion to career entry, residential independence, and family formation. Financial independence, for example, no longer necessarily precedes independent living or cohabitation; nor does childbearing predictably follow marriage. As the normative script of the adolescent-to-adult transition has broken down, the trajectory into adulthood has become more diverse, with profound differences—in length of schooling, age of marriage and childbearing, and rates of unmarried parenthood—developing along lines of class, ethnicity, and immigrant status, even as gender differences have narrowed.

The subjective entry into adult status also takes place more gradually and unevenly than in the early post–World War II era. Some defining experiences, such as sexual initiation, take place much earlier than half a century ago, while others, such as the achievement of financial independence, occur later. Meanwhile, adulthood has come to be defined less by clear rites of passage, such as marriage, college graduation, the purchase of a first house, or the birth of a child, than by subjective feelings of self-sufficiency and autonomy, as well as a sense that one no longer engages in the reckless behavior characteristic of youth.[2]

The forces behind this shift include the expansion of access to higher education, the increased cost of housing, and the lengthier time that it takes to find an occupation that pays a middle-class income. The post–World War II economic boom allowed young men, even those without a high school diploma, to obtain a job sufficient to support a family by their early twenties. But beginning in the 1960s, as the economy shifted away from manufacturing, a middle-class income increasingly required postsecondary education or another educational credential. In recent years, educational attainment has become a key variable predicting when or if young adults marry and whether their children are born inside or outside marriage.[3]

Also contributing to the delay is the increased acceptance of unmarried cohabitation, which means that young adults do not need to marry to have a stable sex life, and of a value system that views young adulthood as a time of exploration and self-discovery. For much of the nineteenth and twentieth centuries, most single young adults resided in their parents' home and contributed to their family's support, a pattern still common among many immigrant groups. But around 1960, a new pattern emerged, as a growing proportion of young adults lived apart from their parents before starting their own families. For many young people, the twenties became the "age of independence." Physically separated from parents, the young were free to experiment with a variety of living arrangements, including unmarried cohabitation and same-sex partnerships. For all the talk about "boomerang kids," a smaller proportion of young adults live with their parents than in the past, and those who do reside with their parents tend to do so temporarily, after a job loss or a relationship breakup.[4]

The prolongation of young adulthood has carried profound consequences for parent-child relationships. The family of origin now serves as the primary safety net for young adults. As a result of lengthier and more costly schooling and delayed achievement of a middle-class income, young people in their twenties are far more likely than their predecessors to rely on financial support from their parents. Indeed, a third of the cost of parenting is spent upon children older than age seventeen. Fully half return home for a period of time during their young adulthood. As the transition to adulthood has grown more uncertain, parents now provide scaffolding for adult children in ways unexpected a generation ago.

Emotional dependence, too, persists. Technology has made it easier for parents to stay connected to their young adult children, but technology has also made it more difficult for some parents to let go. Many parents stay deeply involved in their children's lives even as their kids enter college. These enduring ties, though welcomed by many parents, are nonetheless a mixed blessing. Young people who maintain daily contact with their parents via cell phone, email, and social networking sites are less likely to perceive themselves as adults. Separation from parents is critical for maturation, and for a growing number of the young, psychological independence is achieved more slowly than in previous generations.[5]

The changes that have occurred in the transition to adulthood have provoked anxiety, apprehension, and alarm. A common complaint is that today's twenty-somethings, coddled as children, are aimless, irresponsible, and emotionally immature. Stuck in a perpetual adolescence, they supposedly avoid commitment, spurn entry-level jobs, and are caught in a limbo state of prolonged adolescence, selfishness, self-indulgence, and deferred responsibility. The young, we are told, are entitled, narcissistic exploiters of their parents' good will — and inevitably so, given hovering helicopter parents who infantilize their offspring and raise their material and career expectations to unrealistic levels. Popular culture speaks disparagingly of the "failure to launch" and of over-aged Peter Pans mired in a state of "arrested development."

These complaints are not new. Condemnation of the younger generation is among this country's oldest traditions. The criticisms, however, have varied with each generation and have been wildly contradictory. Seventeenth-century ministers such as Thomas Cobbett vilified the young for acting "proudly, disdainfully, and scornfully toward their parents." During the 1950s, adults were haunted by images of switchblade wielding juvenile delinquents and brass-knuckle armed gangs making trouble for the hell of it. But adults were not satisfied when these "Rebels without a Cause" gave way to waves of young adults flashing peace signs and organizing against social injustice. Contemporary pundits deride the young for relying too much on their parents' advice and direction and being insufficiently self-motivated.[6]

In a society that suffers from a foreshortened historical memory, it is easy to forget that the perception of the twenties as an unsettled, anxious, and uncertain period of life has a long history. Every generation, at least since the early eighteenth century, has had to contend with insecurity and self-doubt in the process of seeking rewarding work or a romantic partner. A century ago, the social critic Randolph Bourne, himself in his twenties, described how "in our artificial civilization many young people at twenty-five are still on the threshold of activity." In the 1960s, the psychologist Kenneth Keniston, drawing on the ideas of Erik Erikson, described this period as a time of "identity exploration" and alienation. What is distinctive today is that many young people enter adulthood carrying heavy levels of debt and facing an increasingly competitive economy in which employers' expectations of experience and credentials have escalated.[7]

A historic transition in the passage to adulthood is occurring across the developed world. Indeed, delayed entry into adulthood independence is even greater in Italy and Japan than it is in the United States. The Japanese voice disgust about "parasite singles" and blame mothers, in particular, for failing to raise independent children. In Italy, where 37 percent of thirty-year-old men have never lived away from home, many speak of a "cult of mammismo," or mamma's boys. In every postindustrial society, delays in the transition to adulthood have evoked alarm.[8]

Thus, it is reassuring to recognize that a protracted transition into adulthood is not a new phenomenon. After Henry David Thoreau graduated from Harvard at the age of nineteen, he was hired as a school teacher, only to resign two weeks later. He then intermittently worked in his parents' pencil factory, served as a tutor, and shoveled manure. As we shall see, vacillation, doubt, uncertainty, and lack of direction have long characterized early adulthood. Except for the brief period following World War II, it was unusual for the young to achieve the markers of full adult status before their mid- or late twenties. Between the seventeenth century and the late nineteenth, those in their teens and early twenties occupied a lengthy transitional stage called "youth," shifting back and forth between residence in the parental household and work experience outside their home.[9]

Today's young adults are experiencing a momentous transformation in the path to a successful job and family life. As recently as 1970, half of all women were married by the age of twenty-one to husbands who tended to be about two years older. With real wages rising rapidly for men, even for high school dropouts, but few opportunities for women to achieve economic independence, there was little reason to shop around, whether for a long-term job or a long-term mate. If you were a young man whose parents could not afford to send you to college, it made sense to go to work immediately and grab the first job you were offered. If you were a young woman, getting married was often the best investment you could make in your future.[10]

But the old model of plunging directly into independent adult living no longer functions well. In fact, it is the young people who try to follow the 1950s model who have the toughest time establishing stable and productive lives. It is not necessarily that young people spurn entry-level jobs. It is that entry-level jobs are too often dead-end jobs. The pay gap between college graduates and everyone else has been widening steadily. And even among college graduates, the best jobs usually go to those who can afford graduate school or an unpaid or low-paid internship or training period.

The young people who do best are those who do not leap out of the nest too soon. Postponing marriage, childbearing, and permanent commitment to a single job actually increases one's chances of having a rewarding career and a lasting marriage. But doing so without parental assistance has become increasingly difficult. The people who are most likely to succeed are those who can rely on their parents to help them make their way through the costly process of completing their education and taking low-wage jobs or internships to improve their resume. Parents' contacts and social networks can also help young adults find an entry- level job. Young adults increasingly depend on parents to support them as they learn advanced job skills and cope with the rising cost of housing.[11]

Understanding these challenges puts the notion of "helicopter parents" and "boomerang kids" in a new light. Whatever the excesses of some parents, it turns out they have good reason to be standing by with a rescue rope as their children try to make their way through the overgrown and traditional paths to adulthood that may no longer secure employment. The twenties have replaced the teens as the most risk-filled decade. Problematic behavior—binge drinking, illicit drug use, unprotected sex that leads to disease or unplanned pregnancies, and violent crime—peaks during this age, and missteps during these years can impose lifelong penalties. Parental support can play a crucial role in preventing their offspring's lives from going severely off track.[12]

From the vantage point of history, it is clear that the transformations that have occurred in the passage to adulthood are only the most recent examples of shifts that have taken place several times before. A series of historical myths surround the transition to adulthood: that it took place much earlier and more seamlessly in the past; that before the twentieth century, most young people followed in their parents' footsteps; and that, accordingly, the transition was smoother and less wrenching than it has recently become. In fact, each of these is profoundly misleading.

Contrary to what many people assume, the overwhelming majority of young people in the past did not enter adulthood at a very young age. To be sure, a few did achieve positions of responsibility while exceptionally young. Alexander Hamilton became General George Washington's aide at the age of seventeen. At the outbreak of the Revolution, Henry Knox, a leading general, was twenty-six, and James Madison and Gouverneur Morris were both twenty-five. Early in the nineteenth century, some observers, such as the British naval officer Captain Frederick Marryatt, were convinced that young Americans achieved independence at a much younger age than their European counterparts. Marryatt claimed that "At fifteen or sixteen, if not at college, the boy assumes the man, he enters into business, as a clerk to some merchant, or in some store. His father's home is abandoned, except when it may suit his convenience, his salary being sufficient for most of his wants. He frequents the bar, calls for gin cocktails, chews tobacco, and talks politics." But Captain Marryatt's observations were not actually accurate. During the early nineteenth century, young men in their teens and even twenties tended to swing between periods of relative independence and phases of dependence when they returned to the parental home.[13]

Nor did most young women and men follow effortlessly in their parents' footsteps. Given constant changes in the economy, replicating parents' lives has generally not been an option. Despite the assumed immobility of the preindustrial world, geographical movement was widespread, and most migrants to the American colonies arrived in their late teens or twenties. As early as the late seventeenth century, land shortages near the Atlantic coast forced many young men to migrate westward if they wished to farm. If they wanted to stay near their birthplace, many had to find some other occupation. During the early nineteenth century, the breakdown of the apprenticeship system meant that young men had to identify new paths into skilled crafts or business.[14]

Neither did marriage and childbearing take place at an especially young age. With the exception of the early post–World War II era, most young people did not marry until their mid-or even late twenties or early thirties—that is, at about the same age as today. Even in the colonial era, young men generally had to delay marriage until they received an inheritance, which usually took place after a father's death. The essential point is that the decade stretching from the late teens to the late twenties has long been a period of uncertainty, hesitation, and indecision.

Take, for instance, the life of John Dane, a tailor, who was born in Berkhampstead, England, around 1612. Around the age of eighteen, his father, a harsh disciplinarian who had severely beaten the boy in the past, thrashed him with a stick, prompting the son to leave his parents' home to seek his fortune. Carrying just "2 shurts," his "best suit," and a "by bull" (Bible), young Dane began a period of wandering from town to town. Over the next several years, he encountered many temptations from harlots, threats from thieves, and misadventures with vagabonds. But through the successful practice of tailoring, he was able to take on an apprentice and a journeyman. Dane nevertheless was dissatisfied with his life and the sinfulness around him: "I find here a deuell [devil] to tempt and a corupt hart to deseue [deceive]." Around the age of twenty-four he migrated to New England, first to Ipswich in Massachusetts Bay Colony and then to Roxbury, near Boston.[15]

The patterns we see in Dane's early life—the movement from one town to another and slow progress toward finding a vocation and defining an identity, are apparent in many other young lives in subsequent centuries. After Herman Melville's father died when he was twelve, the future author of *Moby-Dick* unsuccessfully sought work as a surveyor on the Erie Canal, then served as a ship boy, taught school, worked on a whaling ship, and deserted in the Marqueses Islands—all by the age of twenty-two. Mark Twain's youth was similar. After his father's death, when young Sam Clements was eleven, the boy took jobs as a printer's apprentice in Cincinnati, New York City, Philadelphia, St. Louis, and Washington, D.C., before reaching the age of nineteen. He then served as a riverboat pilot, volunteered briefly as a Confederate soldier during the Civil War, and then made his way west to Nevada, where he mined silver before embarking on a career as a writer at the age of twenty-eight.[16]

Nor were young women's lives as predictable or predetermined as sometimes assumed. Among the first colonial women to keep a diary, Esther Edwards Burr provides as revealing a glimpse into an eighteenth-century American woman's inner life as exists. Born in 1732, the daughter of the prominent theologian Jonathan Edwards, she was twenty years old when she married the second president of the College of New Jersey (now Princeton). At twenty-two, she bore a daughter and two years later had a son, Aaron, who would become vice president under Thomas Jefferson.[17]

As the young wife of a minister and college president, she was constantly harried. "Busy, Busy-hurry, Fly-Run" she wrote in one diary entry. "I feel like an old dead horse," she penned in another. But her journal also offers a vivid record of her religious reflections, including her sense of guilt over her spiritual unworthiness and the coldness of her heart, as well as her complaints about ill health, which she viewed as religious trials and chastisements from God. We learn about her childrearing techniques, including her efforts to "gouvern" her daughter when she was nearly ten months old, by whipping her "on Old Adams account." Especially noteworthy are the repeated insults she received from men who derided women's intelligence, piety, and capacity for friendship. Regarding one of many incidents, she notes: "The Men say (tho' not Mr Burr he is not one of that sort) that Women have no business to concern themselves about [public affairs] but trust to those that know better and be content." From her diary, it is clear that her closest relationship was with a female friend, Sarah Gill; she wished keenly that the two could spend more time together: "O the happy day when we shall meet never to part! No such thing as distance of place or length of time to intercept our joys."[18]

Her life ended tragically and prematurely. Her husband died of malaria in 1757, when she was twenty-five. Six months later, her father died following a smallpox inoculation, and she herself died at the age of twenty-six of unknown causes. Then, her mother died of dysentery while traveling to Princeton to take care of Esther's orphaned children. Each death underscored the precariousness of family relations in the American colonies.

The unpredictability and uncertainty that characterized Esther Edwards Burr's life were typical of many young women's lives. A noted nineteenth-century poet, Lucy Larcom, born in Beverly, Massachusetts, in 1824, was the ninth of ten children. She, too, suffered from the premature death of a parent. Just eight when her father died, she helped support her family by working in a textile mill in Lowell, where she was employed from the age of eleven until twenty-one, rising from the status of a doffer, responsible for replacing bobbins on the spinning frame, to bookkeeper. "I defied the machinery to make me its slave," she would later observe. At the age of twenty-two, she moved westward. Working as a schoolteacher in Illinois, she saved enough money to enroll in college at age twenty-five, graduating three years later, and subsequently taught at Wheaton Seminary (later to become Wheaton College) in Massachusetts.[19]

Five transitions to adulthood—each idiosyncratic, yet each eventful, circuitous, and unpredictable. For much of American history, the transition to adulthood was just as irregular and arduous as it is now. In fact, the young were even more likely to experience dramatic discontinuities in their lives, such as a parent's premature death, movement back and forth between the parental home and residence elsewhere, passage into and out of schooling, dramatic shifts in status, and, in the case of enslaved African Americans, sale, which was most likely to take place during the teens or twenties. Nor did their gender make young women's lives more stable, settled, and predictable than young men's. Nineteenth-century native-born women migrated to cities at even higher rates than their male counterparts, and substantial numbers of immigrants, especially among the Irish and Eastern European Jews, were young women, who frequently traveled alone.[20]

Successfully navigating the transition to adulthood has always required flexibility, adaptability, resilience, and a certain toughness. In the seventeenth and early eighteenth centuries, work, not schooling, occupied a central place in the lives of those in their teens and early twenties. So, too, did adult supervision and authority. As many as half of the early white settlers to the American colonies arrived as indentured servants or laborers, who had to work between four and seven years before they were set free from their bonds and contracts. Most of the newly arrived indentured servants—including convicts, paupers, and boys and girls shanghaied by shipowners—were in their teens or early twenties. Yet even those young people who were nominally free experienced prolonged periods of dependency, often entering into service in another household at the age of seven, eight, or nine, with boys entering an apprenticeship or working as hired labor in their teens. This transitional status, in which a youth was neither a child nor a "freeman" or "free woman," often lasted for years and usually stretched into the twenties or even beyond longer. Indeed, the roots of Americans' acute sensitivity to arbitrary authority are partly planted in the widespread experience of various forms servitude and service. Even in the early nineteenth century, many young people would have shared the sentiments of Abraham Lincoln, who considered himself his father's virtual slave. In an early speech, Lincoln said "I used to be a slave. . . . We were all slaves one time or another."[21]

During the eighteenth century, as the colonies became increasingly integrated into transatlantic trading networks and a series of imperial wars disrupted local economies, this earlier system of patriarchal control began to break down. Choice became young adulthood's defining characteristic: choice in occupation, place of residence, and marriage partner. In 1720, the Presbyterian minister Benjamin Colman underscored this point:

> Now, O young people is your chusing time, and commonly your fixing time; and as your fix now, it is likely to last. Now you commonly chuse your trade; betake yourselvs to your business for life, show what you incline to, and how you intend to be employ'd all your days. Now you chuse your master and your education or occupation, and now you dispose of yourself in marriage ordinarily, place your affections, give away your hearts, look out for some companion of life, whose to be as long as you live.[22]

As the colonies became increasingly integrated into transatlantic networks, employment opportunities expanded, giving young people more vocational options than ever before. With new territory opening to settlement and geographical mobility increasing, young women as well as young men had greater freedom to decide where to live and labor. Most strikingly, young people's choice of marriage partner broadened. Fewer daughters married in birth order, and fewer sisters married into a single family of sons. But greater freedom resulted in heightened risk. During the eighteenth century, rates of illegitimacy shot up as parental control of sexuality broke down. To maintain control over youthful sexuality, some parents embraced the custom of bundling, in which a courting couple who occupied the same bed were wrapped in blankets or separated by a board in order to ensure that no sexual activity took place. If, however, pregnancy followed regardless of these measures, the parents knew the father's identity.[23]

By the early nineteenth century, the prescribed system of apprenticeship and service had collapsed, making coming of age increasingly problematic. Autobiographies and biographies of the era treated the teens and twenties as years of doubt, indecision, uncertainty, and vacillation. The changes in young women's lives were as dramatic as in young men's. During the first years of the century, household production declined sharply, accompanied by a shift from domestic labor to wage labor outside the home. The mechanization of cloth manufacture eliminated a task that had absorbed hours of young women's lives and set them free to leave home to seek work. Thousands of young unmarried women received unprecedented opportunities to attend a school or female academy and to work outside a home, as a mill girl or teacher or, beginning in the 1850s, as a shop girl or female clerk in a countinghouse or business or government office.[24]

No longer able to guarantee their children's economic status, an emerging middle class responded to a "crisis of family succession" by dramatically reducing the birth rate (from an average of seven children in 1800 to five in 1850 and three in 1900) and emphasizing intensive mothering and the nurturing of emotional bonds. These parents kept their children in school well into their teens and had them remain at home into their late teens or twenties. They also sought greater control over their children's entry into the labor force and provided them with the skills and support needed to achieve economic success. Anxiety over the unstructured nature of youth prompted efforts to rationalize, standardize, institutionalize, and systematize the transition to adulthood. Beginning in the 1840s, educators and youth workers created a host of new institutions, including high schools and YMCAs, to insulate the young from the adult world and shield middle-class youth from contamination by the "dangerous classes" and the corruptions of urban life.[25]

Prior to the mid-nineteenth century, youths of different classes had worked side by side in farms or on ships or in small workshops. Regardless of class, youths moved sporadically in and out of the parental home. But with the Industrial Revolution and the growth of white-collar employment, prolonged schooling and delayed entry into the workforce and into marriage became defining attributes of middle-class life. Upward mobility hinged on postponing entrance into full adult status until young men were established financially. A code of values emphasizing self-improvement, self-control, and respectability was embraced by many aspiring middle-class youth. Even though he grew up on the rough-and-tumble Kentucky, Indiana, and Illinois frontier, young Abraham Lincoln embraced this ethos, pursuing self-advancement and eschewing smoking and heavy drinking.[26]

At the same time, working-class youth pursued wage labor from a very young age, often before reaching their teenage years, giving them a greater measure of economic independence from parents. As older mechanisms that had regulated the lives of laboring class youths, such as apprenticeship or indentured servitude, disintegrated, an urban population of free-floating young men (and to a lesser extent, young women) who lived outside a master's household, in boarding houses in distinct working-class neighborhoods, grew rapidly.[27]

Over time, the ladder to adulthood became ever more elaborate, protracted, and prescriptive, embracing working-class as well as middle-class youth. Toward the end of the nineteenth century, a host of reformers sought to universalize a middle-class trajectory into adulthood. These reformers recognized that if working-class youth entered the labor force too soon, without adequate schooling, they would never advance. Their goal was to construct an institutional ladder for all youth that would allow them to attain adulthood through instructed steps. A previously haphazard system of education was replaced by age-graded classrooms, compulsory school attendance laws, and the creation of the high school. Between 1900 and 1940, the country opened, on average, a high school every day, raising the proportion of students graduating from high school from just 6 percent in 1900 to over 50 percent in 1940 and over 70 percent in 1962.[28]

In recent years, the desire to create a smoother pathway into adulthood has taken on a new aim: that of universalizing postsecondary education. Today, roughly seven out of ten white and Hispanic students and six out of ten African American students enroll in college. In practice, however, the educational pipeline has proven to be quite leaky, with just sixty-eight out of every one hundred ninth-graders graduating from high school on time, forty immediately enrolling in college, twenty-seven still enrolled during the sophomore year, and eighteen graduating from college in four years. At one end of the spectrum are the 20 to 25 percent of twenty-somethings who never graduated from high school or received a GED. Some have been in jail or on probation, some suffer from a serious disability or a severe substance abuse problem, some have aged out of foster care or mental health programs, and some had a child as a teenager. At the other end of the spectrum are the three in ten who receive a college diploma (one-third of whom will also earn a master's, doctoral, or professional degree). A plurality fall in between, attending some college, but never receiving an associate or bachelor's degree.[29]

Institutions have long occupied a crucial role in the passage to adulthood. Some institutions hinder it. Involvement in the criminal justice system, not surprisingly, renders the transition especially problematic, as employers are far less likely to hire anyone with a criminal record. But institutions, whether educational or military, can also facilitate this passage. Whether an institution hastens or retards the transition to adulthood depends largely on the kind of structure, support system, mentoring, and social connections it offers, as well as the culture that its participants share.[30]

Over the course of American history, militia or military service was an essential step in growing up for many young men. During the colonial era and well into the nineteenth century, militia service was widespread, and an estimated 40 percent of young men participated in a war. Militia membership was a crucial symbol of civic manhood, and those who were barred from it were not regarded as full members of the polity. From the 1940s into the early 1970s, the military draft served as an especially important entryway into manhood. During the Second World War, about 20 percent of the male population, and a far higher proportion of young male adults, took part in the U.S. military. As recently as 1969, nearly a fifth of young men who graduated high school entered the military. For many young men, military service provided skills, discipline, a sense of accomplishment, and time to mature, though for others, especially those in combat, it produced a variety of medical and mental disabilities.[31]

The establishment of a volunteer army, beginning in 1973, has transformed the military experience of young adults. Not only has a sharply reduced portion of the young come to serve in the military, but those who do are from a far narrower socioeconomic spectrum of the population. For some, the military has remained a two-year coming-of-age experience, providing economic independence from parents and offering travel, discipline, and exposure to a diversity of people and places. But many others have enlisted for educational benefits or training in skills valuable in the civilian workforce. For these young people (about 85 percent of whom are male), the military has become a means to an end. Still others have regarded military service as a career. Access to secure, decently paid employment with relatively generous benefits has encouraged that latter group to marry and bear children earlier than their peers. They have also had more stable marriages than their civilian counterparts.[32]

If certain aspects of life with the volunteer military—such as secure employment, decent wages, and relatively generous benefits—have promoted a relatively early attainment of the traditional markers of full adulthood, other characteristics, including a chest-thumping hyper-masculine culture, which associates physical aggression, heterosexual assertiveness, and dominance with manliness, as well as the physical and psychological dangers of combat, have presented unique challenges. Sexual harassment and assault have been among the factors that lead young women to leave the military more rapidly than young men. Meanwhile, the advantages of military service have declined since the 1950s. In contrast to the veterans of World War II and the Korean War, who tended to achieve significantly higher educational and income levels than nonveterans, more recent veterans have experienced fewer benefits from military service. Indeed, male veterans of the Vietnam era acquired less education than those who did not serve. Veterans of the volunteer army, including officers, outearn their nonserving counterparts very modestly.[33]

During the second half of the twentieth century, college became the dominant institutional space in which the young began the transition from adolescence to adulthood. For a growing majority of young people, college provided the setting in which they separated from parents, started to define an adult identity, and developed deeper, more intimate friendships and romantic relationships than those they had in high school. Much as the early twentieth-century "discovery" of adolescence was a product of the growth of the high school, so the rise of a stage between adolescence and full adulthood known as "emergent adulthood" is shaped by the expansion of postsecondary education.[34]

1.1. Georgetown University graduation, June 9, 1924.

In 1900, just 4 percent of eighteen-to-twenty-two-year-olds attended college. Today, in stark contrast, about 50 percent of all the college-aged youth do so; two-thirds of all high school graduates enter a community college or a four-year college or university; most of the rest enter the labor force: and perhaps one in seven neither attends school nor joins the workforce. But far from equalizing opportunity, colleges tend to reinforce class divisions. The proportion in college varies widely on the basis of gender, ethnicity, and especially income. For 2012 graduates, the college enrollment rate was 71 percent for young women and 61 percent for young men. The college enrollment rate of Asian high school graduates (82 percent) was higher than for recent white (67 percent), black (58 percent), and Hispanic (69 percent) graduates.[35]

Higher education serves disadvantaged students particularly poorly. Young people from economically disadvantaged families are much less likely to enroll in college, and if they do, are more likely to attend for-profit institutions, community colleges, or less-selective four-year institutions, while youth from more affluent and better educated families are more likely to enroll in selective institutions and obtain a bachelor's degree. Only 29 percent of those from the bottom economic quartile enter college, compared to 80 percent of those from the top—a substantial gap. In addition, only 9 percent of those from the bottom quartile of the income groups who enter college actually complete it, compared to 54 percent of those from the top income group.[36]

However incomplete, the increasing democratization of a college education has already fundamentally altered the profile of today's postsecondary students. Although the phrase "college student" conjures up the image of an eighteen-to-twenty-one-year-old attending a residential campus full time, a majority of undergraduates are nontraditional: They are working students, part-time students, commuters, and caregivers. About 40 percent of undergraduates are over twenty-five. Four in ten attend college part-time. Unfortunately, higher education has done an especially poor job of helping these students graduate. Only a quarter of part-time students ever receive a degree.[37]

In the late eighteenth century, only one out of one hundred young men attended one of the colonies' nine colleges. These institutions graduated fewer than forty students a year between 1701 and 1750, and less than 130 between 1751 and 1800. Harvard's entire faculty in 1800 consisted of the college president, a professor of theology, a professor of mathematics, a professor of Hebrew, and four tutors, and graduated roughly the same number of students in 1800 as it had a century earlier. Yet despite limited enrollment, the colonial colleges exerted a disproportionate impact on their society. Although initially founded to train ministers, fewer than half of their graduates entered the clergy. Most of the leaders of the Revolution and the early Republic were college graduates, and Princeton (then known as the College of New Jersey) played a particularly crucial role in disseminating the ideologies that defined the revolutionary cause. Princeton students, during the late colonial era, included a future president, James Madison, a future vice president, Aaron Burr, and the celebrated poet Philip Freneau. The college also produced ten cabinet ministers, sixty members of Congress, twelve governors, fifty-six state legislators, and thirty judges, including three justices of the Supreme Court.[38]

Between 1830 and 1860, the number of colleges shot up, propelled by small-town boosterism and competition among religious denominations. These antebellum colleges were generally small, with just one or two professors, a tutor, and a president, and a very small student body, averaging between twenty-five and eighty students. Tuition, which was equal to about a third of the annual earnings of a skilled worker, was relatively low and allowed many farm boys to attend. These young men, who alternated between school and work, would become leaders in their local communities after graduation. In the antebellum period, the numbers of mechanics' institutes, female academies, normal schools, theological seminaries also grew, and the first public colleges were established.[39]

After the Civil War, the cost of tuition, fees, and room and board rose steadily, until it equaled the yearly wages of a skilled worker. Despite federal land-grant acts in 1862 and 1890, which helped establish many public universities, it became increasingly difficult for young men to pay for a college education by combining their studies with work. Meanwhile, the age range of college students gradually narrowed, and the more elite liberal arts colleges and the newly established universities concentrated on educating the children of the well-to-do. Nevertheless, enrollments increased as educational credentials became increasingly necessary to enter many fields.[40]

It was only with the 1944 GI Bill of Rights that the federal government actively began to promote mass college education. This initiative, which subsidized the tuition and living expenses of returning World War II veterans, was followed by other measures that greatly expanded college access, including the Sputnik-inspired National Defense Education Act of 1958 which provided low-interest loans for college students, and the 1965 Higher Education Act, which provided grants to low-income students and subsidized loans for middle-income students and also established work-study programs to subsidize employment of needy students. The result was to dramatically increase college enrollment. In 1940, less than 5 percent of adults had a college degree. Today, 30 percent of adults have a bachelor's degree and another 10 percent have an associate degree from a two-year institution.[41]

The decline in industrial jobs and the rising financial premium for higher education in an information economy have helped fuel demand for college-educated young adults. Between 1960 and 1975, the percentage of high school graduates enrolling in college tripled, then grew by another 23 percent until 1990, after which it has largely stagnated. As the proportion of young people enrolling in college rose, more and more were women (who now make up three-fifths of undergraduates and an equal share of Master's students) and nontraditional students: working students, commuter students, part-time students, community college students, older students, and family caregivers. Today, only 16 percent of the student population can be described as "traditional" in terms of entering college right out of high school, attending full time, and living on campus. Social class has continued to exert a powerful impact on educational trajectories as tuitions have risen exponentially and fewer lower income students have been able to afford the costs. Since 1980, college graduation rates have risen sharply among the more affluent while stagnating among the poor. Whereas three-quarters of those who grow up in the top quarter of the income spectrum earn a baccalaureate degree by the age of twenty-four, the figure is only one out of three in the next quarter down and one in ten for the poorest quartile.[42]

Today, diversity in mission, finances, and student demographics characterizes higher education. Close to half of all undergraduates, and a higher proportion of nontraditional, non-white, low-income students, attend a community college, attracted by low cost, geographical accessibility, and open enrollment policies. Between 1901, when the first public junior college was established in Joliet, Illinois, and 1920, enrollment in such schools reached only 10,000, but during the 1920s and 1930s, their enrollments grew twenty-fold. From their founding, these institutions were torn between two competing visions: to serve as trade schools offering a vocational education or as college preparatory institutions offering a liberal arts education. In some areas, community colleges were regarded as extensions of high schools; in others, as entry ways into four-year colleges. Yet even though most community college students enter with hopes of obtaining a bachelor's degree, only about one in five students will transfer to a four-year institution, and only a third will receive either an associate's or bachelor's degree within six years. For too many students, community colleges prove to be a dead end.[43]

Nominally, college instills skills, knowledge, and credentials necessary to secure a rewarding job, as well as helping to develop a social and professional network. In actuality, for many undergraduates, college is less about learning than growing up: separating from parents, developing intimate and romantic attachments, taking responsibility for oneself, coping with impersonal bureaucracies, and having fun. It is first and foremost a coming-of-age experience, a time of self-discovery, intense friendship, and informal socializing. On average, college students spend only about twelve to fourteen hours a week on their classes. For full-time students, much of the rest of their time is spent mingling with peers, participating in extracurricular activities, or earning extra money. For all, it is a critical stage on the way to maturity and self-realization.

The defining features of college life — intercollegiate athletics, fraternities and sororities, and an assortment of clubs and extracurricular and intramural activities, ranging from student newspapers and yearbooks to glee clubs and student government — were largely a product of the late nineteenth century, when the modern research university was established and key characteristics of the modern college experience, including semesters, credit hours, tenure, academic departments, majors and minors, and multiple-choice tests, were introduced. The late nineteenth-century words of a Columbia sociologist were equally apt a century later: He called college a "playworld." And, indeed, from the 1910s onward, Hollywood has showed a special interest in colleges' extra curriculum of parties, sophomoric pranks, romance, and bacchanalian football weekends. Only rarely have films offered inspirational portraits of faculty mentors or of outsiders from humble backgrounds, who, through dint and determination, succeed in graduating. Focusing almost exclusively on elite residential colleges, these films abound with stereotypes. Among male students, there is the big man on campus, the stuffed shirt, the dumb jock, the raucous fraternity boy, the snobbish, upper-class preppy, and the campus radical. Coeds are caricatured as big-haired husband hunters, socially inept, glasses-wearing intellectuals, cheery, rosy-cheeked college girls, and seductive sex kittens. Nor are faculty members portrayed any more realistically. Among male professors, there in the lecher, the washed-up pedant, and the dissolute prima donna wearing a tweed sport coat with leather elbow patches; female caricatures include the dowdy, the neurotic, and the sexually repressed. However unrealistic, these films have helped to shape students' expectations about college life and what they hope to get out of it.[44]

The double-edged character of the college experience, in which academics coexist uneasily with its social aspects, is the product of a contentious history involving faculty, administrators, and students themselves. Colonial colleges treated their students like children. Indeed, many, who often entered college at the age of fourteen, would in fact fit current definitions of childhood. In part because of students' young age, American colleges, from the start, assumed greater responsibility for student life, including dormitories and dining halls, than did continental European universities, where students mostly lived off campus. Acting *in loco parentis*, the colonial colleges required students to live under the watchful eye of their professors and tutors. The schedule at Princeton was not atypical. A morning bell rang at 5 A.M., followed by chapel services at 6 A.M.; recitation and study stretched from 9 A.M. to 1 P.M., when a mid-day meal was served, followed by another period of recitation and study. At 5:00 P.M. there were prayers, followed by supper at 7:00 P.M. and bed at 9 P.M. Rules and customs made the college a place of hierarchy and deference, with punishments taking the form of fines and whippings. Students were required to tip their hats to professors. A common custom, not abolished at Yale until 1804, was fagging, in which underclassmen were required to perform menial tasks for upper classmen. The curriculum itself was prescribed, offering few or no electives.[45]

Beginning as early as the 1760s, student resistance erupted. Harvard's first student riot took place in 1766, prompted by an uproar over rotten butter in the dining hall. Protests broke out at many of the early colleges against bad food, compulsory military drilling, antismoking regulations, and limits on freedom of speech, with students bolting classroom doors, smashing campus windows, and stoning faculty members' houses. There were six riots at Princeton between 1800 and 1830. James Fenimore Cooper was dismissed from Yale for hitching a horse to a classroom lectern. This unrest could have serious repercussions. During a riot at Harvard, the historian William H. Prescott lost his eyesight; another riot at Yale resulted in a tutor's death. During the 1830s, one University of Virginia professor was horsewhipped, another stoned, and yet another murdered.[46]

In 1809, the president of the University of Vermont claimed that student unrest originated in a breakdown of older systems of discipline and the impact of the Revolution's democratic, egalitarian ideology. In his words, student rebellions stemmed "from deficiencies in modern, early parental discipline; from erroneous notions of liberty and equality; from the spirit of revolution in the minds of men, constantly progressing, tending to a relinquishment of all ancient systems, discipline and dignities; from an increasing desire to level distinctions, traduce authority and diminish restraint; from licentious political discussions and controversies." Expressing sentiments that would be echoed centuries later, the president of Dickinson College complained, "Our students are generally very averse to reading or thinking."[47]

In a bid to restore discipline, colleges resorted to harsh measures, including mass expulsions. Harvard expelled forty-three of seventy members of the class of 1823. Colleges also began to institute grades, which were shared with parents. A far more successful strategy involved colleges gradually broadening their curriculum beyond the classics (introducing expanded offerings in science, as well as the first courses in social science, starting at Oberlin College in 1858) and inaugurating the first electives. They also started to tolerate a more independent student lifestyle and to permit the establishment of literary societies, fraternities, sporting clubs, and organized athletics. The first fraternity, Kappa Alpha, was formed at Union College in 1825. Organized crew and boat racing were introduced in the 1840s, baseball in the 1850s, and the first intercollegiate football game took place between Rutgers and Princeton in 1869.[48]

At first, various college clubs, fraternities, sororities, campus newspapers, and extracurricular activities were organized and run by students themselves. In the early twentieth century, in part in response to the emerging concept of adolescence, college administrators began to institutionalize and oversee student life. Dormitories were staffed by counselors, and athletic directors took charge of intercollegiate and intramural sports. In recent years, campus administrators have become both more and less involved in undergraduate life. On the one hand, the most restrictive policies, such as parietals, or the dormitory rules governing visits from members of the opposite sex, were abolished during the late 1960s and 1970s. On the other hand, administrative involvement in other areas of student life — ranging from drinking to psychological health and oversight of sex offenses — has greatly expanded.[49]

Today, campus life is defined less by athletics or the fraternity and sorority scene, or even by organized extracurricular activities than by informal socializing — hanging out, flirting, gossiping, visiting, engaging in bull sessions with friends, and partying. Friendships, including cross-gender friendships, which became more common after the introduction of coed dorms starting in the late 1960s, are central to college life. The shift in focus from formality to informality reflects the increasing demands on students' time, as they devote more time to off-campus jobs, internships, study abroad, and other activities. It is also a product of the student body's growing diversity, the longer time needed to acquire a degree, and the growing tendency for students to take courses from multiple institutions. As a result, campus life is far less hierarchical now than previously.[50]

College is indispensable if one is to attain a middle-class life. Those with college degrees make nearly twice as much as those with a high school diploma, and more than 60 percent of jobs require postsecondary education, up from just 28 percent as recently as 1973. Yet despite high levels of reported satisfaction on the part of students and their parents, colleges do not serve many students particularly well in terms of intellectual development or vocational preparation. According to some measures, nearly half of undergraduates demonstrate no significant improvement in critical thinking, complex reasoning, and writing skills during their first two years—a situation that reflects the distractions of work and socializing as well as institutional cultures that place little emphasis on high-quality teaching and mentoring. Worse yet, colleges and universities do a poor job of helping the bulk of their students identify realistic career objectives and a credible plan to achieve those goals. As a result, many students flounder for years before falling into a job that may or may not reflect their academic training or interests.[51]

Despite persistent efforts to ease the route to a productive adulthood by creating a clearly defined institutional pathway through college, the transition remains anything but smooth. The bridge years between adolescence and functioning adulthood, often romanticized as a period of exploration and self-discovery, are, for many, a period of uncertainty, ambiguity, and flailing about. To understand why this is the case, it is necessary to shift our focus to the gradual development of a youth culture intensely ambivalent about adulthood and to the emergence of youthful lifeways that have made the transition to adulthood seem less urgent or compelling.

~✦~

The passage from youth to adulthood is life's unsurpassed drama. During the liminal stage between adolescence and full adulthood, the young separate from their family of origin, define an independent identity, find their calling, establish more mature and intimate relationships, and grapple with profound spiritual and sexual issues. An odyssey of discovery and self-fashioning, this stage requires the young to pass through a series of trials, temptations, and rites of passage as they struggle to achieve mature status. Not surprisingly, literature, especially since the late eighteenth century, has looked to the passage to adulthood for many of its most compelling plots. It reveals and helps shape the expectations, conventions, ideals, and fantasies that color the way readers imagine their own lives. It is from fiction, novels, movies, and television shows that the young have learned what it means to grow up in society and embrace an uncertain future.

Literary treatments of coming of age often center on an education, apprenticeship, or self-formation; on rebellion against a father; on sexual initiation or the experience of first love. Some coming-of-age stories are tales of loss—the loss of innocence, naiveté, and spiritual faith. Others are tales of maturation, forged out of a hard-won experience, in which a young person grows cognitively and emotionally, developing a sense of autonomy, establishing a unique identity, and acquiring a sense of purpose and direction. Still others depict deepening alienation—often estrangement from parental values and from such institutions as schools or churches. All, however, emphasize the young person's agency, regarding their protagonist not as a passive victim but as an active agent, who, for better or worse, make a series of profoundly consequential choices. In these works, we can enter into the youths' psyche, hear young people's voices—cynical, vulgar, humorous, and prematurely wise—and eavesdrop on their fantasies, desires, and dreams.

The late eighteenth century saw the rise of the bildungsroman, the novel of development. In its classic form, the bildungsroman not only traces an author or artist's coming of age, but also explores the transition from innocence to wisdom, ingenuousness to experience, naiveté to maturity. Not simply a picaresque tale of youthful adventures, the bildungsroman presents a young person's process of soul-searching and self-discovery. It chronicles a young person's quest to define a philosophy of life and vocation in the face of a host of moral, intellectual, familial, and social constraints. Becoming an adult, in such novels, is the classic bourgeois declaration of independence and assertion of individuality.

In the archetypal European bildungsroman, the father is the youth's antagonist, hostile to the child's ambitions and aspirations and utterly insensitive to the young person's sensibilities. Geographical mobility, interpersonal conflict, and brooding self-awareness are all characteristics of this literary genre. Sexual awakening also occupies an especially important place in the bildungsroman, as a youth experiences a number of love affairs, some debasing, others uplifting. Separation from the family matrix and from paternal authority and the constraints of lineage and kinship are key elements in these narratives. In some novels, such as Jane

Austen's *Pride and Prejudice* (1813), the coming-of-age process is characterized by closure, as in marriage. But in many others, such as Honoré de Balzac's *Comedie humaine* (1830–1842) or Thomas Wolfe's *Look Homeward, Angel* (1929), the novel ends with rupture, not closure.[52]

This new literary genre arose at a particular moment in time and reflected an intense, secularized interest in the self in the late eighteenth century. The bildungsroman signaled a new emphasis on youth as a social category and as a critical moment of self-definition and initiation into the mysteries of love and sexuality. Especially in the male bildungsroman, coming of age is associated with the development of an autonomous, individuated self and a quest to leave one's mark on society and in these ways very much symbolized and celebrated the triumph of bourgeois aspirations.[53]

The genre also pointed to the fact that the passage to adulthood had become problematic in new ways. Although often called a "novel of apprenticeship," the bildungsroman arose at precisely the time that traditional apprenticeship, involving a period of tutelage under a master's mentorship, was breaking down. Discontinuity between generations was increasing, and the passage to adulthood was anything but linear or predictable. This new uncertainty lies at the heart of the bildungsroman's coming-of-age narrative.

Many of the United States' most enduring works of literature, from Louisa May Alcott's *Little Women* (1868–1869) and Mark Twain's *The Adventures of Huckleberry Finn* (1885) to F. Scott Fitzgerald's *This Side of Paradise* (1920), Carson McCullers's *The Member of the Wedding* (1946), J. D. Salinger's *Catcher in the Rye* (1951), Ralph Ellison's *Invisible Man* (1952) Jack Kerouac's *On the Road* (1957), and Philip Roth's *Goodbye, Columbus* (1959), are American variants on the bildungsroman. These novels are journeys of self-fashioning, odysseys of moral and psychological growth, and quests for experience and self-discovery. Indeed, one might argue that in a nation that has long defined itself in terms of its youth, the coming-of-age tale is the preeminent American literary form, repeatedly retold by outsiders and newcomers. The genre was seized upon by fugitive slaves, immigrants, and women of diverse backgrounds.

Over time, we can detect within these American coming-of-age tales a striking shift in attitude. Whereas the earlier works viewed the achievement of a mature adulthood positively, during the twentieth century, growing numbers expressed disdain and alienation from the attributes of conventional adulthood. Some works, like Mary Antin's *The Promised Land* (1912), continued to associate adulthood with liberation from confining customs and narrow traditions. But many others, like Anzia Yezierska's *Bread Givers* (1925), and especially those that followed *Catcher in the Rye*, are more cynical, critical, or ironic tales of alienation, disaffection, and angst.[54]

In many classic American female bildungsromane, from Susanna Rowson's 1791 novel *Charlotte Temple* through Sylvia Plath's *The Bell Jar* (1963), a patriarchal society thwarts a woman's efforts to fulfill her talents and capacities. Sexuality proves particularly problematic. In African American and Chicana bildungsromane, rape and violence—legacies of slavery, Jim Crow, and colonial subordination—are facets of growing up. Bildungsromane by female African American writers such as Toni Morrison, Gwendolyn Brooks, Gayl Jones, Sapphire, Ntozake Shange, Thulani Davis, and Jacqueline Woodrow explore other issues important to the lives of young black women, including confrontations with western standards of beauty and integrating into unwelcoming white-dominated spaces.[55]

In these literary works, the maturational process is long, arduous, and often painful, and the protagonist's objective is to avoid succumbing to the shortcomings of conventional adult life. Many recent American bildungsromane prove to be less about maturation than celebrations of wanderlust and the unfettered possibilities of young adulthood. Some revel in the pursuit of kicks, the joy and spontaneity of life on the road, and the kinetic energy and recklessness of this phase of life. By contrast, others, especially those by immigrants and marginalized ethnics, are about the traumas of displacement, the challenges of fashioning an identity, and the struggle for acceptance.[56]

If literary depictions of coming of age have grown more ambivalent or even hostile toward conventional adulthood, the same is true in real life. As the passage into adulthood has grown more prolonged and problematic, it has often come to involve a period of transformation in a zone of fluidity more permissive than the world of adolescence and less structured than that of adulthood, in which tattooing, body piercing, hooking up, smoking, and using drugs, and drinking are rituals of separation and initiation. Young adulthood today is characterized by a relative freedom from adult responsibilities and oversight; segregation from interaction with large numbers of older adults; a lack of clearly defined social roles; and immersion in a commercial culture that is highly critical and even dismissive of the constraints of conventional "button-down" adulthood.

The emergence of a more skeptical and even cynical attitude toward adulthood did not occur overnight. Central to a shift in attitude was the growth of youth cultures heavily influenced by commercial mass culture. Over the past two centuries, a middle-class peer culture of "adaptation," which sought to prepare aspiring young women and men for the roles and responsibilities of adulthood, gradually gave way to an alternative youth culture that became resistant and even adversarial toward many of the trappings of adult life.

Far from being a twentieth-century invention, youth cultures were a source of public scrutiny and concern even in the sixteenth and seventeenth centuries. Youth then was a much more amorphous category than the modern conception of adolescence. Not only were youth's chronological boundaries vaguer, but the term was not closely linked to sexual, social, and emotional maturation. Nevertheless, early modern societies did regard youth as an important period of transition, involving profound changes in social behavior and work patterns. It was during this life stage that most young people left home and began to work as servants or apprentices.

In much the same way that our society associates adolescence with such characteristics as moodiness and rebelliousness, sixteenth- and seventeenth-century English society associated youth with certain distinctive traits. Youth were wild, headstrong, frivolous, arrogant, rebellious, and licentious. The young, it was said, were rowdy, steeped in carnal lusts, and absorbed in rioting, swearing, and sensual gratifications. Yet despite the charge that young people preferred dancing, clowning, and play to the word of God, by modern standards, youth in sixteenth- and early seventeenth-century England was primarily a period of self-denial and celibacy. Youth inhabited a sharply sex-segregated world, with little opportunity to establish intimate relations with members of the other sex. Many of the popular activities that involved mixed-sex socializing, such as round dances in which partners were frequently traded, discouraged young people from pairing off. Young people spent large parts of their teen years away from their family and their immediate neighborhood. Unlike modern adolescence, which is a period of prolonged dependency spent living in their parents' home and attending school, the teens and twenties during the sixteenth and seventeenth centuries involved a much greater degree of living apart from one's family in order to earn their sustenance.[57]

Today, a sharp line separates the music, jargon, and clothing styles of adolescents and adults. In the early modern era, the line between youth and adults was much more permeable. We now often think of youth culture as more distinctly separate in its desires and tastes, perhaps even as oppositional with regard to adult society. The closest thing to modern youth culture in the past was to be found in London, where apprentices numbered between 10,000 and 20,000 by the seventeenth century, or about 15 percent of the population. In the capital, apprentices formed a distinctive subculture with a strong sense of fraternity and a tradition of violent collective action. Publishers of chapbooks produced a large literature of escapist as well as religious literature targeted at this subculture.

Nothing quite like that existed in America until the mid-nineteenth century. Then, middle-class and upwardly mobile working-class male youth, from the early teens into the twenties, began to organize a host of collectives, including debating societies, literary clubs, and youth auxiliaries of reform and philanthropic societies, to cultivate organizational and speaking skills and establish social connections that would prove valuable in later life. Meanwhile, many middle-class young women participated in cross-generational church organizations, reform societies, and philanthropic endeavors, which integrated them into the world of adult womanhood. At a time when adult-run youth organizations were in their infancy, young people themselves took the lead in promoting the transition to adulthood. The very uncertainty of youth's status drove these rehearsals for adulthood.[58]

This genteel culture of aspiration coexisted with working-class youth cultures that offered an alternative to the middle-class emphasis on self-control and self-improvement. In rapidly growing cities, there was a high-dressing, fast-talking "b'hoy" culture, a boisterous world of physical prowess and jolly fellowship, made up of urban men of immigrant and native backgrounds, drinking, carousing, flirting, brawling, and taking part in volunteer fire brigades. A middle-class commentator described this figure:

> The hair . . . was one of his chief cares. . . . At the back of the head it was cropped as close as scissors could cut, while the front locks permitted to grow to considerable length were mattered by a lavish application of bear's grease. . . . A black, straight, broad-brimmed hat, polished as highly as a hot iron could effect, was worn with a pitch forward . . . a large shift collar turned down and loosely fastened, school boy fashion, so as to expose the full proportions of a thick, brawny neck; a black frock coat with skirts descending below the knee; a flashy satin or velvet vest. . . . A profusion of jewelry as varied and costly as the b'hoy could procure. His rolling swaggering gait on the promenade on the Bowery; his position, at rest, reclining against a lamp or awning post; the precise angle of the ever-present cigar; the tone of voice, something between a falsetto and a growl; the unwritten slang which constituted his vocabulary cannot be described.[59]

Also challenging middle-class conventions of propriety and deportment were growing numbers of urban working-class women who promenaded on urban streets wearing eye-catching clothing purchased with their own earnings and who openly socialized with men in public. This g'hal culture consisted of laboring young women who worked outside of family households as seamstresses, shop girls, dressmakers, milliners, shoe and book binders, map colorists, and artificial flower makers. Others peddled food and domestic goods on city streets. One observer noted: "Her very walk has a swing of mischief and defiance in it." Another wrote: "Her gait and swing were studied imitations of her lord and master, and she tripped by the side of her beau ideal with an air which plainly said, 'I know no fear and ask no favor.' "⁶⁰

The most dramatic alternative to the youth culture of aspiration was evident in the youth gangs that arose in the new nation's rapidly growing cities in the early nineteenth century. Gangs offered a way for lower-class and working-class young men to assert their manliness and masculinity, to secure a sense of identity and camaraderie, and to police ethnic boundaries. In 1807, the trustees of the African Methodist Episcopal Zion Church, in lower Manhattan, pleaded with the New York's City Council to do something about gangs of white working-class youths who harassed their worshipers on Sundays. By the early twentieth century, gang membership was a normal part of growing up for many urban immigrant and working-class youth. A Jewish teacher in New York recalled: "When I was a youngster . . . a common sight was a street battle between the Jewish and Irish boys. . . . One day the Irish boys would raid 'our' territory, turning over pushcarts, breaking store windows and beating up every Jew in sight. Another day saw 'our' side retaliating on Irish home grounds." Following World War II, public concern mounted as the number of gangs rose sharply and gang conflicts became more violent and more racially charged. Ice picks, knives, and homemade guns replaced sticks, stones, and bottles. Postwar urban renewal, slum clearance, and migration from the rural South, Mexico, and Puerto Rico ignited battles over territory in many of the nation's central cities as black, Latino, and European ethnic gangs fought to control playgrounds, parks, and neighborhoods. The homicide rate for adolescents in New York City in the years after World War II was double what it had been prior to the war. Unable to achieve academic or economic success, these young men sought status and adulation in crime.⁶¹

Challenges to the youth culture of aspiration were not confined to the working class. At the end of the nineteenth century, a burgeoning commercial "fun" culture gradually undercut this earlier youth culture. This vibrant, expanded commercial heterosexual youth culture revolved around dance halls, amusement parks, vaudeville theaters, and nickelodeons redefined the social and sexual relations between young women and men. In cities, commercial amusements attracted growing numbers of young working women, mainly first- and second-generation immigrants who were employed as department store salesgirls and secretaries. These young women worked somewhat shorter hours than earlier female seamstresses, maids, and garment workers and thus had increased leisure time. Their low wages forced these women to rely on men to pay for entertainment, a practice known as "treating." "The shorter work day," recalled one young woman, "brought me my first idea of there being such a thing as pleasure." Their dancing, dress, and less-inhibited lifestyle foreshadowed the flappers of the 1920s.[62]

Following World War II, youth culture became much more self-consciously resistant and oppositional. World War II itself contributed to new attitudes among the young by giving new urgency to seeking pleasure as the world became more dangerous. Many teenagers, too young for military service, worked in war industries and other jobs that gave them a higher disposable income than ever before. The result, according to a Buffalo, New York, newspaper was the "unequalled freedom that money brings," which also produced a growing number of "rowdies" and "would-be toughies." Youth, the newspaper concluded, "is catering to more wild parties and patterning closely behind many adults with whom they work side by side."[63]

Further contributing to this shift in consciousness was the democratization of the high school, where, for the first time, large numbers of middle-class and working-class adolescents interacted. African Americans in their mid-teens and their working-class and second-generation immigrant counterparts, who previously had gone directly from grade school into the workforce, now went to high school. Instead of attending separate vocational and technical high schools, growing numbers enrolled in comprehensive high schools that included college prep and vocational tracks under a single roof. Whereas in 1920, high schools educated less than a third of the nation's population of fourteen-to-seventeen-year-olds, by 1940, the figure had risen to 73 percent. The influx of working-class youth into the high school contributed to the rise of new styles and values, in which youth asserted their independence through music, dance, language, and fashion.[64]

1.2. Doing the twist in the baggage car, 1962. Photograph by Herman Hiller.

During that 1950s, many of the most popular films, novels, and writings aimed at a youth audience in their criticism of conventional middle-class life. Popular films, like Nicholas Ray's *Rebel without a Cause* (1955), starring James Dean, and popular novels, like J. D. Salinger's *Catcher in the Rye*, applauded sensitive, alienated youths unable to conform to the dominant adult values of suburban and corporate America. Meanwhile, during the late 1950s and early 1960s, a series of influential books explored the plight of youth in postwar society and the damage that a culture that emphasized conformity and social adjustment imposed on the young. Edgar Z. Friedenberg's 1959 classic *The Vanishing Adolescent* argued that American society, preoccupied with "the renunciation of individual differences," frustrated young people's efforts to grow psychologically and carve out an independent identity. Youth, in Friedenberg's view, should be a time of identity exploration, but adult society pressured the young to grow up prematurely. Adults, fearful of any deviation from established norms, and especially of any behavior that smacked of homosexuality, responded to young people's attempts at individuality with efforts at cooptation and suppression. Adult-sponsored organizations and activities, such as student councils, were little more than "adults-in-training" programs, while adult hostility toward rock'n' roll, which Friedenberg regarded as a harmless yet authentic expression of young people's hunger for a more vibrant, vital culture of their own, betrayed adults' desire to crush any forms of expression not aligned with middle-class values. Schools, which in Friedenberg's view should promote young people's psychological and interpersonal growth, were little more than custodial and sorting institutions. Rather than helping the young to better understand their own lives and those of others, schools emphasized conventionality and obedience and humiliated those students who failed to conform. With their desire for autonomy thwarted and their self-esteem quashed, many lower-class youth responded by dropping out, enlisting in gangs, and engaging in acts of delinquency.[65]

Anything but objective social science, Paul Goodman's forceful 1960 work of cultural criticism, *Growing Up Absurd,* was "a howl of pain" on behalf of young people who encountered institutions that rendered a "healthy process of growing up" impossible. Offering few opportunities for community or useful or meaningful jobs to aspire to, American society gave the young only two choices: either "cynically join the system" by joining the rat race and taking a meaningless job or rebel by becoming a delinquent or a bohemian. In his words, "Our abundant society is at present simply deficient in many of the most elementary objective opportunities and worth-while goals that could make growing up possible." Instead, a puritanical culture stigmatized adolescent sex and deprived the young of any useful ways to contribute to their society.[66]

James Coleman's 1961 ethnographic study of ten Illinois high schools, *The Adolescent Society,* argued that youth inhabited subcultures that stood apart from adult society. Largely segregated from the adult world, the young sought recognition from their peers. In stark contrast to the portrait drawn by sociologist August Hollingshead a decade earlier, entitled *Elmstown's Youth* (1949), Coleman identified a stark divide between adult and adolescent values. Coleman also emphasized the role of the peer group in the socialization of the young. Within the high schools, a series of distinctive youth subcultures had emerged, each with its own customs, language, music, dress, and value system. Within these peer-oriented subcultures, which flourished apart from adult-supervised activities, sociability, status, and popularity were far more important than brains or grades. Compared to high schools today, Coleman's schools were far more hierarchical, with a clear pecking order, which for young men was defined by athletic prowess and success with the opposite sex, and for young women, by attractiveness and social skills. Today's reader is struck by Coleman's hasty dismissal of the youth subcultures as dysfunctional on the grounds that they did little to prepare the young for an adult world preoccupied, for men, with careers and financial success, and for women, with marriage and motherhood. But Coleman also uses the word "subversive" to describe the youth subcultures, since he recognized, if somewhat hazily, that young people were disseminating a set of values, involving the erotic, the playful, and the quirky, that challenged the value system of adults.[67]

Few books better captured emerging trends in youth culture than Kenneth Keniston's *The Uncommitted* (1965). Based on intensive interviews with twelve Harvard students, the book focused on a segment of youth who aroused particular concern among adults: alienated youth who self-consciously rejected conventional adult values regarding jobs and family roles. The precursor to the hippies and radicals who symbolized the cultural revolution of the later 1960s, these highly privileged young men had a thirst for experience, adventure, heightened awareness, and mystical fusion into a larger community. Some experimented with illicit drugs, others tried out unconventional "beatnik" style living arrangements, and still others participated in radical politics. Their parents found it difficult to grasp why these children of privilege felt nothing but disgust for Harvard or for conventional youth culture, with its emphasis on sports and status. Keniston argued that their alienation was partly rooted in their upbringing as offspring of psychologically absent fathers and of highly sensitive, deeply frustrated mothers, who were convinced that their marriages had prevented them from fulfilling their aspirations. Lacking strong or attractive adult and masculine role models, these young men hunted for alternatives to conventional adulthood. But Keniston also attributed their alienation to a technocratic society that overemphasized technical expertise at the expense of emotions and lacked a strong sense of community, meaningful myths, or an appealing utopian vision.[68]

The cohort born in the late 1930s and 1940s, who reached their twenties during the 1950s, was dismissed, even at the time, as the "Silent Generation," characterized by conformity, conventionality, and risk-aversion. Never before, William Manchester later wrote, "had American youth been so withdrawn, cautious, unimaginative, indifferent, unadventurous—and silent." Coined by *Time* magazine in 1951, the name "Silent Generation" had pejorative echoes of the earlier notion of a "Lost Generation" in the 1920s. Its image was cemented in the popular imagination by photographs of collegians participating in panty raids and piling into telephone booths. In fact, this phrase was a misnomer. Far-reaching changes were occurring in the lives of young people in the wake of World War II. As high school attendance became virtually universal, the young were able to create a world separate and apart from adults. Youth subcultures, at odds with adult values, proliferated, while a new musical style, rock'n' roll, challenged accepted tastes in music, cut across racial lines, and was openly vulgar. Indeed, the very phrase "rock'n' roll" had been used in blues songs to refer to sexual intercourse. Dr. Francis J. Braceland, a noted psychiatrist, denounced the music as "a communicable disease . . . appealing to adolescent insecurity and driving teenagers to do outlandish things," and between 1954 and 1958, there were numerous crusades to ban it from the airwaves. If some young people, dressed in penny loafers, cardigan sweaters, or poodle skirts did indeed fit the Silent Generation stereotype, others would play leading roles in the civil rights movement and Beat culture, while others would become feminists and activists in other struggles for social change.

Nevertheless, it was not until the mid-1960s that youthful alienation from adult values became widely recognized.[69]

During the 1960s, youth loomed larger in American society than any other group. As a result of depressed birthrates during the 1930s and the postwar baby boom, there was a sudden explosion in the number of teenagers and young adults. Unlike their parents, whose values had been shaped by the Great Depression and World War II, young people of the 1960s grew up during a period of prosperity. This allowed them to seek personal fulfillment and to dismiss their parents' generation's success-oriented lives. Blue jeans, long hair, psychedelic drugs, casual sex, hippie communes, campus demonstrations, and rock music all became symbols of the distance separating youth from the world of conventional adulthood; these also gave rise to alarm over a "generation gap." Of course, not all youth subscribed to a common set of ideas. In fact, in 1968, far more young Americans voted for George Wallace, a divisive symbol of segregation, than joined the leading New Left organization, Students for a Democratic Society. Social scientists reported that there was very little divergence of ideas between teens and their parents on moral and social issues, and that the biggest cultural division was not between young people and their parents, but among youth themselves, especially between white middle-class and white working-class adolescents. Nevertheless, it is clear that millions of young people served as the shock troops in a wave of cultural transformations, advancing new hairstyles, modes of dress, aesthetics, cultural practices, and mindsets.[70]

Young people in their teens and twenties during the 1960s served as a cultural avant-garde. Their behavior and attitudes not only came to define the mood and atmosphere of the era, but also contributed to a paradigm shift, a fundamental change in values and behavior. Among the most obvious changes was sexuality, as cohabitation outside of marriage became much more common, and the birth control pill not only gave women greater control over their sex lives but also made it easier for them to enter and remain in the workforce. Equally important were young people's role in movements that drew the nation's attention to the problem of racism,

1.3. Photograph taken near the Woodstock music festival, August 18, 1969. Photograph by Ric Manning.

sexism, and other forms of discrimination and to the moral issues involved in the Vietnam War.

The civil rights movement served as the prototype for other struggles for equality and underscored the role of youth as a force for social change. Many of the most iconic and powerful images of the civil rights movement are of young people: There is the sixteen-year-old Elizabeth Eckford, surrounded by a mob as she walked to Little Rock, Arkansas, Central High School in 1957, or the eighteen-year-old Ronald Martin, Robert Patterson, and Mark Martin staging a sit-in at the F. W. Woolworth luncheon counter in Greensboro, North Carolina, in 1960 after being denied service, or the twenty-year-old Birmingham, Alabama, high school student Walter Gadsden being restrained by a police officer in 1963 as a police dog buries his teeth in the youth's stomach. Images of neatly dressed African American youth sprayed with fire hoses or standing beside a fire-bombed bus or beaten by segregationists made the evils of segregation concrete and played an instrumental role in awakening the American public to the evils of racial discrimination. Civil rights leaders wrestled with the ethics of mobilizing young people, including children, against segregation, but the young proved eager to take an active role in the struggle for racial equality. More than victims of discrimination, the young were agents of transformation.

Civil rights activism on the part of the young first arose in response to the trials of the Scottsboro boys during the 1930s, when nine black youths, ages twelve to nineteen, were falsely accused of raping two white women in Alabama in 1931. To encourage young people to participate in the struggle for equal rights, the NAACP established youth councils in the 1930s, and these organizations served as the training ground for many later civil rights activists. Meanwhile, YMCAs, YWCAs, college fraternities and sororities, and NAACP chapters, from the Great Depression through the 1950s, staged protests against segregation in schools, movie theaters, and swimming pools, as well as challenging racially offensive portrayals of African Americans in television, movies, and newspapers.[71]

Certain circumstances in the 1950s and early 1960s encouraged growing numbers of young African Americans to become involved in civil rights campaigns. Inspired by the rhetoric of freedom and equality spawned by World War II and the cold war, yet also feeling a deep generational divide from their parents, whom they saw as too passive and accommodating in the face of racial injustice, many young African Americans adopted a more militant posture. For some, the murder of fourteen-year-old Emmett Till in Mississippi in 1955 for allegedly whistling at a white woman was instrumental. For rural Mississippian Anne Moody, who was also fourteen in 1955, Till's murder was the event that prompted her to become a civil rights activist. She was appalled when she asked adults about the murder only to be told to shut up. She began to hate her elders "for not standing up and doing something."[77]

Far more combative than their elders, young activists prodded their elders to adopt more confrontational tactics. Organizations such as the Student Nonviolent Coordinating Committee (SNCC) and later the Black

Panthers shifted the focus away from a stress on integration and toward an embrace of Black Power, with its emphasis on racial pride, identification with Africa, the creation of community self-help organizations and black businesses, and political self-determination.

Parallel struggles for social justice engaged Mexican Americans, Native Americans, gays and lesbians, and women of all ethnic backgrounds. Radical feminist groups emerged among college students who were involved in the civil rights movement and the New Left. Women within those movements often found themselves treated as "second-class citizens," responsible for kitchen work, typing, and serving, as feminist activist Anne Koedt put it, "as a sexual supply for their male comrades after hours." In cities across the country, independent women's groups sprouted up, and by 1970 there were at least 500 women's liberation groups. A host of new words and phrases entered the language, such as "consciousness-raising," "Ms.," "bra-burning," "sexism," "male chauvinist pig." In 1970, the more radical feminist writings reached the broader reading public with the publication of Shulamith Firestone's *The Dialectic of Sex,* Germaine Greer's *The Female Eunuch*, and Kate Millett's *Sexual Politics*. These books argued that gender distinctions structure virtually every aspect of individual lives, not only in such areas as law and employment, but also in personal relationships, language, literature, and religion, as well as in an individual's internalized self-perceptions. As examples of misogyny these authors cited pornography, grotesque portrayals of women in literature, sexual harassment, domestic abuse, and rape. Meanwhile, women's organizations battled in courts and legislatures against laws and practices that allowed separate pay scales and want ads targeting men or women; excluded women from juries or set different ages at which women and men became adults; imposed height and weight requirements that excluded women from certain jobs; and barred women from pursuing abortion.[73]

At the same time, Mexican American youth embraced the terms *Chicano* and *Chicana,* drawn from the Nahuatl word for the "poorest of the poor," and launched a series of struggles against police brutality and inequities in school funding and staffing, and for bilingual education and compensation for descendants of families whose lands had been illegally seized. The most publicly visible struggle was on behalf of migrant farm workers, who sought higher wages, enforcement of state labor laws, and union recognition. Native American groups, invoking the phrase "Red Power," brought legal suits against states that had taken Indian land and abolished Indian hunting, fishing, and water rights in violation of federal treaties, and took legal action to prevent strip mining or spraying of pesticides on tribal lands. Young gays and lesbians in growing numbers came "out of the closet," publicly asserting their sexual identity, and then organized politically. In the wake of the 1969 police raid on the Stonewall Inn, a Greenwich Village bar, activist organizations like the Gay Liberation Front transformed sexual orientation into a political issue, attacking customs and laws that defined homosexuality as a sin, a crime, or a mental illness.

Since the 1960s, youth cultures have proliferated, with hippies giving way to hipsters, punks, rappers, slackers, and diverse ethnic youth subcultures, perhaps most evident in a multiplication of musical styles ranging from disco, rap, funk, and punk rock in the 1970s to heavy metal, techno, salsa, hip hop, grunge, alternative rock, and a wide variety of women's music in subsequent years. What links these diverse subcultures is their disconnection and estrangement from the world of conventional adulthood. For them, coming of age means not so much entering the adult world as exiting adolescence and childhood.[74]

⁓

Unlike the United States, Japan observes a holiday called Coming of Age Day, Seijin no Hi. On that day, those who turn twenty dress in a bright kimono or formal *hakama* (a dark color kimono), and a celebration ensues to welcome the youth into adulthood. In stark contrast, the United States has no public, collective, or formal rites to mark a young person's entrance into adulthood. To be sure, contemporary American society has a handful of communal or multigenerational rituals to mark one's coming of age. For Jews, there are the *bat* and *bar mitzvah*, which, today, rather than signifying the transition to adulthood, mark entry into adolescence. For many Protestants and Catholics, confirmation ceremonies serve a somewhat similar function. For many Latinos, the *quinceañera*, a celebration of a girl's fifteenth birthday, nominally marks the transition from girlhood to womanhood. In practice, however, it has become a more elaborate, religiously enveloped version of the sweet-sixteen party, which was common in the post–World War II middle class.[75]

Among the Amish, *rumspringa* is a period of relative freedom and experimentation when young people in their mid- to late teens and early twenties are able to partake in mainstream American culture before deciding whether to formally join the church. For nineteen-year-old Mormon males, missionary work is a fundamental tenet of faith. Among certain elites, there are "debutante balls," "cotillion balls," or "coming-out" parties in which a young woman is formally introduced to polite society. In addition, hazing rituals exist among gangs, fraternities and sororities, sports teams, and military units to initiate newcomers into the group. Unlike the ordeals that young people in traditional societies undergo in order to achieve full adult status, these hazing rituals typically subject initiates to bullying and humiliating sexual or physical abuse. The closest this society has to the formal public rituals of the past are the high school and college graduation ceremonies, during which the graduates' procession is accompanied by Sir Edward Elgar's *Pomp and Circumstance* in a custom inaugurated by Yale in 1905. Yet in recent years even these ceremonies have lost much of their collective or communal character due to their size and scale.[76]

In contemporary American culture, the most meaningful rites of passage are intensely private. These include the first date, the first kiss, the first opportunity to drive a car or drink coffee or smoke a cigarette. These events have become synecdoches for maturity. Yet, however meaningful these rituals may be at a personal level, they lack the communal character that characterized coming of age in more traditional cultures. The absence of such rituals in American society not only reflects the protracted nature of the transition to adulthood; it underscores and reinforces the intensely individualistic character of American culture and the separation between the worlds of youth and full adulthood. Growing up in the contemporary United States consists of a series of individualized, privatized acts lacking public sanction or recognition except among the peer group.[77]

The purpose of rites of passage in more traditional societies is to ease and publicly validate difficult and abrupt transitions in status. In classic works of ethnography, anthropologists discovered that the process of coming of age in small-scale societies involves a series of rituals and experiences involving the crossing of thresholds. These rites of passage separate the young from their previous role and environment, situate them temporarily in a threshold status outside conventional social categories, and then reintegrate them into society with a new status and role to play. These rituals often involve physical tests or ordeals and acquisition of a new name, denoting a new social identity. Among the purposes of these rites are managing conflict between generations, defining gender and distinguishing the realms of the sexes, and assisting the young in the passage from dependence to adulthood responsibilities.[78]

In many early Native American societies, for example, the young went through a variety of rituals of separation, transition, and incorporation. Thus, at the time of first menstruation, a girl might go into seclusion to a special menstrual hut. There, an older woman would care for her and instruct her in her roles as an adult. After her reemergence, she would begin to dress as an adult. Boys also underwent rites of initiation. A number of firsts, including the first tooth, first steps, and the first big game killed by a boy, were recognized in public ceremonies. Among many peoples, when a boy approached adolescence, he went alone to a mountaintop or into a forest to fast and seek a vision from a guardian spirit. On his return, his courage and survival enabled him to assume adult status.[79]

The passage to adulthood in contemporary Western societies bears scant resemblance to this indigenous pattern. In contrast to more traditional societies in which an individual's transition to maturity is public and social, in contemporary Western societies, the process is individual and focused inward. A young person's odyssey is as much a voyage of psychological self-discovery and identity formation as it is a matter of physical movement. As in small-scale societies, coming of age is a time of uncertainty and risk. It is a period when the young begin to detach from parents, abandon older loyalties and form new ones, and experiment with adult forms of behavior. But this process occurs primarily on a personal, not a collective or communal, level.

Many of the most culturally significant signposts of coming of age—a driver's license, a first drink, a first cigarette, a sexual initiation—are private matters, experienced solely by young people themselves. This fact has led some observers to suggest that the difficulty many young people experience in making the transition to adulthood may be related to a deficiency of public rituals that mark off the maturational process. In her classic 1928 ethnographic study, *Coming of Age in Samoa,* the anthropologist Margaret Mead contrasted the supposedly easy and effortless passage to adulthood in Samoa and the conflict-ridden process in the United States. She argued that the stormy familial struggles that American society experienced were not inevitable products of human biology, but were effects of a culture that provided young people with too few ways to express their growing maturity and competence, inhibited expressions of adolescent sexuality, and kept the young psychologically and economically dependent far too long.[80]

For many of the young today, the single most important marker of the transition away from childhood and adolescence involves sexual initiation. Sex, at least since the eighteenth century, represented the most significant symbolic dividing line between childhood innocence and adult sophistication. The early twentieth century marked a fundamental shift in sexual experience. Instead of having their first sexual experience with a prostitute or a woman from a lower social class, young men began to have their first intercourse with young women of their own class, typically with a fiancé. Among those born before 1900, 37 percent of men and only 3 percent of women reported having had premarital intercourse by the age of eighteen. Of those women born between 1900 and 1930, in contrast, about 20 percent had experienced intercourse by age twenty. Up until the 1960s, however, for most young women, loss of virginity was associated with engagement, and premarital intercourse was still largely confined to a single partner. Of those born in the 1920s, 70 percent of men but only 12 percent of women reported having had more than one sexual partner prior to marriage. Some 45 percent of women born around 1940 married their first sexual partner, compared to just 6 percent of those born after 1965. A seismic shift in adolescent sexual behavior took place during the 1970s, when sex before the age of eighteen became an increasingly normative adolescent experience. The percentage of fifteen-to-nineteen-year-old females who had experienced coitus rose from 30 percent in 1971 to 43 percent in 1976, and from 50 percent in 1979 to 77 percent today.[81]

This profound shift in the adolescent sexual script burst into the public spotlight with the publication of Judy Blume's *Forever* (1975), the first young adult novel to candidly describe a sexual relationship between two "typical" high school students. Set in the mid-1970s, it depicted a New Jersey teenager who falls in love, decides to lose her virginity for her boyfriend's sake, and expects the relationship to last forever. Then, after the couple is separated for the summer, she discovers that she has feelings for another boy and is forced to rethink her ideas about love and commitment.

In real life, as in fiction, loss of virginity stands out as one of the most meaningful milestones in the transition to adulthood. Americans transmit many contradictory messages about this moment: that it symbolizes coming of age; that it is often painful, awkward, and disappointing; that it should be confined to loving, romantic relationships; that it is primarily about one's self, one's personal pleasure and maturation. If loss of virginity is eagerly anticipated, it is also associated with risk and danger of pregnancy, pain, and performance anxieties. Even today, remnants of the sexual double standard persist, with the implicit assumption that sex is something that a young man gets and a young woman gives, perhaps eagerly and enthusiastically, but sometimes reluctantly, ambivalently, and half-heartedly. Guilt and shame continue to shadow sexual initiation, at least for some. According to one study, some 70 percent of young women express some regret over the timing or circumstances of sexual initiation.[82]

For some young men and women, virginity is a stigma, and its loss symbolizes becoming a real man or woman. For some young women, "going all the way" is instrumental; it is a means to an end, especially true love. For others, it is a gift, a demonstration that a relationship is loving, trusting, and truly intimate. For still others, it a form of bartering, an exchange of sex for commitment. For a significant and increasing number of women, it is associated with empowerment, agency, pleasure, and taking ownership of their own body.[83]

Sexual initiation cannot be divorced from broad issues of power with profoundly unequal implications for young women and men. For some, first sex is intentional, but for others "it just happened" or was associated with drinking or was a product of coercion or acquiescence. Those young women in their teens and early twenties who have a strong future orientation and high ambitions do appear to be more careful about sex than others and are much more likely to use contraceptives. Regardless, there remains a sense that young women remain the sexual gatekeepers and that young men will apply pressure. Many teenage boys still think of intercourse as conquest or as a rite of passage in which their partner's identity or feelings are inconsequential, an attitude summed up by the phrase "popping the cherry." Nevertheless, there is some indication that an older "battle of the sexes" paradigm is giving way to greater convergence in female and male attitudes toward virginity loss.[84]

A host of myths surround adolescent and early adult sexual behavior. One such myth is that today's adolescents begin sexual activity far earlier than their parents. In fact, since the 1970s, the age of first intercourse has remained roughly constant. Another misconception is that sexual behavior is much more promiscuous and casual than it was a generation ago. In fact, most sexual activity among young adults takes place within ongoing relationships, although what constitutes a serious relationship now has by definition a shorter time span than it did in the past. Contrary to what many think, the history of adolescent and early adult sexuality is not simply a story of the steady liberalization of attitudes and behavior. In fact, even in recent years, rates of intercourse have varied widely. In 1991, 54 percent of high school students engaged in sexual intercourse; a decade later, the figure had fallen to 46 percent. Yet another illusion is that contemporary colleges are latter-day Sodoms and Gomorrahs. In fact, college students are less sexually active than their noncollege peers, and their sexual activity is less promiscuous. That oral sex is a way for the young to remain "pure" or technically virgin is yet another figment of the media's imagination. Oral and anal sex among heterosexual youth does appear to have become more common in recent years, but it is generally a supplement to, not a substitute for, vaginal intercourse.[85]

At the same time that the age of sexual initiation dropped, another aspect of an older sexual script, the romantic date, faded away. The date, which first appeared among the urban working class during the 1910s, was a much more informal alternative to courting, with its presumption that a young man's intentions involved the possibility of engagement and marriage. In its classic form, from the 1930s through the 1950s, dating involved a process of sampling the field in ways that affirmed a young woman or young man's status, followed by a progressive deepening of commitment, and culminating in rituals such as "pinning" or giving a girlfriend a symbol of attachment, such as a letter jacket. During the 1970s, dating as a ritualized experience declined and was replaced by socializing in packs and by partying. An earlier bargain, in which the male paid for a date and sought sexual favors in return, came to be viewed as an example of sexism and gradually gave way to new pathways toward forming relationships.

Highly sensationalized articles in the popular press often associate late adolescent and young adult sexuality with "hooking up," a phrase that suggests consensual sexual activities outside the context of a steady relationship. In actuality, though, the phrase itself eludes clear definition, and the act of hooking up can range from making out to sexual intercourse. Whereas some see hooking up as a way for ambitious female high school and college students to avoid the time-consuming complexities of steady relationships, others view it as a byproduct of gender inequality and thus an unavoidable path for young women who seek a romantic relationship—a path that involves not romance or intimacy or even sexual satisfaction, but alcohol or drug-fueled one-night stands. In fact, even on residential college campuses, hooking up appears to be less common than media reports suggest. Yet the desire for intimate and committed relationships persists. Today, about 15 percent of eighteen-to-twenty-three-year-olds are currently cohabiting, and about a fifth have cohabited at least once by the age of twenty-four.[86]

It is clear that the path toward such relationships has shifted, becoming less stylized, ritualistic, formalized, and dependent upon male initiative.

Especially within colleges with highly skewed sex ratios, the sexual double standard persists, with young men exercising more power over relationships. But two points stand out. First, the definition of an intimate relationship has changed among many young women and men, evolving into something more committed and intimate than a hookup but something less than a steady romantic relationship as previously understood. Second, serial monogamy remains the primary sexual script. In spite of the talk of "friends with benefits" and "booty call," no-strings-attached sex remains unusual. After college, however, dating becomes more common, as young women and men more seriously seek a marriage partner.[87]

Perhaps the most striking shift in sexual scripts involves the open acknowledgment of same-sex desires and a growing willingness to act upon these yearnings at an earlier age and with far less ambivalence than had previously been the case. Instead of waiting to identify oneself as gay or lesbian in the mid- to late twenties or even later, there is a growing willingness to come out in one's teens. There are, however, certain striking gender differences in this development. Young women are three times more likely to report same-sex attraction and activity as young men, but are less likely to describe themselves as homosexual and more likely to identify as bisexual.[88]

It is not that same-sex acts among the young were uncommon in the past. Intensely intimate same-sex friendships were widespread before the Civil War, involving effusive displays of emotion and passionate physicality. One surviving letter by Virgil Maxcy, who would later become a leading Democratic politician prior to the Civil War, is quite explicit. "Sometimes," he wrote to a male friend, "I think I have got hold of your doodle when in reality I have hold of the bedpost." Maxcy signed the note "your cunt humble." In his 1948 study of male sexuality, Alfred Kinsey reported that in rural areas, male same-sex sexuality, in which those involved did not consider themselves homosexual, was common. In the homosocial world of adolescent play during the early and mid-twentieth century, certain acts, like "jerk-offs" among adolescent boys and impassioned kissing and hugging among girls, were widely recorded, though almost never labeled as homosexual. What changed from the late nineteenth century into the mid-twentieth century was the identification of a distinct homosexual identity, which was labeled as unnatural and a psychopathology. Indeed, it was not until 1973 that the American Psychiatric Association removed homosexuality from its list of psychological disorders.[89]

The pathologizing of homosexuality led many with strongly felt same-sex desires to strive to repress or deny their impulses. In the wake of World War II, homophobia intensified, and same-sex desire was stigmatized as a form of immaturity and, in men, as effeminacy. By the 1990s, however, a growing number of early and middle adolescents were also willing to assert a lesbian or gay identity despite the risk of bullying and other expressions of hostility.[90]

Increasing access to sex on the part of young women as well as young men was a crucial step in the erosion of adulthood's special privileges. No longer did one have to be an adult to live independently, cohabit with a member of the opposite sex, or have access to sex on a regular basis. Not surprisingly, the ability to obtain adulthood's most desirable elements, without also assuming its traditional obligations and responsibilities, sharply diminished adulthood's appeal.

⚜

The dozen years from the late teens to the late twenties are the defining decade in American lives. Decisions made during that crucial decade largely determine an individual's life trajectory. This decade is also a time of risk, when young lives are most likely to go seriously off track. By most measures, it is the twenties, not the teens, when young people engage in the riskiest behavior. Binge drinking, illicit drug use, unprotected sex, even speeding peak in the twenties. It is also then that the young are most likely to have an unplanned child. Mental health issues, too, are most likely to manifest themselves during this decade. If teens make mistakes, they often receive second chances. But for those in their twenties, society is less forgiving. This is especially true for young men of color. About 1.5 percent of white men in their twenties serve time in prison, but the figure is 4 percent for Latinos and 10 percent for African Americans. It is not surprising that the twenties are especially risky. The predictable routine and dependency of adolescence has not yet been supplanted by the stabilizing responsibilities of adulthood, including an established career, marriage or some other lasting relationship, and young children.[91]

The idea that the twenties are the decisive decade is not new. In the mid-nineteenth century, in a letter to a friend, Charles W. Eliot, the future president of Harvard, wrote: "What a tremendous question it is—what shall I be?" "The different professions are not different roads converging to the same end; they are different roads, which starting from the same point diverge forever, for all we know." Eliot was not alone in betraying a sense of uncertainty. Another young man gave pointed expression to his unhappiness at his inability to chart a clear course in life: "I am twenty-eight years old today. Twenty eight! And nothing done. My education unfinished—no immediate expectation of being 'settled in life'—rather a sorry picture."[92]

The emphasis on the twenties as the seminal moment in a person's life was as true for young women as for young men. In her autobiography *Twenty Years at Hull House* (1911), Jane Addams wrote about the challenge that faced many young women of her social class after they completed their education—namely, charting a meaningful direction for their lives. "I have seen young girls suffer and grow sensibly lowered in vitality in the first years after they leave school. . . . She is besotted with innocent little ambitions, and does not understand this apparent waste of herself, this elaborate preparation, if no work is provided for her."[93]

For well over a century, young adulthood has been viewed as a time of aimlessness and indecision. It was during the second half of the nineteenth century that young men embraced a new way of thinking about the transition to adulthood. These young men spoke of identifying and pursuing a career—of choosing a clear direction for their ambitions and undergoing a period of intensive training to acquire the skills and experience that would be useful in the years ahead. For a growing number of these ambitious young men, higher education, for the first time, became an indispensable step on the path to a lucrative, high status career.[94]

In the autobiographical *Education of Henry Adams* (privately printed 1907), the author complained that he was educated for success in one world but graduated into a very different world for which he was unprepared. At least part of the difficulty of navigating the transition to adulthood lies in the intense age segmentation of contemporary American society, which ill prepares many young people for adult realities. Most twenty-somethings are more disconnected from mainstream society during that decade than at any other phase of life. As a group, these young women and men are less engaged in civic affairs than their elders as well as their juniors. They are less likely to read a newspaper, vote, attend church, or vote than any other segment of the adult population.[95]

Today, many young adults view the traditional markers of adulthood with suspicion and contempt, associating adulthood with weighty, unwelcomed responsibilities, closed-off options, and stultifying, button-down conformity. As one young adult put it: "If 'adulthood' means being saddled with a mortgage, a life-sucking nine to 5 job, two expensive kids, an equally disgruntled spouse, and lifelong educational debt[,] I hope I never reach adulthood."[96]

Ironically, many of the characteristics ascribed to emerging adults—identity exploration, relationship instability, and job shifting—are not restricted to twenty-somethings. Instability, uncertainty, and a desire to grow, but not grow up and settle down, persist into adults' thirties, forties, fifties, and sixties. A script that shaped expectations of adulthood through much of the twentieth century has unraveled. No longer can a majority of adults expect an unbroken marriage or a single career or a lifelong residence in a single city. Adulthood has become a time of flux and mutability.

CHAPTER TWO

Achieving Intimacy

If childhood today is a time of playmates and playdates, and adolescence, of crushes, infatuations, and peer bonding, then the next phases of life are the time of adult relationships, of emotional attachments that tend to be deeper and more fraught and complex than those experienced as a child or a teenager. Unlike earlier relationships, these connections are more likely to be the products of personal choice and involve a greater degree of intensity and intricacy.

Over the past half century, growing numbers of adults have come to see intimacy as their deepest source of personal happiness and satisfaction in life. At the same time, a code of emotional reticence gradually gave way to more open expressions of intimate affection. Extensive surveys conducted in the 1950s and 1970s saw a marked increase in awareness of the importance of intimacy to people's emotional health, even as difficulties in achieving intimacy came to be regarded as a mounting problem.[1]

Academic researchers and therapists also came to view a capacity for intimacy and deep connection as a critical factor influencing adults' psychological well-being. For Erik Erikson, the primary developmental task of young adulthood was to form intimate bonds. In his view, it was not until individuals had formulated a clear sense of their personal identity that they were capable of forming authentically adult relationships. The "humanistic" psychologist Carl Rogers regarded the development of a capacity for empathy, openness, commitment, deep understanding, nonjudgmental acceptance, and what he called "congruence" as essential to any meaningful long-term adult relationship. Meanwhile, Abraham Maslow placed love, affection, and "belongingness" high on his hierarchy of needs.

A major source of maladjustment and psychological dysfunction, he believed, was the thwarting of these needs for connection by a pathologically individualistic society. Today's positive psychologists, such as Martin E. P. Seligman and Mihaly Csikszentmihalyi, view the capacities for intimacy, nurturance, and empathy as buffers against distress and pain and as essential sources of strength and resilience.[2]

In this era of social networking, computer-mediated communication, and anytime, anywhere connectivity, when individuals can instantly communicate with "friends" who, on Facebook, average over one hundred, many worry that Americans are losing essential human interaction skills, such as the ability to read body language, assess a person's mood, or interact in a sustained and meaningful way. Debate rages over whether social networking sites are an antidote to or manifestation of an atomized, highly individualistic culture, in which social bonds have frayed, civic trust has eroded, and active participation in face-to-face voluntary associations has declined. Historical perspective is clearly called for.

Far from being encased in amber, intimacy, love, and friendship are concepts and experiences that have evolved. Over the past four centuries, the ideal of love was feminized and the concept of friendship reconceptualized in therapeutic terms. During the nineteenth century, the language of religion—transcendence, adoration, union—was projected onto love, as part of a broader cultural drift toward secularization. A feminized conception of romantic love, emphasizing self-disclosure and emotional intimacy, which arose during the eighteenth century, came under attack in the twentieth century, only to be supplanted by the very different idea of romance. Meanwhile, friendship largely lost its public dimension and came to be understood personally, in terms of listening, providing comfort, validating feelings, and massaging a person's ego. Friendship became more important emotionally, but in a highly mobile, work-oriented, couple-centered society, friendship—based on proximity and face-to-face interaction—became more difficult to sustain.

An unconventional source of evidence, folk art, can provide a starting point for an examination of the changes that have taken place in affective life. Two centuries ago, hand-colored valentines, heart-shaped boxes,

2.1. Anne Pitts, "Valentine," 1806.

and jewelry woven from strands of human hair were common tokens of affection, often accompanied by sentimental verses like this one:

> Here I've enclosed a ring of hair
> Which you have often seen me wear
> And when no more my face you see
> Look at this and think of me.[3]

In a post-romantic age, this mid-nineteenth-century folk culture is often dismissed as vapid, mawkish, and overly sentimental. Yet far from being mere adornments, these tokens of affection were endowed with meanings and symbolism far beyond their practical function. They reflected a new vision of the self, in which the true self is thought to be hidden beneath social convention and seeks to disclose itself and its emotions in love and friendship. The cult of sentimentality had a high purpose: Its goal was to elevate, dignify, and lift the self above a competitive, materialistic society. Hair rings, remembrance books, friendship albums, the language of flowers, and obsessive letter exchanges were attempts to bind individuals together by love and affection. The quest for love and friendship was a secular manifestation of the earlier religious search for magic and mystery as signs of God's intentions.[4]

Young women played a central role in creating this new sentimental culture. It was empowering to them in that it represented a radical attack on patriarchal ideas about the family, as well as a counterforce to American society's pervasive commercialism, materialism, and competitiveness. It sought to tame and channel male aggression and arrogance by promoting a feminine definition of love, emphasizing self-disclosure, intimacy, and the effusive expression of emotion. Today's synonyms for the word "sentimental" are uniformly negative: "sappy," "syrupy," "gushy," "maudlin," but the need for attachment, communion, magic, and mystery in relationships remains intense. It is not surprising that marketers and manufacturers strive ceaselessly to exploit these emotional needs.[5]

People's relationships before the rise of early nineteenth-century sentimental culture tended to be more formal and less expressive emotionally. Individuals purportedly married for practical, pragmatic, and prudential reasons. Their family interactions were aloof. Many scraps of evidence reinforce this view. In the seventeenth- and eighteenth-century colonies, wives and husbands addressed each other in their letters as "Mister" or "Dear Child." Surviving spouses frequently remarried within weeks of their partner's death. Parents often named children after recently deceased siblings. But it is a mistake to assume that our ancestors were emotionally inhibited and lacked our capacity for intimacy and emotional expression. All one needs to rebut the idea that love is a historically recent invention is to turn to the works of Shakespeare.[6]

"What is love?" asks the clown in *Twelfth Night*. In *Romeo and Juliet*, Shakespeare answers this question in multiple ways. Romeo's love for Rosaline, at the play's beginning, is immature infatuation; his love for Juliet is a passion so overpowering that it displaces loyalty to family and friends. For Mercutio, Romeo's close friend, love is erotic and adversarial. In Sonnet 116, Shakespeare refers to love as a "marriage of two minds," an "ever fixed mark" that is "never shaken" even when it encounters "tempests." In *Othello*, Desdemona's love is steadfast and unwavering, while her husband's, in contrast, is a raging passion that ultimately overcomes reason. For Iago, love is indistinguishable from lust—"merely a lust of the blood and a permission of the will." In *The Taming of the Shrew*, a platonic notion of love as worship of an ideal (evident in the relationship between Lucentio and Bianca) contrasts with love as an unromantic struggle for domination (in Petruchio's courting of Katherine). *As You Like It* depicts love in its myriad forms: love at first sight, love as folly, romantic love, adultery and cuckoldry, homoerotic love, and unrequited love.[7]

Today, we recognize the many faces of love. Teenage crushes, platonic love, adulterous love, jealous love, immature infatuation, wedded love, elderly love, May-December love, love from afar, love as fantasy, the mature love that grows with years together—these are just a few of love's multiple manifestations. A neurological condition, a sublimated sexual desire, an evolutionary mechanism to promote long-term relationships, a theological virtue, an amalgam of various drives and emotions ranging from self-love to love of humanity to love of children, parents, or relatives—love is all these things and more. It can be frantic, passionate, or tender; it can also be irrational, fickle, unpredictable, fragile, magical, intense, and exalting. It is often marked by jealousy, anxiety, and agony. It can also be a source of self-loathing. Love can fixate on a single person or express more general concern. It can be state of mind or an experience or a pursuit. It can be highly transient and earth-shattering, or it can be calm and enduring. Lust, infatuation, affection, attraction, attachment—these emotions are universal. They also have a history.[8]

Attitudes toward love are profoundly shaped by culture. Many languages have words or phrases to describe intimate relationships that have no precise English equivalent. Examples include *"Unmei no hito,"* a Japanese phrase that translates as "destiny person," the person one is fated to meet. There is the Chinese word *yuanfen*, which is drawn from Buddhism, and which refers to the "binding force" that dictates a person's relationships and encounters. The French speak of *"la douleur exquisite,"* the heart-wrenching pain of wanting someone one cannot have. *Forelsket* is Norwegian for the euphoria that individuals experience when falling in love. Then, there is *saudade*, Portuguese for the longing for a lost love, and *koi no yokan*, Japanese for premonitions of love. These words can be translated into English, but at a price: the words' emotive qualities and evocation of a broader system of social relationships are lost.[9]

Over time, cultural ideals of love have shifted dramatically. In classical Greece, there was *paiderastia*, the idealized relationship between an older male and an adolescent youth; *ludus*, game-playing and flirtatious love; *eros*, passionate sexual love; *storge*, the love that grows out of mutual understanding, respect, companionship, sharing, and concern; *mania*, obsessive, jealous, irrational love; *pragma*, the love based on self-interest and practical concerns; and *philia* and *agape*, the universal love later extolled in the New Testament. Then there is the courtly love of medieval romance and the ethereal Romantic conception of love as an involuntary force that unites distinct selves. Blake, for instance, described the metaphysical union of "Gratified Desire"; Shelley wrote of "one soul of interwoven flame"; and Keats referred to the "Melting . . . Mingling" of love. There is also the notion of rational love, found in the works of Jane Austen and George Eliot, which is seen as the highest form of friendship. During the Victorian era, the asexual and selfless relationship between mother and child and between siblings was extolled as the pinnacle of love. In recent years, love has been interpreted as a product of brain chemistry, with distinct neural circuitries and neurotransmitters associated with feelings of sexual desire, attraction, and attachment. Today, consummate love is widely regarded as combining several elements—passion, intimacy, companionship, and commitment—and the couple relationship has become its paradigm, with the soul-mate who is capable of fulfilling all of a person's emotional and sexual needs being the embodiment of true love.[10]

The late eighteenth century witnessed the emergence of romantic love as a cultural ideal. In a survey of all periodicals published during the thirty years before the American Revolution, one issue out of four contained a reference to romantic love as the proper basis of marriage; during the next twenty years the number of references to romantic love tripled. The heightened emphasis attached to romantic love can be seen in the proliferation of new kinds of love letters. Courtship letters changed by the nineteenth century from brief notes to longer, more effusive expositions of feelings and emotions. Seventeenth-century Puritans tended to moderate expression of affection in love letters. A letter from a Westfield, Connecticut, minister to his sweetheart was not atypical. After describing his passion for her as "a golden ball of pure fire," he added that his affection "must be kept within bounds too. For it must be subordinate to God's Glory."[11]

By the early nineteenth century, love letters, particularly those written by men, had grown more expressive and less formal. Instead of addressing their beloved in highly formalized terms, lovers began to use such terms of endearment as "dearest" or "my beloved." In their love letters, couples described feelings of affection that were deeply romantic. In 1844, Alexander Rice, a student at Union College in Schenectady, New York, described the feeling that overcame him when he first met his fiancée, Augusta McKim: "I felt . . . as I had never felt in the presence of a lady before and there seemed to be a kind of [direction] saying to me that I was now meeting her whom it was appointed should be my special object of affection and love."[12]

Yet even in deeply impassioned love letters such as this one, writers stressed that their love was motivated not by transient emotions, but by mutuality of tastes, companionship, trust, and shared interests. Alexander Rice made this point in typical terms: emotion alone would not have led him "blindly forward had not I discovered in you those elements of character and those qualities of mind which my judgment approved." The kind of love that early nineteenth-century Americans sought was not transient passion, declared Henry Poor, a young Bangor, Maine, attorney, in a letter to his fiancée, but a higher kind of love, "the kind that seeks its gratification in mutual sympathy."[13]

Although romantic love had historical roots in the traditions of courtly love, Neoplatonism, and Christian mysticism, it was a product of a particular epoch and culture. Romantic love reflected new ideas about the self, privacy, intimacy, equality, and personal choice. Romantic love represented a metaphysical or transcendental state in which couples were joined together in spiritual union and communion. Popular definitions elevated love into a soul-saving experience. Romantic love was disembodied; it was pure emotion, not a physical act. The sacralization of love represented a response to many women's fears about sex and an attempt to bridge the distance between women and men. It gave tangible expression to personal longings that arose partly in response to the displacement of religion from the core of imaginative life. Above all, the ideology of romantic love arose from a series of social developments that made marriage more problematic. For many young women, marriage threatened a loss of freedom and a loss of self in ways that were unprecedented. In the early nineteenth century, large numbers of young women worked outside a home and began to view marriage as a closing off of freedoms enjoyed in girlhood.[14]

An early nineteenth-century courtship illustrates the emerging middle-class ideal of love. In 1838, Theodore Dwight Weld, a thirty-nine-year-old abolitionist, wrote a letter to Angelina Grimké, the daughter of a wealthy, slaveholding South Carolina family who had left her birth state and turned against slavery, in which he disclosed "that for a long time you have had my whole heart." He had "no expectation and almost no hope that [his] feelings are in any degree RECIPROCATED BY YOU." Nevertheless, he asked her to reveal her true feelings. Angelina replied by acknowledging her own love for him: "I feel, my Theodore, that we are the two halves of one whole, a twain one, two bodies animated by one soul and that the Lord has given us to each other."[15]

Like many early nineteenth-century middle-class couples, Theodore and Angelina devoted much of their courtship to disclosing their personal faults and dissecting their reasons for marriage. They considered passion a childish and unreliable motive for marriage and instead sought a love that was more tender and rational. In his love letters, Theodore listed his flaws and worried that he was not deserving of Angelina's love. He was a "vile groveling selfish wretch"—reckless, impatient, careless in appearance, and poorly educated.[16]

Angelina responded by confessing her own faults—her temper, her pride, and the fact that she had once loved another man—and revealed her fear that the vast majority of men "believe most seriously that women were made to gratify their animal appetites, expressly to minister to their pleasure." Only after Theodore and Angelina were convinced that they were emotionally ready for "the most important step of Life," did they finally marry.[17]

Their romantic courtship rested on their belief in personal choice, including the principle that a woman should choose a spouse free from parental interference; the revelation of an authentic self; and an assumption of female moral and emotional superiority. Nineteenth-century courtship progressed through a series of predictable stages. It began with intimate self-disclosure and effusive expressions of inner feelings. It culminated in a series of crises, usually initiated by the woman, to test her suitor's commitment and affection. These emotional scenes enacted doubt, frustration, and anxiety and were followed by demonstrations of reassurance and praise. In a number of instances, women underwent severe doubt on the verge of marriage. In an increasingly mobile society, a woman's choice of life partner determined her future status and well-being. This was a decision fraught with tension. Perhaps not surprisingly, an unprecedented number of women declined to marry.[18]

Did romantic love provide the basis for emotionally intense and fulfilling unions? Often the answer was "no." The couples had grown up in a homosocial world and felt less comfortable with members of the opposite sex. The gender equality promised by romantic love often proved illusory. Although the male was expected to initiate the courtship and almost invariably wrote the longest love letters, after marriage many women and men retreated to separate spheres. Many women maintained their deepest and most intense emotional ties with other women.[19]

Around the turn of the twentieth century, ideas about love underwent a major new interpretation that sought to de-romanticize and demystify it. There were scientific realists who sought to lay bare love's physiological, neurological, and psychological roots; secular moralists who viewed love as a source of jealousy, possessiveness, and obsession; and feminist critiques that associated love with female dependency and loss of self.[20]

According to Freud, adult love is grounded in an infant's suckling of the mother's breast; in sublimation of libidinal impulses; in self-love projected onto an idealized love object; and in a mixture of erotic and aggressive impulses. In his words, romantic love is nothing more than "lust plus the ordeal of civility," a way to sacralize or elevate carnal impulses. According to Marxists, romantic love was an expression of bourgeois values: A belief in the exclusiveness and sanctity of love epitomized the bourgeois adoration of private property. T. S Eliot thought that "no human relations are adequate to human desires," while Proust considered love relations as "reciprocal torture." For Sartre, love was, first and foremost, an expression of egotism and an exercise of power: "Love consists merely in a desire to be loved." For the psychoanalyst Erich Fromm, love was a way to overcome existential loneliness. Writing eight years before her own marriage, Gloria Steinem declared: "The truth is that finding ourselves brings more excitement and well-being than anything romance has to offer." In our age of careerist individualism and diminished expectations, many fear that lasting love is unattainable and perhaps even undesirable, since it may lead to complacency and dependence. Oscar Hammerstein II made the point most forcefully in the 1938 musical *The Boys from Syracuse* (itself based on Shakespeare's *Comedy of Errors*) when he wrote that "falling in love with love is falling for make-believe."[21]

More recently, romantic love's demystification has taken a new form, as neuroscience associated love with brain chemistry. The passion, obsessiveness, joy, giddiness, and jealousy associated with romantic love have been connected to the production of phenylethylamine, a natural amphetamine, which also clouds judgment and makes individuals reckless and manic. Attraction has been linked to increased levels of dopamine and norepinephrine and a decrease in serotonin, while attachment has been cor-

2.2. "Love's Reward," c. 1908.

related with vasopressin and oxytocin, two neurotransmitters. Far from being a mystery—a heart-wrenching, visceral, overpowering feeling and a longing for connection and completion—love is a chemical cocktail combined with emotional neediness.[22]

Yet at the very time that a host of critics sought to demystify romantic love, an emerging mass commercial culture idealized unbridled romantic passion and elevated it to new heights. A 1912 play by George Bernard Shaw, entitled *Overruled,* was the first to use the word "romance" to refer to an emotionally passionate, sexually charged love affair. In the work's most memorable line, Shaw wrote: "I felt my youth slipping away without ever having had a romance in my life; for marriage is all very well, but it isn't romance." Romance resembles, but also differs profoundly from, the older ideal of romantic love. Like romantic love, it involves a powerful fantasy of emotional intensity, union, and self-transcendence. But unlike romantic love, it is more sensual and erotic and less tied to a single other person. It is a psychically intense, seemingly mystical experience rather than a spiritual bond. It is also tied to leisure and consumption in a way that romantic love was not.[23]

During the twentieth century, a commercial "love culture" emerged, directed primarily, but not exclusively, at women and girls. It encompassed popular magazines like *True Romance* and *Dream World,* which first appeared during the 1920s, romance novels, romantic movies, and soap operas. A defining message conveyed by the love culture was that individuals' lives were incomplete unless they experienced romantic love, culminating in marriage. Film, fiction, and advertising helped to shape popular images and the story of romance. Key components of the early and mid-twentieth-century romantic fantasy were that love happens; it is not chosen; nor is it the product of conscious agency or control. It is a product of fate, it is mysterious and magical, and it is the very opposite of everyday experience. Romance was deeply integrated into the realm of commodity exchange. Certain products and exotic experiences acquired romantic auras: engagement rings, champagne, candle-lit dinners, isolated tropical beaches, and, for a time, cigarettes.[24]

In his last book, the philosopher and social critic Allan Bloom complained that contemporary culture had demeaned and devalued love, reducing the emotion that lies at the heart of the greatest works of literature and art to sex and using the term indiscriminately to refer to anything that one likes. For Bloom, twentieth-century society had increasingly adopted the pseudo-psychological and faux sociological language of relationships for older words of love, downgrading lovers into self-enclosed individuals whose interactions invariably involve self-love, libido, elements of masochism and sadism, and relations of power, control, and dependence.[25]

Yet if some disdained and demystified love, their doing so did not reduce its power. The need for fusion, adoration, and transcendence only grew greater over time. One of the classic themes of social science is that modernization produces emotional relationships that are far more fragile and transient than those in the past, leaving individuals more atomized and

2.3. Teenage couple embrace on the bank of the Frio Canyon River, 1973.

anomic. If individualism and secularization breed a yearning for solitude and autonomy, modernization, with its emphasis on mobility and the independent self, also increases the need for emotional connection, support, and companionship, which can only be met through love and friendship.

❦

Aristotle thought friendship the most important thing in the world. "No one would choose to live without friends," he wrote, "even if he had all other good things." Montaigne regarded friendship as the "perfection" of social relations, since it was a product of free choice and entertained "no dealings or business except with itself." St. Augustine was left devastated by a friend's death. "Grief . . . torment . . . misery. All that we had done together was now a grim ordeal without him. . . . I wondered that he should die and I remain alive, for I was his second self." How many today would claim to have a friend who meets Dr. Samuel Johnson's benchmark of being one "who supports you and comforts you while others do not . . . with whom to compare minds and cherish private virtues"?[26]

Today, as more and more of adults' interactions with friends take place virtually, through email, tweets, or online postings, fears have mounted that friendship has grown shallower and less demanding than in the past. Some claim that the very concept of friendship has been degraded, as the word "friend" has been transformed into a verb or gerund and reduced to social networking. As one wit put it, adults watch *Friends* on television but have few friends in real life.[27]

Nags contrast today's e-friendships with the ideal of friendship advanced by Aristotle or Cicero or Augustine or Montaigne. Aristotle described friendship as "one soul inhabiting two bodies." Cicero, writing in 44 BCE, defined true friendship as "a complete identity of feeling about all things in heaven and Earth. . . . With the single exception of wisdom, I am inclined to regard it as the greatest of all gifts the gods have bestowed on mankind." Compared to these high standards — the friend as second self and friendship as a moral bond, indeed, life's most meaningful moral relationship — it is easy to conclude that today's friendships are weaker. Contemporary friendship, we are often told, have been reduced to participation in shared activities or to a therapeutic relationship: Friendship is supposedly little more than a nonjudgmental, largely friction-free relationship in which validating a friend's feelings and decisions is uppermost.[28]

In a highly mobile, time-stressed society, where adults are working longer and socializing less and television viewing and computer use have increased, friendship appears to many to be a casualty. Exacerbating this concern are sociological studies that suggest that adults are becoming lonelier and more friendless. One study found that the average American had only two close friends in whom he or she would confide on important matters, down from an average of three in 1985. One in five Americans reportedly has only one confidante, generally a spouse. These research findings have sparked a spasm of cultural self-reproach. Adult friendship, many fear, has been reduced to an occasional phone call or email message or a visit once or twice a year. No longer, many fear, is friendship a moral matter, as its connotations of trust, loyalty, and obligation in times of trouble, illness, or financial difficulty have seemingly eroded.[29]

Such fears are almost certainly exaggerated. Cross-gender friendships are far more common than at any time in history, and other kinds of sociability have proliferated too, including friendships that arise out of children's sports or Lamaze classes. With marriage no longer structuring a majority of adult life, friendships inevitably fill the void. In fact, fears of social isolation have a long, hyperbolic history. David Riesman's 1950 sociological analysis, *The Lonely Crowd,* and Philip Slater's 1970 blistering cultural critique, *The Pursuit of Loneliness,* were successors to earlier works by pioneering social scientists such as Emil Durkheim, Georg Simmel, and Ferdinand Tönnies, who claimed that the process of modernization frayed social ties and militated against life-long friendships. To be sure, the pressures on friendship are strong, arising especially from the demands of work and the competing claims of children and intimate partners. Fewer adults have life-long neighborhood chums; fewer are actively involved in civic organizations, such as PTAs, and voluntary associations; fewer participate in bowling leagues or socialize in neighborhood bars. Yet it is a mistake to assume that most adults are lonelier, more atomized, or socially isolated than those in the recent past. Standards of intimacy within friendship have risen, and the average person's core social network is actually broader than in the past. No longer is geographic proximity the primary means by which friendships are established and maintained. Nevertheless, worries about social isolation are not misplaced. Loneliness and social disconnection may well kill more people than auto accidents or cancer. Social isolation is linked to mental and physical illness, higher rates of stress and depression, and lower levels of civic engagement. As Ecclesiastes 6:16 put it: "A faithful friend is the medicine of life."[30]

Unlike family connections, rooted in consanguinity, friendship is voluntary and elective and free from the binding obligations associated with family life. In general, in contemporary society, friends tend to be far less judgmental and more fun than relatives. The rules of friendship are ambiguous, but generally involve reciprocity and mutual emotional support. Friendships vary dramatically: in intensity, duration, and salience. There are friendships of individuals, but there are also group friendships, which can constitute distinct subcultures. There are casual or close friends or best friends forever, confidantes, comforters, chums, companions, and compadres. Then, too, there are business associates, high school and college buddies, alter egos, fun friends, life-long friends, and fossil friends from a person's past. In recent years, the boundaries between friendship and other relationships have blurred. Parents aspire to befriend their children, spouses aspire to be best friends, and even siblings are supposed to be friends.[31]

In contemporary society, friendship is a life-course phenomenon, with adolescence and early adulthood being friendship's golden age. This has long been the case. In the seventeenth century, friendships were commonly formed in youth, when many young people lived apart from their parents as servants, apprentices, or school chums. Young men not only drank together, but in a society that prevented male and female youth from coupling, kissed, danced, and shared beds. Lord Byron called friendship "the dear peculiar bond of youth."[32]

Today, friendship remains tied to the life course. Around three or four, children begin to describe playmates as friends. Between nine and fifteen, young people begin to comment on the nature of interactions with their friends. But it is during the twenties that many of the most lasting adult relationships form. The friends acquired during the twenties are self-consciously chosen in a way that earlier friends are not. These friendships are also the result of adult decisions about one's identity, rather than geographical proximity. Marriage, however, has often, but not always, led to a diminishment of friendship ties. In 1662, an Anglo-Welsh poet, Katherine Philips, noted: "We may generally conclude the marriage of a friend to be the funeral of a friendship." As adults grow older, age differences seem to matter less to friendships. In a society in which many wives outlive their husbands, late life has also become an important time for women's friendships.[33]

Contemporary friendships also tend to be gender asymmetrical. Although the point can be exaggerated, the generalization that women's friendships are face-to-face and men's side-by-side contains a kernel of truth. For many adult men, trusting and intimate relationships are often confined to their wives. For others, intimate self-disclosure and requests for emotional support are reserved for relationships with female friends, with whom men feel they can be more vulnerable.[34]

In classical antiquity, friendship represented an important philosophic topic and literary subject. Classical Greece upheld an ideal of *synomosy*, a fellowship bound by solemn oath. A true friendship involved oneness of mind and spirit, and was characterized by loyalty and frankness. In the *Nicomachean Ethics*, Aristotle devised the most enduring classification system, dividing friendship into three kinds: friendships based in pleasure and on companionship and mutual activities; friendship rooted in utility, resting on advantage or material benefits; and friendship rooted in disinterested affection, mutual feelings, virtuous character, and shared interests. In the world of classical antiquity, philosophers claimed that true friendship was possible only among social equals. The classical world did not define friendship precisely as people do today. Friendship had a public dimension that has since declined. Civic friendship was an underpinning of the political order.[35]

In stark contrast to the classical world in which friendship was deemed possible only among equals, contemporary Americans can envision friendships not only across lines of race, class, and gender, but species, too. Decades earlier, cross-class and interracial friendships symbolized democracy's promise. In the late eighteenth century, revolutionaries on both sides of the Atlantic upheld fraternity as both a force for political transformation and the ultimate objective of politics. Canonical works of nineteenth-century American literature sentimentalized interracial friendships, such as those between Hawkeye and Chingachgook, Ishmael and Queequeg, and Huck and Jim, although it is noteworthy that these relationships took place outside the confines of civilization. Nineteenth-century workers viewed unions and even political parties as resting on bonds of fraternity; men socialized in lodges, fraternal orders, and college fraternities in which members called themselves "brothers." At the same time, middle-class and upper-class reformers founded friendly societies and staged friendly visits to bridge divisions of social class. Much more than an interpersonal relationship, friendship carried profound political implications.

Unlike Aristotle and Cicero, who focused on friendship as a bond uniting two individuals, the early Christian Church praised universal friendship, while regarding exclusive friendships as detracting from one's obligations to the Church and to humanity as a whole. The Church also feared that love of God could be subordinated by love of friends. Yet the early Christian and medieval eras also regarded friendship as a fundamental social bond that established social obligations and knit society together. Early Christianity attached a high value to nonsexual relationships that overcame social division, such as siblinghood and fraternity, and had a variety of friendship rituals that subsequently disappeared. The early Christian ceremony of *kolouthia* (occasionally *eukhe*) *eis adelphopoiesin* involved the ritualized "creation of brothers." These "brother-making" ceremonies offered a way for men to formalize alliances or to reconcile clans or households. During the Middle Ages, the bonds between lords and vassals were made official through formal oaths of friendship.[36]

In a self-conscious effort to resurrect classical ideals, Renaissance humanists, including Michel de Montaigne and Francis Bacon, sought to revive the Aristotelian notion of perfect friendship as involving a second self or one soul in two bodies. But even as the Renaissance revived the classical conception of friendship as the supreme human tie, there was a crucial difference. The treatment of friendship by such key figures as Montaigne and Shakespeare was self-reflexive in a way that that the classical discussions were not; it also exhibited a self-conscious awareness of the sexual and power dynamics embedded in friendship. Montaigne, drawing on Aristotle's arguments, contrasted "a true and perfect friendship" with those based on utility, pleasure, sex, or sociability. But in addition to describing friendship as a form of fraternal love, Montaigne self-consciously reflected on the loss of friendship, a friend's essential and enduring otherness, and the role of friendship in defining the self.[37]

In early modern England friendship had a public as well as a private dimension. If, on the one hand, friendship was a personal bond involving companionship and camaraderie, it was also, on the other, a social tie that linked patrons and clients and social superiors and inferiors. Friendship was the glue that bound together a hierarchical, deferential, patronage society. One's friends included extended kin, patrons, protectors, clients, associates, guarantors, and guardians as well as one's neighbors. Friendship involved more than sociability and affection; male friendships served instrumental as well as emotional functions. Friendships were part of a broader system of patronage, clientage, reciprocity, and solidarity and played an important public role in politics and economics. Similarly, in colonial America, the term "friendship" referred not to interpersonal relationships involving bonds of affection, intimacy, loyalty, disclosure, and emotional support, but to prudential ties of assistance, support, and interest that characterized a hierarchical society.[38]

During the seventeenth and eighteenth centuries, the word "friendship" was used increasingly broadly, to refer to intimates, patrons, clients, neighbors, and associates. But as early as the seventeenth century, friendship came to be contrasted more and more with market relations. Disinterested affection was friendship's defining characteristic. Francis Bacon made this point bluntly: "It is friendship, when a man can say to himself, I love this man without respect of utility." By the mid-eighteenth century, the notion that friendship was a private relationship based on free choice, affection, mutual sympathy, empathy, and affinity had grown more common. Indeed, such mid-eighteenth-century Scottish philosophers as David Hume and Adam Smith asserted that one of the benefits that accompanied the rise of commercial society was that it was now possible to have relationships wholly free of self-interest and mercenary calculation.[39]

The Romantic movement complicated notions of friendship. Romantic poets viewed friendship as an essential antidote or counterweight to the anonymity and rootlessness of urban life. Individuals no longer inhabiting an intricate matrix of roles and relationships with kin and neighbors, and now possessing previously unimaginable opportunities for privacy and solitude, attached heightened value to the intimate connections symbolized by friendship. At the same time, an effusive physical and emotional intimacy began to characterize same-sex friendship—emotional energies that would later be redirected toward spousal or parent-child relations.

Passionate romantic friendships could be found among men as well as women. Eighteenth-century American men addressed friends as "dearly beloved" and partook in a culture of jolly fellowship, involving drinking, gambling, whoring, hugs, bloody fistfights, and rough and tumble matches. In 1786, James Gibson wrote in his diary, with no apparent sense of impropriety, "Went to Leander—he gave me a hair ribbon and I promised to sleep with him tonight." Similarly, when Charles Brockden Brown recorded his sudden infatuation with a law student in 1792, he was thinking not of possible sexual fulfillment but of ideals of friendship: "No sooner did I see and converse with him, than I felt myself attached to him by an inconceivable and irresistible charm that, like the lightning of love, left me not at liberty to pause or deliberate."[40]

As young men, leading political figures such as Daniel Webster and Abraham Lincoln shared beds with close male friends. Abraham Lincoln shared a bed with Joshua Speed for four years, leading gay members of the GOP to call themselves "Log Cabin Republicans." In the twentieth century, such behavior suggests homoerotic attachment. Meanwhile, many women maintained intense intimate relations with other women throughout their lives. In the nineteenth century, given the disparate upbringings and spheres of activity of women and men, women turned to other women for intimacy. When a female friend visited, a married woman might spend the night kissing, hugging, and sharing her most intimate thoughts and feelings with this woman.[41]

In a context of separate sexual spheres, friendship circles played a crucial role in the provision of emotional support. They were especially important not only to the Romantic poets, but to abolitionists, pioneering feminists, and early twentieth-century modernists. The friendship group offered a tangible alternative to conventional society, an idea that resurfaced in the guise of the 1960s communes and in television's idealized images of group friendships in shows like *Seinfeld, Sex and the City, Friends,* and *The Big Bang Theory.*[42]

It was not until the eighteenth century that women's friendships garnered public notice. For centuries, Western literature associated true friendship exclusively with men. The paradigms of true friendship, with few exceptions, such as Ruth and Naomi, consisted of males: Damon and Pythias, Achilles and Patroclus, and Hamlet and Horatio. War, in particular, supposedly produced bonds of loyalty and understanding that lay outside women's experience. Indeed, Aristotle, Cicero, and Montaigne believed that true friendship was possible only among men. The American literary canon was populated with tales of male bonding, and the idealization of male friendship remained a hallmark of popular culture well into the twentieth century, evident in the pairings of Laurel and Hardy, Tonto and the Lone Ranger, and Butch Cassidy and the Sundance Kid.[43]

During the eighteenth century, the notion of friendship as a male monopoly came under attack. In a letter written in 1757 to her friend Sarah Gill, Esther Edwards Burr, the mother of Aaron Burr, recounted an incident in which a tutor at the college that would become Princeton asserted that women "did not know what Friendship is" and that "they were hardly capable of anything so cool and rational as friendship." Appalled, she spoke out forcefully: "I retorted several severe things upon him before he had a time to speak again. He blushed and seemed confused. . . . We carried on our dispute for an hour—I talked him quite silent." The letters between Burr and Gill reveal an extraordinarily intense friendship. Burr addressed her friend with deep affection, calling Gill "the Sister of my heart." Describing her feelings as "unfeighned" and her friend as her "beloved," she wrote effusively: "I could not help weeping for joy to hear once more from my dear, very dear Fidelia [Burr's affectionate nickname for Gill]. . . . I broke it open with [as] much eagerness as ever a fond lover imbraced the dearest joy and delight of his soul." Her love for her friend was intense and uninhibited:

> As you say, I believe tis true that I love you too much, that is I am too fond of you, but I cant esteem and value too greatly, that is sertain—Consider my friend how rare a thing tis to meet with such a friend as I have in my Fidelia—Who would not value and prize such a friendship above gold, or honour, or any thing that the World can afford? . . . I am trying to be weaned from you my dear, and all other dear friends, but for the present it seems vain. I seem more attached to'em than ever.[44]

Women's friendships, Virginia Woolf observed in *A Room of One's Own*, were notable in their absence from canonical literature. To be sure there were a few memorable exceptions, such as Chaucer's wife of Bath, who says of her gossip (a Middle English term for a woman's close companion), "she knew my heart and my secrets. . . . To her I revealed everything." Shakespeare's plays offer a number of examples of close female friendships, including Beatrice and Hero in *Much Ado About Nothing*, Paulina and Hermione in *The Winter's Tale*, Celia and Rosalind in *As You Like It*, and Hermia and Helena in *A Midsummer's Night's Dream*. Later, Jane Austen and George Eliot produced vivid images of female friendship, including the relationship between Charlotte Lucas and Elizabeth Darcy in *Pride and Prejudice* and Lucy Deane and Maggie Tulliver in *The Mill on the Floss*. In some of these works, the friends are comforting confidantes who offer support and loyalty, even at the risk of their lives. In other instances, the friendships are broken by petty jealousies and misunderstandings. For the most part, however, women's literary friendships were depicted as catty and competitive, involving little more than blather, gossip, tittle-tattle, distrust, suspicion, jealousy, and envy. Clare Boothe Luce's wickedly funny 1936 play *The Women*, with its snappy, razor sharp, backbiting invective, epitomized the view of women's friendships as shallow, superficial, and conflict-ridden.[45]

In recent years, in stark contrast, female friendship has become the gold standard of a meaningful friendship. Women's friendships are upheld as far deeper, more intense, and longer lasting than men's. Now, it is male friendships that are derided as shallow and superficial, supposedly based on little more than camaraderie, companionship, and shared interests and activities. Female friendships, by contrast, rest on intimate self-disclosure, emotional expressiveness, sharing, and mutual support, and in these ways reflect the triumph of a therapeutic conception of friendship.[46]

Perhaps the most important development in friendship in recent years is the growing frequency of nonsexual cross-sex platonic friendships. While these are nothing like the bonds that Plato discussed in *The Symposium*, which are anything but ethereal, the notion of platonic friendship was put forth by the Renaissance scholar Marsilio Ficino to describe an affection that was spiritual and intellectual, not sexual. The phrase was introduced into English in 1636 by the English playwright Sir William Devanant, who poked fun at the idea of a nonsexual relationship between the sexes in his satirical comedy of manners *Platonick Lovers.*[47]

Casual relationships between adult women and men were uncommon before the twentieth century. The first sign of change was the introduction of the terms "boyfriend" and "girlfriend" in the 1890s. The words betokened a relationship that involved companionship as well as romantic attachment. Informal relations across gender lines also became more common at that time in high schools. But it was not until surprisingly recently that cross-sex adult friendships were considered unexceptional. Before the 1980s, many believed that platonic friendships across gender lines were impossible in part for the reason given in the 1989 film *When Harry Met Sally* where, as Harry says, "the sex part always gets in the way." Decades earlier, James Joyce made the same point. In *A Painful Case,* he wrote that "friendship between man and woman is impossible because there must be sexual intercourse." But the absence of genuine male-female friendships also reflected men's tendency to put women on a pedestal, which inhibited genuine interaction. As recently as 1979, a *Psychology Today* article reported that nearly three-fourths of the respondents agreed that "friendships with someone of the opposite sex are different from same-sex friendships." Major reasons were that "sexual tensions complicate the relationship," "members of the opposite sex have less in common," and "society does not encourage such friendships."[48]

Prior to the eighteenth century, such relationships were deemed impossible not because of erotic attraction, but because of the widely held male belief that women lacked the capabilities required for intense friendships. In Montaigne's words, "women are in truth not normally capable of responding to such familiarity and mutual confidence as to sustain that holy bond of friendship." The philosopher and essayist George Santayana laid out the obstacles to cross-sex friendships this way: "Friendship with a woman is therefore apt to be more or less than friendship; less, because there is no intellectual parity; more, because (even when the relation remains wholly dispassionate, as in respect to old ladies) there is something mysterious and oracular about a woman's mind which inspires a certain instinctive deference and puts it out of the question to judge what she says by male standards."[49]

Now that women and men are more likely to work together as equals, it has become easier for many to establish platonic friendships. For many men, such friendships allow for an intimacy that they fail to find in their friendships with men, while for some women, cross-sex friendships involve a playfulness and joking camaraderie that they do not find with other women.[50]

The drift toward a feminized, therapeutic ideal of friendship rooted in self-disclosure raised expectations for intimate connection, but also proved, even in the nineteenth century, to be problematic. In his famous 1841 essay on "Friendship," Ralph Waldo Emerson described a friend as a "paradox in nature," "a beautiful enemy." A friend was part blessing and part albatross, a threat to one's independence. In Emerson's eyes, friendship was as much a fantasy as a reality. "Friendship," he wrote, "like the immortality of the soul, is too good to be believed." In a true friendship, he added, "there is no winter and no night; all tragedies, all ennuis vanish, all duties even." Friendship occupies an uneasy place in a culture that emphasizes competition, individualism, and mobility.[51]

Compared to the romantic friendships of the nineteenth century, twentieth-century friendships were, in general, more repressed, especially among men. This reflected a deepening preoccupation with the family and fears of the homoerotic overtones of same-sex friendships. Also, compared to adults in the previous century, twentieth-century women and men had a limited repertoire of words and gestures to express affection for same-sex friends. In twentieth-century America, friendship became increasingly privatized and marginalized. No longer were friendships expected to serve certain instrumental functions, meet certain obligations, or provide services. Friendships were unacknowledged by the legal system as a relationship worthy of public recognition; indeed, friendship came to be viewed as a source of danger in the form of favoritism and cronyism. Even obituaries failed to recognize friendships. Meanwhile, many of the institutions that supported male friendship, such as fraternal orders and lodges, withered away. The gravest threats to friendship came from the new economy and the dual-earner family. The time Americans spend socializing with others off the job declined by almost 25 percent after 1965. Free hours were increasingly spent with spouses and children.[52]

Today, work and an intense, inward-turning family life are close friendship's worst enemy. Over the course of the twentieth century, romantic partnerships become the primary or exclusive relationship expected to provide intimacy, affection, and emotional support. However, work, family, and friendship have not always been at odds. For male and female workers prior to the 1970s, the workplace promoted sociability. At the same time, children provided a basis for parental friendships, and neighbors were especially likely to socialize together. In a highly mobile, time-stressed age, in which marriage occupies a smaller proportion of adult life, spousal bonds have grown increasingly fragile, and extended family ties have become less intense, a reversal is now taking place, with friendship becoming increasingly important as a source of care, intimacy, and connection. Indeed, intimate friendship has, in recent years, become the paradigm for interpersonal relationships. Adults not only seek romantic partners who are their best friends, but also want to be friends with their children.[53]

A key question is whether electronic communication can replace face-to-face encounters and whether so-called "families of choice," rooted in ties of friendship, can in fact serve as adequate substitutes for the forms of support that so many once expected to find in family life. The answer, one fears, is a qualified "no." Friendship, especially the therapeutic conception that is widely extolled as its very essence, rests on conversation—on banter, gossip, and intimate self-disclosure—which is extremely difficult to recapture online. The sharing of secrets, fears, and fantasies, the disclosure of vulnerabilities and disappointments, requires face-to-face time that many adults seem to lack. The online world may help keep friendships alive, but much online communication is shallow, casual, and transient. Online communication has expanded social circles, but friendships are not measured by numbers but by their depth and intensity. As Aristotle noted, "He has no friend who has many friends."[54]

Equally worrisome is the fact that many feel forced to hire ersatz friends. Even close friendships often prove unable to bear the weight of life's most profound problems, leading many to turn to clinical psychologists, therapists, and counselors as substitute confidantes. Nor do friendship networks generally prove capable of meeting caregiving needs over prolonged periods of time in the way that kinship networks frequently do. Lacking the intense sense of moral obligation felt by close relatives, friends often prove unable or unwilling to provide the prolonged day-to-day support necessary during severe illnesses or other ordeals. If friends are those one can share experiences with, converse with, and celebrate with, it is not clear that even close friends are those one can borrow money from or ask to care for one's children or aging parents. The sad fact is that contemporary society makes friendships more necessary, yet less sustainable and less able to serve as reliable sources of support.

CHAPTER THREE

I Do: The Evolution of Marriage

Much as nineteenth-century editors and biographers expurgated personal papers and omitted crucial details to sustain selective images of their subjects and not taint their illustrious reputations, so, too, do we often paper over the complex realities in our images of marriage in the past. Sentimentality blinds us to the tensions that lay beneath projections of marital bliss. Our understanding of marriage has changed dramatically in recent years, but the struggles for conjugal power, individuality, and fulfillment within marriage have remained constant.

Take the twenty-two-year-long marriage of Nathaniel Hawthorne and Sophia Peabody. The couple began to keep a diary the month they married in 1842. His first entry waxes romantic: "A rainy day—a rainy day, and I do verily believe there is no sunshine in this world, except what beams from my wife's eyes." He went on euphorically: "It is usually supposed that the cares of life come with matrimony, but I seem to have cast off all care, and live on with as much easy trust in Providence as Adam could possibly have felt before he had learned that there was a world beyond his Paradise." Her words were as ardent as his: "I rejoice that I am, because I am his, wholly, unreservedly his."[1]

Margaret Fuller described the Hawthornes' marriage as "holy and equal," but in reality, the union was beset by tensions over domination and submission. Hawthorne claimed to worship his wife, but also sought to submerge her identity in his own and to subordinate her needs to his. "Awe," he wrote his wife, "does not prevent me from feeling that it is I who have the charge of you, and that my Dove will follow my guidance and do my bidding." Superficially submissive, Sophia expressed her absolute devotion to her husband even as she exercised power through indirection and vented, indirectly, her frustrations over his trips alone and his repeated attempts to stop her from painting or sewing. "I once thought that no power on earth should ever induce me to live without thee, and especially thought an ocean should never roll between us," Sophia once wrote to her husband in a passive-aggressive fashion. Children proved particularly disruptive of the perfect union that the couple envisioned for themselves. A stillbirth was followed by the birth of a daughter, Una, who proved to be a source of extraordinary anxiety for her parents, even before she fell ill, experienced a mental breakdown, and descended into madness. Such trials took their toll on this "holy and equal" marriage.[2]

Marriage, George Eliot wrote in *Middlemarch*, is the great beginning. Like Adam and Eve, we honeymoon in Eden, and then face life's thorns and thistles. Marriage can be a true union of souls that "makes the advancing years a climax, and age the harvest of sweet memories in common." Or it can be, as Shakespeare put it in *Othello*, a "curse," marred by sparring, conflict, and estrangement. Flagrant infidelity and violent abuse have been as much a part of marriage as mutuality and intimate affection. The disruption of the rigid social hierarchies of the colonial era gave rise to a deepening divide between female and male spheres and to women's rising expectations for self-fulfillment. The emergence of the emotionally intense, inward-turning, tightly bounded, and highly sentimentalized middle-class family gave disputes over marital power heightened symbolic, ideological, and emotional significance.[3]

In the popular imagination, the history of marriage falls into one of two narratives. There is a Whiggish account in which marriages based on practical and prudential considerations gradually gave way to relationships based on love and intimacy. Expectations for communication, companionship, and sexual satisfaction slowly rose, and gender roles, at a snail's pace, became more equal. Then there is a narrative of decline, in which divorce and unmarried cohabitation and the single life have placed marriage on the road to extinction. Supporting this narrative is a seemingly endless stream of signs of marital decay. Today, fewer than half of American households are headed by married couples and less than half of the average adult life span is spent within marriage. Half of first marriages, and nearly two-thirds of remarriages, end in divorce. Meanwhile, child-bearing, childrearing, and sexual relations are almost as likely to take place outside of marriage as within it. Fully half of young adults consider marriage obsolete.[4]

The actual history of marriage, however, is far more complex than any Whiggish or declensionist narrative can suggest. Conjugal love was never wholly absent from marriage even in the sixteenth and seventeenth centuries. Indeed, outside of the elite circles, love and companionship were widely regarded as essential and expected components of marriage, even as women and men calculated the need for a partner to maintain a farm or a shop. And today, many marriages are far less companionate and egalitarian than many accounts would have it. To be sure, there does appear to be a greater emphasis on emotional expressiveness among spouses than in the past, and those husbands and fathers who are present do engage more in the care of young children and perform a wider range of domestic responsibilities. Nevertheless, it would be a mistake to exaggerate the advances over the past. Many contemporary spouses lead parallel lives, and, in many instances, spend less time interacting than in the mid-twentieth century due to the escalating demands of work and hands-on child care. Nor should one overemphasize the blurring of gender roles. Especially after the birth of children, marriage roles tend to gravitate toward a more "traditional" division of labor.

There are certain striking continuities in the history of marriage, as well as discontinuities. Many couples, then as now, married for children, and not simply because kids were an economic asset. Indeed, many parents in the past considered children to be economic burdens. Unlike today, dynastic considerations were more explicit motives for marriage, as many men spoke of a desire to keep the family name alive. Respectability, too, was a more commonly cited reason for marriage. Yet even today, a partner's money-earning potential remains an important element in selecting a spouse. In recent years, marriages across educational and class lines have declined. Among the more affluent and best-educated, a shared socioeconomic status has become the norm, as older notions of marrying up or down have faded, and individuals seek partners who share their interests and experiences and can truly be a life partner. Among the poor and working class, many women hesitate to marry a man whose potential financial input does not enable sharing the cost of living together.[5]

Instead of viewing marriage through a Whiggish or declensionist lens, it is more accurate to identify a series of far-reaching transformations that radically reshaped marriage over the past four centuries. One involves the shift of marriage from a status and a social institution, with clearly defined roles, to a contractual relationship worked out by the partners. The "institutional" conception viewed marriage as the only socially sanctioned way to combine sex, procreation, childrearing, economic cooperation, and emotional intimacy into a stable union. This conception of marriage has been succeeded by an "affective" conception, which considers love, intimacy, communication, and personal fulfillment central to marriage, with no reference to gender difference, procreation, childrearing, or permanence.[6]

In addition, the history of marriage is inextricably tied to the transition from the "corporate family economy," a productive unit typified by the colonial family farm or artisanal household, to the "family wage economy," in which the husband or father was the family's sole or primary wage earner, to the contemporary "individual wage economy," in which each adult is expected to earn an independent income. Each of these family economies has been accompanied by its own distinctive ideology, demographic characteristics, division of domestic roles, and emotional and power relations. Historically, male authority was rooted in ownership of property, control of craft skills, or role as the family's chief wage earner. In recent years, as increasing numbers of married women have entered the paid workforce, breadwinning, the central component of male identity for a century and a half and the critical factor defining men's time commitment to their family, has become a shared responsibility. It is no surprise that this development has thrown into question older assumptions about men's proper domestic roles.[7]

Equally important has been the increase in women's empowerment within marriage. In the past, women's diaries often focused on the need for resignation in the face of an unhappy marriage. Women frequently wrote about their need for the patience or strength to cope with "the cross I have to bear." But over time, the tension between women's desire for self-fulfillment and the expectation that women should sacrifice their individuality for the sake of their marriage and especially their children intensified. This tension became much more explicit during the nineteenth century. The process of asserting an independent identity was evident as early as the 1830s and 1840s, manifest in a growing number of court cases in which women challenged their husband's patriarchal authority. By the mid-nineteenth century, it was already clear that divorce was primarily a woman's weapon against marital abuse and distress; today, wives initiate about two-thirds of divorces.

In recent years, fewer women have been willing to limit their aspirations or sacrifice their individuality to make themselves more agreeable to their husbands. As recently as the early 1970s, nearly three-quarters of women said it was more important to help their husbands' career than to have a career themselves. Yet today wives no longer see it as their job to cheer their husbands' accomplishments and console them on their failures. Nevertheless, women remain, as one magazine editor put it, "wife, mother, baby-sitting and housekeeping manager, cook, social secretary, gardener, tutor, chauffeur, interior decorator, general contractor and laundress." As a result, contemporary marriage has become a site of struggle, where women and men tussle self-consciously over issues of equity and fairness, and parents, but especially mothers, wrestle with work-family conflicts.[8]

The sexual revolution, shifting gender norms, and profound economic transformations (including the shift to a service economy and the declining economic prospects of less-educated working-class men) have altered the way Americans perceive marriage. Most couples today come to marriage having led more independent lives and with more experience in prior relationships than did their predecessors. Many also bring to marriage a more sophisticated psychological understanding that encourages a heightened attention to the emotional quality of the relationship. No doubt expectations about the fulfillment that marriage can bring is higher than in the past, as many seek an equal partner, lover, soul-mate, and best friend. But broader changes, including the increasing isolation of the conjugal unit from extended kin, a decline in shared friendships, and separate work lives, make successful marriages more difficult to sustain even as these developments increase the need for intimate marital connection and support.[9]

There is, of course, no history of marriage in the singular. Marriage has varied profoundly across class, religion, and ethnicity. The dramatis personae include same-sex couples, interfaith and interracial couples, cohabiting couples, and "open" marriages. Well before the divorce revolution of the last third of the twentieth century, many marriages broke up and many couples lived apart for prolonged periods of time. "Happily ever after" is a sentiment suited only for fairy tales, not for grown-up marriages, in which harmony is inevitably joined with conflict and sorrow is inseparable from joy. History reveals that many of the features that characterize marriage today—delayed marriage, the prevalence of informal, legally unsanctioned unions, marital breakups, and frequent remarriage—were more common in the past than many suspect. However, a feature of married life that we take for granted today, the concentration of intimacy within the conjugal couple, is unusual and represents a sharp break from the past, when emotional relationships tended to be more diffuse.

Over a twenty-year span, stretching from the late 1960s to the late 1980s, the institution of marriage underwent more radical transformations than in any other period in history. The age of marriage climbed sharply, from an average of just twenty-one for young women and twenty-three for young men as recently as 1970 to twenty-seven for women and twenty-nine for men today. Meanwhile, the birthrate fell by half, married women's participation in the workforce doubled, and the divorce rate tripled. The path into marriage experienced a far-reaching shift, as cohabitation became a normative step toward marriage; it also became a widespread alternative to marriage. In addition, the link between sex and marriage unraveled as did the link between marriage and parenthood, as fewer women delayed sex until engagement and the stigma against unwed motherhood faded. Family arrangements grew much more diverse, as the nuclear family consisting of a male breadwinner and female homemaker was joined by increasing numbers of dual-earner, single-parent, multigener-ational, same-sex, and complex, extended families formed by remarriage and step-relationships, as well as by other family units not defined by blood or marital ties. Especially striking was a sharp increase in the number of remarriages. Today, because of remarriage, more than four in ten adults have a step-relative in their family. Lacking well-defined precedents, step-parents innovate and negotiate how to parent or assist step-relatives in their familial relations.[10]

Alongside these demographic shifts were profound changes in mar-riage's legal definition and in means of entry into and exit from the insti-tution. In 1967, the U.S. Supreme Court struck down laws prohibiting in-terracial intermarriage, which, at various times, had been adopted in forty-one states. The next year, the court invalidated many state laws that treated "illegitimate" children differently from children born within wedlock. In 1974 and 1977, the Court overturned zoning laws that dis-criminated against nontraditional households. Marital rape began to be criminalized in the mid-1970s and had become illegal in every state by 1993. In 1980, the U.S. Bureau of the Census eliminated the presumption that a man was automatically deemed head of his household. Perhaps the most dramatic changes took place in the nature of the marriage contract. Many states abandoned their traditional reluctance to enforce prenuptial agreements, which allowed the couple themselves to define the nature of their obligations independent of the state. Enactment of no-fault divorce laws, beginning in California in 1969 and subsequently by every state, meant that dissolution of a marriage no longer required proof of serious fault. A marriage could be ended unilaterally without any punishment for the "guilty" party, and alimony was replaced by temporary maintenance. At the same time, state laws that barred divorcees who were behind on child support payments from remarrying were also struck down. Mean-while, marriage's privileged legal status faded somewhat, as businesses extended benefits to unmarried partners, and some states recognized alternatives to marriage such as civil partnerships.[11]

These dramatic developments have prompted fear among some that marriage is on the verge of extinction. However, that is highly unlikely.

A substantial majority of Americans continue to marry or enter into a marriage-like relationship. The institution of marriage persists as the most powerful cultural symbol of commitment and the most sustained and intimate relationship that most adults experience. Although marriage rates have declined sharply, this is due more to postponing, than to abandoning, marriage. More than eight in ten women marry by the age of forty, and three-quarters remarry within ten years of a divorce.[12]

Nevertheless, there can be no doubt that marriage occupies a very different place in adult life than it did half a century ago. Marriage has become an option rather than an expectation. Whereas in 1960, over three-fifths of adulthood was spent with a spouse and a child, today the proportion spent within a marriage with children has fallen to the lowest point in history, occupying just two-fifths of the adult life course. Rather than being regarded, as it was in the 1950s, as the gateway to adulthood, with its attendant responsibilities, duties, obligations, and privileges, marriage has become, for many, a capstone experience, signifying completion of an education, entry into a full-time job, and attainment of economic independence. At the same time, marriage has been dethroned from its primary position in adult life. No longer is it the predominant way that adults structure sexuality, childbearing, and childrearing. As many of the prescriptive norms, roles, behaviors, rules, and expectations associated with married life have lost their power, couples have to decide on their own how to apportion responsibilities for wage-earning, childrearing, and housework. In this sense, marriage has been deinstitutionalized and has become what each couple makes it.[13]

It is remarkable how swiftly profound changes in attitudes and expectations have taken place. Whereas adults in the 1950s and early 1960s defined a happy marriage in terms of clearly delineated marital roles, such as being a good provider or good homemaker and a responsible parent, marriage partners have become far more likely to assess a marriage based on the relationship's quality, including the level of communication and the degree of sexual fulfillment. No longer is it enough for a man to be a good breadwinner; he also has to be a good parent and bed partner. Instead of focusing on companionship, work, responsibility, and duty, marriage has come to be viewed as an emotional partnership involving mutual care, support, and compatibility. An earlier assumption that spouses should be regarded as a single entity, symbolized by the wife's adoption of her husband's last name, gave way to a new view: that spouses maintain their separate identity even after marriage. The very language used to describe spouses has shifted. The word "partner" signifies a growing emphasis on equality within marriage, in which both spouses are wage earners and co-parents.[14]

No longer the sole route to adult status and respectability, marriage, in recent years, has become merely one of a number of ways, widely regarded as equally valid, that adults organize their personal lives. Recent justices on the U.S. Supreme Court exemplify the diversity that characterizes contemporary arrangements. These include several divorcees, a widow, a justice who has never been wed, a husband who married late in life, an adoptive parent, and partners in an interfaith and an interracial marriage.[15]

Contemporary marriage is, at once, highly valued, increasingly optional, and decidedly fragile. The overwhelming majority of adults aspire to marry, but more live outside of marriage than at any time in the past century and a half. Most adults conceive of marriage as a lifelong commitment, but are more likely to divorce or to have short-term cohabiting relationships than any other people in the developed world. Many couples idealize marriage as a source of romance, intimate communication, companionship, and emotional support, but, on average, spend less time interacting than did their parents. From a cross-cultural perspective, Americans have more partners than their counterparts in Europe, Australia, New Zealand, and Japan, and their children are much more likely to experience their parents' breakup. About 40 percent of children experience their parents' divorce by their fifteenth birthday.[16]

As far-reaching as these disruptive changes in marriage have been, they are not without precedent. Change, diversity, and contestation have been constants in the history of marriage. Far from a static or unvarying entity, marriage has taken a multiplicity of forms and evolved in ways small and large over the past four centuries. For all the talk about the traditional family, marriage is a surprisingly malleable institution, and it is marriage's plasticity in its roles, functions, and emotional and power dynamics that has made it adaptable to shifting cultural, demographic, economic, and social circumstances.

Lewis Henry Morgan, a nineteenth-century New York attorney and one of ethnography's founding fathers, was among the first anthropologists to compare and contrast marriage rules and practices, kinship terminology, and family forms cross-culturally. His studies of the Iroquois Indians found patterns that diverged sharply from American Victorian norms. The Iroquois were encouraged to marry cross cousins (the children of a mother's brother or father's sister) but not parallel cousins (the children of a mother's sister or father's brother). Upon marriage, a husband resided in his wife's longhouse, which might house twenty or more families related matrilineally. Authority within the longhouse was exercised largely by female elders, and women were free to leave their husbands at will.[17]

In later works on descent and marriage, Morgan found that while virtually all societies had regularized partnerships, the nature of these ties varied widely, and included sibling and cousin marriages and multiple partner relationships, such as polygynous and polyandrous marriages. Many aspects of Morgan's work have been subsequently discarded, such as his speculative theories about marriage's evolution, but his comparative ethnographic perspective not only underscored the diversity of marriage forms and kinship systems, but inspired later anthropologists to recognize the wide range of critical social functions marriage serves in various cultural settings—functions that include establishing alliances within or across social groups; organizing sexuality, production, and consumption; legitimating and rearing children; and consolidating and transmitting property. As diverse as its forms are, its functions need to be fulfilled.[18]

Monogamous heterosexual marriage is not universal across cultures. In many societies, other arrangements exist, such as polygyny, concubinage, and temporary "traveler's marriages," along with a tolerance of prostitution. Many cultures place less emphasis on the spousal relationship than on the kinship unit or lineage or mother-child bond. From a cross-cultural perspective, the emotionally isolated, inward-turning, tightly bounded, child-centered, and highly mobile nuclear family—the form that most Americans associate with the word "family"—is extremely unusual. Societies vary markedly in the value attached to marriage, with not all cultures regarding it as the highest form of human relationship. Many early Christian theologians considered celibacy superior to marriage and agreed with St. Paul's conclusion that the best thing that could be said for marriage was that it was better to marry than to burn. In addition, the ease with which spouses can separate or divorce and establish new unions has ranged widely. Divorce on demand, by either spouse, was permitted by many societies, including many early Native American societies.[19]

Marriage is not only diverse across cultures, but across historical eras. Over the past four centuries, marital ideals have ranged from the patriarchal, in which the husband was expected to govern his household, to the complementary, based on a highly gendered division of labor, and the symmetrical (or parallel), in which spouses' roles are interchangeable and decision-making is shared. Contemporary marriage has evolved out of a number of conflicting traditions that date back half a millennium. In sixteenth- and seventeenth-century Europe, three conceptions of marriage coexisted. The Catholic view, officially promulgated at the Council of Trent of 1563, regarded marriage as one of the seven sacraments, a symbol of the eternal union between Christ and his church and a remedy for humanity's sinful nature. This view, which emphasized the fusion of spouses into a single entity, was justified in part by its procreative role. Accordingly, canon law condemned contraception, abortion, infanticide, and child abuse as violations of marriage's natural functions. Despite regarding marriage as distinctly inferior to celibacy, the church treated marriage as a source of sanctifying grace.[20]

A second tradition, associated with the Protestant reformers, denied that marriage was a sacrament. Though ordained by God, marriage was a natural, and not a distinctly Christian, institution, which proved useful to society in a variety of ways: in providing intimate companionship and mutual support, preventing sexual sin, rearing godly children, teaching love, self-control, and virtue, and serving as an essential foundation for social order. Marriage was, in Martin Luther's words, a "worldly thing . . . that belongs to the realm of government." Rather than being governed by the church, marriage was to be regulated by civil government, and marriages themselves were presided over by magistrates or other public officials. A covenant, or a solemn agreement among the parties, the community, and God, marriage was an honorable estate, preferable to celibacy, which the reformers thought served only to encourage sodomy, concubinage, and prostitution. William Gouge, an English clergyman and author of a widely known treatise on domestic duties, underscored the Protestant view of marriage as a microcosm of the social order. He considered the family "a Bee-hive, in which is the stocke, and out of which are sent many swarmes of Bees: for in families are all sorts of people bred and brought up and out of families are they sent into the Church and commonwealth." The male's role as head was an essential element in many early Protestant conceptions of marriage.[21]

A third tradition considered marriage a contractual arrangement formed by mutual consent. It was, first and foremost, a personal relationship intended to provide mutual love. A sixteenth-century English theologian, Thomas Gataker, regarded intimacy as the essence of marriage. "Husband and Wife are neerer than Friends, and Brethren," he wrote, "or than Parents and Children." John Milton went much further, regarding unhappy marriages as loveless shams lacking legitimacy. "The apt and cheerful conversation of man with woman is the chief and noblest purpose of marriage," he wrote. "Where loving [conversation] cannot be, there can be left of wedlock nothing but the empty husk of an outside matrimony." The seventeenth-century struggles over royal absolutism reinforced a drift toward a more contractual view of marriage, since marriages too could be disrupted by abuses of power and authority.[22]

In certain respects these marital traditions overlapped. Catholics and Protestants alike prohibited fornication and adultery, barred marriages with close relatives for being incestuous, and condemned sodomy, abortion, and contraception as a violation of marriage's procreative functions. These groups, too, agreed that marriage merged husband and wife into a single entity under the man's authority, a notion that was institutionalized in the legal doctrine of coverture, which held that, upon marriage, a wife ceded her property and legal rights to her husband. He alone had the right to buy or sell property, make contracts, or, in certain instances, be held accountable for a crime. But in other respects, these traditions conflicted. For example, many Protestant reformers, unlike Catholics, considered wedding rings idolatrous, while some in the contractual tradition viewed rings as symbols of ownership and male proprietorship. Also, the Protestant and contractual traditions treated marriage as a civil arrangement, and all Protestant countries except England allowed a marriage to be dissolved if one of the parties breached marriage's responsibilities and duties.

In sixteenth- and seventeenth-century England, the law of marriage was mystifyingly complex. A marriage did not necessarily require parental approval, prior publicity, witnesses, or church sanction. A pledge by mutual consent was sufficient. Such a pledge was known by various terms, including "espousals," "betrothings," "assurings," "contractings," "affirmings," and "troth-plightings," and could be immediately binding (a vow *per verba di presenti*) or a conditional promise to marry (a contract *de futuro*). The only impediments to marriage by consent were bigamy, deceit, duress, non-consummation, or an impermissible consanguineous or affined relationship. But a growing number of voices, Catholic and Protestant alike, considered a marriage contracted without advance notice, parental consent, and solemnization sinful. Marriages made without solemnization were deemed clandestine or illicit.

Marriage in sixteenth- and seventeenth-century England was far from universal. Many, like Queen Elizabeth herself, did not marry. Among the elite, about a fifth of the younger sons in propertied families never wed. Many others, including apprentices and servants, spent much of their adult lives unmarried. Marriage then was a somewhat privileged status, most common among householders and property holders who needed a marital union to organize production and support a household. Because marriage involved the exchange of property, the involvement of family and the larger community was taken for granted, though their role in the marriage process varied widely, depending on the social status of the bride and groom and the amount of property at stake. Among the gentry and aristocracy, families might arrange a marriage to form an alliance or consolidate property. At the other end of the social spectrum, the head of a household would play an instrumental role in forming a marriage among apprentices, servants, or wards. In cases involving fornication (and sometimes involving rape), a court might force a couple to marry. In other instances, however, the involvement of family and other interested parties was limited to blessing the child's marriage or helping to negotiate a dowry, the property or money brought by a bride to the groom, or to bargaining over dower or jointure, the widow's share of her husband's estate. Parents could and sometimes did use financial and other pressures to influence the choice of a marriage partner, but lacked the legal authority to invalidate a marriage that a child formed on the basis of consent.[23]

Shakespeare's plays offer a fascinating glimpse into attitudes toward marriage in late-sixteenth- and early seventeenth-England, on the eve of English colonization. Marriage occupies a pivotal place within virtually every Shakespearean play. In the histories, marriage ignites conflicts, reconciles opposing factions, and provides continuity across generations. In the comedies, marriage is often the play's end point in which protagonists, initially divided by law, custom, misunderstanding, or a harsh, unreasonable authority figure, are united and wed. In the tragedies, marriage frequently sets in motion the train of events that result in violence, disorder, and death.

In a highly litigious society in which a population of four million brought a million cases to court each year, it is not surprising that many of Shakespeare's plays touch on issues in matrimonial law and legal practice and procedure, such as the validity of a marriage, the parents' role in contracting marriages, and marriage and property. In *All's Well That Ends Well*, Shakespeare parodied the three reasons for marriage spelled out in the Elizabethan Book of Common Prayer: to procreate, avoid fornication, and receive the help and comfort of a spouse. The Countess of Roussillon asks Lavatch, the Clown, to enumerate "thy reasons why thou wilt marry." The Clown replies: "My poor body, madam, requires it: I am driven on by the flesh." He then offers another reason: "I have been, madam, a wicked creature. . . . I do marry that I may repent." Then one more reason, a double entendre: "I am out of friends, madam, and I hope to have friends for my wife's sake." In *The Taming of the Shrew,* Shakespeare toys with marriage's patriarchal character, though his own perspective is enigmatic. It is not at all clear how one should read Katherine's memorable last speech, in which she calls a husband a woman's "lord," "life," "keeper," "head," and "sovereign." Do these words signify Katherine's acceptance of patriarchy? Or are her words ironic or caustically critical of the dominant view of the age? Or is she only pretending to accept a subordinate position within the household, and intends to manipulate her seeming deference to exercise her will?[24]

Shakespeare's plays allow us to enter a world at once alien and familiar. On the one hand, one comes across customs, such as the exchange of tokens in the form of gifts or coins as a symbol of betrothal, and of terms, like "espousals," "dower," and "jointure," unfamiliar to a modern day audience. On the other hand, marital relations appear that are instantly recognizable, involving spousal jealousy, skirmishes for dominance, accusation of infidelity, fears of cuckoldry, marital abuse, and spousal murder. At times, Shakespeare portrays marriage as a yoke or a ball and chain, a harness that binds a man to certain obligations. "Here comes my clog" (a heavy block) says Bertram, the Count of Rousillon, referring to his wife, Helena, in *All's Well that Ends Well.* But one also comes across conceptions of marriage as a source of bliss. In *Henry IV,* Shakespeare depicts forced marriage as "a hell / An age of discord and continual strife," in contrast to a marriage freely chosen, which "bringeth bliss /And is a pattern of celestial peace."[25]

In the seventeenth-century English colonies, where the structure of institutions was far less developed than in England, marriage was the foundation of the social and economic order. Marriage transformed a man into a master and a woman into a mistress or goodwife. Together, a master and mistress presided over a household that had a far broader and more expansive range of functions than today's families and whose boundaries were much more elastic and permeable. The household was a unit of production that served a variety of educational and welfare functions later transferred to other institutions. Its membership expanded and contracted depending on its labor needs. Marriage was a necessity, and, when demographic conditions allowed, virtually every free adult married. After a spouse's death, a master or mistress remarried rapidly. This, it must be stressed, did not mean that spouses did not love one another and grieve their partner's death. Rather, it was out of economic necessity that people remarried. As for young unmarried adults, these women and men were kept under strict oversight. Fearful that unmarried men might become rakes or sodomites, New England required bachelors to pay a tax and to live in a family household.[26]

In theory, the household was a patriarchal and hierarchical unit, part of the great chain of being, the ladder of authority that flowed from God to the lowliest living beings. Patriarchy was symbolized in a variety of ways. The husband and father sat in an armchair, his symbolic throne, whereas other family members sat on benches or stools. In letters, husbands rarely asked their wives for advice, and generally addressed their wives with condescending terms such as "Dear Child," while wives signed their letters, "your faithful and obedient wife."[27]

Realities were far more complex. Although law rested on the principle of coverture, that upon marriage a woman's legal identity was absorbed into her husband's, in practice, married women frequently served as "deputy husbands." Marriage in the colonial era rests on a paradox. It was a hierarchal institution, founded on inequality, but also a genuine partnership that depended on the close cooperation of a mistress and master to survive.[28]

By the mid- and late eighteenth century, in the face of rapid population growth, increasing geographical mobility, and the expansion of a consumer economy, this early model of marriage began to break down. As economic opportunities expanded and fathers had less land to bequeath to their offspring, fewer sons and daughters were willing to delay marriage. Parental control over courtship weakened, as is evident in the fact that more and more daughters married out of birth order and that about a third of women were already pregnant on their wedding day. Most striking of all, rates of out-of-wedlock births steadily rose, indicating that earlier mechanisms of social control no longer functioned effectively.[29]

Women's futures began to depend, more than in the past, upon their husband's status. Given both high rates of male outmigration from the more settled areas near the eastern seaboard and increasing economic stratification, it also became more difficult to find an acceptable husband. In the face of these developments, a new sentimentalized conception of courtship and marriage arose, which sought to reinvigorate marriage as an ideal. Popularized in an outpouring of novels, this sentimental view contrasted marriages resting on love, friendship, and mutuality with those founded on more instrumental or mercenary motives. An ideal marriage, in this view, was a meeting of true minds.[30]

But by the early nineteenth century, marriage involved a closing off of freedoms enjoyed in girlhood—freedoms that had a real novelty. For the first time, large numbers of young women enjoyed a period when they were not under the control of a father, a master or mistress, or a husband; this could occur while attending school, working in a mill, migrating to a city, or simply being released from earlier obligations to spend their time spinning, weaving, or taking part in some other productive activity. If marriage marked an important turning point in women's lives, along with the termination of certain girlhood freedoms, it is not surprising that many women hesitated when faced with marriage. Marriage was such an awesome step that few women in the late eighteenth or early nineteenth centuries entered into the relationship lightly. Many underwent a marriage trauma as they decided whether or not to wed.[31]

Many women wrote that they "trembled" as their wedding day approached, that their "spirits were much depressed," and that their minds were "loaded with doubts and fears." One woman, Sarah Williams, noted that she felt "rather depressed than elevated" at her impending marriage, and Catharine Beecher, a prominent educator, worried that once her betrothed got over the "novelty" of marriage, he would be "so engrossed in science and study as to forget I existed." After her husband died in 1767, Mary Fish, a Connecticut widow, remained unmarried for nine years despite at least three proposals of marriage. She finally remarried in 1776, but only after her future husband read a document Mary had composed describing the qualities she wanted in a spouse. Entitled "Portrait of a Good Husband," the document stated that he should "gratify" her "reasonable inclinations," enter into her grief and participate in her joys, should not be jealous or abuse his wife or stepchildren, and should not mismanage or dissipate her inheritance.[32] Whereas in colonial New England, marriage was regarded as a social obligation and an economic necessity, and virtually all adults married, by the early nineteenth century, the number of unmarried women increased to an unprecedented 11 percent.[33]

It is not accidental that it was during this period that new rituals began to surround marriage, practices that we now think of as traditional. There was the white wedding gown, symbolizing the bride's virginity, and the bridal veil, with its reference to female modesty. There was the seating of families on opposite sides of the church, signaling the joining together of two separate kinship groups. There was the father escorting and giving away the bride, demonstrating his blessing of the union and the transfer of his daughter's care to her husband. Then there was the placement of the ring, a symbol of ownership upon the bride's finger, with its allusion to intercourse, and the rice toss, with its associations with fertility.

These rituals represented an abrupt shift from seventeenth- and eighteenth-century practices in the colonies. The staunchly antiritualistic Puritans made the wedding ceremony a private and austere event and rejected elements associated with Catholicism, such as the custom of giving a bride a wedding ring. As late as the beginning of the nineteenth century, weddings typically took place within a home, and a bride might wear a dress of any color. By the 1840s, in stark contrast, a host of elaborate, formal new rituals had arisen, which helped young women and men maneuver the difficult steps toward marriage. To signify their intention to marry, men and women began to give each other engagement rings. (Over time, it became more common for only the man to present a ring to his fiancée.) Families began to announce their children's engagement in letters to friends and family or in newspapers.[34] At the same time, marriage ceremonies increasingly became larger and more formal affairs, attended

3.1. John Lewis Krimmel, *Country Wedding, Bishop White Officiating,* 1814. Oil on canvas. Accession number 1842.2.1. Courtesy of the Pennsylvania Academy of the Fine Arts.

not simply by near kin (which had been the custom during the colonial period) but by a much larger number of family members and friends. Guests received printed invitations to the ceremony and were, in turn, expected to give wedding gifts.[35]

Rituals, anthropologists tell us, help individuals navigate difficult life-course transitions, and marriage has long represented one of life's most profound shifts in status. In seventeenth- and early eighteenth-century America, among male property holders, marriage not only transformed a youth into a master, responsible for heading a household, but often took place in conjunction with a series of other key life transitions: the death of a father, inheritance of land, and exit from an apprenticeship. By the mid- and late eighteenth century and early nineteenth

3.2. "The Wedding March," c. 1897.

century, the transition to marriage became especially difficult for women, whose future well-being was tied up with her choice of a husband. The new rituals marked off marriage as an especially beautiful and solemn occasion, the supreme occurrence of a woman's life. It is noteworthy that at the very time when civil marriage was becoming prevalent on the European continent, it was only in Britain and America, the twin archetypes of the emerging market economy, that a sacramental conception of marriage, exemplified by the church-based "white" wedding, triumphed.[36]

It was during the early nineteenth century that the household economy began to gradually give way to a wage economy in which work took place outside of the household, in a factory, a workshop, a countinghouse, or elsewhere. For the first time, large numbers of ordinary women and men spent their days in wholly separate realms. Accompanying this fateful division between the household and the workplace came an extreme sentimentalization of the home as a "walled garden" or "haven in a heartless world." A growing number of women defined their identity as wives and mothers, while men were the providers and breadwinners. During this early nineteenth-century period of transition, fathers often continued to occupy the position of primary parent—of the family's "governor," in the parlance of the time. But a shift was underway, apparent in legal changes, such as the "tender years" doctrine that gave women custody of young children following a separation or divorce, and in childrearing manuals, which, for the first time, were directed toward mothers rather than fathers.[37]

Within the family, gender relations shifted. Instead of referring to their spouses as "Mr." or "Madam" couples used terms of endearment such as "dear" or "beloved." Birth rates began to fall (from an average of seven to ten children to about five in 1850 and just three in 1900), and the techniques that couples relied on—abstinence, withdrawal, and the rhythm method—depended heavily on male cooperation. Men regarded their wives in a new light, as figures who should not be subjected to an endless round of pregnancy, childbearing, and childrearing, and a growing number of women, too, saw themselves as individuals who could and should take control of this facet of their lives. In a letter to her sister, written in elliptical language, Harriet Beecher Stowe expressed her determination to limit her number of births, declaring that "she shall not have any more *children, she knows for certain* for one while."[38]

Over the course of the nineteenth century, married men gradually withdrew from the domestic sphere into a homosocial world, spending more of their leisure hours in saloons, barber shops, cigar stores, fraternal lodges, political ward offices, and, in the case of the wealthy, men's clubs. Victorian novels may have popularized a marital ideal resting on intimate

3.3. "She Was Led to the Altar," c. 1908.

friendship, but at dinners and parties, women and men tended to retreat into same sex groupings.[39]

Toward the end of the nineteenth century, the discovery that the American divorce rate was by far the Western world's highest and that the native born birth rate was falling sharply prompted a national debate over the future of marriage. At first, there were efforts to shore up marriage by tightening grounds for divorce and criminalizing the circulation of birth-control information and abortion. But by the 1910s and especially the 1920s, marriage-savers began to popularize a new ideal, which would come to be known as "companionate" marriage. According to this ideal, spouses were to be friends and lovers. Male-only bastions of recreation came under attack, culminating with attempts to eliminate red-light districts and prohibit the manufacture and sale of alcoholic beverages. Leading foundations financed research into birth control in the belief that more satisfying sex lives might strengthen marriage. In actuality, the companionate ideal was at odds with the reality that marriage was based on separate but supposedly complementary spousal roles. As the number of farm families rapidly declined, the male breadwinner household became the norm.[40]

The Great Depression imposed enormous strains on marriage. During the early years of the depression, when nearly a quarter of the workforce was unemployed, the divorce rate fell by about 25 percent from the 1929 level, but this reflected the fact that couples could not afford to divorce. Abandonments, however, soared. The 1940 Census recorded a million wives and husbands living apart. Also, by 1940, the divorce rate was significantly higher than before the depression. Meanwhile, the depression exacted an especially heavy toll on husbands. Initially, husbands responded to joblessness by tirelessly searching for work. But these men quickly grew discouraged, and their relationships with their wives and teenage children often deteriorated.[41]

The post–World War II era has been aptly called "the age of mandatory marriage." Those who were unmarried were deemed immature, or homosexual, and companies expected white-collar employees to be married. The age of marriage fell to a record low. In the late 1950s, more women married at the age of seventeen than any other age, and fully half of women were married by the age of twenty. Early marriage, however, set the stage for the domestic upheavals of the 1960s and 1970s. By the mid-1960s, many women's deepening unhappiness with their domestic lives could no longer be repressed or redirected. Even before enactment of no-fault divorce laws, divorce rates were rising. Increasingly divorce was viewed as a way to end unequal, conflict-ridden, or unfulfilling marriages. As expectations for communication, romance, and sharing of responsibilities escalated, individual marriages became more likely to disappoint. Then, in the 1970s, a fundamental shift occurred in the division of domestic roles. In the face of rising inflation and stagnating family incomes, married women in unprecedented numbers entered the wage labor force.[42]

It is not an accident that divorce rates peaked in the late 1970s. The upsurge reflected an institution in transition. In some instances, women viewed divorce as liberation from an oppressive, limiting, sexist institution.

But even more significant was the wrenching adjustment as an older marital bargain, in which a husband supported his wife, gave way to a new reality, in which couples were expected to be co-providers, co-parents, and co-housekeepers, and as women's growing authority as wage earners meant that husbands had to accommodate their concerns.[43]

～✲～

In the 1972 book on *The Future of Marriage,* the sociologist Jesse Bernard argued that every marriage actually contains two marriages: hers and his. His, she found, was much more satisfying than hers. By almost every measure, including physical health, psychological well-being, and career success, men's marriages were more beneficial than women's. More wives than husbands reported negative feelings about their marriage, deemed themselves unhappy, and had considered separation or divorce. Women were also much more likely to report high levels of stress, anxiety, and depression. Women and men not only experienced marriage differently, but took on very different responsibilities. Wives assumed a disproportionate share of household responsibilities for cooking, cleaning, shopping, and child care, as well as emotional and relational work, nurturing family members and serving as intermediaries with relatives, neighbors, and friends. Bernard concluded that the future of marriage was problematic if it failed to become a more attractive option for women. That would require men not only to share in housework and parenting, but to better meet women's emotional needs for intimacy, romance, and psychological succor and to become more supportive of women's aspirations for fulfillment.[44]

At the time that Bernard wrote her book, just 24 percent of married women were in the labor force, compared to 70 percent forty years later. Half of all women and men in the early 1970s said that the most satisfying lifestyle was a marriage where the husband worked and the wife stayed home and took care of the house and children. Today, when women are the sole or primary earner in four of ten households with children under age eighteen—which is four times the proportion in 1960—a radical change in values has taken place. And yet, in spite of far-reaching changes in attitudes toward married women and work, truly egalitarian marriages prove to be difficult for most couples. Wives not only remain responsible for a disproportionate share of domestic chores, child care, and management of household tasks, but for handling the family's emotional relations with friends and relatives.[45]

The words that earlier generations used to describe husbands and wives denote a clarity in marital roles that no longer exists. In the colonial era, there was the "master" and "head of household" and the "mistress" and "goodwife." During the nineteenth century, there was the "paterfamilias" or "governor" and the "angel of the house." The twentieth century brought the "breadwinner" and "homemaker." Today, gender neutral words like "partner" and "spouse" abound. In short, in the past, marriage was institutionalized in a sociological sense. Certain normative expectations were taken for granted. In recent years, marriage has been deinstitutionalized, in that norms pertaining to marital roles have been increasingly contested and are in many ways collapsing. Yet, the drift toward a blurring of female and male family roles is far from complete.[46]

In seventeenth-century New England, a goodwife was a deputy husband, engaging in household crafts, trade, and gardening. Far from being locked into a single domestic role or devoting her time to childrearing and housework, a mistress performed many duties and functions. These included spinning and fabricating clothing, supervising servants, engaging in crafts, such as brewing, manufacturing household goods, and participating in trade. A goodwife might farm, serve as an accountant or her husband's attorney, and handle business matters in her husband's absence. To be sure, early colonial society drew a sharp division of the sexes, and derogatory comments about women's capabilities were commonplace. Indeed, one Puritan minister called "pride and haughtiness" "the special sin of woman" and deemed women to be "ignorant and Worthless." Women's access to schooling was limited, their literacy rates were far lower than men's, and their inheritances were typically half the size of their brothers'. But crossing gender boundaries in the interests of the family took place frequently without upsetting the patriarchal order.[47]

By the mid-nineteenth century, a very different gender division of labor existed among the rapidly growing urban middle class. The popular mid-nineteenth century chromolithographs of Currier and Ives depict mothers with children ten times more frequently than fathers with children. During the early nineteenth century, the gradual separation of the household and the workplace was accompanied by a radical redefinition of women's domestic identities. Women in the rapidly expanding urban middle class embraced an identity as mother and homemaker. In 1931, Virginia Woolf would describe the Victorian wife and mother as "the angel in the house." She was the figure who sacrificed her individuality for her family's sake. "She was utterly unselfish. She excelled in the difficult arts of family life. She sacrificed herself daily. If there was chicken, she took the leg; if there was a draught she sat in it." It was her responsibility to support and console her husband emotionally.[48]

By the late 1960s, women became less willing to temper their ambitions and to play a subordinate role within the household. Men, however, benefited as much as women from the women's liberation movement. Feminism freed husbands from total responsibility for their family's economic well-being, liberated men to take a more active role in parenting, and released men from cultural constraints that inhibited disclosure of their emotions.[49]

Today, two contrasting images of fatherhood pervade contemporary American popular culture. One is the image of the sensitive "new" husband and father, actively sharing in housework and fully involved in the nurture of his children; the other is the negative stereotype of the deadbeat dad, who is neglectful, physically and emotionally distant, abusive, or simply absent. These contrasting cultural images reflect contemporary realities yet also have deep historical roots. On the one hand, as a result of divorce, out-of-wedlock births, and short-term cohabiting relationships, fewer fathers are in touch with their biological offspring than at any other time in American history. On the other hand, the dominant ideal of fatherhood, and to a lesser extent, its reality, calls on men to invest substantial amounts of time and emotion in their relationship with their wives and children and to play an active role in their household.[50]

In Puritan New England, ministers, magistrates, and other authority figures charged fathers with responsibility for heading their households and for leading family prayers, instilling values, and guiding and disciplining children. Even though mothers were responsible for the day-to-day care of young children, fathers played a central role in rearing older sons. Law reflected this patriarchal conception. Childrearing manuals were addressed to fathers rather than mothers, and fathers received custody of children after a separation or divorce. This emphasis on the father-centered family persisted into the mid-nineteenth century.[51]

Yet changes were already underway that would relegate the father to the margins of the family circle. As the family was gradually stripped of its role as a productive unit, husbands and fathers came to conceive of themselves primarily as providers and breadwinners. This conception of the paternal role restricted the time fathers had available for their children and justified men's limited commitment to child care. Children came to see their mothers as the primary parent and caregiver.[52]

Following the Civil War, urban men retreated from the family circle, with an elite spending more and more time in men's clubs, and the less affluent joining lodges and fraternal orders and spending their leisure time in saloons, pool halls, barber shops, political clubs, brothels, and other bastions of male-only sociability. Turn-of-the-century industrial workers, often unable to support their families on their own wages or suffering chronic unemployment, spent much of their time in leisure activities with other men.[53]

During the first two decades of the twentieth century, Progressive reformers succeeded in eliminating or restricting many male retreats, by closing red-light districts and supporting prohibition. The therapeutic culture that sought to focus on the feelings of spouses began to take root during the 1920s and further marginalized fathers. Efforts to popularize a new image of the father, as his wife's caring companion and his children's big pal, largely failed. Since the 1920s, family professionals have lamented fathers' aloofness from their wives and offspring and called on them to cultivate closer involvement in their family's life. An emerging masculine ideal — tough, laconic, virile, and unemotional — reinforced the drift from the family's center, as did certain key twentieth-century developments. Immigration undercut paternal authority, as children absorbed the language and mores of American culture and moved away from their fathers' values. The Great Depression further reduced the status of unemployed or underemployed fathers, who lost power as primary decision-makers, as well as self-respect, and turned to alcohol, became abusive to family members, or walked out the door, never to return. Popular culture began to teem with images of bumbling, incompetent fathers and husbands, like the comic strip figure Dagwood.[54]

The upheavals of World War II and the affluence of the cold-war era led many child-guidance experts to emphasize the psychological indispensability of fathers in helping their children establish a proper sex-role identity, emotional health, and a well-adjusted personality. But many men refused this role because they were unwilling to relinquish the role of family provider, their self-absorption in work, their reluctance to perform "women's" work, or out of learned helplessness. Images of fatherhood in popular culture ranged from the idealized, ever-dependable, wisdom-dispensing sage, exemplified by Jim Anderson of *Father Knows Best* and Ward Cleaver of *Leave It to Beaver,* to the cartoonish doofus, clueless, hapless, and bumbling. The upheavals of the 1960s and early 1970s brought very different images of men: Archie Bunker, the white working-class husband, aggrieved, buffoonish, and stubborn, but also bewildered by the cultural changes around him; Mike Brady, the first of many television husbands in a blended family; Michael Keaton as Mr. Dad, the house husband; and the "new" husband, the Cliff Huxtable character who is nurturing, authoritative, and emotionally available; as well as the self-consciously irreverent anti-dad, Al Bundy, in *All in the Family*. The proliferation of popular cultural images reflects, like a fun house mirror, the dramatic changes in men's roles in the past half century. Husbands, in mass culture, run the gamut from overbearing authoritarians and remote, self-contained, uncommunicative husbands to the deadbeat dad, who has abandoned his biological children and is reduced to little more than a sperm donor.[55]

During the late 1960s and 1970s, the rapid influx of mothers into the workforce and the reemergence of feminism challenged the definition of a good father as family breadwinner, part-time chum, and role model for sons and marriageable daughters. For the first time, there were widespread calls to alter or abolish the gender division of labor. Then, in the 1980s, fatherhood became a pressing political issue. Social conservatives charged that society's most intractable problems — crime and delinquency, teenage births, substance abuse, persistent poverty, and declining school achievement—were linked to fatherlessness. Today, an unresolved conflict pits a masculine self-image as primary provider against an androgynous cultural ideal of an emotionally sensitive and expressive man who is capable of caregiving as well as wage-earning. A question looms: Are the majority of fathers willing to become equal participants in their children's care or will men continue to leave to their wives the dual roles of worker and family caretakers?[56]

⁓⁂⁓

In six visual sequences spanning just two minutes, *Citizen Kane* (1941) presented Hollywood's most memorable portrait of a marriage. Charles Foster Kane's estranged best friend describes Charles's first marriage tersely: "Well, after the first couple of months, she and Charlie didn't see much of each other except at breakfast. It was a marriage just like any other marriage." The pithy succession of images illustrates how adoring, talkative newlyweds retreat into icy silence and seething resentment over the course of nine years.

For a century, Hollywood was the country's most important educator. Whether humorous, poignant, or shocking, whether depicted comically, tragically, or melodramatically, cinematic portraits of marriage showed how couples can drift apart, and marriage can become a conflict zone. In a culture prone to sentimentality and denial, the movies laid bare the dynamics, tensions, and complex realities of marriage and therefore contributed to the popular understanding of the most intimate, intense relationship that adults inhabit. "Marriage ain't a party dress," Beulah Bondi warns Joan Crawford in *The Gorgeous Hussy* (1936). "You gotta wear it mornin', noon and night."[57]

The movies provided surprisingly few examples of happy marriages. Perhaps the most celebrated cinematic marriage was found in *The Thin Man* television series (1957–1959), which pairs the alcoholic detective Nick

Charles and his heiress wife, foil, and sparring partner, Nora, who matches him quip for quip and drink for drink. But most screen portrayals of marriage were either comic or melodramatic. There were madcap comedies of remarriage, like *His Girl Friday* (1940), in which couples reunite after a separation or divorce, and sexless battles of the sexes, like the 1942 Spencer Tracy-Katherine Hepburn dramatic comedy *Woman of the Year*. Marital comedies often paired partners who are polar opposites — a theme developed most vividly in films featuring two men, like *The Odd Couple* (1968) or *La Cage Aux Folles* (1968), or who reverse traditional gender roles, like *Mr. Mom* (1983).[58]

The melodramas put marriages to the test. There were tear-jerking sob stories, like *Penny Serenade* (1941), involving a miscarriage and the loss of a child to a fatal illness, and loveless marriages faced with alcoholism and drug addiction, such as *The Man with the Golden Arm* (1955). On the screen, audiences witnessed searing portraits of couples slinging verbal insults, as in *Who's Afraid of Virginia Woolf?* (1966), or wrestling with the consequences of infidelity, as in *Fatal Attraction* (1987) or *Terms of Endearment* (1983). Then there are the dutiful couples who seek different things from marriage and who end up bored and alienated, as in *Citizen Kane*.[59]

Marriage, unlike romance, has long presented a host of challenges to moviemakers. After all, who wants to see movies featuring financially hard-pressed couples, intrusive in-laws, or sick children? The issues raised by marriage, such as who wears the pants in the family or whether the loving spouse is everything she or he seems, had little intrinsic dramatic appeal to a fantasy-craving audience. During the silent and studio eras, many cinematic marriages were ultimately reassuring, showing that despite a host of trials and tribulations, marital problems could be resolved and couples reconciled. But during and after World War II, filmmakers placed a greater focus on dysfunctional families, beset by constant bickering, brazen infidelity, and attempts at spousal murder, in such examples as *Gaslight* (1944) or film noir like *Double Indemnity* (1944) and *The Postman Always Rings Twice* (1946). "Our marriage is not a sick one," the couple in *The Marrying Kind* (1952) tell the judge; "it's a dead one."[60]

The 1970s brought a string of films that depicted marriage as an obsolete or oppressive institution, populated by cold, uncaring, and abusive husbands, as in *Diary of a Mad Housewife* (1970); others presented divorce as an opportunity for personal and sexual liberation, as in *An Unmarried Woman* (1978). A number of influential films traced the disintegration of a marriage, like Ingmar Bergman's wrenching *Scenes from a Marriage* (1973) or John Cassavetes's *Faces* (1978). But each wave of filmmaking produced a reaction, and the feminist films of the period were accompanied by a number of anti-divorce films, like *Kramer vs. Kramer* (1979), which criticized the notion of divorce as an opportunity for self-discovery, as well as cautionary tales, like *Fatal Attraction,* which underscored the dangers of straying from one's marriage vows.

If, on the one hand, a handful of movies or shows like *The Thin Man* series (six films were released between 1934 and 1947, and weekly television episodes followed from 1957–1959) presented an appealing vision of marriage — where partners trade clever remarks and share adventures, and illustrate what a companionate marriage might look like — most movies cast marriage in less flattering terms, featuring impulsive or shotgun marriages, long-suffering wives, and searing conflict. It would be a gross exaggeration, however, to conclude that Hollywood films are largely anti-marriage. Romantic comedies consistently portrayed marriage as love's ultimate affirmation and any intimate relationship's ultimate endpoint. In the free-floating fantasy world of Hollywood cinema, viewers could see both the idealization and sentimentalization of marriage alongside vivid depictions of the kinds of vexing realities that all marriages face.[61]

Americans are more likely to marry than any other people in the Western world, but they are also the most likely to divorce, and more likely to remarry and divorce again. In an effort to improve the quality of their marriages, enhance their sex lives, and prevent divorce, growing numbers of twentieth-century adults, primarily women, turned to clergy, social workers, and licensed marriage counselors for help. In the late 1920s, a new profession, marriage counseling, arose to help couples deal with the marital dysfunctions that they confronted. When the first professional association in the field of marriage counseling was established in 1942, it had just thirty-five members. Today, the American Association for Marriage and Family Therapy has more than 25,000 members in the United States, Canada, and abroad.[62]

Marriage counseling emerged in the early twentieth century in response to twin discoveries: that the United States had the highest divorce rate in the Western world and that the birth rate of more affluent women was falling sharply and was far below that of working-class and immigrant women. Rising divorce rates became a focus for advocates of eugenics (the pseudoscience which sought to improve hereditary qualities by discouraging reproduction among those with undesirable traits and encouraging it among those with desirable traits), social hygiene (the movement to reduce the incidence of venereal disease), and mental hygiene (an early twentieth-century movement to promote mental health and prevent mental defects by combating maladjustments and improving family interactions). These and other Progressive-era reformers began to study the reasons for marital failure, offer marriage preparation courses in colleges, and provide private counseling. Paul Popenoe, who founded one of the first marriage counseling clinics in Los Angeles in 1930, was himself a eugenicist who advocated the institutionalization and sterilization of the feebleminded. He also wanted the "fit" to have more harmonious marriages in order to raise their birth rate. Other pioneers in marriage counseling who belonged to groups such as the American Eugenics Society or the Association for Voluntary Sterilization or had eugenicist backgrounds included Robert Latou Dickinson, Emily Hartshorne Mudd, Robert Laidlaw, and Abraham and Hannah Stone.[63]

Among the messages that Popenoe and other family educators and counselors popularized was that sustaining marriage required hard work and that with proper expert advice and a correct attitude, most marriages could be saved, a view that reinforced the popular American faith in self-help and positive thinking, and the belief that every problem can be corrected. "Marital adjustment" was their catchphrase. Spouses must adapt to a new marital role and think of themselves as part of a couple rather than as separate beings. Marital adjustment required not only communication but a willingness to share a partner's interests and values. In practice, marriage counselors worked primarily with wives and encouraged them to adjust to their husbands' needs. Yet even as counselors sought to lower women's marital expectations to improve chances for marital success, marriage counseling also contributed to a fundamental change in the meaning and goals of marriage from duty, sacrifice, economic partnership, and spiritual union to intimacy, romance, sexual compatibility, and communication.

Marriage counseling was popularized through advice columns, like *Ladies' Home Journal*'s "Can This Marriage Be Saved?" A segment on the popular radio and television show, Art Linkletter's *House Party*, which appeared on weekday afternoons from 1944 to 1969, featured Paul Popenoe, as did a show entitled *Divorce Hearing*, which was broadcast from 1957 to 1960. There were even grassroots movements that sought to save failing marriages by advancing the gospel of marriage adjustment. Divorcees Anonymous was founded in 1949 by divorced women who counseled those who were contemplating divorce. Modeling the program on Alcoholics Anonymous, its leaders offered advice about how a woman might salvage her marriage by forgiving an adulterous husband or improving her wardrobe and hairstyle. The clergy also became actively involved in marriage counseling. A Catholic group, Marriage Encounter, invoked secular therapeutic language to promote the church's opposition to contraception and divorce.[64]

Developments often considered as recent innovations were pioneered by marriage counselors. Tests of couple compatibility to predict and encourage marital success, precursors to online dating questionnaires, were introduced in the 1930s. These early tests rested on the assumption that only marriages between individuals of the same religion, race, and ethnicity were likely to be stable. As one leading counselor warned, "mixed marriages do not turn out well." During the 1940s, marriage counselors incorporated Freudian theory into their practices, and began to treat marriage problems as outgrowths of personality disorders and maladjustment to traditional spousal roles. Largely ignoring problems like alcoholism and physical and emotional abuse, many therapists regarded wife's complaints about their domestic lot as a failure to accept their femininity.

But approaches to marital counseling were far from monolithic. Some sought to temper excessive expectations about romance, while others promoted emotional intimacy.[65]

Making marriage work, women were repeatedly told, was a wife's responsibility. In her 1953 book *How to Help Your Husband Get Ahead*, Dorothy Carnegie, wife of self-help guru Dale Carnegie, argued that a wife should encourage her husband's success in business, monitor his diet, tend to the emotional and spiritual health of the marriage, and be willing to create spontaneous moments of romance and sexual intrigue to break up the monotony of family obligations. Reflecting the fact that most of the clients who flocked to marriage counseling clinics were women, therapy largely involved self-disclosure and introspection. The advice that these women received reflected the counselors' commitment to the idea that therapy involved adjustment and that the goal was marital reconciliation. Women were often told to endure abuse, infidelity, and alcoholism for the sake of familial unity.[66]

But not every marriage counselor held that all marriages were worth saving. The psychologist Emily Mudd (1898–1998), whose Marriage Council of Philadelphia was one of the country's first marriage clinics, took as her motto "save people, not marriages." She questioned gender norms and rejected the view that all women should find happiness in marriage, motherhood, and homemaking, thus anticipating the views of many marriage counselors of the 1960s and 1970s. Not surprisingly, a backlash accompanied the rise of this revisionist view. In 1973, Marabel Morgan's bestseller, *The Total Woman*, argued that a subservient wife who catered to her husband's every desire was the key to a successful American marriage.[67]

Marriage brings along with it inevitable strains. A major challenge all couples face is managing and resolving marital conflicts. The kinds of issues discussed in marriage counseling sessions provides a barometer measuring changes in women's concerns. In the early 1960s, "lack of communication" was seventh on the list of things that couples complained about in marital counseling sessions. By the early 1970s, it topped the list. Today, alongside the classic problems facing marriage — namely, finances and relations with in-laws—are problems involving the division of household labor and career conflicts.[68]

❦

During the early 1980s, American marriage began moving in two divergent directions. Among college graduates, the age of marriage rose sharply and the divorce rate fell, by the early twenty-first century, to the lowest level since the late 1960s. These degree-holders delayed marriage not only to complete their education and begin their careers, but to identify an appropriate partner. Less than a third were divorced by the age of forty-six. Among noncollege graduates, a very different pattern emerged, characterized by early marriage and significantly higher rates of divorce and unmarried cohabitation. Whereas college-educated men and women were twenty-seven or older when they married, nongraduates were less than twenty-three. And while the divorce rate for college graduates at age forty-six was less than 30 percent, for those with some college but no degree it was 50 percent higher, and for high school dropouts, the divorce rate was nearly 60 percent.[69]

Historically, social class has exerted a powerful impact on marriage patterns. When Helen and Robert Lynd conducted the first of their Middletown studies during the mid-1920s, class differences in Muncie, Indiana, were so profound that the Lynds described the business class and the working class as separate tribes. The most basic difference lay in exposure to unemployment, with working-class husbands undergoing frequent bouts of joblessness, during which their wives had to work to keep the family afloat. Residing in homes without running water or central heat and frequently exposed to unemployment, the working class had little money to spend on leisure activities. When together, working-class wives and husbands had little to say to one another and reportedly fell into an "apathetic silence." Many of the working-class women describe the four hours a day most spent on household chores as drudgery. The business-class men were no more willing than the working-class men to carve out time for their children. When asked whom they would go to "when thoroughly discouraged," not one working-class wife mentioned her husband.[70]

3.4. A couple leaving the altar, 2004. Photograph by David Ball.

Women in the business class took it for granted that they would use birth control, but only half of the working-class women did, and the Lynds describe their methods as primitive, relying largely on "being careful." Although working-class women were desperate to reduce the number of births — one said she hoped "to heaven she'll have no more children" — many, like this woman, did not dare mention the topic to their husbands. Another said that her approach to birth control was to stay away from her husband, adding, "He don't care — only at times." Perhaps it was due to such disaffection that the Lynds found that prostitution flourished in Muncie during the 1920s.[71]

The Lynds's portrait of marriage in Muncie in the early twentieth century is bleak. For all the talk about companionate marriage in the popular press, most marriages, especially among the working class, remained strongly sex-segregated. Men defined their identity as breadwinners and women as homemakers, as being responsible for childrearing, and, among the business class, as being social pace-setters. Men viewed women as purer than men, but also as impractical, emotional, unstable, easily hurt, and incapable of facing facts. Women, in turn, saw men as nothing but big little boys. Companionship was not seen as essential for marriage. In social interactions, husbands and wives gravitated apart. Although couples sometimes played cards with friends, her activities took place largely with female kin, neighbors, and friends, while his occurred with men. When the Lynds conducted interviews, many of the working-class wives didn't want them to leave. "I never have anyone to talk to," said one woman. "My husband never goes anyplace and never does anything," said another. "In the evenings he comes home and sits down and says nothing. I like to talk and be sociable, but I can hardly ever get anything out of him." Divorce rates were high, not much lower than today, especially among the working class. Between 1890 and 1920, the number had increased by 87 percent, in part because Indiana liberalized its divorce law, allowing judges to terminate marriages on grounds other than adultery and abandonment. Local attorneys estimated that 75 percent of those seeking divorce were women; the primary grounds were non-support and cruelty.[72]

Class differences in marital relations are longstanding. The standard sociological and ethnographic studies of family life from the 1920s through the early 1960s underscored the importance of income, occupation, and education as variables influencing spousal roles and relationships and marital dynamics. Before children were born, couples across the class spectrum shared activities and spent time together. But after children were born, working-class marriages became more sex-segregated than their middle-class counterparts. Drinking was an issue of concern to many working-class wives. It symbolized various threats to marriage, since husbands who drank were more likely than others to be unreliable, abusive, and unfaithful. The rates of violence within marriage were also higher. In one study, only 30 percent of the working-class marriages reported no violence.[73]

Working-class mothers were less likely to use contraception, and not only because a higher proportion of these women were Catholic and rejected contraception on religious grounds. Many regarded contraception as unnatural and artificial and considered a woman with just one child to be selfish. A lack of communication and mutuality within marriage also led to hesitation about using use contraception, as did a fatalistic attitude that pregnancy was inevitable. In interviews from the 1920s and 1930s, many of working-class women viewed sexual intercourse as the means for having babies and less as a source of sexual pleasure. Many did not recognize the word "orgasm."[74]

Compared to their business-, professional-, or managerial-class counterparts, working-class mothers had less time to supervise children, and their family life was more adult-centered than child-centered. At the same time, however, children provided a wife with compensation for her husband's lack of affection. Meanwhile, segregated interests and separate leisure and work activities impeded communication among spouses. Sociological studies found less communication and conversation and less gratification of emotional needs in working-class marriages. Spouses proved less likely to take their troubles to each other than to siblings, other relatives, or same-sex friends. Talk was a woman's weapon to address power inequities with their husbands, and many husbands dismissed their wives' complaints as nagging and retreated into stony silence. Levels of gender distrust were higher in working-class marriages, with fathers more likely to tell their sons to regard women warily. Yet, if in certain respects these marriages were more sex-segregated, they were also embedded more firmly within an extended kinship network. Even though families lived in nuclear households, there was much more contact with kin of various generations within working-class families than in those of higher economic status.[75]

The world of work in all times intrudes on family dynamics in diverse ways. The industrial workplace from the early twentieth century into the 1960s was a place of rigid hierarchies and strict rules and commands in which tough guys were admired or feared. It seems likely that the workplace model affected the home as well, with the father as a "boss" who made the rules.[76]

Race, like class, has been a significant determinant of marital and familial relations.

Today, African Americans are three times less likely to be married by the age of forty-six than others in the population and are much less likely to remarry after a divorce. However, if one looks closely at differences commonly attributed to race, it becomes clear that many are in fact byproducts of social class.

Few government reports have ignited a firestorm equal to Daniel Patrick Moynihan's *The Negro Family: The Case for National Action*. In 1965, Moynihan, then an obscure assistant secretary of labor, warned that an alarming decline in marriage rates and a surge in out-of-wedlock births threatened to obstruct government efforts to promote black advancement. "The white family has achieved a high degree of stability and is maintaining that stability," the report said. "By contrast, the family structure of lower class Negroes is highly unstable, and in many urban centers is approaching complete breakdown." Attributing the breakdown of the black family to the troubled past of slavery, segregation, urbanization, migration, and a half century of depression-level unemployment, Moynihan claimed that broken, mother-centered families and emasculated men lay at the root of African American problems of chronic poverty and crime.[77]

Moynihan's arguments drew upon, but distorted, the scholarship of a series of African American scholars, including W. E. B. DuBois, E. Franklin Frazier, and Charles S. Johnson, who had stressed the importance of class stratification within the black population. Frazier argued that slavery had undermined African customs surrounding sexuality and marriage, that urban migration produced a relatively high nonmarital birth rate (which he estimated at 10 to 20 percent during the 1930s), and that lower-class black men's lack of access to stable, well-paying jobs contributed to high levels of cohabitation, common-law marriages, informal divorces, and female-headed households. In retrospect, it seems clear that these earlier scholars were correct: Class, education, and occupational status, rather than race, accounted for differences in rates of marriage, family instability, and unwed parenthood.

In the decades before the Civil War, slavery subjected African American families to severe strains. Although slave codes forbade legal marriage, most enslaved African Americans entered into de facto marriages that lasted, barring forcible disruption, until death. The internal slave market, however, broke many unions. A sale, a lease, or a master's death divided at least a third of slave couples and separated an even higher proportion of parents from their children. Even when marriages were not forcibly split, many husbands and wives lived apart and could visit each other only with their masters' permission. Only about a third of spouses on small farms resided together, and even on the largest plantations, about a third resided at another unit. A death rate substantially greater than among southern whites further terminated slave marriages.[78]

Despite these obstacles, enslaved African Americans were able to forge strong family and kinship ties. Most slave children were born into two-parent homes, and most were named for family members — circumstances that suggest strong links between generations and to an extended kin network. Many children were named for their father or members of their father's family, thereby indicating his importance within the family unit. Prenuptial intercourse and childbearing were more common among southern blacks than whites, but within the context of plantation life, they proved to be compatible with marriage. Spousal roles among African Americans also tended to be more egalitarian than those found among whites, North or South, in ways that reflected African traditions as well as the fact that enslaved women participated in field labor alongside men. Instead of describing the slave household as matriarchal, it is more accurate to call it double-headed.[79]

Conditions following the Civil War intensified the pressures upon African American families. In the rural South, a substantial proportion of couples lived in consensual unions. In the North, African American men were denied access to the industrial economy and found themselves forced into unstable, low-paying jobs. Women found domestic work, which was also low-paying and unstable. Consequently, many had to travel in search of work. From 1880 to 1960, black children were two to three times as likely as white children to live apart from one or both parents.[80]

In the middle of the twentieth century, blacks were about as likely to marry as whites. However, higher rates of separation, divorce, abandonment, and mortality meant that those marriages were more likely to be prematurely disrupted. Although the nonmarital birthrate was higher than among whites, out-of-wedlock childbirths were relatively rare. Then, in the last third of the twentieth century, marriage rates began to fall and unmarried births to rise. Some blamed this upon a series of Supreme Court decisions between 1968 and 1971 that struck down rules restricting unmarried women's access to welfare benefits. These decisions invalidated regulations that denied benefits to women who were not local residents for a certain period of time, who had a man in their home, or who were deemed employable. A much more important factor was the falling birthrate among better-educated and more prosperous women, black and white, deepening distrust between poor women and men, and the growing isolation of low-income blacks from the cultural and economic mainstream. Especially significant was a declining number of "marriageable" men as a result of chronic unemployment, low earnings, and rising incarceration rates.[81]

The Moynihan report claimed that the black family was caught in a "tangle of pathology." In fact, however, low-income blacks proved highly resourceful, developing a variety of strategies for coping with poverty and prejudice. Grandmothers and networks of kin proved to be especially valuable resources. Clusters of kin spread across several different households swapped goods, pooled and shared money, provided services, and cared for each other's children. Derogatory stereotypes to the contrary, many unwed fathers remained involved in their children's lives, and contributed financially to their support, at least for several years. In many instances a father's relatives helped pay hospital bills, provided diapers and clothes, and babysat for the mother. But the strength and security of the kin network tended to work against long-term male-female relationships, as did welfare policies that reduced benefits if a woman married a wage earner.[82]

Issues like out-of-wedlock births, absent fathers, and serial unmarried cohabitation, once viewed through a racial lens, can no longer be attributed to race. The current rate of single parenthood among non-Hispanic whites, 29 percent, is higher than the 25 percent it was among African Americans in 1960. As the rates of unmarried cohabitation, single parenthood, and births outside of wedlock have risen among whites, it has become increasingly clear that the retreat from marriage is less a matter of race or culture than of divergent social and economic circumstances.[83]

Marriage increasingly divides American society along class and educational lines. It has become a class marker and a symbol of social and economic advantage. In recent years, couples with similar levels of education have grown much more likely to marry one another. This phenomenon, known as "educational homogamy" or "assortative mating," intensifies class stratification and income inequality. Deepening class differences in household structure carry far-reaching consequences for children. All parents, regardless of social class, now spend a greater share of their income on children than in the 1970s because of rising expenditures on child care, preschool, and postsecondary education. But those children who grow up in households with two married college graduates receive significantly greater investment in enrichment activities—by some measures, nine times more than in lower-income households. These children also have greater access to social connections. Meanwhile, those who live with cohabiting parents who are unmarried are much more likely to experience multiple disruptions in their family arrangements.[84]

In recent years, a mounting conviction that the breakdown of marriage intensified every social ill, from poverty to juvenile delinquency, teen pregnancy, and low school achievement, convinced a range of U.S. lawmakers to fund a variety of marriage promotion programs including marriage education and couples' counseling. A handful of states instituted "covenant" marriage as an alternative to standard marriage. First enacted in Louisiana in 1997, covenant marriage requires couples to undergo premarital counseling and restricts the grounds for divorce. In the four states—Arizona, Arkansas, Kansas, and Louisiana—that made covenant marriage an option, less than 1 percent of couples made this selection.[85]

As part of the 1996 welfare reform act, Congress allowed states to expend welfare funds on measures to promote marriage. Nine years later, Congress committed $100 million for five years to a "healthy marriage" initiative and earmarked another $50 million annually to promote "responsible fatherhood." Within fifteen years, the states had spent some $600 million on marriage promotion. A $5 million media campaign extolled the virtues of marriage with the slogan "Friend me forever." None of these efforts significantly increased the marriage rate among low-income couples nor demonstrably reduced poverty.[86]

The appeal of marriage promotion seemed self-evident. Household income, reported life satisfaction, and children's outcomes tend to be higher among married couples than among single parents. Among married couples where both partners work full-time, the poverty rate is virtually nonexistent; when one partner works, the rate is under 10 percent. In contrast, a third of single parents and nearly half the children in single-parent households live in poverty. Why, then, was the effect of the interventions small? The factors contributing to the low rates of stable marriages among the poor are not something that relationship-training courses can effectively address. The downward trend in marriage rates among poorer women dates to the 1940s and reflects, in part, the limited number of "marriageable" men. The men whom impoverished women are most likely to marry—who often lack a high school diploma, have been incarcerated, experience substance abuse problems, and have children from other relationships—are not good candidates for stable marriages, and nearly two-thirds of single mothers who do marry are divorced by the time they reach forty-four years of age. To be sure, some welfare programs, such as the Earned Income Tax Credit, Medicaid, and child care credits, unintentionally penalize low-income married couples. But the effect of "War on Poverty" and later welfare programs on marriage rates has proven to be small. Far more effective than marriage promotion initiatives in assisting the poor are programs that target nutritional, income, employment, and educational needs. These include programs to prevent unwanted births, increase educational attainment, insure that work pays adequately, and provide the kinds of support, especially in the area of child care, women in poverty need in order to work full time.

~~⁓~

In 1969, Troy Perry, the founder of Los Angeles's Metropolitan Community Church, presided over the first public same-sex marriage ceremony in the United States. The wedding involved two women, Neva Heckman and Judith Belew. A year later, a Minnesota couple, Jack Baker and James Michael McConnell, sued a county clerk who denied them a marriage license. Even before the Supreme Court refused to hear their case, another county clerk issued them a marriage license.[87]

During the Supreme Court's deliberations about the constitutionality of a California referendum banning same-sex marriages, Justice Samuel Alito called same-sex unions "an institution which is newer than cellphones or the Internet." In fact, the battle for same-sex unions already had a forty year history, which was intimately connected to a broader evolution in marriage. What framed the Court's 2013 majority decision striking down the 1996 Defense of Marriage Act, which allowed states to refuse to recognize same-sex marriages granted by other states, was "the community's . . . evolving understanding" of marriage. Marriage, which historically had served a variety of functions—to unite kin groups, regulate inheritance, organize production, bind couples together, and provide a context in which children were born and raised—had become primarily a unit of consumption and of social reproduction (that is, the bearing and raising of the next generation). Over time, marriage focused more and more on two functions—providing emotional sustenance to the partners and socializing children—neither of which depended on the partners' gender. If equality between the partners was presumed, if earlier marriage restrictions based on race seemed absurd, if procreation was no longer viewed as marriage's primary purpose, if marriage was justified as a public expression of love and commitment, and if marriage had become the primary mechanism through which many rights and benefits are conferred, then why should same-sex couples be denied the same rights that heterosexual couples enjoy?[88]

Today's dominant marital ideal, emphasizing emotional intimacy, has nothing to do with gender. Currently, marriage's foremost public function is to distribute legal, governmental, and employment benefits such as those involving health insurance, Social Security, and inheritance, making it all the more valuable for same-sex couples. At the beginning of the twenty-first century, the federal government identified 1,138 statutory provisions in which marital status was a factor in determining benefits, rights, and privileges. These included tax benefits, such as the ability to file a joint income-tax return or create a family partnership or receive an exemption from estate and gift taxes; employment benefits, such as Social Security, Medicare, and disability benefits; visitation rights in hospitals or jails; legal benefits such as right to sue for wrongful death or loss of consortium and a privilege against disclosing confidential communication with a spouse; and immigration and citizenship privileges for non-citizen spouses.[89]

Two broad themes characterize the legal history of marriage in the United States. The first is the decline of coverture, the notion that a married woman's identity is subsumed in her husband's. A second theme is the overturning of earlier restrictions about who can marry whom. In an 1849 letter, Lucy Stone, a prominent women's rights reformer, denounced the legal doctrine of coverture, which denied a married woman a separate legal identity. Under this doctrine, a wife had a duty to obey her husband; he, in turn, controlled his wife's property and earnings and was obligated to support her. Stone attacked this principle with stinging language: "It seems to me that no man who deserved the name of MAN, when he knows what a mere thing, the law makes a married woman, would ever insult a woman by asking her to marry."[90]

Stone was not alone in her condemnation of patriarchal marriage. Twelve years earlier, another women's rights advocate, Sarah Grimké, had charged that there was no greater source of discrimination against women "than the laws . . . enacted to destroy her independence and crush her individuality." During the 1840s and 1850s, women's rights activists argued that coverture reduced every woman to the status of a slave and a slave breeder, and denied women protection against abusive, intemperate, and impecunious husbands. Their arguments met heated resistance from defenders of older notions of paternal authority. At the New York State constitutional convention in 1846, a delegate declared: "If . . . man and wife [were] converted as it were into mere partners, . . . a most essential injury would result to the endearing relations of married life."[91]

During the 1840s, ordinary women went to court in growing numbers to challenge the notion that economically their lives depended on their husband's generosity. It was this economic and legal dependence that forced women to accept the guidance of those writers who advised women to be self-effacing and to dissemble or deny their personal wishes to propitiate their husbands. These legal battles gradually eroded the doctrines that denied women the right to sue, control their own wages, and manage their separate property. But it was not until the 1970s that the courts began to see women as full rights bearers within marriage. The most powerful symbols of this shift are prosecutions for marital rape and elimination of the presumption that a husband is head of the household for legal purposes. In important respects, marriage, like the economy, was being deregulated. Not only were laws restricting racial intermarriage repealed, so too were laws that restricted remarriage for those behind in their child-support payments, that permitted divorce only on grounds of fault, or that distinguished between legitimate and illegitimate children. Slowly and unevenly, American society also abolished restrictions on marriage based on people's identity. As recently as the 1920s, thirty-eight states barred marriages between whites and blacks, Chinese, Filipinos, Japanese, Indians, "Malays," and "Mongolians." It was not until 1967 in *Loving v. Virginia*, the Supreme

Court decision that threw out a Virginia ban on black-white marriages, that racial and ethnic restrictions were outlawed.[92]

The struggle for same-sex marriage, which began in the late 1960s, is the latest chapter in a long-term battle to remove a host of legal restrictions. Marriage today bears scant resemblance to marriage even half a century ago, when the male breadwinner family prevailed and dual-earner and single-parent households were far rarer than today. The contemporary notion of marriage as an equal, gender-neutral partnership differs markedly not only from the patriarchal and hierarchical ideal of the colonial era, but from the notion of complementary spousal roles that predominated from the 1920s into the mid-1960s. Change, not continuity, has been a hallmark of the history of marriage. Even before the twentieth century, marriage underwent certain profound transformations. Landmarks in this history included enactment of the first Married Women's Property laws in the 1830s and 1840s, which established women's right to control property and earnings separate and apart from their husbands; passage of the first adoption laws in the mid-nineteenth century, allowing those unable to bear children to rear a child born to other parents as their own; increased access to divorce, beginning with judicial divorce supplanting legislative divorce; and the criminalization of spousal abuse starting in the 1870s.

Marriage's persistence has reflected this adaptability. The Defense of Marriage Act represented an unprecedented federal attempt to fix the definition of marriage and impose this definition upon the states and their inhabitants. It stigmatized a specific group of Americans, lesbians and gays, and barred them from the same civil rights and benefits available to other citizens on the basis of a particular religious point of view. In Justice Anthony Kennedy's ringing words: "The federal statute is invalid, for no legitimate purpose overcomes the purpose and effect to disparage and to injure those whom the state, by its marriage laws, sought to protect in personhood and dignity." History laid bare the misleading assumption that same-sex marriage deviates from a timeless, unchanging marital norm.[93]

It is a stunning irony that at the very moment that many heterosexuals were retreating from marriage, many gay and lesbian couples sought to gain access to marriage. Between 1969 and 2013, same-sex marriage

3.5. Recently married couples leaving City Hall in Seattle on the first day of same-sex marriage in Washington State, 2012. Photograph by Dennis Bratland.

was transformed from something largely unimaginable into something embraced by a substantial majority of the public and legalized in a growing number of states. In 1989, Denmark became the first country to legalize same-sex partnerships. Civil unions or registered partnerships among same-sex couples were subsequently recognized in Norway in 1993, Israel in 1994, Sweden in 1995, France in 1999, and Germany and Portugal in 2001. Same-sex marriage was permitted in the Netherlands in 2001 and Belgium in 2003. In 2004, Massachusetts became the first American state to recognize same-sex marriages. Marriage, like every other social institution, has evolved over time, and the embrace of same-sex marriage is the latest readjustment in an ongoing history of transformation.[94]

What makes this period of transformation distinctive is that it is taking place in a context of deepening economic inequality, which has profoundly different implications for those who are more or less advantaged. The more affluent and college-educated are the most likely to marry and remain married, while the poor and nearly poor are much more likely to divorce or to live in unstable cohabiting relationships. Whereas the affluent and college-educated have embraced a gender-neutral ideal of marriage emphasizing companionship, intimacy, and shared pleasures, and tend to marry partners who share similar values, interests, and a common educational background, growing numbers of women who are less well-off see few advantages in marriage, since the men they are likely to marry are often unable to find stable, well-paying jobs. As a result, increasing numbers of economically disadvantaged children are growing up in unstable, complex households, where relationships with the father and paternal kin are often tenuous and the resources invested in their upbringing extremely limited. Nowhere is the impact of mounting economic inequality more palpable than in the increasingly class-stratified patterns of family life.[95]

CHAPTER FOUR

I Don't: Alternatives to Marriage

In 1860, Elizabeth Parsons Ware Packard's husband, an orthodox Congregationalist minister, fourteen years her senior, committed his wife to an Illinois insane asylum, where she remained for three years. It was the same asylum where Mary Todd Lincoln's son Robert would commit his mother fifteen years later. Placed in a ward alongside "violent maniacs" who physically attacked her, Packard was medicated with opium and various stimulants.[1]

After twenty-one years of marriage and the birth of six children, Elizabeth had begun to question her husband's religious views and refuse to perform various household responsibilities. She associated with Spiritualists and Swedenborgians as well as with abolitionists and women's rights advocates, and threatened to leave her husband's congregation and join the Methodist Church. Fearful that his wife's heretical religious beliefs and associations endangered his children, Reverend Theophilus Packard had her placed in the state asylum against her will. There she was diagnosed as suffering from moral insanity and monomania on the subject of religion. Under Illinois law, a husband could commit a wife without a public hearing. All that was required was the asylum keeper's permission. Three years later, Packard was released into her husband's custody after the asylum keeper deemed her incurable and accused her of fomenting "discontent and insubordination" among the other inmates. Upon her return home, her husband locked her into her room each night.[2]

A group of neighbors filed a petition with a state court charging that she was "unlawfully restrained of her liberty" and "cruelly abuse[d]" by her husband. A trial was subsequently held, not to determine whether she was unlawfully imprisoned, but whether she was insane. A jury deliberated just seven minutes before concluding that Packard was in fact sane. Her husband responded by moving from Illinois to Massachusetts with two of the children and placing a third child in a sister's custody. He also put all of Packard's possessions into storage.[3]

This case became the pivot for a fiery public debate over a husband's authority, child custody, married women's property rights, and the treatment of mental illness. Calling herself one of the "slaves of the marriage union," Packard wrote that she had staged a "notorious family rebellion" brought on by "the Calvinist law of marriage, which enslaves the wife." She claimed that her husband had sought to "chain my thought . . . by calling me 'insane.'"[4]

Her experience inspired Packard to become a leading advocate for laws to protect married women's child custody and property rights and for expanded protections for the mentally ill, including the right to a public hearing prior to commitment. She lobbied for an investigation of the Illinois asylum system, which disclosed that 205 patients had been confined without evidence of insanity and that many patients were subjected to severe treatment, which included having their heads submerged in water. She also convinced the Illinois legislature to pass a law giving patients the right to conduct uncensored correspondence with those outside the asylum, providing inmates a vehicle to contest their confinement and obtain legal representation.

Today, when divorce is commonplace, it is easy to be nostalgic about the past when marriage was, supposedly, more enduring and stable, and the spousal relationship more interdependent. In fact, this rose-colored view of the past is deceptive. From the mid-eighteenth century onward, criticisms of marriage were widespread. Even at a time when divorce was rare, marriages frequently broke down and couples regularly found ways to end unhappy unions — this, despite the fact that the primary methods for ending marriage, separation and abandonment, left many women without means of support. Under the doctrine of coverture, a separated or deserted wife was generally unable to sign a contract or have a guaranteed right to her own earnings.

Although the late eighteenth and nineteenth centuries are often associated with the extreme sentimentalization of marriage, it was during these years that the institution came to be viewed as more problematic than in the past. In his 1759 novel *Rasselas,* Samuel Johnson wrote: "I know not . . . whether marriage be more than one of the innumerable modes of human misery. When I see and reckon the various forms of connubial infelicity, the unexpected causes of lasting discord, the diversities of temper, the oppositions of opinion, the rude collisions of contrary desire . . . I am sometimes disposed to think . . . that marriage is rather permitted than approved, and that none, but by the instigation of a passion too much indulged, entangle themselves with indissoluble compacts."[5]

Classic nineteenth-century novels are replete with images of noxious, abusive, loveless, and conflict-ridden marriages. The domestic novels of the era, the successors to the cautionary tales of seduction and betrayal of the late eighteenth century, not only contain romantic fantasies of young women finding their ideal mate, like Elizabeth Bennet in *Pride and Prejudice* or the title character in *Jane Eyre,* but multiple examples of failed marriages, in which a promising union disintegrates into mutual alienation or dissolves into separation or divorce. These failed marriage plots include mercenary marriages undertaken for status and security, like Charlotte Lucas's to Mr. Collins in *Pride and Prejudice,* and monstrous marriages, like Dorothea Brooke's to Edward Casaubon in *Middlemarch,* which rest not on intimacy, companionship, and love, but on intellectual admiration, a sense of duty, or a woman's desire to sacrifice her individuality for some larger good. Scattered through the Victorian novel are marriages that are power struggles rather than partnerships, and are preoccupied with status and acquisition. The very novelists who celebrated marriages of true minds also illustrated unsettling marital failures.[6]

Women's rights activists, freethinkers, and ordinary women spoke out forcefully about marriage. In the midst of the American Revolution, in 1777, Lucy Knox, in a letter to her husband, General Henry Knox, whom she called her "dearest friend," expressed her hope that "you will not consider yourself as commander in chief of your own house, but be convinced that there is such a thing as equal command." Others were more blunt. Of the fifteen abuses against women specified in the 1848 Women's Rights Convention's Declaration of Sentiments, drafted by Elizabeth Cady Stanton, a third dealt with marriage. In one of the document's most stinging passages, one of the most glaring inequities "in the covenant of marriage" is singled out: namely, that a wife "is compelled to promise obedience to her husband, he becoming, to all intents and purposes, her master — the law giving him power to deprive her of her liberty, and to administer chastisement."[7]

But outspoken doubts about marriage were not confined to the novels of George Eliot, Anthony Trollope, Thomas Hardy, or George Meredith, or to advocates of women's rights. In a series of letters to her daughter Victoria, Princess Royal, Queen Victoria, expressed her misgivings about marriage. "I think people really marry too much," she wrote in 1858; "it is such a lottery after all, and for a poor woman a very doubtful happiness." In a letter written two years later, her words were even more pointed: "The poor woman is bodily and morally the husband's slave. That always sticks in my throat. When I think of a merry, happy, free young girl — and look at the ailing, aching state a young wife is generally doomed to — which you can't deny is the penalty of marriage."[8]

The nineteenth-century view of marriage as a problematic institution was expressed in a variety of legal reforms: expanded access to divorce; statutes enacted to protect women within marriage's confines, including married women's property rights acts and laws protecting women against spousal cruelty; and new principles governing child custody after a separation or divorce. If the Victorian era romanticized marriage as a joining of hands and hearts, it also recognized, as Dickens wrote in *Little Dorritt,* that marital unions could be a "jolt through a Slough of Despond, and through a long avenue of wrack and ruin."[9]

To be sure, marital breakdown was not a new phenomenon in the late eighteenth or nineteenth centuries. The seventeenth-century New England poet, Anne Bradstreet, who married an assistant in the Massachusetts Bay Company and the son of a Puritan minister when she was only sixteen, apparently delighted in her marriage. In her poem "To My Dear and Loving Husband," she wrote:

> If ever two were one, then surely we.
> If ever man were lov'd by wife, then thee.
> If ever wife was happy in a man,
> Compare with me, ye women, if you can.

Her younger sister, Sarah Dudley, however, had a profoundly unhappy marriage. Seven years after her marriage, her husband, Benjamin Keayne, a soldier and a merchant, abandoned her, and later attacked her in a series of letters, accusing her of failing to obey his instructions and of having "impoysoned" his body with syphilis. Her father succeeded in obtaining a divorce on her behalf.[10]

Sarah Dudley's plight was not hers alone. In 1686, a Boston spinster, Comfort Wilkins, publicly spoke out about the "Tears, and Jars, and Discontents, and Jealousies" that marred many Puritan marriages. Between 1630 and 1699, at least 128 men were tried for abusing their wives. In one case, a Maine resident kicked and beat his wife with a club when she refused to feed a pig. In another case, an Ipswich man poured ratsbane, a poison, into his wife's broth in an attempt to kill her. The punishments for wife abuse were mild, usually amounting only to a fine, a lashing, a public admonition, or supervision by a town-appointed guardian. Five seventeenth-century New England men, however, did lose their lives for murdering their wives, including Peter Abbot of Stratford, Connecticut, who slit his wife's throat while she was asleep, and Hugh Stone of Andover in Massachusetts Bay Colony, who slashed his wife's neck after the couple argued about the sale of a plot of land.[11]

Even in cases of abuse, Puritan authorities commanded wives to be submissive and obedient. They were told not to resist or strike their husbands, but to reform their spouses' behavior. Some women refused to conform to this rigid standard. At least thirty-two seventeenth-century Puritan women deserted their husbands and set up separate residences, despite the risk of losing their dower rights and facing criminal charges of adultery or theft. Another eight women were brought to court for refusing to have sexual relations with their husbands over extended periods. Seventy-six New England women petitioned for divorce or separation, usually on grounds of desertion, adultery, or bigamy.[12]

Women who refused to obey Puritan injunctions about wifely obedience were subject to harsh punishment. Some 278 New England women were brought to court for heaping abuse on their husbands, which was punishable by fines or whippings. Joan Miller of Taunton, Massachusetts, was punished "for beating and reviling her husband and egging her children to healp her, biding them knock him in the head." How widespread these deviations from Puritan ideals were, we do not know.[13]

But if marital unions had broken down in the past, and scattered individuals, like the seventeenth-century English poet John Milton, publicly defended divorce on grounds of spousal incompatibility, it was only during the nineteenth century that criticism of the institution became commonplace, and a host of reforms were enacted to try to improve women's situation within marriage. Various alternatives to monogamous marriage were raised and utopian experiments with plural marriage and other alternatives to conventional marriage proliferated. One such alternative was the "complex marriage," practiced at Oneida Community in western New York State, in which all women in a community were wives to all the men, and all men were all the women's husbands. Also, for the first time, same-sex unions, such as Boston marriages, or long-lasting living arrangements among two women, came to public notice.

Today, in the early twenty-first century, about half of all marriages end in divorce. This is three times the rate than that of the mid-1960s. Given these statistics, it is easy to assume that marriages were far more secure and lasting in the past. But clearly this was not so. Divorce is a legal process and, in its current no-fault form, a relatively recent innovation. Marital breakdown, before accessible divorce, has a far longer history. Even though marriage was an economic necessity for most adults, and low wages and a lack of economic opportunities and residential options discouraged women from exiting loveless or abusive marriages, marriages were terminated, through separation, desertion, suicide, and murder.[14]

In notices appearing in the Bennington *Vermont Gazette* in 1796, Enoch Darling denounced his wife, Phebe, as undutiful and accused her of eloping from his bed and board. He also declared that he would no longer be responsible for her debts. She responded by accusing her husband of treating her "in so improper and cruel a manner, as to destroy my happiness and endanger my life." Rather than properly providing for her "as a husband ought," he had spent his time and money in taverns. Theirs were among thousands of desertion notices that appeared in newspapers from the mid-eighteenth century onward. One scholar has identified 3,300 notices of separation in newspapers in several states between 1700 and 1800. The vast majority of these were published by men, who placed the ads in a bid to withhold economic support from their wives. But these ads also testify to these men's inability to stop their wives from leaving their household, spending their money, or deserting their household chores. The women's responses, in turn, undercut stereotypes of female docility or dependence. In a bid for community support, women's ads refer to their husband's adultery, desertion, intolerable cruelty, and refusal to adequately provide food or clothing. At times, the notices were part of a negotiating process in which the victimized spouses aired their complaints publicly and then made up. In New England, about a third of these ads between 1790 and 1830 were followed by the reconciliation of the couple.[15]

The expansion of a market economy in the nineteenth century intensified marital conflicts. In an increasingly commercial economy, many men failed in their provider role, running up debts, drinking excessively, losing jobs, and going bankrupt. Many newspaper ads specify a wife's "unreasonable" debts as the cause of marital strife, while many women cite their husband's inability to adequately provide for his family. Some of the most notable women writers of the early Republic, like Judith Sargent Murray and Lydia Maria Child, turned to writing fiction in response to their husbands' economic failures.[16]

By the third decade of the nineteenth century, the number of desertion notices in newspapers declined, partly reflecting the mounting sense that marital disputes should not be aired in public and that the courts were the proper mechanism for addressing them. Instead of informally separating from their husbands, a growing number of women sued for divorce, and courts became the stage on which many marital conflicts were played out. During the early nineteenth century, wives in growing numbers used the legal system to force their husbands to provide financial support for food and shelter, win custody of children, control their own earnings, confirm their property rights, obtain a share of marital assets, or get a legal separation or divorce.[17]

Far from a golden age of marriage stability, the nineteenth century was chockfull of marital separations, abandonments, desertions, and bigamy. By moving across state lines or even to another part of a state, a husband might free himself to start a new union. Extremely high rates of geographical mobility and inadequate record-keeping made it difficult to determine whether a woman or man had been married previously. Judges, in turn, were reluctant to convict individuals of bigamy, out of a fear of casting doubts on children's legitimacy or the validity of a spouse's identity as a wife or husband. An absence of ministers in frontier areas meant that many marriages were contracted informally, and might be broken just as casually. Perhaps the most famous example involved Andrew Jackson's wife, Rachel, who married her first husband at the age of seventeen and separated from him four years later. It is unclear when she and Jackson wed; the couple claimed to have married in 1791, while other sources reported that the two were living together a year earlier. Regardless, her first husband did not file for divorce on grounds of infidelity and desertion until 1792, and the divorce was not granted until the next year. Much marital discord remains hidden in the private lives of the past.

~ఎక్~

The history of divorce is anything but straightforward. It is a story that involves starts, stops, and reversals, as well as bitter contestation. Although divorce was accepted under Greek, Jewish, Roman, Germanic, Frankish, and Scandinavian legal codes, the Christian Church ruled in the ninth century that marriage was indissoluble. The church, however, did allow a marriage to be annulled on various grounds. Since a valid Catholic marriage required that the ceremony follow prescribed canonical forms and that the couple be free to marry, freely consent to the union, and agree to assume the obligations of marriage, an ecclesiastical tribunal could declare a marriage to be void if these conditions were not met. A marriage could also be nullified if it was not contracted before a priest or deacon; if one of the parties was not of proper age, suffered from impotence, or was deceitful; if the spouses were too closely related; or if one spouse was not committed to an exclusive, permanent relationship and the bearing of children at the time of the ceremony.

The Protestant reformers viewed marriage as a secular contract, and every Protestant country except England allowed divorce on grounds of serious fault such as adultery, desertion, cruelty, or impotence, and many allowed the innocent party to remarry. Seventeenth-century England was unique among Protestant nations in forbidding divorce except by private act of Parliament (the first was granted in 1669) and restricting annulment to very limited grounds, such as bigamy and non-consummation. Altogether, the House of Lords approved only ninety acts of divorce between 1697 and 1785, with all awarded to men. Given the lack of alternatives, unhappy couples resorted to informal solutions: separation for prolonged periods of time, desertion, and a folk custom known as "wife sale," in which one man informally deeded his wife to another man in exchange for a symbolic payment.[18]

History books often imply that from the early days of settlement, the American colonies adopted a much more liberal stance toward divorce than that found in the mother country, making divorce "an American tradition." Divorce, such works suggest, was part of the fabric of American life from the onset of colonization. Many works report that the first divorce in the colonies was granted in 1639 to the wife of James Luxford. After uncovering Luxford's bigamy, the Massachusetts General Court voided the marriage, fined the husband one hundred pounds, and placed him "in the stocks an hour upon the market day." His property was given to the now husbandless woman, who was pregnant with her second child, and Luxford was ordered expelled to England "at the first opportunity." Technically, however, this was an annulment rather than a divorce, and this episode did not mark the beginning of a steady stream of divorces.

Indeed, the next dissolution of a marriage did not take place for another five years.[19]

Access to divorce in colonial America was quite limited, confined largely to Connecticut and Massachusetts. Those two colonies granted divorces on such grounds as female adultery, male cruelty, bigamy, desertion, failure to provide, and even impotence, but the numbers were quite small. There were only some 229 divorce suits in Massachusetts between 1692 and 1785, of which only 143 were granted. In a number of colonies, especially in the South, divorce was unavailable, and in many colonies where legal divorce was possible, it could only be on the limited grounds of adultery, nonsupport, abandonment, and prolonged absence (usually after a period of seven years). Even in colonies that made a provision for divorce, the law might forbid an injured spouse to remarry, except in instances in which the previous marriage could be annulled. In many colonies divorce was available only through a special act of the colonial legislature. There were some colonial efforts to liberalize divorce statutes in other colonies, but the British Parliament rejected any proposal that conflicted with English law. Far more common than divorce were informal separations, desertions, and abandonments.[20]

It was not until the era of the American Revolution that access to divorce began to increase. This shift reflected the impact of revolutionary ideas about natural rights, a development illustrated by Thomas Jefferson's legal arguments about divorce. In 1772, Jefferson, then an attorney and a member of the Virginia House of Burgesses, prepared a set of notes for a divorce suit that he intended to bring before the General Assembly. At the time, Virginia had never awarded a legislative divorce. Jefferson planned to base his case on natural law, a series of principles inherent in human nature and discoverable through human reason. It was, he wrote, "Cruel to continue by violence a union made at first by mutual love, but now dissolved by hatred." It was unjust to "chain a man to misery till death." The "End of marriage is Propagation & Happiness. Where can be neither, [the marriage] should be dissolved." Because of the plaintiff's death, Jefferson never argued the case. But in the wake of the Revolution, the principles that Jefferson advanced were widely embraced, if only as being applicable to men.[21]

The American Revolution marked a decisive turning point in the history of American marital law. The ideology of the Revolution, with its opposition to tyranny and misrule and its proclaimed right to the pursuit of happiness, gave divorce a new justification. The revolutionary ideas of liberty, equality, and government by consent, many believed, should apply to the domestic sphere as well as to the public realm. The Revolution's implications seemed clear-cut: Tyrannical relationships should be dissolved; marital bonds, like the bonds of empire, depended on consent; and wives should have an equal right to terminate a union that failed to serve marriage's proper goals. The Revolution also freed the former British colonies to adopt approaches to divorce that differed fundamentally from the mother country's. During the eighteenth century, the divorce rate had not risen at all. But by 1799, twelve states and the Northwest Territory permitted divorce. In succeeding years, the northern states made divorce more accessible by substituting judicial divorce for legislative divorce and broadening the grounds for the dissolution of a marriage. The slave South proved much more resistant to the liberalization of divorce laws. The region's leaders regarded marriage as an essential component of social stability. South Carolina, in fact, did not permit divorce until 1949.

Under the United States' system of federalism, marriage and divorce are considered a state responsibility, and state laws on divorce have always varied widely. Long before the current controversies surrounding same-sex marriage, an ongoing source of debate was whether states with stringent divorce statutes had to recognize divorces from states with more liberal laws. Article IV of the Constitution declares that the states must recognize the legislative acts and judicial decisions of other states. But it would not be until 1942, in a case known as *Williams v. North Carolina*, that the Supreme Court would begin to settle this issue of disparate state laws.[22]

The conception of divorce that arose in the early nineteenth century was fault-based. Rather than focusing on the irretrievable breakdown of the marital relationship, divorce law took the position that one spouse, by committing a grievous wrong, had broken the marriage covenant. This attribution of fault cast an aura of shamefulness around divorce that lingered into the 1970s. Yet if the primary object of marriage was to promote personal happiness and the welfare of society, then divorce could be justified on broader grounds. As early as the 1820s, a growing number of reformers argued that the grounds for divorce should be expanded to include physical cruelty, willful desertion, intemperance, and temperamental incompatibility. Connecticut and a number of other states moved in this direction by adopting "omnibus" divorce laws, which allowed a judge to grant a divorce for any misconduct that "permanently destroys the happiness of the petitioner and defeats the purpose of the marriage relation."[23]

In a culture generally hostile to divorce, some unhappy couples dealt with marital discord by formally negotiating a separate maintenance agreement for the wife. In other instances, a wife might invoke the legal principle of "marital unity" in order to obtain a court order guaranteeing financial support and requiring her husband to pay her debts. Nineteenth-century court dockets abound with suits in which wives describe husbands who have abandoned them to form a new family or simply to pursue new opportunities. Many, and perhaps most, nineteenth-century divorces were an effort to get the court to recognize a separation that had already taken place. Indeed, much of the impetus behind married women's property rights laws and the shift from legislative to judicial divorce came from a desire to ensure that the community would not have to assume the burden of supporting indigent wives who had already been abandoned by their husbands.[24]

Typically, men would file suit to free themselves from the obligation to support their wives. Women, in contrast, sought to reclaim their property and ensure the right to control their own earnings. From the beginning of the nineteenth century, it was clear that divorce was largely a woman's weapon as it was women who were most vulnerable to physical and financial abuse. Women, in disproportionate numbers, filed for divorce, even though they would have to pay fees to bring a case forward and hire a lawyer. This was an act that also took great courage, since the woman and her attorney would have to convince an all-male jury to accept her arguments. Since it was rare for a woman to receive alimony or a financial or property settlement following a divorce, suits for divorce came largely from women in the propertied classes, who had an ability to support themselves in a divorce's wake. The arguments advanced in court tended to reinforce gender stereotypes. Women insisted that they had properly performed their household and marital duties, and men swore that they had provided for their wives. By the 1830s, it was routine for women to receive custody of young children. However, decisions over children's custody were at a judge's discretion and depended upon his assessment of the woman's moral character and financial circumstances.[25]

Apart from desertion, adultery and extreme physical cruelty were other common grounds for divorce. Over time, however, judges proved more willing to grant divorces on such grounds as a husband's habitual drunkenness, physical cruelty, gambling, and failure to fulfill his duty to support his wife. Acceptance of mental cruelty as a legitimate basis for divorce took place much more slowly. In the early nineteenth century, American courts followed a 1790 precedent set by the English jurist Lord Stowell, who declared, "What merely wounds the mental feelings is in few instances to be admitted, where not accompanied with bodily injury, either actual or menaced." Marriage, he insisted, was too valuable a source of social stability to be terminated on the basis of "mere austerity of temper, petulance of manners, rudeness of language, [or] a want of civil attention." Yet even evidence of violent injury might not be sufficient to justify a divorce. In 1836, New Hampshire's highest court rejected a divorce petition despite evidence that the husband had locked his wife in the cellar and lashed her at least twice, since she was "impatient of control . . . and not always ready to submit, even to the legitimate authority of her husband." Nevertheless, attitudes were evolving. By 1860, six states permitted divorce when a spouse had suffered "indignities," which might include vulgarity or ridicule, and which "render[ed] his or her condition intolerable."[26]

Heated public debates accompanied expanded access to divorce. Far more complex than a simple contest between liberals and conservatives, the divorce debate pitted pro-divorce feminists, such as Elizabeth Cady Stanton and Ernestine Rose, who viewed divorce as a way to liberate women from patriarchal strictures, against anti-divorce feminists, like Antoinette Brown, Elizabeth Oakes Smith, and Elizabeth Packard, who feared that divorce would harm the interests of aging women by enabling husbands to be rid of them. Packard's goal was to increase wives' legal rights within marriage to shield them "from an unmanly husband who failed to honor and protect her rights." During the 1840s and 1850s, as utopian socialists, such as Robert Owen and John Humphrey Noyes, and free thinkers, such as Francis Barry, Ezra Heywood, Robert Dale Owen, Mary Gove Nichols, Victoria Woodhull, and Frances Wright, advocated ideas that critics deemed "free love," and as women's rights advocates like Elizabeth Cady Stanton defended divorce as a way to strengthen women's autonomy and transform marriage into a relationship of equals, anti-divorce sentiment mounted. Defenders of liberalized divorce laws regarded these statutes as Emancipation Proclamations that would fundamentally alter gender relations within the home by requiring husbands to be on their best behavior, as though they were in courtship. Opponents, in turn, regarded liberal divorce as a fundamental threat to monogamous marriage and to the proper relationship between the sexes, including a husband's duty to support his wife. In the early twentieth century, controversy swirled around proposals for a restrictive national divorce code that would ban "migratory" divorces, in which a spouse would acquire residency in a state with a lax law in order to terminate a marriage.[27]

Increasing access to divorce is often interpreted in unambiguously positive terms, as a vehicle through which individuals can assert their own personal declaration of independence and pursue their own definition of happiness. Certainly, the liberalization of divorce laws strengthened marriage as an institution by providing a safety valve for abusive and loveless unions. It also opened the possibility of alimony and provided a formal mechanism for women to recover their property and earnings. But enactment of liberal divorce laws was not simply a way to free a spouse from an abusive and loveless marriage. Divorce also represented an alternative to extra-legal marital dissolutions and informal remarriage. It was the prevalence

4.1. Udo J. Keppler, "Divorce, the Lesser Evil," February 7, 1900.

of desertion and abandonment that led many state legislatures to try to end self-divorce and bring marriage under the purview of state regulation.

The trend in divorce rates was upward, with sharp increases following wars and a few plateaus. In 1867, the number of divorces reached 10,000 for the first time. About 5 percent of the marriages contracted in that year eventually ended in divorce. The discovery, in 1889, that the United States had the highest divorce rate in the Western world led state legislatures across the country to tighten divorce statutes, reducing the grounds for divorce from over 400 to fewer than twenty. Only three states continued to allow courts to grant divorces on any grounds they deemed proper. In addition, the process of applying for divorce was made more stringent. A number of states prolonged the waiting period between divorce and re-marriage, prohibited the guilty party from remarrying for a period of time, imposed longer residency requirements before divorce proceedings could begin, and required more adequate notice to the defendants in divorce cases and more adequate defense of divorce suits.[28]

These restrictions made surprisingly little difference. In the half century between 1870 and 1920, the number of divorces rose fifteen-fold. By 1924, one marriage in seven ended in divorce. Legal restrictions made little difference when couples were willing to participate in a charade to liberate themselves from an unsatisfying marriage. By 1920, reformers, convinced that the law's adversarial approach to divorce was harmful for both spouse and children, recommended mandatory counseling of parties seeking divorce, non-adversarial divorce proceedings, and greater availability of divorce on grounds of mental cruelty and incompatibility. Many states established separate family courts, specifically charged with a resolving a variety of family-related problems, including desertion, adoption, maltreatment of children, and juvenile delinquency, as well as divorce. Many sponsors of family courts were inspired by the example of divorce proctors, who had been hired by a number of jurisdictions prior to World War I to investigate petitions for divorce, make recommendations to the court, and try to achieve a reconciliation of the parties. In practice, however, a lack of funds and overcrowded dockets prevented family courts from conducting careful investigations or counseling the spouses. However, they did underscore the state's concern about marriage and its stability.[29]

Variation among the states widened. While many states lengthened residence requirements and imposed longer waiting periods, some judges diluted stringent legal statues. In 1931, only seven states specifically permitted divorce on grounds of mental cruelty, but judges in most jurisdictions broadly reinterpreted physical cruelty to encompass constant nagging, humiliating language, unfounded and false accusations, insults, and excessive sexual demands. As the Indiana appellate court ruled in 1910, "Anything that tends to humiliate or annoy may as effectively endanger life and health as personal violence and affords grounds for divorce." But the economic impact of divorce elicited surprisingly little debate. Awards of alimony were rare as was stringent enforcement. Few spouses requested alimony (just 20 percent in 1916) and even fewer were awarded payments (just 15 percent in that year). Only five states made imprisonment the punishment for nonpayment of court-ordered alimony awards.[30]

In 1969, California adopted the nation's first "no-fault" divorce law, allowing a couple to institute divorce proceedings without first proving that either was at fault for the breakup. A husband or wife could obtain a divorce by mutual consent or on such grounds as incompatibility, living apart for a specified period, or irretrievable breakdown. In many states, a single partner could obtain a divorce unilaterally, without regard to the wishes of the other partner. Within a span of just five years, all but five states adopted the principle of no-fault divorce. The goal was to provide couples with a way to avoid long, acrimonious legal battles over who was to blame for a failed marriage and how marital property was to be divided. In an effort to reduce the bitterness associated with divorce, many states changed the terminology used in divorce proceedings, substituting "dissolution" for "divorce," replacing "alimony" with "spousal support" or "maintenance," and eliminating any terms denoting fault or guilt. But ironically, no-fault divorce laws, precisely because they were nominally gender-neutral, failed to adequately account for the inequities and disabilities that many women face, and unintentionally exacerbated clashes over children and finances.[31]

Many women's groups, which initially favored no-fault divorce, have called for sharp modifications of the laws. Convinced that "divorce is a financial catastrophe for most women," these groups worry that the laws are based on certain false assumptions. Courts, following the principle of equality, generally require husbands to pay only half of what is needed to raise the children, on the assumption that the wife will provide the remainder. In many instances, divorced women, who modified their career trajectories during a marriage, face difficulties in reentering the workforce full time.[32]

As the legal system moved away from the principle of lifelong alimony, growing attention began to be placed on the distribution of the couple's assets at the time of divorce. In community property states, in which spouses are considered to own their property, assets, and income jointly, property acquired during marriage is divided equally. Other states allow judges to award property equitably. In dividing property, a majority of states require courts to place monetary value on the wife's contributions as homemaker and mother and require judges to consider such sources of family wealth as insurance policies, pensions, deferred income, and licenses to practice a profession. Nevertheless, most women suffer a significant loss of income in the wake of a divorce.[33]

In 1897, Henry James published what was almost certainly the first novel to explore the effects of divorce on a child. Set in the late nineteenth century along the shady margins of the English upper class, the quasi-comic *What Maisie Knew* dissects the aftermath of a broken marriage. The mother, a society beauty, is shallow and self-absorbed; the father, a retired diplomat, is narcissistic and hollow. The two share joint custody of their six-year-old daughter, Maisie. Though the story is told by a sophisticated adult narrator, the novel foregrounds the child's point of view as Maisie is shipped between households, "rebounding from racket to racket like a tennis ball or a shuttlecock." The novel explores how a precociously observant child attempts to make sense of the doings around her, as the adults in her life shift from one adulterous affair to another. It also shows the parents cynically manipulating the innocent child's affections and loyalties out of spite, anger, egotism, and self-righteousness. At the work's heart is Maisie's transformation from a precocious yet inexperienced child into a sophisticated, yet wounded, adolescent, who gradually realizes that her parents regard her as an inconvenience.[34]

4.2. Cover of sheet music for "Divorced," 1893.

Each year in the United States, about one and a half million children live through their parents' divorce. A relatively small number experience serious academic, emotional, or behavior problems following the breakup, with the most severe problems associated with high levels of parental discord before, during, and after the divorce. The most common problems in a divorce's aftermath involve family finances, parental stress, adjustment issues related to movement from a familiar neighborhood and school, multiple transitions in family make-up as new partners enter and exit the household, and, in many cases, loss of regular contact with the father. Since divorce is now a normative experience, and the divorce rate is unlikely to fall significantly, the great public policy challenge is to ameliorate its negative consequences by reducing postmarital conflict and providing greater stability in children's lives.[35]

Whether one initiates a divorce or unexpectedly discovers that a marriage is over, the disruption is one of adulthood's greatest sources of stress. In 1967, two psychiatrists, Thomas Holmes and Richard Rahe, devised a scale to rate stress. A spouse's death topped the scale, achieving a score of 100. A divorce averaged 73. Even an amicable divorce represents a shattering end to the hopes, dreams, and expectations that a person brought to the marriage. But if a divorce can be stressful, it is important to remember that marriage, too, can be a source of great suffering, whether it is abusive, conflict-ridden, or simply unhappy and unfulfilling.

In the late 1830s, Eliza Jumel sued her husband, former Vice President Aaron Burr, for divorce, accusing him of committing adultery with Jane McManus, a journalist fifty years his junior. A servant testified that she had seen Burr, who was then almost eighty years old, on several occasions with his pants down and his hand under McManus's clothing. Adultery is a common factor in divorce. When asked to explain why they divorce, couples today cite infidelity as the third leading reason, behind "lack of commitment" and "too much arguing," but ahead of "marrying too young," "unrealistic expectations," "lack of equality in the relationship," "lack of preparation for marriage," and "abuse." Whether a cause of divorce, or a symptom of a troubled marriage, infidelity nearly doubles the chance that a couple will get divorced.[36]

The seventh of the Ten Commandments, a prohibition on adultery, evokes images of surreptitious phone calls and text messages, dimly lit bars, and clandestine visits to seedy hotel rooms. In today's era, with divorce readily accessible and casual sexual affairs far more accepted than in the past, infidelity seems less scandalous than cheap, crude, and tasteless. But in many canonical works of Western literature, tales of adultery, cuckoldry, forbidden love, and sexual transgression occupy a central place, beginning with Tristan and Isolde and Lancelot and Guinevere. In Chaucer's *Canterbury Tales*, the Merchant's Tale, the Miller's Tale, the Shipman's Tale, and the Franklin's Tale, in various ways, make a more tragic case for adultery: sexually inadequate husbands, dissatisfied and frustrated wives, marriages based solely on economic motives, and extended spousal separation. Literary depictions of adultery, however, assumed a new dimension and significance with the rise of bourgeois society and the veneration of marriage and motherhood as society's sacred foundation. What was at stake in adultery, as demonstrated in *The Scarlet Letter*, were the guilty parties' souls. Conversely, betrayal of marriage vows represented a revolt against social convention and all that implied—a boring, routinized life, and a rigid and hypocritical sexual code that denied women's erotic passions. In the twentieth-century works of Harold Pinter, Philip Roth, John Updike, and Fay Weldon, adultery can be recreation, a growth experience, or a hazard to one's personal system of values. Its sinfulness has dissipated along with its greater social visibility.[37]

Infidelity and its consequences have long been among film's most popular plot devices. Cinematic depictions of adultery have ranged from tawdry flings and momentary dalliances to elegant and sometimes lasting affairs. Some popular films depict adultery negatively, as a threat to the family or as the action of a home-wrecking seductress or a heartless cad. Others subtly glamorize adultery as a desperate response to marital boredom and spousal incompatibility, as a reaction to a loveless sham of a marriage, or as a dramatic act of romantic courage. *A Brief Affair, Double Indemnity, The Postman Always Rings Twice, From Here to Eternity, Dr. Zhivago,* and

Fatal Attraction are only a few of the feature films that place adultery at the heart of the film's plot. Off-screen, too, adulterous romances, especially those involving Clark Gable and Loretta Young, Kathryn Hepburn and Spencer Tracy, Ingrid Bergman and Roberto Rossellini, and Elizabeth Taylor and Richard Burton, captivated public attention and sympathy.[38]

Even today, adultery remains a crime in twenty-three states. Almost never enforced, such laws, which have no counterpart in other Western nations, are a vestige of a time when it was assumed that government had an obligation to confine sexual relations to marriage. Over time, the justification for such laws shifted—away from the fear, as an 1838 court decision put it, that infidelity threatened "to adulterate the issue of an innocent husband, and to turn the inheritance away from his own blood, to that of a stranger," to a view that adultery violated a couple's exclusive right to one another's affection and support.[39]

Whether adultery has grown more common over time, however, is unclear, despite the widespread view that a heightened emphasis on romance, passion, and sex as central to personal fulfillment has intensified marital discontent. The statistics compiled by Alfred Kinsey, covering the 1930s and 1940s, estimated that about half of married men and a quarter of married women had extramarital sex. Those figures are not dissimilar from current estimates. There is some indication that extramarital sex has become more common among older adults, thanks to erectile dysfunction drugs, and that rates of infidelity among women and men have grown more similar in recent years.[40]

What does seem clear is that American adults continue to be intolerant of infidelity, even as large numbers cheat on their spouse. According to the National Science Foundation's General Social Survey, Americans feel more strongly than ever about sexual exclusivity, with over 80 percent considering extramarital relationships always wrong and another 15 percent "almost always wrong," up significantly from a decade earlier. Yet at the same time, many studies put the lifetime infidelity rate at about 30 percent for men and nearly as high for women. The desire for sexual fidelity and the belief in its centrality to marital happiness remain firm.[41]

Marriage is in retreat in the United States and globally. In the half century after 1950, the marriage rate in the United States fell by two-thirds. Were this trend to continue, the marriage rate would reach zero in 2042. Not a distinctively American phenomenon, the drift away from marriage is worldwide. About 87 percent of the world's population has lived in countries where the marriage rate has fallen since the 1980s.[42]

As the marriage rate has fallen, alternatives to marriage have proliferated. Even though the two-earner couple remains a norm, no single household type predominates in the way that the male breadwinner–female homemaker model did in the early post–World War II era. These postmodern arrangements are highly diverse, fluid, flexible, and fragile. Often, they arise in response to distinctive personal circumstances, challenges, and opportunities. A layoff, a health problem, a rent increase, an issue involving children—any might precipitate a change in living arrangements. Divorce has created a dizzying array of configurations of ex-spouses, former in-laws, stepparents, and half siblings. Some of the marital arrangements are minimalist—that is, they are compatible with highly independent lives. These include live-in companions or relationships involving separate residences. Others represent novel kinds of support networks, which consist of kin and non-kin in various caring and sharing arrangements. These might include multigenerational arrangements and units constructed around sibling ties as well as networks providing emotional, social, and material support, which may or may not occupy a single residence. Many families, which are products of the postindustrial information and service economies, also take certain feminist ideas—about the legitimacy of diverse family arrangements, shared household responsibilities, a gender-neutral definition of marital roles, and women's right to independence and self-fulfillment—for granted. Unlike the United States, many European countries have sought to institutionalize alternative familial arrangements by allowing cohabiting couples to register civil partnerships (which are known in France as "civil solidarity pacts"), which legally define inheritance and pension benefits and next-of-kin rights in hospitals. But in the

United States, where personal freedom is often defined in opposition to governmental authority, resistance to the legal regulation of alternatives to marriage is fierce.[43]

Over the course of American history there have been a variety of alternatives to monogamous marriage. Among the early Mormons, there was "plural marriage" modeled after the forms of polygamy described in the Old Testament. Utopian socialists experimented with a variety of marital forms involving divorce on demand, communal childrearing, and, in a few instances, nonexclusive pairings of partners. Yet, among the variety, three alternatives to monogamous marriage have been primary: single motherhood, unmarried cohabitation, and the single life.

In April 1747, a London newspaper printed a speech purported to have been delivered by a certain Polly Baker in a courtroom "at Connecticut near Boston in New England." Baker "was being prosecuted for the fifth time for bearing a bastard child." In her speech, she denied that what she had done was immoral: "I have brought five fine children into the world at the Risque of my life," she declared. She had not "debauched any woman's husband or enticed any youth," nor had she ever refused "any bonafide proposal of marriage." After stating that the man who had originally impregnated her was now a magistrate of the court, she asked if "her offense [could] have angered heaven" when God had furnished her children "with rational and immortal souls."[44]

The account was a fiction written by Benjamin Franklin, who himself had fathered a child out of wedlock. It was a protest against a legal system that defamed a woman for having an illegitimate child, while not similarly branding the father or ensuring that he supported his offspring. As for Polly, she personified the New World woman: outspoken, irreverent, and noncompliant.

Marriage is no longer obligatory. Not only has much of the stigma attached to alternate living arrangements eroded, but marriage itself is often viewed negatively, in terms of antiquated gender roles and hierarchies. A growing number of women have found an alternative to marriage in single parenthood. Today, a quarter of children live with a single mother and another 6 percent live with a single father. A majority of African American children (and 88 percent below the poverty line) live in a single-parent household, as do two-fifths of Hispanic children. In 1,500 neighborhoods nationwide, a majority of white children live in single-parent families.[45]

Single motherhood and female-headed households are anything but new phenomena. Indeed, the proportion of children living with a single parent in 1900 was about the same as in 1960. In both years, about one child in eleven lived with an unmarried mother. Nor have the causes of single motherhood changed as much as some imagine. To be sure, in the past, a higher proportion of single-parent households resulted from a parent's death. Three-quarters of single mothers claimed to be widows. But a quarter reported that they were separated or divorced or never married. As recently as 1940, a million women who identified themselves as married headed a single-parent household.[46]

Contrary to what some have speculated, single parenthood in 1900 was not primarily an urban phenomenon nor was it associated primarily with immigrants. Far from being more susceptible to single parenthood, immigrants were slightly less likely to reside in mother-headed homes, and the children of immigrants were somewhat more likely than the native-born to live with two parents. The supposed centrifugal effects of urbanization and immigration are not apparent. Neither the anonymity nor the stresses of urban life generated higher rates of single parenthood.[47]

While it is the case that a higher proportion of African American children in 1900 lived in a single-parent home, the figure was relatively low. About one black child in seven lived with one parent and a small but noticeable number lived with extended kin. In cities, however, roughly 40 percent of African American children resided in a single-parent home, nearly twice the rate for whites, suggesting that the restricted employment opportunities for black men in industry and commerce were the major factor contributing to black single-parent households. In 1900, over nine in ten African Americans lived in rural areas, but as the number of urban blacks rose, so, too, did the proportion living with a single parent.[10]

One of the crowning achievements of the Progressive era was the provision of "mother's pensions" to women who were raising children on their own. Between 1911 and 1931, virtually every state enacted pensions to allow widows to keep their children at home, rather than placing them into an orphanage or another institution in order to feed them. The amount of aid provided was pitifully small, and the states instituted various morality tests to ensure that only "worthy" or "deserving" mothers received relief. Many counties provided no benefits at all, and African American mothers were largely denied assistance. Stigma was not only attached to poor-relief, but to fatherless children themselves, whose birth certificates were stamped with the word "illegitimate." Meanwhile, the emerging profession of social work devoted a great deal of attention to single-parent families, defining standards for proper mothering, housekeeping, and a healthy diet. Nevertheless, the innovations of the Progressive era did establish a crucial precedent of material support for single mothers precisely because they were mothers, in the face of widespread hostility toward the poor for their dependence, supposed irresponsibility, and deviant family structures.[49]

During the Great Depression, the New Deal constructed a two-tiered system of economic support, which distinguished between "welfare" for single-mother families (officially known as "Aid to Children," and later as "Aid to Families with Dependent Children") and "social insurance" for male breadwinners. Social security was a right of citizenship and an earned benefit, while welfare was a form of charity. The benefits received by the unemployed and the elderly were entitlements financed by employee and employer contributions; Aid to Children, in contrast, was state-funded, with benefit levels varying across the states. These latter benefits were contingent on the mother's full-time care of children and subject to strict supervision to ensure that there was no outside income or man in the house. The constraints on single mothers were considerable.[50]

If single motherhood is not new, there is no doubt that its frequency greatly accelerated beginning in the mid-1960s. Many social conservatives cast blame on Great Society welfare programs, which supposedly provided financial incentives to young women who had children outside of marriage, or on feminism, with its critique of marriage as an outmoded patriarchal institution. Although it is certainly true that welfare programs had a limited impact on births outside of wedlock, the underlying cause for the upsurge in nonmarital births was more straightforward: the extremely high rate of dissolution among marriages contracted by persons in their teens or early twenties. During the 1950s, fully half of all women were married by the age of twenty, with the single largest number of marriages occurring at the age of seventeen. Most of these marriages were contracted quickly, before the partners knew each other well. The average length of courtship was just six months. Roughly half of these were shotgun marriages. That is, half of the brides were already pregnant on their wedding day. Young women in the 1950s proved increasingly willing to engage in premarital intercourse precisely because they felt confident that their boyfriend would marry them if they got pregnant. If he did not, putting the newborn up for adoption was a common practice among whites.[51]

Growing doubts about the wisdom of early marriage first emerged among low-income African Americans. As semiskilled industrial job opportunities began to fade in the wake of World War II, fewer young men could afford marriage and children. At the same time, a growing number of mothers, who had themselves married and divorced early, discouraged their daughters from repeating their mistake. Premarital sexual activity did not decline; the result was a growing number of births outside of wedlock. Since nonmarital childbearing had limited impact on these low-income women's future life prospects, there was little incentive to postpone childbearing, though these young women did take active steps to limit the number of births.

More affluent women also delayed marriage, partly to pursue advanced education and a career. These women, like their poorer counterparts, were eager to postpone marriage until they had found an appropriate partner and had achieved a degree of economic independence. Access to the birth control pill and other forms of contraception allowed these young women to engage in premarital intercourse with a much reduced risk of pregnancy. Nevertheless, with these women spending more years outside of marriage, nonmarital childbirths have inevitably risen.

It is often argued that single motherhood is a recipe for lifelong poverty, but in fact unwed mothers have made significant gains in education, income, and employment rates in recent years. The proportion of single mothers who are high school dropouts has fallen since the 1960s by nearly 80 percent. Neither moralism nor marriage promotion initiatives have done much to reduce out-of-wedlock births or single parenthood. The trend toward unmarried childbearing and single-parent households is longstanding; it began in the 1940s, and reflects factors unlikely to be reversed, including shifting cultural norms, increased options for women (including cohabitation), and the decline in the availability of "marriageable" men (due in part to deindustrialization and partly to high rates of incarceration).[52]

There are, however, proven ways that public policy can assist lone mothers in an environment in which fewer children are being raised by two parents. Single mothers are far more likely to work part-time than married mothers, reflecting the difficulty of juggling child care, other household responsibilities, and a job. Today, 80 percent of married mothers work full-time, compared to just 60 percent of single mothers. Child care subsidies, refundable earned income and child tax credits, and paid maternity leave, sick days, and vacation time would, at once, allow single mothers to raise their household income and ease the burden of raising a child by oneself.[53]

Few changes in American life over the past half century have been more profound or consequential than the growing incidence of unmarried cohabitation. As recently as 1972, lewd and lascivious cohabitation was a crime in thirty states. Twelve states, mainly in the West, abolished such laws between 1972 and 1979. What had once been derided as "living in sin" came to seem normal, and even expected among college students and twenty-somethings. "Shacking up" among young adults, the poor living in informal unions, cohabiting gay and lesbian partners, and unmarried couples households among the elderly began to evoke no surprise. Diversity has become a defining characteristic of cohabitation, which is no longer simply a prelude to marriage, confined to childless young adults. It has increasingly become an alternative to marriage. About half of cohabiting couples are over the age of thirty-five, one in seven is over fifty-five, and nearly half of cohabiting couples live with children. Unlike marriage, cohabitation, in many cases, is not a self-conscious choice. A majority of cohabitating couples said they either "slid into it" or "talked about it, but then it just sort of happened."[54]

Unmarried cohabitation is not as novel as one might think. Earlier in American history many famous marriages lacked legal sanction. Benjamin Franklin and Deborah Read never formally married because she was not able to secure a divorce from her first husband, John Rodgers. Nor did Frederick Douglass legally marry Anna Murray, since enslaved African Americans were barred from legal marriage. Today, in most states, marriage requires a formal civil or religious ceremony. But in a small number of states, marriage rests on consent. Spouses who hold themselves up publicly as a married couple are considered to have a legal, binding "common law" marriage. Given the shortage of magistrates and ministers especially in frontier regions, common-law marriages were widely recognized until the end of the nineteenth century, when many states imposed a host of legal requirements upon marriage. Common law rendered informal unions respectable and guaranteed partners and their children legal claims on the man's earnings.[55]

In 1882, in an effort to reduce the cost of Civil War pensions, which accounted for 40 percent of the federal budget, the Democratic Congress barred pensions for widows who were cohabiting with another man and for wives who had not legally married their husband. The attack on cohabitation was part of a much broader concern with public morality, evident in efforts to criminalize wife beating and child neglect, to outlaw abortion and the distribution of contraceptive devices or birth-control information, and to tighten divorce laws.[56]

Informal unions, however, remained common among the poor and among interracial couples, who were legally barred from marriage. In 1964, the Supreme Court overturned a Florida law that criminalized interracial cohabitation. Meanwhile, many states (primarily, but not exclusively, in the South) had "suitable home" regulations that barred welfare benefits to women in cohabiting relationships. In 1968, the Supreme Court invalidated welfare rules that allowed authorities to make unannounced searches to determine if a woman had "a man in the house." The Court unanimously held that "Destitute children who are legally fatherless cannot be flatly denied federally funded assistance on the transparent fiction that they have a substitute father." Other successful challenges were launched against state rules that prohibited cohabitation in public housing.[57]

During the 1970s and 1980s, the more liberal states extended inheritance rights and unemployment insurance and the right to sue for loss of consortium (that is, for the loss of the benefits of marriage, including sexual relations) to cohabiting couples, while some cities barred housing discrimination on the basis of marital status. But in many states, law and public policy have failed to take account of the growth of cohabitation. Many states still refuse to recognize "unsanctioned" relationships — those not based on marriage, adoption, or descent — and thus deny health benefits, hospital visitation rights, and many government benefits, fail to prohibit employment or housing discrimination against cohabitors, and allow judges to take cohabitation into account in making child custody decisions.[58]

Alongside the growth of unmarried cohabitation has come a growing defense of singledom as a chosen identity. In 1950, solos accounted for about 9 percent of all U.S. households; today that figure is roughly 28 percent. In Manhattan and Washington, D.C., half the population consists of singles; in cities as diverse as Atlanta, Denver, Minneapolis, San Francisco, and Seattle, the figure is over 40 percent. The growth of singledom, which marks a fundamental change in the way adults live, has much to do with shifting demographics and social norms, including delayed marriage, longer life spans, and increased affluence.[59]

Singles evoke many contrasting images. Among women, most images have been pejorative, conjuring up Miss Havisham, the lonely spinster, the "bag" lady, and the "cat" woman who supposedly lead an empty life. Then there is the "cougar," the post-forty woman on the prowl for younger men, and the thirty-something, epitomized by Carrie Bradshaw and Bridget Jones, who are insecure, emotionally needy, and obsessed with their love life. Isolation, desperation, awkwardness, and eccentricity — these are among the traits associated with single women, suggesting that for women an unmarried status is unnatural. Among men, certain bachelors are considered immature and unmanly—effeminate dandies, sexual deviants, self-indulgent idlers, or lonely losers—but others, especially cowboys, soldiers, urbane, sophisticated playboys, and hard-boiled detectives and private investigators, are paragons of independence and thought to embody the desires of married men.[60]

The word "bachelor" appeared in the seventeenth century to refer to non-property-holding single men. The New England colonies regarded bachelors as a threat to the stability of a community, and a number of the colonies subjected such men to special taxes and the requirement to live within a family household. Some colonies also mandated militia service for bachelors, and denied single men who had no property the right to vote, hold office, or serve on juries. But the term "bachelor" was not necessarily derogatory. As early as 1677, Harvard College students founded the Friday Evening Association of Bachelors, which was among the first of many literary and debating societies that provided unmarried men with opportunities for same-sex sociability. In contrast to New England, the southern colonies had a sharply skewed sex ratio, and many men remained unmarried into their thirties or later.[61]

During the nineteenth century, mass immigration and increased geographical mobility made bachelors more common and visible. In some cities and frontier areas, single adult males made up well over half the population, with many concentrated in distinct "bachelor districts" and residing in boarding houses. But during the nineteenth century, it is important to stress, most single native-born men (and women) lived in their parental home. Nevertheless, a host of institutions arose to meet bachelors' needs for camaraderie and conviviality: barber shops, billiard halls, brothels, saloons, as well as fraternal lodges and, for the social elite, men's clubs. There was a respectable bachelor culture, organized around mutual improvement societies, reform societies, and YMCAs, and a sporting culture, emphasizing gambling, drinking, horseracing, card games, smoking, virility, and rough and tumble fisticuffs. Friendly competitiveness was a part of bachelor culture, shifting, over time from organizational activities, including debate clubs and urban volunteer fire companies, to team sports, beginning with baseball in the 1830s and 1840s.[62]

As the average age of marriage fell during the first half of the twentieth century, bachelor culture diminished, only to resurface in new forms during the century's second half. As early as the 1950s, there were mounting attacks against the "bondage" of breadwinning, which made men fully responsible for their family's financial well-being. The *Playboy* philosophy that self-indulgence was not incompatible with manliness emerged to counter the straitjacket that confined the conventional husband. At the same time, a medical and psychiatric critique of modern manhood identified the health-endangering stresses of men's work and the ways that the rigid male role produced tension, anxiety, and bad temper. By the late 1960s, gay cultures had become increasingly visible, followed by other bachelor cultures, including today's bro culture, with their emphasis upon male bonding. The overarching message was that an adult male could be a "real" man, mature, happy, and sexually fulfilled, outside of marriage.[63]

In an influential 1862 article entitled "Why Are Women Redundant?" an English journalist, W. R. Greg, described singleness among women, which was growing much more common, as "an unwholesome social state, and is both productive and prognostic of much wretchedness and wrong." Rather than "completing, sweetening, and embellishing the existence of others," these women "are compelled to lead an independent and incomplete existence of their own." To this male observer, they were superfluous women. Like their male counterparts, they were not fulfilling their marital role.[64]

To be sure, some women remained single as a result of circumstances. In the New England and Middle Atlantic states, rapid male westward migration resulted in a sharply skewed sex ratio among the native-born, with women outnumbering men by about 20,000 in each region in 1850 and by double that over the next decade. But many of these women freely chose to remain unmarried, considering liberty "a better husband than love." Some felt that it was better to remain unmarried than to marry badly. As the *Ladies' Literary Cabinet* put this, "A single lady, though advanced in life, / Is much more happy than an ill-match'd wife." Many, however, self-consciously rejected marriage because it would deny them the opportunity to pursue a career or a life of service, economic independence, or the intimacy they would enjoy with their family or with other women. In 1853, the astronomer Maria Mitchell explained why she avoided marriage:

> Woman is expected to know how to do all kinds of sewing, all kinds of cooking, all kind of woman's work, and the consequence is that life is passed in learning these only, while the universe of truth beyond remains unentered.

Many of these single women remain well known today, including Susan B. Anthony, Emily Dickinson, Louisa May Alcott, and Clara Barton. In the early nineteenth century, many embraced the phrase "single blessedness" to describe their lives, with its connotations of sanctification. Alice Cary, a mid-nineteenth-century poet, defended the single life as "a higher, more expansive, and expressive life." The reformer and educator Emily Howland chose as her epitaph the words, "I strove to realize myself and to serve."[65]

Some single women defined their identity as daughters who devoted their lives to the care of other family members, but others engaged in activities outside the home. The six Weston sisters of Weymouth, Massachusetts, were dedicated abolitionists who lived together and provided each other with nurture and emotional support. As a friend observed, "Nothing but a most desperate falling in love could carry them off. They are married to each other and cannot imagine at present, that any man could supply the society of the sisters." It was an aura of service and self-sacrifice that freed some single women to overcome the social pressures, gender-role definitions, and ideological constraints that prevented other older women in the nineteenth century from taking an active role outside the home in reform, nursing, school teaching, and charity work. In the late nineteenth and early twentieth century, single women were responsible for the establishment and staffing of women's colleges and the founding of the nursing and social work professions.[66]

Not all lived alone. During the late eighteenth century, one finds references to "passing couples," in which a woman would dress as a man to make her attachment to another woman socially acceptable. Toward the end of the nineteenth century, the phrase "Boston marriage" (apparently first used by Henry James in his 1886 novel *The Bostonians*) was widely adopted to describe a long-term, intimate relationship between two women. One noteworthy example involved Charity Bryant, the niece of poet William Cullen Bryant, and Sylvia Drake, who lived together and ran a tailoring shop in Weybridge, Vermont, between 1807 and 1851. In a letter to a friend, the poet Bryant described his niece's union as "no less sacred than the tie of marriage." He went on to relate

> how they slept on the same pillow and had a common purse, and adopted each other's relations, and how one of them, more enterprising and spirited than the other, might be said to represent the male head of the family, and took upon herself their transactions with the world without.[67]

Later in time, during the New Deal, nearly a third of the leading female social welfare advocates lived in stable unions with other women.[68]

The proportion of unmarried women, which rose sharply after the eighteenth century, peaked at the end of the nineteenth century, reflecting gender differences in migration patterns and the emergence of "she" and "he" towns with distinctly different labor needs, which made it difficult for many women and men to find a spouse. The most common forms of wage employment for unmarried nineteenth-century women—domestic service, household manufacture, laundering, dressmaking, millinery, shoe-binding, and small proprietorships—were considered appropriate only for the working class. There were very few respectable jobs, apart from teaching or taking in boarders, available for middle-class women. Thus few lived free of family authority; most resided with parents or siblings or in an extended family household, often tending to the needs of aging parents and siblings. Like single men's culture, theirs was homosocial, organized largely around churches and various reform, philanthropic, and religious organizations.[69]

The late nineteenth and early twentieth centuries brought expanded job opportunities that allowed growing numbers of older single middle-class women to live apart from a family. Since most forms of paid professional employment were viewed as incompatible with marriage until the 1960s, many of the first generation of women professionals resided in institutional settings including settlement houses, hospitals, and teacher-training and women's colleges that provided close ties with other women. In fact, over half of women's college graduates in the period from 1870 to 1910 remained single. Despite a public image as dour, grave, grim-faced, and unsmiling lady superiors, many, like the settlement house founders Jane Addams and Lillian Wald and crucial figures in women's education like M. Carey Thomas, found a sense of community, joy, and sisterhood in intense, intimate friendships and, apparently, in discrete, homoerotic relations with other women. During the late nineteenth century and the early twentieth, it was easier for single women to meet their emotional and physical needs than it would be later. The cult of romantic friendship allowed women to hug, hold hands, and cuddle in bed without embarrassment or the stigma of lesbianism, which would become a source of shame and scandal in the mid-twentieth century.

Alongside these working professionals were substantial numbers of female live-in servants, many of whom were first- or second-generation immigrants, who were expected to remain unmarried. Others were day servants and factory operatives. In 1900, about one-third of all women workers lived apart from their family. Those who were not live-in servants usually lived as boarders and lodgers. The growth of wage-earning opportunities in offices and retailing and the development of apartment buildings during the late nineteenth and early twentieth centuries made a single life more practical for a larger swath of women. Nor was the single life confined to the Northeast. The numbers may have been even greater in the South. In antebellum Charleston, South Carolina, half the white women were unmarried, despite the value attached to marriage in slave society. Mass male deaths during the Civil War meant that a significant portion of the South's white female population remained unmarried during the postwar era. Certainly, fewer single white women in the South sought a vocation, but many took the lead in various civic endeavors and works of charity and benevolence. It was among African American women that the single life was most visible. African American women were significantly less likely to marry than white women from the late nineteenth century onward.[70]

The proportion of never-married women reached a high point in the late nineteenth and early twentieth centuries, rising from 7.3 percent for women born between 1835 and 1838 to 11 percent for those born between 1865 and 1875. That average figure of one in nine is only now being matched. In the early twentieth century, hostility toward single women intensified. Popularized versions of Freudian psychoanalysis associated the single life increasingly with lesbianism, precipitating attacks during the 1920s and later that such women were physically, psychologically, and sexually deviant. This was a topic that Lillian Hellman critically explored in her 1934 drama, *The Children's Hour*, which told the story of two head-mistresses at an exclusive all-girls boarding school accused of having a lesbian relationship.[71]

Eugenics, with its fear that the "less advanced" groups would out-reproduce the better-educated classes, further stigmatized single women, as did the association of singleness with "old-style" feminism, with its presumptions of women's moral superiority, purity, and capacity for caring and self-sacrifice, which seemed far out of step with the burgeoning consumer culture. Nevertheless, single women were not the "women adrift" (a phase first used in a 1910 federal report) who aroused widespread public anxiety during the early twentieth century. We know that some larger cities such as Chicago had an active lesbian subculture that flourished as early as the 1920s and was based in shared apartments.[72]

The growth of the single life is intimately linked to a shifting view toward childbearing and childrearing. For much of American history, adulthood and parenthood were treated as synonymous. Today, however, bearing children is seen as a choice, and one that a growing number of adults are declining. One in five American women never bear children, twice as many as in the previous generation. About half are childless by choice; the other half, due to physiological infertility or to circumstances (for example, choosing not to have a child without a partner or marrying later). The fact that childless women are better educated and more affluent than other women has contributed to a myth that these women choose to sacrifice motherhood because they center their lives on themselves and their career. Yet far from being self-centered, childless women are more likely than women with children to care for aging parents and to keep in close contact with siblings, friends, and neighbors.[73]

Seventeenth- and eighteenth-century colonists took the biblical injunction to "Be fruitful and multiply" seriously. A woman might bear her first child in her early twenties and not cease childbearing until her early forties. On average, a mother might bear between seven and ten children, or about one every eighteen months to two years. But many women bore no children. Over the periods in which reliable records are available, the infertility rate has remained relatively constant at between 10 and 13 percent of married couples.[74]

Barrenness, as it was then known, was regarded as an act of God, a punishment for sin or a test of faith. During the colonial period, as in much later periods, childlessness was regarded as a woman's problem. George Washington attributed his lack of children to a defect in his wife, Martha, even though she had borne four children in a previous marriage. Male potency was assumed if a man could have an erection. For many colonial women, childlessness was a source of anguish, leading them to seek out folk remedies. Few turned to physicians, however, since doing so might be interpreted as defiance of God's will. The association of infertility with women would persist. In the late nineteenth century, gynecologists often blamed childlessness upon women's diverting their reproductive energies into a career or intellectual activities. During the 1940s and 1950s, psychiatrists claimed that some women did not conceive because they unconsciously resisted motherhood. Meanwhile, physicians were reluctant to attribute infertility to men, whether it was caused by venereal disease or a low sperm count.[75]

But infertility did not mean that a woman would live without children. There were many opportunities for informal adoption or guardianship. An unmarried aunt or childless couple might take in orphans or raise the extra children of neighbors or relatives. During the Great Depression, some parents, including the journalist Russell Baker's mother, gave an "excess" daughter to a childless relative. Even today, child placement strategies that place a child in a relative's home temporarily or more permanently due to economic distress are not uncommon among many immigrant groups and

African Americans. It is only in the mid- and late twentieth century that the dominant culture came to view a parent's to share her or his children with another parent as unnatural.[76]

During the late twentieth century, attitudes toward childbearing moved in two contradictory directions. On the one hand, improvements in birth control and the decriminalization of abortion allowed women to limit births, while fears of global overpopulation contributed to the rise of anti-natalist sentiments. Beginning in the mid-1970s, the first public defenses of a child-free lifestyle emerged, apparent in the publication of books with titles like *The Childfree Alternative* and *Childfree by Choice*. Yet as the ability to reduce the number of births increased, so, too, did the desire to have a child of one's own. As opportunities for informal adoption declined and the association between female identity and mothering increased, a growing number of single women sought children either through formal adoption or through assisted reproduction.[77]

Many current techniques of assisted reproduction have a surprisingly long history. The first experiments with donor insemination took place in the middle of the nineteenth century, with the first successful fertilization of human eggs in vitro taking place in 1944. Artificial insemination drew widespread public attention in the 1930s, which was the same decade in which fertility drugs were introduced. Advances in endocrinology and the spread of in vitro fertilization and surrogate mothering held out the promise that with enough money and time any woman might have a child. But in practice, this promise often proves false. Today, only about half of the women who undergo fertility treatments, which are often highly invasive and dangerous, bear a child.[78]

In recent years, the stereotype of singles as lonely, isolated, and unfulfilled has been thoroughly rebutted. Many are more actively engaged in social and civic life than their married counterparts and are more likely to volunteer or to attend classes, concerts, and public events. Delayed marriage, high rates of cohabitation and divorce, longer life expectancies, increased affluence, and the deepening gender divide in education with young women now receiving nearly three-fifths of all bachelor's and master's degrees—all suggest that the single life will become more common in the future and extend for more years and even more broadly across the life course. In a society in which caregiving is, first and foremost, a familial responsibility, a looming question involves whether new kinds of support networks will be adequate to provide care to the growing number of aging singles.[79]

⁓

Many of the changes that are occurring in and to marriage are international in scope. In Western Europe, unmarried cohabitation and out-of-wedlock births are even more common than in the United States, reflecting growing affluence, women's independence, and the destigmatization of sex outside of marriage. What makes the United States distinctive is a significantly higher turnover in relationships—and in the economic consequences of relationship instability. Compared to Europeans, Americans marry and divorce more frequently and have more live-in partners and short-term cohabiting relationships. This turnover, and children's exposure to multiple parenting figures, appears to have adverse effects on at least some children's psychological well-being.[80]

Americans not only marry more and divorce and remarry more frequently than adults in any other postindustrial society, but agonize more about marriage's future—about the optimal age of marriage, the proper way to allocate spousal roles, and appropriate reasons for divorce. Political debates swirl around issues like covenant marriage (in which couples waive their right to no-fault divorce) and government-sponsored efforts to promote marriage and boost marriage rates, which have no counterpart in other countries. The reasons are simple and straightforward. One of the main ones has to do with the fact that this country has a much less developed welfare state than that of many others in Western Europe; consequently, marriage plays a larger role in caregiving in the United States. Indeed, many Americans regard marriage as the country's most effective and least costly antipoverty program. Concern about marriage reflects this society's preoccupation with children's well-being and future success. A stable and nurturing marriage is seen as the best predictor of healthy children. In addition, marriage provides a thinly veiled way to discuss issues relating to race, gender, and sexuality, with social conservatives decrying those who fail to conform to an ideal of heterosexual marriage that they deem traditional.[81]

If the United States wishes to raise marriage rates and reduce rates of divorce or cohabitation, it should not invest government resources in marriage promotion, which have had negligible or nonexistent effects. The only proven tool for increasing marriage rates are higher levels of education and steady, well-paying jobs. It turns out that nothing raises the marriage rate better than higher educational levels, which give young people an incentive to delay marriage and the skills necessary to sustain a marriage, as well as yielding higher incomes, which make marriage a more feasible and attractive proposition. Whatever efforts this society makes to stimulate marriage, it seems likely that the proliferation of ways that adults organize their private lives is irreversible, since these reflect long-term attitudinal, cultural, economic, and legal transformations. Under the circumstances, it makes more sense to better meet the needs of all families irrespective of their structure or composition.

CHAPTER FIVE

The Trials of Parenting

Childrearing is more contentious in the United States than in any other postindustrial society. Every facet of childrearing—breastfeeding versus bottle-feeding, crib-sleeping versus co-sleeping, spanking versus time outs or reasoning with children, home care versus institutional child care, strict versus permissive parenting—elicits bitter debate. American parents are also more sensitive to threats to their children's safety and physical and psychological well-being than those elsewhere. American debates over overprotected or overscheduled children, oversolicitous mothers, or helicopter parents have no European parallels. At the same time, panics over childhood sexual abuse and stranger abductions, or the impact of divorce or unmarried cohabitation or same-sex parenting, or even circumcision or the possible negative consequences of childhood vaccinations evoke far more controversy in the United States than in other societies. Not surprisingly, there has been far greater concern in the United States that irrational parental fears have a damaging impact upon children.[1]

Anxiety is the hallmark of contemporary American parenting. Even before a child's birth, many parents agonize incessantly about threats to a fetus's health from drinking, smoking, and toxins. After birth, contemporary parents worry intensely about sudden infant death syndrome, and later about their child's personality development, psychological and physical well-being, and academic performance. None of this unease is new, although the intensity has certainly increased, and the sources of anxiety have shifted dramatically over time. Few parents today agonize over their children's posture or over infant feeding schedules, which were once major sources of concern. Today's parents, in contrast, are far more worried than their predecessors about sleep disorders, hyperactivity, Asperger's syndrome, autism, and whether their children are bored or unhappy. They also fret more about their children's future economic prospects. Compared to American parents in the past, those today are far more likely to view their children as fragile creatures, who are vulnerable psychologically as well as physically. Whereas for much of the twentieth century there was a tendency to regard children as hardy and resilient, there has been an increase, over time, in fears that damage inflicted in the "critical years" of early childhood persists into later life. Meanwhile, the injuries and impairments that worry contemporary parents the most are defined largely in psychological terms. Indeed, among the greatest sources of parental anxiety are threats to their children's self-confidence, self-image, and self-esteem. Even in the case of childhood sexual abuse, much of the worry focuses on the psychological damage rather than the physical harm.

Given American society's diversity, parenting practices have always differed significantly along lines of ethnicity, parental age and education, religion, and social class. Recent immigrants tend to raise their children far differently than do the native born, and older, highly educated parents also do so differently from those who are younger and less well-educated. A child's sex and age, too, prompt different approaches to child-drearing. Nevertheless, certain generalizations carry some validity. Since the early nineteenth century, foreign observers have agreed that American children are more independent, indulged, and resistant to authority than their European counterparts. For generations, foreign commentators have deemed American children less deferential, polite, and respectful than those abroad, as well as being more embedded in a peer culture. Nonetheless, a decisive shift in American parenting practices has occurred in recent years. With fewer children and higher disposable incomes, parents spend much more money on children than in the past, provide them with many more store-bought toys, which are now given year round, and seek their children's affection, rather than expecting their children to earn their love.

Another broad generalization is that the introduction of every new form of media has evoked intense nervousness. The Internet and videogames are only the most recent sources of alarm, but in the past, movies, radio, pinball machines, and television provoked similar concerns about a loss of parental control and influence. What is different today is the exaggerated perception that digital diversions are more addictive, isolating, and violent than the earlier entertainment forms. To these generalizations, we might add that American children have always swung between periods of freedom and of close adult supervision. What is distinctive now is that children spend much more of their time alone, indoors, in front of a videogame, a computer monitor, or a television screen. The geographical space that children traverse on their own has shrunk significantly, and kids' outdoor activities are far more likely to be adult-organized and adult-supervised than in the past.[2]

All of these developments have triggered a host of fears: that by depriving children of sufficient opportunities to explore the outdoors on their own, parents have made them less competent physically, more anxious psychologically, and less imaginative and creative; that by coddling children, parents deprive them of the very risks and challenges that kids need to grow up and achieve independence; that by purchasing toys and videogames with prepackaged storylines, parents teach kids to become avid consumers and rob them of the opportunity to invent and fabricate their own toys and construct and negotiate rules; that by failing to assign children household chores from a very young age, parents unintentionally raise freeloaders with little sense of responsibility. Many commentators speak disparagingly about "bubble-wrapped kids," of "hurried children," growing up too fast and too soon, and of kids who are no more than "walking résumés."[3]

What accounts for the emergence of a highly self-conscious, risk-averse, intensely involved approach to parenting? Smaller families have led parents to invest more resources and attention into each individual child. Overabundant information, disseminated by physicians, psychologists, journalists, and advocacy groups, has contributed to parental anxieties. Guilt, too, has played a significant role, as mothers, in particular, have overcompensated for time spent on the job. Today's working mothers actually spend more face-to-face time with their children than did the stay-at-home moms of the 1950s. Meanwhile, a competitive, winner-take-all economy, coupled with fears that children's economic status will not equal their parents', has further intensified the importance attached to childrearing, since parents want to give their offspring a leg up. But of all the factors that have contributed to a fixation on parenting, perhaps the most important is the widespread perception among today's middle- and upper-middle-class parents that they are unable to provide their offspring with the kind of relaxed, unpressured, playful childhood that they themselves enjoyed.[4]

For many baby boomers and their parents, the golden age of American childhood did not occur in the mythic past: It existed within living memory. The early post–World War II era, many believe, was far more child-centered than today, and childhood itself was much less pressured, structured, or hurried than it has since become. To be sure, nostalgia colors many of those fond memories. It is easy to forget the childhood-centered panics of the early cold war era—over comic books, Strontium-90 in milk, juvenile delinquency, and especially polio. Likewise, the sacrifices made by many women, who were expected to forego career ambitions for their family's sake, can be overlooked. Affectionate memories also obscure the racial, class, and gender inequities of the era, the mistreatment of children with disabilities, the fistfights that were considered a normal part of boyhood, and the way boys teased and tormented girls and sometimes openly abused animals.

Nevertheless, a cold war childhood remains the yardstick against which Americans assess contemporary childhood. And according to that measure, contemporary childhood stacks up poorly. If childhood during the early post–World War II era was often filled with prolonged periods of boredom, many girls and boys, regardless of class and ethnicity, personally recall a childhood characterized by unsupervised play in vacant lots, fields, and streets, bicycling without helmets, and sandlot sports that were not organized by adults. This, many believe, was a childhood that encouraged imagination and creativity, in stark contrast to the seemingly careworn, overly organized, if also overly indulged, middle-class childhood of today.

A declension model dominates popular thinking about childhood. Some adults point to the introduction of school classes in friendship as a sign that kids no longer know how to make or keep friends. Others lament the loss of older childhood rituals and pastimes, such as playing marbles, chasing fireflies, or indulging in kick the can—activities that supposedly nourished children's resourcefulness and taught valuable social skills. Many worry that today's society, in its efforts to reduce risks of all kinds, has deprived middle-class children of opportunities for maturation and the acquisition of significant life experiences. Indeed, a number of recent best-sellers, including *The Dangerous Book for Boys* and *The Daring Book for Girls,* as well as a television series, *Kid Nation,* have sought to exploit adults' desire to recreate a seemingly lost world of childhood as a time of playful adventure, risk, and discovery.

"Revolution" is a word that historians use warily, but at least superficially the changes that have occurred in childrearing since the early 1970s meet that standard. One notable development was that the decision to have a child became much more a matter of conscious choice as a result of a sharp increase in international adoption, the advent of in vitro fertilization, surrogate motherhood, and other novel birth technologies, and the decline in the stigma against childlessness. By the early twenty-first century, some five million babies worldwide had been born with the aid of reproduction technologies, even as one in five American women ended their childbearing years without having borne a child, compared to one in ten in the 1970s. Another noteworthy change involves delayed parenthood. A majority of women now delay childbearing into their late twenties or thirties, rather than concentrating their births in the early and mid-twenties as was the case through the 1960s. In general, older parents are more mature and economically secure than those who were younger, but also more anxious and apprehensive. With over two-thirds of mothers of young children in the paid labor force, an especially striking transformation involves the care of young children. By the early twenty-first century, about 40 percent of children under four were cared for by a day care center or by a nonrelative, and half were cared for primarily by a relative other than their mother. Equally important was the increasing complexity and diversity of the makeup of the households in which children grew up. Today, over half of children under thirteen live with a stepparent, who is married or cohabiting with the biological parent, or with step-siblings or half siblings. At the same time, an unprecedented proportion of children, about one-third, are only children.

Accompanying these demographic shifts are profound changes in attitude. Among the most striking are the "discovery of risk," intensifying anxieties over threats to children's well-being; a growing revulsion against corporal punishment, evident not only in prohibitions on paddling in schools, which was banned in thirty states after 1971, but in a gradual drift away from spanking; and a rejection of the view that children will mature naturally without self-conscious parental intervention. In a more competitive economic environment, middle-class parents have become more prone to regard their children as extensions of themselves and to view their child's achievements and accomplishments as measures of their own competence. These mothers and fathers are more likely than previous generations of parents or parents in similar societies to assist in their child's homework or to intervene on their child's behalf in school or sports or other activities. The term "helicopter parent" refers to parents' growing tendency to view their children as their alter egos and close friends. These tendencies have prompted criticism that fewer contemporary mothers and fathers are willing to parent—that is, to impose discipline, set boundaries, and enforce guidelines.[5]

These shifts in parenting practices, which are most pronounced among the middle class and upper middle class, carry profound public policy consequences. The 1996 welfare reform law required low-income mothers of young children to work or take part in job training or educational programs in exchange for benefits. The belief that economically disadvantaged families produced an ecology that inhibited their children's intellectual development, by not providing sufficient verbal stimulation or exposure to reading, led to the establishment of a host of programs designed to give children in poverty a "head start." The long-term effectiveness of early childhood educational programs, in the absence of policies to promote employment for their parents at decent wages, remains unclear.[6]

The behavioral, attitudinal, and demographic transformations in childrearing practices and in parent-child relations have produced many misgivings. But the story is far more complicated than a tale of decline. The changes that have taken place in children's everyday lives have occurred far more incrementally then the declension model supposes. In addition, the causes of change lie less in a transformation of values — such as a growing selfishness or intrusiveness among adults — than in structural shifts in demography, the economy, and technology. In fact, there is no compelling evidence that indicates that children's resourcefulness, imagination, or ability to play independently have diminished over time; nor is there any empirical evidence to suggest that children are less outgoing or socially competent than in the past. Rather than viewing the recent history of childrearing as a history of decline, we would do better to see how the contemporary emphasis on *intensive* and *intentional* parenting, the self-conscious cultivation of certain traits within their children, arose.

Around the turn of the nineteenth century, several prominent men embarked on experiments, some intriguing, others appalling, to shape the next generation. The best known example involved James Mill, the Scottish economist and father of the philosopher John Stuart Mill. Determined to create a genius, he taught his son Greek at the age of three and Latin around eight. Before he was eight the younger Mill had read *Don Quixote* and the *Arabian Nights* and had intensively studied geometry, algebra, history, and read (in the original) Virgil, Horace, Ovid, Sophocles, Euripides, Aristophanes, Thucydides, and many other classical authors. Around the age of twelve, he began a thorough study of Scholastic logic; at thirteen he studied the works of the Scottish political economist and philosopher Adam Smith and the English economist David Ricardo; and at fifteen, he studied law. At twenty, however, the younger Mill underwent a "mental crisis," which he attributed to his upbringing. He was "left stranded at the commencement of my voyage, with a well-equipped ship and rudder, but no sail."[7]

The American painter Charles Willson Peale, who fathered seventeen children, eleven of whom survived infancy, was eager to inspire his children to careers in science and the arts. To this end, he named his children after prominent scientists and artists. His sons included Raphaelle, Rembrandt, Titian Ramsay, Rubens, Charles Linnaeus, and Benjamin Franklin; his daughters, Angelica Kauffmann, Rosalba Carriera, and Sophonisba Angusciola.[8]

Richard Lovell Edgeworth, the Anglo-Irish inventor and father of twenty-one children, including the author Maria Edgeworth, sought to raise his first-born son according to the principles of Jean-Jacques Rousseau's *Emile*. In response to the stultifying system of rote learning and corporal punishment prevalent at the time, Rousseau advanced an alternative vision of a natural education emphasizing experiential learning and self-discovery (but which also involved a high degree of behavioral manipulation). His larger goal was to allow the individual to retain the natural virtues that would otherwise be distorted by society's corrupting influences. In Rousseau's novel, Emile is breastfed, not dispatched to a wet nurse; nor is he swaddled or scolded. Edgeworth sought to follow Rousseau's philosophy, and refused to constrain his oldest son's impulses. The father attributed his son's mechanical abilities to Rousseau's emphasis on learning by doing, but his son also developed an uncontrollable temper. It proved "difficult to urge him to anything that did not suit his fancy, and more difficult to restrain him from what he wished to follow. In short, he was self-willed, from a spirit of independence, which had been inculcated by his early education." The father placed his son in a Catholic seminary and eventually disowned him.[9]

Then there was Thomas Day, a British humanitarian, who, in 1769, visited a foundling home and, pretending to be seeking maidservant apprentices for a married friend, acquired two girls, aged twelve and eleven whom he renamed Lucretia and Sabrina. Inspired, like his friend Edgeworth, by Rousseau's vision of raising the young according to enlightened principles, his goal was to create the perfect wife for himself. His story helped inspire George Bernard Shaw's Pygmalion. He dismissed Lucretia as intransigent and "invincibly stupid," and subjected Sabrina to ordeals to build up her constitution: He dripped hot wax on her shoulders and arms, stuck her with pins, forced her to wade in a frigidly cold lake, and even fired a pistol at her.[10]

These are only the most extreme examples of a kind of intentional parenting that became increasingly common in the late eighteenth and early nineteenth centuries, inspired by the Enlightenment faith in the power of nurture and environmental conditioning. But the roots of intentional parenting go back somewhat earlier in time. A more explicit attention to childrearing practice became apparent in the sixteenth and seventeenth centuries and was a product of the religious upheavals of the era. Parenting has evolved through a series of successive and overlapping phases. It has also been continually contested. In early modern Europe, several conflicting conceptions of childhood coexisted. One viewpoint, associated with the early Protestant reformers, considered children as tainted by original sin, and charged parents with responsibility for suppressing their selfish and lustful impulses. John Calvin called on fathers to regard their children as a gift of God and recommended them "diligently to form their children under a system of holy discipline." A second view, associated with Christian humanists, saw children as inexperienced and malleable creatures in ways that anticipated John Locke's description of children as blank slates, or tabula rasa. As early as the 1520s, the Christian humanist Desiderius Erasmus (1466?–1536), published a series of books and pamphlets stressing the importance of proper nurture, guidance, and discipline:

> [A child] ought to imbibe, as it were, with the milk that he suckles, the nectar of education, [for] he will most certainly turn out to be an unproductive brute unless at once and without delay he is subjected to the process of intensive instruction.

A third view, associated in England with the royal court, idealized the young's childlike faith and naïve innocence.[11]

Sixteenth- and seventeenth-century conceptions of childrearing cannot be divorced from the broader political and philosophical debates of the era. The humanist view reflected a new understanding of the legitimacy of authority, which depended upon rational consent. As articulated by John Locke, the goal of childrearing was to prepare the young for an independent life by instilling a capacity for self-government and respect for legitimate authority. In contrast, the royalist view was expressed most extensively by the English political theorist and defender of patriarchy and royal absolutism Robert Filmer, who viewed the imposition of deference and respect for hierarchy as essential to social stability. The Puritan view, in turn, reflected a commitment to a social order governed by divine law. According to a number of Puritan reformers, childhood needed to be viewed as a preparatory stage and childrearing transformed into a rational art involving the inculcation of virtues and values. Children needed to be sequestered from the adult world and greater attention needed to be paid to their spiritual education. Spoiling was to be avoided, and deference to patriarchal authority cultivated.[12]

Between the sixteenth and the late eighteenth centuries, a radical new idea gained traction: that childhood was life's formative stage. Prior to the eighteenth century, neither novelists nor biographers betrayed much interest in the first years of life, and autobiographies revealed scant nostalgia for childhood. In his 1749 novel *The History of Tom Jones, a Foundling,* Henry Fielding dismissed the title character's childhood in six words: "nothing happened worthy of being recorded." Especially striking is the apparent inattention to childhood risks, evident in the fact that many children died from causes that seem easily preventable, such as falling down wells or crawling into fireplaces. But by 1802, when the Romantic poet William Wordsworth included the phrase that "the child is father of the man" in his poem "My Heart Leaps Up," it had already become a commonplace that childhood experiences shaped adult character, thereby giving intense significance to proper childrearing.[13]

By the mid-eighteenth century, there was a growing consensus among authorities that without expert guidance and instruction, childrearing was sure to go wrong. William Cadogan, an eighteenth-century British physician and writer on child care made the point forcefully in his 1748 *Essay on Nursing:*

> It is with great Pleasure I see at last the Preservation of Children become the Care of Men of Sense. In my opinion this Business has been too long fatally left to the management of Women who cannot be supposed to have a proper Knowledge to fit them for the Task, notwithstanding they look upon it to be their own Province.[14]

A shift in attitudes toward play also became apparent in the eighteenth century. As late as the 1740s, it was still a commonplace to regard play as something that should be abandoned when a child reached the "age of reason," around the age of seven. In his popular letters to his son, Lord Chesterfield recommended: "No more levity: childish toys and playthings must be thrown aside, and your mind directed to serious objects." But at the very time that he wrote those words, others, notably Jean-Jacques Rousseau, contended that play could be instructive and build a child's physical strength. Play also became the defining symbol of children's essential innocence and the freedom that supposedly characterized childhood.[15]

Childrearing has never conformed to a single model. It has always been diverse and contested. This was certainly the case in the American colonies. Parenting took quite different forms among Native Americans and European colonists of various regions and religious backgrounds. If one objective of Native American childrearing practices was to instill stoicism and an independent spirit within children, then English parents during the seventeenth century had a very different goal: to prepare children for a hierarchical, patriarchal society, in which deference and submission were expected on the part of social inferiors.

European observers were shocked by the differences between their childrearing customs and those of the Indian peoples of the eastern woodlands. There were certain superficial similarities. Native peoples, like Europeans, surrounded pregnancy with rituals to ensure the newborn's health, and practiced rites following a childbirth that Europeans regarded as perversions of baptism and circumcision (such as rubbing an infant in bear's fat and piercing the newborn's tongue, nose, or ears). The differences in childrearing practices, however, were especially striking. A primary objective of Native Americans' was to instill self-sufficiency and fortitude within children. Girls were not expected to spin, weave, or knit, as they were in Europe, and boys were not expected to farm. Nor were children subjected to corporal punishment, since this was believed to produce timidity and submissiveness.[16]

Maturation among Indians was much more enmeshed in religious and communal rituals than among Europeans, and these rites were intended to encourage the young to achieve certain adult competencies and status as early as possible. For boys, there were ceremonies to mark one's first tooth, killing of one's first large game, and a vision quest, in which boys went alone into the wilderness to find a guardian spirit. Many girls were secluded at the time of first menstruation. Among certain southeastern tribes, there was a ceremony called *huskinaw* through which boys and girls shed their childish identity and assumed adult status.[17]

English colonists regarded children as "adults-in-training." They recognized that children differed from adults in their mental, moral, and physical capabilities, and drew distinctions between childhood, an intermediate stage they called "youth," and adulthood. But these colonists did not rigidly segregate children by age. Size and physical strength were more important than chronological age in defining a young person's roles and responsibilities. Parents wanted children to speak, read, reason, and contribute to their family's economic well-being as soon as possible.

Infancy was regarded as a state of deficiency. Unable to speak or stand, infants lacked two essential attributes of full humanity. Parents discouraged infants from crawling, and placed them in "walking stools," similar to modern walkers. To ensure proper adult posture, young girls wore leather corsets, and parents placed rods along the spines of very young children of both sexes. The colonists, unlike their European counterparts, rarely swaddled their infants, and not surprisingly some youngsters had serious accidents in fireplaces or wells.[18]

Colonial America's varied religious cultures exerted a profound influence on childrearing. Even today, the image of Puritans as killjoys owes a great deal to their ministers' attitude toward childhood, especially the sect's emphasis on infant depravity. As the Reverend Cotton Mather put it: "Are they Young? Yet the Devil has been with them already. . . . They go astray as soon as they are born. They no sooner step than they stray, they no sooner lisp than they ly." The New England Puritans urged children to exhibit religious piety and to conquer their sinful nature. To encourage children to reflect on their morality, the Puritans spoke frequently about death. They also took children to hangings so that they would contemplate the consequences of sin. To encourage youthful piety, Puritan parents held daily household prayers; read books, such as James Janeway's *Token for Children,* offering examples of early conversion; and expected even young children to attend hours-long Sabbath services. One of the Puritans' most important legacies was the notion that parents were responsible not only for their children's physical well-being, but also for their choice of vocation and the state of their soul.[19]

In the Middle Colonies (New York, New Jersey, Pennsylvania, and Delaware), a very different pattern of parenting arose. Quaker households, in particular, were much less authoritarian and patriarchal than the Puritans'. They were also more isolated since fewer families took in other families' children as servants than Puritans did. Instead of emphasizing sinfulness, Quaker parents sought to gently nurture each child's "Light Within," the spark of divinity that they believed was implanted in each child's soul, through "holy conversation." Quaker parents, unlike those in New England, emphasized early independence and provided their children with land at a relatively early age.[20]

In the Chesapeake colonies of Maryland and Virginia, a sharply skewed sex ratio and a high death rate produced patterns of parenting very different from those in the Middle Colonies or New England. Marriages in the seventeenth-century Chesapeake were brief (averaging just seven years), and orphanhood and stepparenthood were extremely common. Fathers, who could not expect to see their children reach adulthood, granted their children economic independence at an early age. But if the children of landowners and slaveholders were treated indulgently, the seventeenth-century Chesapeake also included large numbers of teenage indentured servants who were under very strict discipline and frequently suffered corporal punishment.[21]

During the eighteenth century, the world of childhood underwent dramatic shifts. The Great Awakening of the 1730s and 1740s, the most important religious event of the eighteenth century in America, witnessed furious religious debates over the doctrine of infant depravity, which contributed to a further splintering of attitudes toward children. At one end of the spectrum were New Lights, who emphasized the importance of breaking a child's sinful will around the age of two or three; at the other end were religious liberals who sought to bend, not break, a child's will, inculcate values gradually, and motivate children through a sense of duty rather than fear.[22]

Over the course of the eighteenth century, fewer first children were named for parents, who also abandoned the custom of naming later-born children for recently deceased siblings. Children received middle names, suggesting a greater recognition of each child's individuality. Representations of childhood also changed. Stiffly posed portraits depicting children as miniature adults gave way to more romantic depictions of childhood, showing young people playing or reading. Meanwhile, such educational toys as globes, jigsaw puzzles, and board games appeared, as did children's books, with wide margins, large type, and pictures. Animal stories, morality tales, and science books sought to entertain as well as instruct.[23]

Eighteenth-century childrearing tracts suggest a shift in parental attitudes, as well. Alongside an earlier emphasis on instilling religious piety, there was a growing stress on implanting virtue and a capacity for self-government by teaching "the Government of themselves, their Passions and Appetites." Many manuals embraced John Locke's argument that "a Love of Credit, and an Apprehension of Shame and Disgrace" was much more effective in shaping children's behavior than physical beatings. Yet the eighteenth century also saw a growing obsession with masturbation, following the publication in 1710 of *Onania: Or the Heinous Sin of Self Pollution*. As childhood became associated with asexual innocence, behavior that ran counter to this ideal was rigorously repressed.[24]

Contrasting conceptions of childhood coexisted in late-eighteenth-century America. These included the Lockean notion of the child as plastic and malleable, whose character could be shaped for good or bad; a Romantic association of childhood with purity, imagination, and organic wholeness; and an evangelical conception of children as potentially sinful creatures who needed to be sheltered from the evil influences of the outside world and whose willfulness must be broken in infancy. These views of childhood tended to be associated with distinct social groups. The evangelical emphasis on submission to authority and early conversion was most often found among rural Baptist, Methodist, and Presbyterian families. The southern gentry and northern merchants were especially likely to shower children with affection, since day-to-day discipline was in the hands of servants or slaves. Meanwhile, the middling orders, especially upwardly mobile farm, shop-keeping, and artisan families, emphasized self-control and internalized discipline.[25]

The American Revolution accelerated antipatriarchal currents already underway. An emphasis on order and restraint gave way to a Romantic insistence on the importance of personal feeling and affection. Fewer parents expected children to bow or doff their hats in their presence or stand during meals. Instead of addressing parents as "sir" and "madam," children began to call them "papa" and "mama." By the end of the eighteenth century, furniture specifically designed for children, painted in pastel colors and decorated with pictures of animals or figures from nursery rhymes, started to be widely produced, reflecting the popular notion of childhood as a time of innocence and playfulness.[26]

Toward the end of the eighteenth century, a growing number of parental letters to children appear. A theme that runs through these documents is the manipulation of love as an instrument for shaping children's character. For some parents, love was quite explicitly conditional. In a letter to his eleven-year-old daughter, Patsy, written a year after his wife's death in 1782, Thomas Jefferson expressed his love, but made it clear that she would lose his affection if she disappointed him:

> I have placed my happiness on seeing you good and accomplished, and no distress which this world can now bring on me could equal that of your disappointing my hopes. If you love me, then strive to be good under every situation and to all living creatures, and to acquire those accomplishments

which I have put in your power, and which will go far toward ensuring the warmest love of your affectionate father.

A 1778 letter from Abigail Adams to her son John Quincy conveys a similar message in a more moralistic tone:

> Remember that you are accountable to your maker for all your words and actions. Let me injoin it upon you to attend constantly and steadfastly to the precepts and instructions of your father as you value the happiness of your mother and your own welfare . . . , for dear as you are to me, I had much rather you should have found your grave in the ocean you have crossed, or any untimely death crop you in your infant years, rather than see you an immoral profligate or graceless child.
>
> Yet you must keep a strict guard upon yourself, or the odious monster [i.e., vice] will soon lose its terror, by becoming familiar to you.[27]

According to the ideal of "republican motherhood," which flourished in the late eighteenth century, mothers were responsible for implanting the republican virtues of civility and self-restraint in their sons and ensuring that America's republican experiment not follow the path of the Greek and Roman republics. To make sure that women could fulfill this responsibility, the late eighteenth century saw a surge in female academies and a marked increase in female literacy. By the early nineteenth century, mothers in the rapidly expanding northeastern middle class increasingly embraced an amalgam of earlier childrearing ideas. From John Locke, they absorbed the notion that children were highly malleable creatures and that a republican form of government required parents to instill a capacity for self-government in their children. From Jean-Jacques Rousseau and the Romantic poets middle-class parents acquired the idea of childhood as a special stage of life, intimately connected with nature and purer and morally superior to adulthood. From evangelicals, the middle class adopted the idea that the primary task of parenthood was to implant proper moral character in children and to insulate them from the corruptions of the adult world.[28]

As early as the second quarter of the nineteenth century, a new kind of urban middle-class family, far more emotionally intense and

5.1. Portrait of the Smith Family, c. 1807. Attributed to Captain James Smith.

inward-turning than in the past, was emerging. These families were much smaller than their colonial counterparts, as parents rapidly reduced the birth rate from an average of seven to ten children in 1800 to five children in 1850 and three in 1900. These families were also more sharply divided along generational lines, as childrearing was increasingly concentrated in the early years of marriage. In addition, these families were more mother-centered, as fathers left home to go to work and mothers assumed nearly exclusive responsibility for childrearing. Whereas earlier childrearing manuals had been directed at fathers, these tracts were now addressed to mothers. Meanwhile, middle-class children remained within their parents' home longer than in the past. Instead of shifting back and forth between the home and work experiences outside the home, the young remained at home into their late teens or early twenties.[29]

As socialization within the home was prolonged and intensified, childrearing became an increasingly self-conscious activity, a development underscored by a proliferation of advice manuals, mothers' magazines, and maternal societies, where pious mothers discussed methods for properly raising and disciplining children. The advice, which increasingly came from secular authorities rather than ministers, emphasized several themes. One was the crucial significance of the early years. As the Reverend Horace Bushnell wrote in 1843, "Let every Christian father and mother understand, when the child is three years old, that they have done more than half of what they will do for his character." Another key theme was the critical importance of mothering. As Lydia Maria Child put it in 1832, a mother's "every look, every movement, every expression does something toward forming the character of the little heir to immortal life." At the same time, the goals and methods of childrearing were conceived of in new terms. Mothers were to nurture children, especially sons, to be resourceful and self-directed; they were to do so by internalizing a capacity for inner discipline and self-control, not through physical punishment, but through various forms of maternal influence, including maternal example, appeals to a child's conscience, and threats to withdraw love.[30]

Even as the northeastern urban middle class embraced the idea of intensive mothering and a sheltered childhood, very different patterns pre-

5.2. Family of slaves at the Gaines' house, 1861 or 1862. Photograph by G. H. (George Harper) Houghton.

vailed among slave, farm, frontier, mining, and urban working-class families. Their children actively contributed to their family's well-being by hunting and fishing, assisting in parents' work activities, tending gardens or livestock, toiling in mines or mills, scavenging or participating in street trades, and caring for younger siblings.[31]

Parenting under slavery was especially difficult. As a result of poor nutrition and heavy labor during pregnancy, half of all slave newborns weighed five-and-a-half pounds or less, or what we would consider dangerously underweight, and fewer than two out of three slave children reached the age of ten. Nearly half of the former slaves interviewed by the Works Progress Administration were raised apart from their father, either because he resided on another plantation, because their mother was unmarried or widowed, or because their father was a white man. By the time they reached the age of sixteen, fully a third of those interviewed had been sold or transferred to another owner.[32]

Childhood represented a battlefield in which parents and masters competed over who would exercise primary authority over children. One of enslaved children's harshest memories was discovering that their parents were helpless to protect them from abuse. Still, slave parents managed to convey a sense of pride to their children and to educate them about how to maneuver through the complexities of slavery. Through their naming patterns and their transmission of craft skills, religious customs, music, and folklore, slave parents both gave their children the will and skills necessary to endure slavery and sustained a sense of history, morality, and distinctive identity.[33]

Urban working-class and immigrant families depended for subsistence on a cooperative family economy in which all family members, including children, were expected to contribute to the family's material support. During the nineteenth century, as much as 20 percent of many working-class families' income was earned by children under the age of fifteen. Key decisions—regarding emigration, school attendance, and the timing of entry into the workforce and marriage—were based on family needs rather than individual choice, and working-class and immigrant parents frequently invoked their authority to ensure that children handed over their unopened paychecks.[34]

Rural families, too, depended heavily on their children's labor. On the western frontier, parents encouraged children to act independently and to assume essential family responsibilities at an early age. Even very young children were expected to perform essential tasks such as cutting hay, herding cattle and sheep, burning brush, gathering eggs, churning butter, and assisting with plowing, planting, and harvesting. In rural areas schooling tended to be sporadic and intermittent.[35]

In the late nineteenth and early twentieth century, parents began to acquire a greater sense of control over their children's lives, including their health, as physicians successfully treated digestive problems such as diarrhea, dysentery, and worms; respiratory problems such as consumption, croup, pneumonia, and whooping cough; diseases such as scarlet fever; and infections. The pasteurization of milk was particularly important in reducing child mortality. These medical successes encouraged well-educated parents to embrace the notion that childrearing itself should be more scientific. During the 1880s and 1890s, the Child Study movement, spearheaded by the pioneering psychologist G. Stanley Hall, collected information from mothers and teachers, promoted greater awareness of the stages of childhood development (including adolescence, a term that he popularized), and encouraged increased sensitivity to children's fears, insecurities, and anxieties. The early twentieth century saw the rise of "Better Baby Contests," scientifically judged competitions to determine the healthiest infants in a region. Held at forty state fairs, these events spread across the nation, reaching a peak in 1913, 1914, and 1915. These contests also taught parents how diet, hygiene, and scientifically informed childrearing techniques could produce a "superior crop" of babies.[36]

Meanwhile, the belief that scientific principles had not been properly applied to childrearing produced new kinds of childrearing manuals, written by physicians rather than ministers and other moralists. The most influential was Dr. Luther Emmett Holt's *The Care and Feeding of Children*, first published in 1894. Holt emphasized rigid scheduling of feeding, bathing, sleeping, and bowel movements, and advised mothers to guard vigilantly against germs and undue stimulation of infants. At a time when a well-adjusted adult was viewed as a creature of habit and self-control, he stressed the importance of imposing regular habits on infants. He discouraged mothers from kissing their babies, and told them to ignore their crying and to break such habits as thumb-sucking. Upper-class and upper-middle-class mothers, like Dr. Benjamin Spock's mother, were much more likely to adopt Holt's advice than were working-class mothers. The behaviorist psychologist John B. Watson—who, in the 1920s, told mothers to "never hug and kiss" their children or "let them sit in your lap"—claimed Holt as his inspiration.[37]

The twentieth century brought profound changes to parent-child relations. For one thing, the reduction in the birth rate and in multigenerational households meant that there were fewer siblings, grandparents, and aunts and uncles to serve as buffers between the generations. As schooling became more extended and widespread, grades and homework became a mounting concern. In an increasingly urban environment, children's responsibility for household chores declined even as parents' responsibility for overseeing children's leisure activities grew. While parents and their children struggled over dating, dress, and commercial entertainment, as early as the 1910s, adolescent rebellion emerged as a widely recognized problem. One result was a hunger for expert advice. The Children's Bureau, established by the federal government in 1912, received as many as 125,000 letters a year with questions about how to raise a child.[38]

During the 1920s and 1930s, the field of child psychology exerted a growing influence on middle-class parenting. It provided a new language to describe children's emotional problems, such as "sibling rivalry," "phobia," "maladjustment," "inferiority complex," and "Oedipus complex." It also offered new insights into forms of parenting based on such variables as demandingness or permissiveness. Especially influential were the writings of Arnold Gesell and his colleagues Frances L. Ilg and Louise Bates Ames, who identified a series of stages and milestones in children's development and the characteristics of children at particular ages. It was Gesell who popularized the phrase the "terrible twos," but of greater consequence was his role in defining developmental timetables and norms, and thereby giving guidelines and expectations that describe "normal" childhood development. Gesell's notion of a universal developmental sequencing and uniform expectations for the timing of sitting, crawling, walking, grasping, and speaking has since been shown to be incorrect. But it contributed both to parental anxiety over whether their child was normal or abnormal or on-track or off-track and to professional support for such anxiety.[39]

The "discovery" of sibling rivalry was one example of the increasing psychologizing of childhood. Tattling, hair pulling, name calling, and shoving were just a few signs of sibling rivalry that drew increasing attention from childrearing experts. Although awareness of sibling rivalry is at least as old as the biblical stories of Cain and Abel, Esau and Isaac, Rachel and Leah, and Joseph and his brothers, the squabbling and animosity associated with this phenomenon became the subject of psychological analysis only in the 1920s, and the phrase itself was introduced only in 1930. The psychoanalyst Alfred Adler, who helped popularize the concept, argued that birth order had a profound effect on children's personality. He claimed that single children preferred adult company and had difficulty interacting with peers, that first-born children received the highest parental expectations, and that younger children acted out and misbehaved to gain attention or due to pampering. In *King Lear,* the classic drama of sibling rivalry, conflict is rooted in a struggle over material resources and status, but in the modern family, it represented a struggle over maternal affection. Sibling relations, however, had the positive effect of serving as a laboratory in which the young learned to deal with resentment, hostility, and envy.[40]

The growing prosperity of the 1920s made the earlier emphasis on regularity and rigid self-control associated with scientific childrearing seem outmoded. A well-adjusted adult was now regarded as a more easygoing figure, capable of enjoying leisure. By the 1920s, a consumer society increasingly sought to nurture children to become socially adept. Rejecting the mechanistic and behaviorist notion that children's behavior could be molded by scientific control, popular dispensers of advice favored a more relaxed approach to child rearing, emphasizing the importance of meeting babies' emotional needs. The title of a 1936 book by pediatrician C. Anderson Aldrich, *Babies Are Human Beings,* summed up the new attitude.[41]

Child Guidance clinics, founded in the late 1910s to treat juvenile delinquency, attracted an expanding clientele of middle-class parents who were concerned about eating and sleeping disorders, nail-biting, bedwetting, phobias, sibling rivalry, and temper tantrums, as well as about problems involving school failure, running away, disobedience, and rebellious behavior. Yet many parents failed to address children's informational needs regarding sexuality, especially girls' need for information about menstruation, and increasingly turned to schools to assume this responsibility. As early as 1922, in response to a growing concern over the prevalence of venereal disease, half of all schools offered some instruction in "social hygiene," an early form of sex education.[42]

The Great Depression imposed severe strains on the nation's parents. It not only threw breadwinners out of jobs and impoverished families; it also forced many families to share living quarters and put off having

5.3. Employed miner's family, Scott's Run, West Virginia, 1937. Photograph by Lewis Hine.

children. More than 200,000 vagrant children wandered the country. Many fathers were overwhelmed by guilt because they were unable to support their families, and unemployment significantly lowered their status within the family. The father's diminished stature was mirrored by a great increase in the money-saving and wage-earning roles of mothers.[43]

Upheavals caused by World War II ensued and also had a profound impact on parenting. The war produced a sudden upsurge in the marriage and birth rate; spurred an unprecedented tide of family separation and migration; and thrust millions of mothers into the workforce. The war also accelerated a trend toward more affectionate childrearing, as mothers took the position that it was normal and healthy to embrace their children, given that so many families had been ravaged by depression and war. At the same time, the war temporarily reduced opposition to child labor in terms of both paid and volunteer work—such as gathering scrap materials or tending victory gardens—since work might reduce juvenile delinquency, which appeared to be a mounting problem.[44]

World War II produced intense concerns about "faulty" mothering, especially maternal overprotectiveness and its mirror opposite, maternal neglect. Americans were shocked by the number of men, more than five million, who were rejected for military service on the basis of physical or psychological deficiencies. Philip Wylie, author of the 1942 bestseller *A Generation of Vipers*, blamed such problems on the combination of a dominant, overly protective mother and a passive or absent father. There was also a tendency to blame juvenile delinquency, latchkey children, illegitimacy, truancy, and runaways not on unsettled wartime conditions, but on neglectful mothers. An important wartime legacy, based on John Bowlby's studies of British children separated from their parents during the war, was a heightened stress on the significance of maternal attachment in developing feelings of security and competence in children.[45]

No families were more deeply affected by the war than Japanese Americans, who were deemed suspect and potentially disloyal. In the spring of 1942, about 120,000—two-thirds of them U.S. citizens—were relocated from homes on the West Coast to detention camps located in barren and forbidding parts of Arizona, Arkansas, California, Colorado, Idaho, Utah, and Wyoming. Toilets, showers, and dining facilities were communal, precluding family privacy. The internment camps inverted traditional family roles and loosened parental controls, as children were given greater freedom and responsibility than their parents and grandparents.[46]

Severe problems of family adjustment followed the war. Many returning GIs found it difficult to communicate with their children after a prolonged absence, while many wives and children found the men excessively strict, nervous, or intolerant. Estrangement and problems with alcohol were not infrequent as fathers tried to readjust after the war and Americans became familiar with the toll war takes on soldiers. The next decade witnessed a sharp reaction to the psychological stresses of wartime. Americans married at a younger age and had more children than in preceding generations. Responding to the postwar housing shortage, millions moved to new single-family homes in the suburbs. Many war-weary parents, scornful of the childrearing homilies of their parents and grandparents, embraced the advice of Dr. Benjamin Spock, who rejected the idea of rigid feeding, bathing, and sleeping schedules, and told parents to pick up their babies and enjoy them. "Your baby is born to be a reasonable, friendly human being," Spock informed mothers. "If you treat him nicely, he won't take advantage of you."[47]

Spock's advice became a synonym for permissiveness in childrearing, and his critics would later blame him for producing a generation of unkempt, irresponsible, hedonistic young people. In fact, Spock called on parents to balance responsiveness with firmness. More important, however, was Spock's success in popularizing Freudian notions without using psychoanalytic language. Without invoking such phrases as "infantile sexuality" or the "Oedipus complex," Spock helped convince many parents that they should not be alarmed by children's misbehavior but, rather, should worry about the effects of repression and a failure to sufficiently express love toward their child. Spock helped accelerate the shift toward greater expressions of love and affection in childrearing and toward efforts to reduce repression of instinctual behaviors and a child's sense of frustration. Nevertheless, class and ethnic differences in parenting practices remained widespread. The sociologists Allison Davis and Robert Havighurst found that middle-class parents began training children in achievement, initiative, personal responsibility, and cleanliness earlier than working-class parents, who placed a higher premium on obedience and relied more on corporal punishment, and that African-American parents had a more relaxed attitude toward infant feeding and weaning than their white counterparts.[48]

Postwar parenting was characterized by an undercurrent of anxiety, sparked partly by concern over children's physical and mental health. The early 1950s was the last period when large numbers of children were left crippled by polio or meningitis. At the same time, psychologists such as Theodore Lidz, Irving Bieber, and Erik Erikson linked schizophrenia, homosexuality, and identity diffusion to mothers who displaced their frustrations and needs for independence onto their children. A major concern was that many boys, raised almost exclusively by women, failed to develop an appropriate sex-role identity. In retrospect, it seems clear that an underlying source of anxiety lay in the fact that mothers, increasingly remote from their own mothers, grandmothers, and sisters, were raising their children with an exclusivity and in an isolation unparalleled in American history.[49]

During the 1960s, there was a growing sense that something had gone wrong in American parenting. Maverick social critics, including Edgar Z. Friedenberg and Paul Goodman, argued that middle-class parents were failing their children by conveying mixed messages, stressing independence and accomplishment but giving their offspring few avenues of achievement or autonomy. At the same time, books with titles like *Suburbia's Coddled Kids* (1962) criticized permissive childrearing and parents who let their children bully them. By the 1970s, the challenge to permissive parenting had escalated, as conservative ministers, including James Dobson and John Rosemond, called on parents to "dare to discipline."[50]

Since the early 1970s, parental anxieties greatly increased both in scope and intensity. Many parents sought to protect children from harm by baby-proofing their homes, using car seats, and requiring bicycle helmets. Meanwhile, as more mothers joined the labor force, parents arranged more structured, supervised activities for their children. Unstructured play and outdoor activities for children three to eleven declined nearly 40 percent between the early 1980s and late 1990s.[51]

A variety of factors contributed to this surge in anxiety. One factor was medical: The expanded use of prenatal testing, including ultrasound, amniocentesis, and genetic testing, held out the prospect of children free from inheritable and congenital diseases, defects, and deformities. Yet far from providing reassurance and increasing maternal control over the birth process, these diagnostic practices had the unintended effect of intensifying pregnant women's anxieties and making the fetus, rather than the mother, the focus of medical attention.

Today, the number of conditions diagnosable with prenatal testing has increased substantially; it had already reached 940 by 1999. Techniques such as maternal serum alpha-fetoprotein screen, chorionic villus sampling, and preimplantation genetic diagnosis have carried profound implications for thinking about disabilities and physical imperfections. Prenatal tests inspired efforts to screen not only "at-risk" mothers (usually defined as those over the age of thirty-five or those who have given birth to a child with a disability) but all pregnant women, and encouraged an attitude that disabilities, far from being a natural part of human difference, should be avoided at all costs and that imperfect pregnancies should be terminated. In fact, about one in fifty babies has an abnormality of varying medical or cosmetic significance.[52]

A heightened concern with children's psychological well-being further intensified parental anxiety. In 1969, the psychotherapist Nathaniel Branden published *The Psychology of Self-Esteem*, which argued that a healthy sense of self-worth was the key to a young person's future success. Later childrearing authorities reinforced Branden's concern with the importance of noncognitive factors—such as conscientiousness, curiosity, optimism, resilience, grit, and perseverance—in ensuring success in life. As ambitious middle-class parents attempted to provide their children with every possible opportunity by filling up their afterschool time with lessons, enrichment activities, and sports, excessive overloading of children led experts such as David Elkind to decry a tendency toward "hyperparenting." These experts feared that overscheduling and overprogramming placed excessive pressure on children and deprived them of the opportunity for free play and hanging out.[53]

Shocking news reports intensified parental fears, including the revelation in 1973 of the serial murders of twenty-seven juveniles by Elmer Wayne Henley and Dean Corll and the poisoning of eight-year-old Timothy O'Bryan by cyanide-laced Halloween candy in 1974. These incidents were followed by highly publicized claims that young people's well-being was rapidly declining. During the mid-1970s there was alarm about a supposed epidemic of teenage pregnancy. This was followed by a panic over stranger abductions of children, triggered by the mysterious disappearance of Etan Patz in New York City in 1979 and the abduction and murder of Adam Walsh in 1981 in Florida. Other panics followed, involving the sexual abuse of children in day care centers, violent youth gangs and juvenile "superpredators," youthful substance abuse, and declining student performance on standardized tests.[54]

These panics were grossly exaggerated. The teenage pregnancy rate had peaked in 1957 and was declining, not rising. A federal investigation disclosed that few missing children were abducted by strangers; the overwhelming majority were taken by noncustodial parents or were runaways. No cases of multiple caretaker sexual abuse in day care centers were substantiated. Although youth violence did rise in the late 1980s and early 1990s (in tandem with violence by adults), the rate fell sharply in the mid- and late 1990s, declining to levels unseen since the mid-1960s. Similarly, rates of drug, alcohol, and tobacco use by juveniles dropped until they were lower than those reported in the 1970s. Finally, the reported decline in student performance on standardized tests reflected an increase in the range of students taking the tests, not deteriorating student achievement. Nevertheless, these panics produced a nagging, if inaccurate, sense that recent shifts in family life, especially the increased divorce rate and the growing number of single-parent households and working mothers, had disastrous consequences for children's well-being. They also left an imprint on public policy, as many municipalities instituted curfews for juveniles; many schools introduced dress codes, random drug tests for student athletes, and "abstinence-only" sex education programs; and states raised the drinking age, adopted graduated driver's licenses, and made it easier to try juvenile offenders as adults in the court system. Other efforts to restore parental authority and discipline included the establishment of a rating system for CDs and video games; installation of v-chips in TVs to allow parents to restrict children's television viewing; and enactment in some states of laws requiring parental notification when minors sought abortions.[55]

In evaluating recent changes in parenting, there is a tendency to exaggerate evidence of decline and ignore the genuine gains that have occurred. There is no evidence to suggest that most parents are less engaged in child care than in the past or that adults have become "anti-child." While fewer parents participate in PTAs, many more take an active role in soccer leagues and Little League. Although parents are having fewer children, they are investing more time and resources in those they do have. Better-educated parents are much more aware of children's developmental needs and of the dangers of abuse, and most fathers are more engaged in childrearing than their fathers were. Meanwhile, neither rising divorce rates nor increasing numbers of working mothers have had the negative psychological consequences that some predicted. Research suggests that children suffer more when their parents stay together but have high levels of conflict than when they divorce. Moreover, working mothers are less likely to be depressed than stay-at-home mothers; they also provide valuable role models, especially for their daughters.[56]

Parental anxieties are historically contingent, taking very different forms at particular points in time. To be sure, there are certain continuities. During the twentieth century, the introduction of every new entertainment technology, from radio and the movies to television, videogames, and the Internet, has provoked concern that an insidious force threatens children's well-being. But over time there has been a marked shift in the nature of parental fears. In the early and mid-nineteenth century, parents were primarily concerned about their children's health, religious piety, and moral development. In the late nineteenth century, parents became increasingly attentive to children's emotional and psychological well-being. During World War II, concern swirled around father absence and over-solicitous mothers, while the early postwar era worries focused incessantly on polio, despite the fact that it killed fewer children than diseases like whooping cough. For parents whose childhood had been disrupted by the Great Depression and World War II, images of breadlines and mushroom clouds provoked intense anxiety about their ability to shelter their children from external threats. In addition, during the mid-twentieth century, parental anxieties centered on children's gender identity and their ability to interact with peers in conventional and acceptable ways. Today, much more than in the past, insecure parents worry that their children not suffer from boredom, low self-esteem, learning disabilities, and excessive school pressures, all of which may lead to depression.

In an environment in which parents are bombarded with contradictory advice, it is impossible to raise a child unselfconsciously or instinctively. Of course, a concern with proper childrearing is not new; childrearing manuals are virtually as old as the printing press. What has changed, however, is authorship — as tracts written by clergy and educators gave way to those written by physicians and psychologists, and more recently, by mothers and fathers themselves — as have parental concerns, which shifted from moral education and physical health to topics that aroused little concern in the past, such as early academic achievement, the quality of peer relationships, and children's happiness. Perhaps the most notable change was the growing attention to children's psychic health. Over the course of the twentieth century, a new psychologically informed vocabulary of parenting emerged. By the late 1920s, expert opinion had begun to embrace the notion that children's experiences during the first three years of life mold their personality, lay the foundation for future cognitive and psychosocial development, and leave a lasting imprint on children's emotional life. In addition, there is a widespread consensus that even very young children have the capacity to learn, that intellectual development depends on the kind of stimulation that children receive, and that play serves valuable developmental functions. Furthermore, there is a sense that growing up requires children to bond with peers and separate emotionally and psychologically from their parents.[57]

During the 1940s and 1950s, child psychologists identified a series of behaviors that helped define parent-child relations. These include warmth, responsiveness, demandingness, protectiveness, sensitivity, and control. The last can take various forms, from monitoring and reasoning to shaming and harsh physical discipline. In 1966, the developmental psychologist Diana Baumrind identified three distinct parenting styles, general orientations that reflected parents' fundamental values and personality. There was an authoritarian style (a strict approach that emphasized compliance with a parent's rules and directions), an authoritative style (a warm but firm, demanding, but responsive, approach), and permissive style (a lenient, non-directive, and indulgent approach). Subsequent observers added a fourth parenting style, negligent or uninvolved. It turns out that these categories do not effectively describe the parenting practices within many immigrant or ethnic minority families, which have higher levels of parental protectiveness and distinctive forms of control that combine supportiveness with a greater reliance on shaming. Yet they do serve as a guide to the ways parents viewed their possibilities for parenting.[58]

Since the 1970s, a host of parenting styles has been held out as ideal. Among the most influential is "attachment parenting," a phrase coined by the pediatrician William Sears in 1992. Sears argued that a child's psychological well-being depended on developing a secure emotional and physical connection to his or her parents. This, in theory, could be best reinforced through breastfeeding upon demand, co-sleeping, and baby-carrying, all of which involve maintaining close bodily contact with an infant or young child. According to this model, parents were to be highly attentive, emotionally available, and responsive to children's emotional needs. They were to avoid unrealistic expectations, in order to prevent their child from becoming frustrated, and were to use nonpunitive forms of discipline: redirection, setting boundaries, and time-outs. Such a style demanded a great deal of patience on a mother's part.[59]

Then there was helicopter parenting, a pejorative phrase coined around 1990 to refer to overprotective, hyper-attentive, overinvolved parents who hover over their children, step in to solve their problems, and assist with their homework and social life. A less pejorative description of this approach is "concerted cultivation," since the self-conscious goal is to stimulate children's development. To this end, parents provide their children with a rich language environment, and seek to reason with their children and ask frequent questions. But parents are also expected to do more: entertain their children and ensure that they are happy; provide a wide range of adult-supervised and structured enrichment activities such as music lessons, organized sports, and play dates; and run interference for their children in schools and other settings, thus providing a model for asserting oneself in bureaucratic settings. More recently the phrase "tiger parenting" emerged, which criticized "Western-style" childrearing as overly concerned with children's self-esteem, desires, and preferences, and insufficiently attentive to their need for achievement. The polar opposite of this approach is "free-range" or "slow" parenting, which encourages children to develop at their own pace, and discourages attempts to over-structure

5.4. Homecoming, 2006. Photograph by Cassandra Locke.

their activities. Each childrearing style underscores contemporary society's intense concern with parent-child relations and the extreme pressure this puts on parents, especially mothers.[60]

When viewed from a cross-cultural, cross-temporal perspective, it is striking how narrowly childrearing is defined in the United States compared to many non-Western societies. In this country, the focus is almost exclusively on the nature of the parent-child bond, especially the parent's responsiveness to a child's distress, approaches to discipline, and strictness of scheduling. More difficult to measure, but equally important are the values that the parents teach and the behavior they model. In many other societies, childrearing, rather than being monopolized by parents and usually the mother, is diffused among a variety of nurturing figures (termed "allomothers" or "alloparents" by anthropologists), which may include older siblings as well as a variety of kin and non-kin. Parenting practices, of course, account for only some of the influences on children's socialization and development. Other influences include the child's temperament, interactions with siblings, relatives, and peers, and various cultural influences. Yet in the United States, it is parent-child relationships that are in the spotlight.[61]

The terms widely used today may be new, but the concerns with parents who are oversolicitous or overinvolved or who are psychologically absent date back to the late 1920s and early 1930s, when childrearing became increasingly influenced by psychoanalytically informed theories of child development and debate began to rage over the impact of "improper" mothering. Motherhood, viewed as a public calling and civic duty in the nineteenth and early twentieth century, was transformed, by the middle decades of the twentieth century, into a solely private, domestic role, and one that, if improperly conducted, could produce psychopathologies in children, especially sons. In few areas did the spread of psychological thinking have a greater, or more negative, impact than upon childrearing. Mother-blame — the tendency to attribute a child's maladjustments to improper mothering — absorbed far more popular attention than did authoritarian or abusive fathering.[62]

At a time when many mothers are accused of intrusion in their children's lives and of keeping them emotionally dependent into their twenties and thirties, it is important to remember that the pejorative image of the overprotective, overbearing mother is not new. It found its classic image in the portrayal of the Jewish mother. The "Yiddishe Mother" popularized by George Jessel, Al Jolson, Sophie Tucker, Gertrude Berg, and, more recently, by *The Big Bang Theory*, is, according to the popular stereotype, self-sacrificing, doting, overbearing, guilt-manipulating, overprotective, and relentlessly ambitious for her children.[63]

Jokes, sometimes endearing, sometimes vicious, provided a way to deal with a radical change in authority patterns within the family during the twentieth century, as the mother not only became the family's chief domestic authority, but the supposed key to children's future success. The issue was especially pronounced in immigrant families, where many rigid, traditionalist fathers found it difficult to adapt to a new environment. An expanded maternal role produced a great deal of ambivalence, and double-edged humor provided a vehicle for addressing the tension between assimilation and the maintenance of custom and between family solidarity and personal freedom. As guilt became an increasingly important mechanism for maintaining filial obligation, Jewish mother jokes played on the way that such figures supposedly manipulated their children's conscience. As one popular joke put it: "How many Jewish mothers does it take to change a light bulb? None—I'll just sit here in the dark." A Columbia University research project, conducted between 1947 and 1951, initially led by the anthropologists Ruth Benedict and Margaret Mead, helped reinforce an image of Jewish families presided over by a matriarch who was assertive, intrusive, and overly solicitous, a worrier, guilt monger, and family caretaker, and whose insatiable demands might emasculate her husband and produce neurosis in her sons. This portrait received its classic literary depiction in Philip Roth's *Portnoy's Complaint* (1969). The Jewish mother provided an often humorous slant on a far more pejorative image: the bad mother.[64]

If motherhood in the United States has often been idealized as a source of unconditional love and identified with self-sacrifice, "bad" mothers—who are supposedly smothering, overindulgent, rejecting, or emasculating—have been repeatedly stigmatized. Older examples include the pushy stage mother, which has been succeeded in recent years by attacks on mothers with ambitious careers, welfare mothers, crack-addicted mothers, and teenage mothers. At various points in time, hostile, neglectful, emotionally over-involved mothers have been blamed for mental retardation, schizophrenia, homosexuality, and autism.[65]

Contradictory images of motherhood have received especially vivid portrayal in the movies. Over the past century, cinematic depictions of motherhood have undergone a series of radical transformations in response to broad demographic, social, and cultural changes in American society. During the 1910s and 1920s, mothers on the screen largely conformed to the conventions of Victorian melodrama. Films as different as *The Eternal Mother* (1912) and *The Jazz Singer* (1927) presented highly sentimental portraits of mothers as paragons of wisdom and warmth. Serving as their family's emotional core, these mothers indulged their children and represented a rock of stability amid a sea of change. Then there was the selfless mother, the epitome of female self-sacrifice, who foregoes her own well-being for her children's sake. Tear-jerkers, like *Madame X* (1916), *Stella Dallas* (1925), and *Blonde Venus* (1932), depicted mothers who broke their ties to their offspring to ensure their children's happiness.[66]

The Great Depression reinforced highly idealized and sentimentalized images of motherhood. In such box-office hits as *The Good Earth* (1937) and *The Grapes of Wrath* (1940), strong-willed mothers sustained their families in the face of hardship. World War II, however, brought about a marked shift. Although some depictions of motherhood conformed to old stereotypes, such as *Mrs. Miniver* (1942) and *Since You Went Away* (1944), others, like *Now, Voyager* (1942), in which a cold, repressive, domineering mother drives her daughter to a nervous breakdown, offered a new view of the mother as the source of a child's psychological problems. Meanwhile, the value of maternal sacrifice was, for the first time, called into question in films like *Mildred Pierce*, the 1945 film noir that depicts a loving mother's tormented relationship with her spoiled, ungrateful daughter. Although there were a number of positive depictions of motherhood in films like *Cheaper by the Dozen* (1950), succeeding years witnessed a proliferation of harshly negative images, including the overbearing, manipulative mother in *The Manchurian Candidate* (1962), the emotionally abusive mother in *Psycho* (1960), and the delusional mother in *Carrie* (1976), all of whom were the sources of their children's psychological ills.[67]

The view of mothers as the root cause of various social and psychological ills was not confined to the movies. Leading psychologists, psychiatrists, and sociologists, influenced partly by Freudian psychoanalysis, deemed maternal self-sacrifice to be a disguised form of narcissism and possessiveness, and claimed that intense mother-son intimacy, or its mirror image, rejecting, emotionally absent mothers, contributed to male effeminacy, alcoholism, schizophrenia, and a host of other problems. Trapped in loveless or unfulfilling marriages and denied other outlets for their ambitions, mothers supposedly displaced their emotional energies upon their offspring to their children's detriment. As one journalist put it as early as 1935, "Iron-willed, frustrated, self-sacrificing mothers, trying to live a dream life through their progeny, have wrecked more lives than has syphilis."[68]

The Second World War was accompanied by an almost obsessive concern with improper mothering as men went off to war and left women to manage the family on their own. Maternal neglect was blamed for problems ranging from truancy from school, sleeping and eating disorders, and running away from home. Thumb-sucking, bedwetting, whining, and other infantile patterns of behavior were all seen as evidence of deprivation of maternal care rather than the absence of fathers. But social commentators were as deeply disturbed about the mirror image of neglect—that is, oversolicitousness, or "momism," as it was known. Edward A. Strecker, the psychiatric consultant to the U.S. surgeon general, made front-page headlines by blaming America's devoted, self-sacrificing moms as responsible for the 350,000 men who evaded military service, often by dressing up in female clothing. The bestseller of 1942 was Philip Wylie's scathing, misogynistic *A Generation of Vipers,* which maintained that America's mothers produced psychiatric disorders in their children by being overly protective. In his view, they infantilized their sons, making it impossible for them to achieve a well-adjusted maturity. Among the most disturbing examples of this indulgence in mother-blaming was the charge that cold, uncaring "refrigerator" mothers were responsible for autism.[69]

Alongside the mounting concern with faulty mothering came a heightened concern over the damaging psychological consequences of the physical punishment of children. Certain passages from Proverbs provided generations of parents with justification for physically disciplining their children: "He that spareth the rod hateth his son" and "Withhold not correction from a child: for if thou strike him with the rod, he shall not die. Thou shalt beat him with the rod, and deliver his soul from hell."

Today, the overwhelming majority of parents still punish young children physically. Their approaches to punishment range from taps on the buttocks to spankings, whippings, and brutal beatings.[70]

Child discipline has long been synonymous with whippings or spankings. Indeed, a survey of autobiographies, biographies, and letters from the first half of the nineteenth century found that every single individual had been whipped or hit with a physical instrument as a child; in the second half of the century, the figure was 73 percent. Even today, nearly all parents of three and four year olds spank their child. A 2010 survey reported that 75 percent of men and 64 percent of women who were between eighteen and sixty-five years old agreed that a child sometimes needs a "good hard spanking."[71]

Physical punishment of children was justified, first and foremost, by religion. The more orthodox forms of Protestantism tended to place a heavy emphasis on the importance of authority, filial obedience, and the redemptive nature of punishment. The rod would "save the child" from defiance, disobedience, intransigence, and obstinacy. A negative attitude toward the body and toward individual autonomy combined with a belief in children's natural depravity contributed to a view that it was legitimate to exercise authority through corporal punishment. Secular defenses of physical punishment echoed those derived from religion, including the need to sustain order, uphold authority, and suppress children's willfulness.[72]

The meaning of physical punishment was different when it was not solely confined to children. Corporal punishment was a common practice from the seventeenth through the mid-nineteenth centuries. Physical discipline was considered a legitimate way to punish misbehavior. Laws permitted masters to physically chastise servants, apprentices, and slaves. Flogging was imposed for such crimes as Sabbath breaking, petty larceny, and rape. Teachers frequently used rods, whips, and their hands to punish unruly or disobedient pupils. Beginning in the eighteenth century, however, advice books began to advocate limiting the use of corporal punishment and substituting spanking (a word introduced in the 1780s) and psychological suasion for whipping. Around the middle of the nineteenth century, corporal punishment, which had previously been applied to a variety of adults as well as children, was increasingly restricted to children, and usually younger children.[73]

Reformers, including Walter Colton, Richard Henry Dana, John W. Edmonds, Eliza W. Farnham, John P. Hale, Horace Mann, and Elizabeth Cady Stanton, attacked corporal punishment on several grounds. It was archaic and outmoded, cruel and tyrannical, a relic of barbarism, and contrary to the spirit of a democratic society, which rejected older notions of hierarchy and arbitrary authority. Its capriciousness hindered efforts to promote more productive, efficient workplaces and undercut the effort to promote the dignity of labor. Physical punishment and shaming ran counter to educational reformers' goal of instilling morality and self-discipline within students' character. It was also regarded as contrary to the growing emphasis on familial warmth and intimacy and the conception of the home as an emotional haven in a heartless world.

In many northern states, the reform campaigns succeeded in curbing the use of corporal punishment in schools and prisons, while Congress abolished flogging in the Navy. In the South, where physical violence was viewed as essential to sustain a social order resting on slavery, flogging and whipping persisted, and today the only states that permit corporal punishment in schools are located in the South.[74]

The crusade against corporal punishment, however, proved less successful within the home. During the twentieth century there were repeated attempts to separate abusive forms of discipline from those that are acceptable, and to substitute more "therapeutic" approaches to discipline for spankings and paddlings. In 1957 and 1958, Charles Ferster and Arthur Staats introduced the concept of "time-out," in which the punishment consisted of separating a misbehaving child from parents, siblings, or playmates for a period of time. There were growing calls for nonphysical interventions involving "positive" discipline like praise, encouragement, and hugs, as well as "negative" feedback like reprimands, snubbing the child, and stern looks. Positive discipline techniques called on parents to reason with their children, citing facts rather than making demands, using distraction to steer kids away from danger, and working out solutions as a family.[75]

Despite the many suggestions from professionals, today child discipline remains a private matter that parents decide for themselves. Efforts to end the physical punishment of children failed because of a commitment to the notion that the family is an inviolate refuge and sanctuary that should be free from outside interference. Most Americans believe that preserving the family should be society's highest priority. Repeatedly, an emphasis on parental rights and on family privacy, stability, and preservation has stymied efforts at reform. Unlike Sweden, which, in 1979, became the first country to criminalize corporal punishment of children, the United States places few limits on the authority of parents to discipline their children as they see fit.[76]

The movement to restrict corporal punishment of children was part of a broadening concern with child welfare and a growing awareness of the abuse of children. Today, few issues arouse greater moral condemnation than the sexual or physical abuse and neglect of children, yet these were recognized as serious problems only a little more than a century ago, and since then, public concern with them has waxed and waned. In fact, there has never been an era when abuse did not take place, and perhaps most has taken place at the hands of parents, usually the father or a parental surrogate. Yet a persistent belief in parental rights and the sanctity and inviolability of the family and the home, regardless of the cost to individual family members, deterred effective public action.[77]

A single case of child abuse played a pivotal role in bringing the issue to public notice. In 1874, Etta Angell Wheeler, an urban missionary, heard about the plight of a child named Mary Ellen, who was left locked in an apartment by herself and was cruelly beaten by her caretakers. Mary Ellen had no shoes or stockings. She slept on an old bit of carpet and was not allowed to go outside to play with other children. She was whipped almost every day and was cut with scissors. Unsuccessful in persuading the police to remove the child from her foster parents, Wheeler turned to Henry Bergh, the president of New York's Society for the Prevention of Cruelty to Animals. According to legend, he responded by saying: "The child is an animal. If there is no justice for it as a human being, it shall at least have the right of the cur in the street. . . . It shall not be abused." In fact, for several years, Bergh had been asked to intervene in cases of cruelty to children, but had refused. In the case of nine-year-old Mary Ellen, he asked his society's counsel, Elbridge Gerry, to investigate, and it was Gerry who brought the child before a magistrate. Mary Ellen's caretaker was found guilty of assault and battery and sentenced to a year of hard labor in a penitentiary. The girl was placed in an institution for dependent children.[78]

Earlier in 1874, the *New York Times* reported that a thirteen-year-old boy had been beaten to death by his father for "refusing to go after beer without the money to pay for it." But for the most part, horrendous acts of child abuse were largely ignored by the press and public. Several factors, however, made the case of Mary Ellen difficult to overlook. Etta Angell Wheeler's husband worked for a newspaper, and elicited help from journalists in publicizing this case. Because Mary Ellen was beaten by someone other than her natural parents, the case did not challenge a mother and a father's prerogative to discipline their child as they saw fit. In addition, Mary Ellen was an attractive girl, and such girls have long attracted public sympathy. Equally important, the case revealed the failure of public authorities to supervise the placement of children into foster families. Public outrage also reflected a sea-change in public attitudes toward government in the wake of the Civil War, which was now held to have a responsibility to protect the defenseless.[79]

The problem of child abuse has been discovered and rediscovered several times in American history. In colonial America, corporal punishment of children, apprentices, servants, and slaves was considered essential to the proper management of a household. There is some reason to believe that at least in New England, close supervision of households by neighbors and town officials (such as tithingmen, who oversaw ten or twelve households to ensure domestic harmony) provided some restraints on abuse. Indeed, Massachusetts Bay and Plymouth colonies were the first jurisdictions in the world to declare "unnatural severity" against children or women a crime. But as the family came to be regarded as a private institution, public discussion of child abuse faded. Abuse did continue to occur, however, and with shocking regularity. As early as 1852, an article on "The Rights of Children," published in a New England periodical, spoke of the need to "protect" children from parental "tyranny." That the young were sexually abused was well known to nineteenth-century Americans. In New York City, between 1790 and 1876, between a third and a half of rape victims were under the age of nineteen; during the 1820s, the figure was 76 percent. There were more than 500 published newspaper reports of father-daughter incest between 1817 and 1899. An 1894 textbook, *A System of Legal Medicine,* reported that the "rape of children is the most frequent form of sexual crime."[80]

But it was not until the 1870s that the first societies to prevent cruelty toward children were formed. By 1912, there were more than 346 anti-cruelty societies, though many were inactive or defunct, and those that continued to function focused more on neglect than abuse. Then, for half a century, public concern over child abuse again disappeared. Gravitating from child abuse to child neglect, public and professional attention shifted the focus from fathers to mothers. There was an inaccurate claim that "the grosser forms of physical cruelty are not so prevalent as they were a few decades ago." Several factors contributed to this prolonged period of omission: the public's inclination to blame abuse on strangers, the dirty old men of legend; the court's propensity to emphasize the rehabilitation of abusers in the name of family preservation; the willingness of police and physicians to accept claims that fractures, bruises, and burns were the result of accidents; and psychiatrists' tendency to treat children's complaints as fantasies and to stress children's resilience in the face of abuse.[81]

Public concern over child abuse does not appear to reflect actual increases in the incidence of mistreatment, but rather broader social anxieties as well as the influence of groups willing to bring a pressing problem to public light. Following the Civil War, the rapid growth of cities, a massive influx of immigrants, and a sharp rise in the divorce rate provoked fears for the future of the family and alarm over the supposed impact of the breakdown of the family upon children. During the Progressive era of the early twentieth century, anxieties over mass immigration, divorce, child labor, and juvenile delinquency helped stimulate public concern over the abuse and neglect of children. During World War II, concerns about working mothers, latchkey children, and absent fathers sparked public anxiety. Then, in the 1970s, a sharp increase in divorce, single parenthood, and working mothers contributed to a heightened sensitivity to childhood abuse.

A 1962 article by C. Henry Kempe and his colleagues published in the *Journal of the American Medical Association* made it clear that child abuse was not an insignificant problem and that much abuse took place in families. Entitled "The Battered-Child Syndrome," the article concluded, on the basis of X-rays of children's broken bones, that in many instances the breaks were not the result of accidents, but of a pattern of intentional injury. As a result of the Kempe article, by 1967 medical personnel were required to report cases of battered children. To deal with an overwhelming number of abuse reports, states established child protective services, but these agencies lacked the resources to provide effective preventative, therapeutic, or rehabilitative services or to ensure that children placed into foster care were well cared for. Currently, roughly 400,000 abused or neglected children reside with foster families or in institutions or group homes, down from over a million in 1994, at the height of the crack epidemic.[82]

In recent years, debate has raged about whether definitions of abuse and neglect reflect class or ethnic bias. About half of all reports of maltreatment involve racial minorities, and low-income children are by far the most likely to be removed from their family, partly because such families are subject to more scrutiny by social service providers and are less able to conceal abuse or neglect and partly because the stressful conditions of life under extreme poverty tend to make neglect or abuse more likely. Families that are strapped for resources and that lack ready access to childcare while mothers work are especially vulnerable to charges of neglect. About half of all confirmed cases of child maltreatment, and nearly 40 percent of all child fatalities, involve neglect, which usually consists of failure to provide health care; inadequate attention to hazards in the home; providing the child with inadequate nutrition, clothing, or hygiene; lack of supervision; or reckless disregard for a child's safety (such as drunk driving with a child in the car or hazardous living conditions). Neglect, in particular, often reflects the parent's inability to secure a babysitter or other form of child care. In nearly three-quarters of the cases where children were left unattended, this occurred while the parent was working, attending school, or running errands. The ecology of chronic poverty can at times foster abuse or neglect in another way: Poverty's stresses contribute to alcoholism, drug abuse, and depression and other psychological disorders. Still, it is important to note that while attitudes regarding acceptable physical punishment, bathing practices, sleeping arrangements, and physical contact do vary across ethnic and racial group, there does seem to be agreement among all groups that it is wrong to intentionally inflict harm or injury to a child.[83]

The form of maltreatment that has elicited the most intense public concern is child sexual abuse. In 1976, there was less than one report of sexual abuse for every 10,000 children. By 1985, the figure had jumped to eighteen reports for every 10,000 children. In three-quarters of the cases, the reported abuser was a close relative, most often the father or stepfather. Currently, an estimated 20,000 children annually testify in sex abuse trials and as many as 100,000 children each year are involved in sex abuse investigations. To combat abuse, many schools now instruct children in how to distinguish "good touching" from "bad touching." There is, however, no clear consensus about what constitutes sexual abuse. It can include exposure of intimate body parts, voyeurism, fondling, and penetration. Girls appear to suffer sexual abuse more frequently than boys, making up about 71 percent of victims, though boys may well be less likely to report maltreatment. While children of any age can suffer sexual abuse, vulnerability appears to increase at around age ten. Factors that tend to be associated with sexual abuse include the presence of a stepfather and extreme marital conflict.[84]

Public concern over sexual abuse of children has mirrored the pattern of other forms of maltreatment and neglect, with awareness ebbing and flowing over time. At first, concern over child sexual abuse focused on the very young, those ten or younger. But beginning in the late nineteenth century, philanthropists and reformers brought attention to a somewhat older group of those aged eleven to seventeen. Reformers fought to raise the age of sexual consent from as young as seven to sixteen and to enact laws to prevent those younger than sixteen from entering any place that sold intoxicants, as well as pool halls and dance halls. In courthouses, the treatment of sexual abuse was colored by a young person's age, gender, and willingness to conform to cultural stereotypes. For a long time, jurors treated young girls very differently from boys and older girls. Sexual activity with very young girls was clearly regarded as pathological by the late nineteenth century, but proving cases of abuse proved very difficult. Jurors expected a young girl to reveal her innocence by using vague, simple, euphemistic language, while expecting older girls to put up resistance or demonstrate immaturity and a lack of sexual understanding. Interestingly, men charged with sodomizing pubescent boys were convicted in the same proportions as those whose victims were young boys, but this was not the case with girls.[85]

Initially, in cases involving sexual abuse, the focus was on physical harm to the young person or ruin to their reputation; nothing was said about the psychological scars caused by sexual abuse until the 1930s. In fact, 30 percent of statutory rape cases from 1896 to 1926 sought to resolve the case by marriage or financial payment. For much of the twentieth century, sexual abuse of children, like other forms of abuse, was treated as an anomaly and aberration, perpetrated by moral monsters, who were increasingly understood in psychological terms: as sex fiends, perverts, pedophiles, or sexual psychopaths. Evidence such as venereal infections in children, which indicated that sexual abuse of children was not confined to a small number of sex predators, was dismissed, and the infections were blamed on such nonsexual causes as unhygienic toilet seats. It is striking that in his landmark study of female sexual behavior, published in 1953, Alfred Kinsey reported that fully a quarter of all girls under the age of fourteen reported that they had experienced some form of sexual abuse, including exhibitionism, fondling, or incest (at rates roughly similar to those reported today). Yet when these findings were reported, they evoked virtually no public interest, although Kinsey's statistics about premarital sexual activity and adultery provoked a huge public outcry.[86]

The twentieth century witnessed a number of attempts to understand the sexual abuse of minors. The emergence of theories of young peoples' psychosexual development and especially the embrace of the Freudian notion of the sexual child carried ambiguous consequences for the understanding of sexual abuse. During the 1940s, when the influence of psychoanalytic understandings of sexual abuse reached its zenith, there was a tendency to dismiss such claims as fantasies or as the product of a girls' seductive behavior, ideas reinforced by such popular works as Vladimir Nabokov's *Lolita* (1955) and William March's *The Bad Seed* (1956). There was also a tendency to deny that sexual abuse had lasting consequences. But among a few experts, there was a recognition that abuse, even abuse short of genital penetration, caused long-term psychological damage. It is important to stress the contestation that surrounded the impact of abuse, with race and class coloring expert opinion on the sexual abuse of minors. By mid-century, expert opinion tended to regard working-class, and especially black, children as more prematurely sexualized and more endowed with sexual instincts and desire than their middle-class white counterparts. Meanwhile, sexual offenders were frequently regarded as mentally ill and treatable through psychotherapy. Their problem, purportedly, was that they lacked emotional and sexual maturity.[87]

In a society that has grown less judgmental and moralistic, condemnation of child abuse remains one of the few moral issues that command a consensus. Yet while child abuse is reviled, a substantial majority of American adults remain deeply ambivalent about challenging traditional notions of family privacy and parental authority and autonomy. And there remains considerable disagreement about what constitutes abuse, especially psychological abuse. Today, laws require physicians as well as others who work with children — including teachers, social workers, day care workers, and mental health workers — to report all cases of suspected neglect and sexual abuse as well as physical battery. Forty-one states specifically require mandated individuals to report emotional and psychological abuse as well. Eighteen states authorize reporting of abuse by "any person."[88]

Kempe and his colleagues regarded child maltreatment as a mental health problem, rooted in parental pathology. One of their findings was that most abusers had themselves been victims of childhood maltreatment, in a cycle that passed from one generation to the next. One of Kempe's associates, Ray E. Helfer, concluded that abusers had unrealistic expectations that led to frustration and abuse, and that those expectations were rooted in their own early feelings of worthlessness. The public often associates abuse with stepparents or mothers' boyfriends, but the research on these points is inconclusive. While some researchers continue to emphasize certain personality attributes that contribute to neglect—for example, parents who are non-nurturing, hostile, impulsive, or depressed—the characteristics most closely associated with abuse are not psychological, but environmental and ecological, conditions that tend to be exacerbated by poverty. These include an unplanned or a difficult pregnancy, a hyperactive, fussy baby with abnormal sleep patterns, or children with physical abnormalities. Profoundly mentally retarded children are less likely to be abused, apparently because caretakers have lower expectations of the child's behavior and therefore are less likely to be frustrated by misbehavior. While child maltreatment cuts across lines of class, race, and ethnicity, there is no doubt that most parents who abuse and neglect their children tend to share certain common elements in their background, including poverty, unemployment, alcohol or drug abuse, limited education, depression and emotional strain, severe mental or physical illness, and social isolation and a lack of support from neighbors or relatives. Reducing the stresses of poverty upon parents is certainly one of the surest ways to reduce the incidence of child abuse and neglect.[89]

Contemporary society is acutely attuned to the physical and sexual abuse of children, but it is less sensitive to other forms of abuse. These include the violence of expectations in which children are pushed beyond their social, physical, and academic capabilities, largely as an expression of their parents' needs. Then there is the violence of labeling, which diagnoses normal childish behavior as pathological; current examples include confusing any form of impulsivity with an attention deficit disorder or introversion and self-consciousness with autism. There is also the violence of representation, as prepubescent girls, in particular, are sexualized by marketers and advertisers. These forms of abuse may pose lesser threats to children's physical health, but are detrimental nonetheless and deserve far greater attention than they now receive.[90]

⁓⳽⳽⁓

Now that two-thirds of mothers work outside the home, one of the greatest trials of parenting involves providing care for preschoolers and school-aged children after school has let out. Given the cost of professional day care, which is higher than the cost of college tuition in thirty-one states, one might ask why child care has not become a pressing political issue. To a large degree, the answer lies in history—in the fact that child care has been viewed exclusively as a maternal responsibility, and custodial day care has long been underfunded, overcrowded, poorly organized, and associated with poverty.[91]

The first day nursery was established in Philadelphia in 1798 as charity for impoverished working mothers and a way to provide care and supervision for neglected or vagrant children. Established at a time when scarcely any urban middle-class mothers worked outside the home, the nurseries' founders were deeply concerned that the nurseries might undermine mother's sense of maternal responsibility. In fact, most of the women who made use of the nurseries were single mothers; those working women with husbands were far less likely to put their children in the nurseries. The association of nurseries with single mothers attached a stigma to child care that persisted through the 1960s.[92]

During the late nineteenth century, many ethnic groups, including African Americans, Catholics, and Jews, established day nurseries in their own communities. In 1898, a group of prominent New York philanthropists led by Josephine Jewell Dodge founded the National Federation of Day Nurseries (NFDN), the first nationwide organization devoted to this issue. By 1910, philanthropic organizations, settlement houses, and private individuals had established more than 450 charitable day nurseries in urban working-class neighborhoods. The nurseries not only provided custodial care for children whose mothers worked, but also sought to "Americanize" immigrant children through instruction in proper manners, eating habits, and personal hygiene. Many reformers viewed day nurseries as a "more humane and less costly substitute" for orphan asylums, where many working parents, lacking other forms of child care, temporarily placed children. In New York City alone, parents placed 15,000 children in orphanages in 1899. In fact, many of the day nurseries were little more than baby farms. At one Chicago nursery, Jane Addams reported, a child fell out of a third floor window; another suffered serious burns; a third had been tied to the leg of a kitchen table.[93]

The first concerted government efforts to assist working mothers sought not to expand child care but to encourage these women to leave the workforce. By 1909, when the first White House conference on dependent children was held, there was growing consensus that dependent children should be kept in their own families. Outraged by the warehousing of the young in huge institutions, states enacted "mother's pensions" to allow widows and other "deserving" single mothers to care for children in their own homes. After the first such pension was adopted in Illinois in 1911, the idea quickly spread, with twenty states enacting mothers' pensions by 1913 and thirty-nine states and the territories of Alaska and Hawaii doing so by 1919. These measures would serve as the prototype for the system of Aid to Dependent Children that was adopted by the federal government as part of the Social Security Act of 1935. That act provided just six dollars a month for the first child and four dollars a month for every subsequent child.[94]

It is important not to exaggerate the impact of these pensions. The amount of aid provided was so small that most eligible mothers had to work to support their families. Because of "local option" provisions in the laws, many counties, probably around 60 percent, offered no pensions at all. Further, eligibility was severely restrictive. In a number of states, African Americans were excluded from receiving such pensions. Most states established "suitable home" provisions for receiving aid, barring divorced mothers, unmarried mothers, and even women separated from their husbands from receiving pensions. Drinking, smoking, or failure to attend church could be grounds for denial of aid as well. Clearly, need was not the essential criterion for the pension.[95]

The 1920s witnessed the growing popularity of nursery schools, educational institutions for young children of the urban upper middle class. By the end of the decade there were some 300, compared to 800 day nurseries for the working class. During the Great Depression, the New Deal Emergency Nursery School Program set a precedent for federally funded child care. Primarily intended to offer employment opportunities to unemployed teachers, these schools were also seen as a means of compensating for the "physical and mental handicaps" caused by the economic downturn. Nearly 3,000 schools, enrolling more than 64,000 children, were started between 1933 and 1934; over the next year, these were consolidated into 1,900 schools with a capacity for approximately 75,000 students. The program covered forty-three states and the District of Columbia, Puerto Rico, and the Virgin Islands. Unlike the earlier nursery schools, which were largely private, charged fees, and served a middle-class clientele, these free, government-sponsored schools were open to children of all classes.[96]

World War II underscored the inadequacy of child care provisions. Working mothers were able to make only haphazard arrangements for child care. Although most left their children in the care of grandparents or neighbors, some children inevitably had to fend for themselves. Newspaper reports called them "8-hour orphans" or "latchkey" children and experts predicted harmful social consequences from such abandonment. But public child care facilities were woefully inadequate. At the beginning of the war, the Federal War Manpower Commission took the position that mothers with young children should not seek work until childless women had been employed. In 1942, under the Lanham Act, the federal government allowed public works funds to be used for child care in war-disrupted areas and made all mothers eligible regardless of income. By the end of 1943, the federal government had financed approximately 2,000 centers, serving 58,682 children. At its peak, in mid-1944, after the federal program began to accept children under the age of two, it served about 110,000 children. Federally financed extended-school programs provided afterschool care for between 100,000 and 300,000 children. But high fees and inconvenient locations inhibited the wider use of these facilities.[97]

Despite the pressing need for child care, wartime nurseries remained underutilized because many mothers opposed institutionalized care. Numerous wartime child care centers were overcrowded, ill-equipped, and poorly located. One wartime nursery near Baltimore was initially housed in a pair of trailers. After the trailers were found to violate public health standards, the children were moved into a room in an administration building, where they shared a single bathroom with the building's employees. Many centers were located in churches and private residences, often lacking outdoor space for sports and play. The high fees war nurseries charged further limited the use of public childcare. Daily fees typically ranged from fifty to seventy-five cents, or nearly a quarter of a day's wages, discouraging many poorer parents from making use of the centers. Most families stayed with informal solutions to problems of child care. One grandmother called World War II the "grandmother's war," because "the father goes off to war . . . ; mother goes to the factory to go to work, which is a very patriotic, important thing to do; the kids stay with grandmother."[98]

In 1964, a Department of Labor study counted almost a million "latchkey" children who were unsupervised for large portions of the day. In succeeding years, the number skyrocketed. In the space of twelve years in the late 1960s and early 1970s, the number of working mothers with children five or under who worked outside the home tripled. Today, two-thirds of all children under the age of six have a mother who works, more than three out of every five children under the age of four are in a regularly scheduled child care program, and nearly half of all one-year-olds spend part of their day in non-parental care. As the number of working mothers grew, many family experts advocated organized day care or preschool programs as a necessary response.[99]

Liberals, led by Democratic Senator Walter Mondale, called for a national system of comprehensive child development and day care centers. Building on the model of Head Start, the federally funded early education and child development program launched in 1965, Mondale proposed in 1971 that the federal government establish a care system that would include day care, nutritional aid for pregnant mothers, and after-school programs for teens. President Richard Nixon vetoed the bill in a stinging message that called the proposal fiscally irresponsible, administratively unworkable, and a threat to "diminish both parental authority and parental involvement with children." Tapping into the widespread view that child-care was a parental responsibility, the president warned against committing "the vast authority of the national government to the side of communal approaches to child rearing over against the family-centered approach."[100]

Following the presidential veto, congressional support for a comprehensive system of federally funded centers evaporated. Nevertheless, a fragmentary patchwork emerged, consisting of ad hoc, makeshift arrangements by individual parents; informal, family-style care in private homes; and a wide variety of nonprofit and for-profit centers. This crazy-quilt included regulated, unregulated, custodial, and educationally oriented programs. In the United States, child care is thought of primarily as a family responsibility, unlike Europe, where it is regarded as a public responsibility. Yet despite ingrained hostility toward state intervention in the family, public involvement in child care gradually increased. Direct federal funding was restricted almost exclusively to the poor and to military personnel, but the federal government indirectly subsidized child care through grants to organizations that operate day care centers as well as through tax incentives and credits to individual families. In contrast, corporate support for child care for employees has remained negligible, with only about 5 percent of employees eligible for corporate childcare benefits. In the early twenty-first century, forty-three states provided part-time prekindergarten programs, usually targeted at four-year-olds.[101]

While most parents say that they are satisfied with the care that their children receive, expert studies have concluded that the care is of poor or mediocre quality for half of children in child care arrangements. Cost remains a pressing problem. In twenty-two states, parents pay on average more for child care than they do for rent. The most significant problem is inequality of access to educationally oriented programs, with 75 percent of the three-to-five-year-olds of wealthier parents and only 45 percent of those of low-income parents in such programs. Other problems include the low status and pay of child care workers, minimal standards for training, high staff turnover, prohibitive fees, and widely varied, loosely enforced regulations.[102]

Even today, Americans regard institutional child care with ambivalence. There has been far greater public support for educational programs, such as kindergartens, nursery schools, and Head Start, than for custodial care. Even though child care is a necessity for a majority of families with young children, child care is viewed as a familial, indeed generally as a maternal, responsibility rather than as a public good. There is, however, a historical precedent for child care as a public responsibility. In the late nineteenth and early twentieth centuries, there was a similar debate over kindergartens. That debate—which persisted over five decades and required the National Kindergarten Association to lobby state by state and town to town—hinged on the question of cost and ended with a consensus that care for five-year-olds should be educational and provided through public schools.[103]

❧

In a society that strives to raise the perfect child, the challenge of rearing a child with mental or physical disabilities is particularly intense. In an article published in 1962 in the *Saturday Evening Post* magazine, Eunice Kennedy Shriver discussed the tragic life of her sister, Rosemary, who suffered developmental delays, learning disabilities, and, perhaps, a neurological or psychiatric disorder. Her family's third child, Rosemary was slower to crawl, walk, and speak than her older brothers. As she grew older, she became increasingly irritable, experienced violent rages, and had difficulty with her memory, concentration, and judgment. Unable to cope with his daughter's behavior, Joseph Kennedy decided to take drastic action. In 1941, when Rosemary was twenty-three, she became the first person who was diagnosed as mentally retarded to undergo a prefrontal lobotomy. Left incapacitated by the surgery, she spent most of the remaining fifty-seven years of her life in an institution in Wisconsin.[104]

Before the 1970s and 1980s, children with mental or physical disabilities frequently aroused shame and embarrassment among parents, who often institutionalized children deemed "feebleminded" or kept them from public view. Largely in response to the efforts of activist parents and relatives, an abrupt shift in attitudes took place. The new goal was to "mainstream" these children by placing them into regular school classrooms and providing them with opportunities to participate in the same activities as any other child. Although the incidence of premature death of children has fallen sharply in recent years, this decline has been accompanied by a sharp increase in the number and proportion of children suffering from severe disabilities or chronic illnesses. Additionally, while there is heated debate over whether the prevalence of autism or attention deficit disorder has increased, or is, rather, diagnosed more frequently, there is widespread agreement that autoimmune and respiratory disorders and other chronic conditions among children have surged over the past half century.[105]

A shift in attitudes toward the treatment of children with disabilities represents one of the most far-reaching transformations in American culture. Prior to the 1930s, the Children's Bureau supported the sterilization of mentally handicapped girls in the belief that disabilities were transmitted genetically. Until the mid-1970s, most states allowed school districts to refuse to enroll students they considered "uneducable," while physically disabled students of normal intelligence were routinely grouped with mentally retarded students. A 1949 Pennsylvania law was typical: a school district could refuse to enroll or retain any student who did not have a mental age of at least five years. Such children were considered "uneducable or unable to profit from school attendance." In Washington, D.C., eight-year old George Liddell Jr., who was mentally retarded, was denied admission to an elementary school because he would have required a special class. Sixteen-year-old Michael Williams, who suffered from epilepsy, was expelled from another Washington, D.C., school because of frequent absences due to health problems. Altogether, an estimated 12,340 children with disabilities were excluded from school in the nation's capital during the 1971–1972 school year.[106]

Not until 1966 did the federal government give grants to school districts to provide services to students with disabilities. Two landmark 1971 court cases—*Pennsylvania Association for Retarded Children v. Commonwealth of Pennsylvania* and *Mills v. Board of Education*—established the principle that states had a constitutional duty to provide a free public education to children with mental or behavioral disabilities. Yet despite more than thirty federal court decisions that upheld the principle that states had to provide these children with an education appropriate to their learning capacities, as late as 1975 almost a million children with disabilities received no education at all, and only seventeen states provided an education to even half of the known physically or mentally disabled children. In 1973, Congress enacted legislation prohibiting any recipient of federal aid from discriminating in offering services to people with disabilities, and empowering individuals to bring lawsuits to end discriminatory practices. Two years later, it passed the Education for All Handicapped Children Act, which required that students with disabilities receive a free public education appropriate to their unique needs. The law required that students be educated in regular classrooms, whenever appropriate, and mandated parental involvement in all decisions regarding students with special needs.[107]

Yet for all the changes in public policy, responsibility for raising a child with severe physical, developmental, or mental disabilities rests primarily upon parents' shoulders. Parents of children who differ from the norm face several great challenges, which include navigating an intricate maze involving insurance guidelines, medical procedures, therapy sessions, and school policies and coping with onerous expenses, callous and insensitive professionals, disparaging comments from relatives, friends, and associates, derogatory labels, discouragement, pity, and worries about their child's future. Above all, these parents need to deal with shattered expectations and emotional and financial burdens, as well as feelings of grief, rage, guilt, denial, disappointment, and hopelessness, while treating their girl or boy as a unique and special human being, and not simply as disabled or defective. In a highly individualistic society with strict expectations regarding normality and an undeveloped social welfare system, these parents must be their child's foremost advocate and care providers.[108]

When Jason Kingsley was born, on June 27, 1974, with Down syndrome, the doctors advised his mother, a writer for *Sesame Street*, and father to place him in an institution. "They told me he wouldn't be able to distinguish us from other adults," his mother later wrote. The doctors predicted that the infant would "never read or write or have a single meaningful thought or idea." "They advised, 'Never see him again, and tell your friends and family that he died in childbirth.' "[109]

Down syndrome is a chromosome disorder that affects one in every 800 to 1,000 children. A child is born with three rather than the usual two copies of the twenty-first chromosome, which can cause mild to severe effects on a person's physical and cognitive development. Prior to the 1970s, institutionalization was a common response to what was still termed "Mongoloid idiocy." Indeed, just two years before Jason was born, an exposé revealed that sixty children, many naked, some in straitjackets, were warehoused at Willowbrook, a New York state institution on Staten Island, and cared for by a single attendant.[110]

Kingsley's parents took charge of their child's upbringing, providing intense stimulation, especially visual, and physical therapy, including vigorously exercising his arms and legs. Through early intervention, the parents sought to develop their son's motor and cognitive skills. After he was old enough to enter school, the parents persuaded the public school to classify their child not as mentally retarded but as suffering from a learning disability and to place him into special needs and mainstream classrooms.

If Kingsley's life rebuts the assumption of "uneducability," it also undercuts the sentimental stereotype of the carefree, cheerful Down syndrome child. As he grew older, Kingsley sought greater independence from his parents, who, he feared, sought to micromanage his life. In a 1992 letter written when he was seventeen, he said: "I am utterly alone and stressfully upset. You will have to let go of me. I'm not a kid and a teen-ager. Seventeen years I'm dying to be a man. 'Get off my back, please!' " Perhaps the greatest parenting challenge of all is to achieve the middle ground between caring and controlling, concern and constraint, and knowing when and how to let go.[111]

✣

Among history's greatest benefits is that it challenges cultural provincialism and problematizes practices that seem natural, inevitable, or unquestionable, thereby reminding us that things taken for granted are unusual from a historical perspective. Contemporary American childrearing practices are distinctive in a number of ways. For one thing, American parents, like those in most other Western societies, emphasize face-to-face interaction with their babies, whereas in many other societies, the newborn is carried facing outward while touching the caregiver's body. Even compared to other postindustrial societies, U.S. parents also place greater emphasis on the dyadic relationship between mother and infant. Far less attention is attached to the infant's bonds with a broader range of nurturing figures. Middle-class American mothers devote twice as much time to face-to-face interactions with their babies as do their Japanese counterparts. Eye-to-eye contact in the United States is much more common than skin-to-skin contact.[112]

In a culture that prizes individuality, it is not surprising to discover that U.S. childrearing practices reinforce a sense of self and autonomy from a very early age. To be sure, in a society as diverse as that of the United States, there is a great deal of variation in parenting practices. Nevertheless, certain patterns stand out. These include having babies sleep in cribs, apart from their mother, a practice that became common only around the turn of the twentieth century, when parents began to give infants and young children "transition" objects like stuffed animals to cuddle with. Also, in the United States, a single mothering figure provides the overwhelming bulk of care, as opposed to societies that feature multiple nurturing figures, such as related kin. Then, too, there is mother-infant communication in which the spoken references refer almost exclusively to the infant or the infant's mother. In an achievement-oriented culture, it makes sense that parents seek to stimulate their child, perceptually, aurally, and in other ways, even in the crib. Parent-child play is far more common in the United States than in many other cultures, or than in the United States prior to the twentieth century, as is play with objects, which is encouraged from a very early age.[113]

How parents speak about their children varies across cultures and historical eras as well. The very words that contemporary American middle-class parents most frequently use to describe infants and young children reveals something about this country's distinctive values. Whereas the most common word that Spanish parents use to describe a young child translates to "easy," and while Swedish and Australian parents use "happy," American parents are most likely to praise the child who "asks questions," or to remark on a child who is "independent," "rebellious," or "adaptable." These words, in turn, reflect a distinctive American middle-class preoccupation with intelligence, inquisitiveness, independence, flexibility, and resilience. To be sure, American parents are also concerned about whether their child is well-behaved, even-tempered, emotionally secure, and socially competent, but many appear to be preoccupied with their child's developmental status, especially the level of cognitive development, and need to be reassured that the child is well within the normal average realm. Also, contemporary American middle-class parents are far more likely than their European counterparts to refer to the quality time or special time that they spend with their child as something to be proud of and worthwhile. Observers have also identified some other striking differences that make American middle-class childrearing practices distinctive. French parents, according to some accounts, are more likely to let infants cry if they are not sleeping through the night at the age of four months. Also, French children are far less likely to receive medication to control their behavior (less than 0.5 percent as opposed to about 9 percent in the United States), and less likely to snack during the day.[114]

Variation over time is as important as variation across cultures. Studies conducted during the 1940s reported that middle-class children were more restrictively reared than working-class and lower-class children. This contrasted with studies conducted during the 1960s, which concluded that middle-class parenting was more permissive in its childrearing practices. More recent findings suggest that middle-class parents are more likely to embrace more self-conscious and intensive childrearing techniques than working-class and lower-class parents, who are more likely to follow a "natural growth" model, which posits that children develop without intrusive parental intervention.[115]

Naming practices also offer a window into how values and tastes have shifted over time. The historical record provides a particularly rich source of insights into why certain names grow in popularity while others go out of style. It is striking that many of today's most popular children's names, especially girls' names, were virtually unknown just half a century ago. Some popular names fell out of favor, like Lisa or Beth, while others, including Jayden, Justin, and Jason for boys, and Mia or Maya, Kayla, and Madison among girls, became much more common. Generalizations must be made with care, since naming patterns vary by ethnicity and region. Nevertheless, certain long-term trends stand out. Many traditional family or ethnic group customs declined over the course of the twentieth century, such as the common practice of naming a first born child for a father or mother. Fathers' influence on children's names appears to have waned, with many fathers ceding the choice of a first name to the mother in exchange for using his last name. Today's parents appear to spend more time musing over a child's name than parents in the past. The most striking trend in recent years has been a heightened emphasis on individuality, originality, and adventurousness in names. The range of variation in names has greatly increased as has the rate of change, especially among girls. Names that are tied to a particular era—like Barbara, Nancy, Karen, or Susan—or ethnic groups—like Giuseppe and Helga—have declined in popularity, although biblical and antique names (like Abigail, Hannah, Caleb, and Oliver) have grown in frequency as have names associated with defunct occupations (like Cooper, Carter, and Mason).[116]

Particular eras tend to adopt common naming practices. About half of all boys in Roanoke Colony were named John, Thomas, or William, and more than half of newborn girls in the Massachusetts Bay Colony were named Mary, Elizabeth, or Sarah. It was also common for Puritan girls to receive names that resonated with Puritan religious values, such as Charity and Patience. In the past, there were particularly marked regional differences in naming patterns, with antebellum white Southern males especially likely to use surnames or ancestral names as first names (such as

Ambrose, Ashley, Braxton, Jubal, Kirby, or Porter), reflecting an emphasis on family honor.[117]

After the Civil War, former slaves tended to give their children names that had previously been common among whites, while Southern whites altered their naming patterns to distance themselves from freed people. The parents of baby boomers were especially likely to give their children informal names (like Tom or Jeff or Judy) or diminutives (like Stevie or Tommy or Suzy), and to confine their names to a relatively small pool of conventional options, while their children often gave more formal, exotic, or idiosyncratic names (such as Jonathan instead of John or Elizabeth instead of Beth) to their offspring.[118]

Semantic associations and sound preferences appear to have a strong impact on the names parents bestow on their children. In recent years, there has been a tendency to adopt names that begin with a hard "k" (as opposed to baby boomer names that often ended with a "k," like Frank, Jack, Mark, or Rock) or end with "-er" or "-a", while girls' names that end with "-ly" (like Emily) have declined in frequency. In recent years place names have grown more common, while girls' names associated with flowers or decoration (like Violet), have declined as have names that seem old fashioned (like Gladys). Names are signals that send out messages, and parents today seek to emphasize their children's individuality and to give them names that will seem appropriate when they enter adulthood.

There is a tendency among the general public to assume that mass media have a particularly great impact on naming practices, but it does not appear to be the case that the names of public figures, entertainers, celebrities, or characters in television shows or movies exert an outsized influence. However, negative associations, such as those with scandal or a reviled or comic figure (Adolf Hitler or Donald Duck or Donald Trump), do affect names' popularity. Social movements, especially feminism, have had an impact on naming, with girls now more likely to receive cross-gender or androgynous names.[119]

The relationship between ethnicity and social class and naming patterns is complex. Curiously, religious names came into fashion at precisely the time that church attendance was dropping; parents who were most active religiously were least likely to give their children Old Testament names. Today, fewer practicing Catholics name their children after saints. Some ethnic groups, notably Irish Americans, tend to draw upon names with a clear ethnic identification (such as Megan, Kelly, Caitlin, Erin), while other groups, such as Italian Americans, do not. Currently, it is common among Mexican Americans to adopt girls' names that end with an "–a" or names that have both traditional and Anglo counterparts (like Angela); among boys, certain names with clear ethnic connotations, like Jose or Jesus, have declined, while others, like Carlos, have grown more common. Meanwhile, highly educated mothers are more likely to give daughters names that connote strength and substance (such as Elizabeth or Catherine).[120]

❦

The changes that have taken place in parenting as in the naming of children are illuminated by an historical perspective. The major concern as to whether today's children are better off than those in the past has a surprisingly positive response. Despite high rates of divorce, single parenthood, and out-of wedlock births, by most measures of well-being and protection, children are doing better than ever. Adolescents are less likely than their parents to smoke, take drugs, or become pregnant. Juvenile crime and suicide rates have fallen, school achievement has improved, and college attendance has climbed substantially. The explanation is straightforward. Today's parents are better educated than their predecessors. Fathers are more nurturing. Mothers, in general, are happier and more fulfilled. Lower birthrates have meant that parents can devote more material resources to the children whom they have.[121]

Yet in several important respects, the young may be worse off. They have less access to free spaces outside the home. They have fewer opportunities for unstructured physical play and fewer ways to demonstrate their growing maturity and competence. Indeed, the one area in which this society allows the young to demonstrate their maturity is sports, and involvement in athletics peaks in seventh grade. Even in the area of children's health, where the gains are most obvious, more children now suffer from chronic illnesses, congenital health problems, and physical and psychological disabilities than in the past. Whether that is a consequence of increased professional oversight and concern or simply contemporary culture is impossible to measure[122]

Americans certainly treasure their own children, but society as a whole tends to conceive of children as problems to be solved. No other Western society has a greater range of institutions, products, or services devoted to children, or spends as much on children's education, health care, child care, or toys—or juvenile justice and children's protective services. Nor does any other advanced society allow as many children to grow up in poverty. Compared to other Western societies, the United States makes fewer accommodations for children while parents work. Despite talk about children's rights, children have little say in custody decisions and can be punished for status offenses that would not be crimes if committed by adults. At the same time, marketers prey on children with an aggressiveness previously reserved for adults. America's focus on children leads many middle-class parents to treat their own children as projects to be perfected for their future engagement in adult society. A corollary is that they tend to regard other parents' children as potential competitors or threats to their own children's well-being.[123]

With the many social and economic shifts experienced in the first decades of the twenty-first century, a particular definition of childhood seems to be disappearing. This is the notion of childhood as a protected, prolonged stage of innocence and naiveté. Middle-class children have grown far more knowing than their counterparts a generation or two earlier. In terms of health, material resources, and even parental time and attention, childhood today is better treated than at any time in the past. And yet, as many parents strive to organize and structure their children's lives effectively, something is missing. Too many young people find the social roles that they have been assigned, as full-time students and consumers, profoundly unsatisfying. Too many feel marginalized and treated as immature. Children need not only protection and nurture, but also a respite from the pressures of adult expectations. They need to feel worthwhile as individuals without producing results or achieving scores. Parents today sometimes overlook the need to connect with that developing person emotionally and to spend time together with no point other than to enjoy the child for who she or he is. It is precisely this bond of connection that many young people crave and that otherwise well-meaning parents fail to provide.[124]

CHAPTER SIX

Finding Fulfillment in Work

In his classic 1974 oral history, *Working*, Studs Terkel, the author, broadcaster, and master chronicler of American life asked a hundred interviewees—from washroom attendant and waitress to plant manager and editor—to speak about their dislikes, problems, and joys on the job. Some hated their jobs, feeling trapped and beaten down. But most did not. The vast majority were content in their work roles. Alongside the predictable complaints, about annoying coworkers, abusive bosses, and underpay, many expressed pride in their work. A bookbinder said that he loved repairing books because "a book is a life." A grave digger made sure that the edges were square because "A human body is goin' into this grave." Said a waitress, "When I put a plate down, you don't hear a sound. If I drop a fork, there is a certain way I pick it up. I know they can see how delicately I can do it. I'm on stage."[1]

To be sure, there were tensions between the women's and men's hopes and dreams and the humdrum realities of their jobs. Many of the blue-collar job holders drew a sharp distinction between who they were and what they did, insisting that their work did not define them or give full expression to their talents, interests, and capabilities. Still, the most surprising aspect of the interviews was the insistence that their jobs were meaningful. A garbage man, far from grousing over the stigma attached to his job, spoke about the pleasure he took in supporting his family and performing an essential task.[2]

Written in the waning days of the "old" economy—an economy still dominated by manufacturing and large corporate bureaucracies, before information technology and heightened global competition had transformed the American workplace—*Working* argued that even in the most menial jobs, working women and men sought meaning, not simply an income. In one of the book's most oft-quoted lines, an editor, Nora Watson, said: "Most of us are looking for a calling, not a job. Most of us . . . have jobs that are too small for our spirit. Jobs are not big enough for people."[3]

Twenty-eight years later, a group of interviewers sought to duplicate Terkel's effort. Their first-person vignettes covered a broader range of occupations than Terkel's blue-collar emphasis, with a substantial number of jobs reflecting the growth of the "knowledge," "information," and "service" sectors. The differences in the interviews were striking, colored by the downsizing, outsourcing, privatizing, and contingent employment characteristic of the "new" economy. The reflections on work were far more negative, with much more talk about job-related stress, work-family tensions, and insecurity about layoffs. Equally noticeable was a change in the way the interviewees conceived of their work lives. Many spoke of their career but the word did not denote what it had in the past: a period of training followed by the pursuit of a single occupation. Rather, a career now involved any number or kinds of jobs pursued over an adult's work life.[4]

Over the last four decades, the landscape of work has shifted radically. During the 1970s, the proportion of married women working for wages jumped by over 50 percent. At the same time, in the face of mounting foreign competition, many unionized factory jobs disappeared. Over three decades, manufacturing employment dropped 40 percent, and union membership in the private sector, which peaked in 1970, fell from 17 million to just 7 million. Meanwhile, administrative hierarchies flattened and there was a shift toward more "flexible" employment arrangements, including more freelancers and an increasing number of temporary jobs without benefits, more automated hiring procedures, and greater disparities in pay. For many adults, the boundaries separating their work lives and personal lives eroded, due, in large measure, to new communication technologies that made employees available at any time. Yet despite the work-related strains, conflicts, and tensions that had accompanied these developments, work had come to assume a more central role in defining adult identities.[5]

In the space of forty years, there was a marked shift in attitudes toward work. This is epitomized by General Motors's Lordstown stamping and assembly plants in northeastern Ohio. During the early 1970s, this facility became a national symbol of worker discontent, labor unrest, and the unwillingness of young workers to tolerate assembly line regimentation. GM accused the facility's workers of sabotaging cars, vandalizing the plant, and conducting deliberate slowdowns. *Time* magazine reported: "Autos regularly roll off the line with slit upholstery, scratched paint, dented bodies, bent gearshift levers, cut ignition wires, and loose or missing bolts. In some cars, the trunk key is broken off right in the lock, thereby jamming it." Journalists termed the worker unrest "assembly line blues." Wages were not the issue. Rather, the facility's problems involved the pace of work and the alienation that accompanied the repetitive performance of a single, simple job. Relatively high wages proved insufficient to curb exceptionally high rates of absenteeism and turnover. Once regarded as the prototype for the factory of the future, the Lordstown facility was the fastest and most automated in the industry, capable of producing a car every thirty-six seconds. The assembly line was supposed to turn out one hundred cars an hour, instead of fifty or sixty as at other plants. Ultimately, the machinery itself could not keep up the pace and repeatedly broke down.[6]

Opened in 1966 as part of GM's battle against low-priced imports, the Lordstown complex was intentionally located in isolated farmlands in order to attract a rural labor force that GM thought would be less recalcitrant and more tractable than workers from urban areas and more willing to accept a faster pace of work. In fact, the plant's nearly 10,000 workers, which had an average age of twenty-five, the youngest in the industry, consisted of large numbers of Vietnam War veterans, who bristled at the plant's strict discipline, as well as workers from Youngstown, with strong ties to the United Steel Workers. Gradually, if unevenly, the workers' militancy faded. As foreign competition and job security worries mounted, as use of outside contractors increased, and as the labor force aged and watched closures at other plants, the mood at Lordstown shifted from confrontation to relative cooperation. Although the number of grievances remained high, workers proved increasingly willing to accommodate themselves to company demands.[7]

The shift that took place at Lordstown resonated elsewhere, as work grew less reliable yet ever more central to an adult sense of self for both men and women. Careerism, the rat race, and the grind, widely derided during the boom years of the 1960s, gave way by the 1980s to a heightened dedication to work. The language of alienation — of work as stultifying, soul-sapping, and stress- and disease-inducing — faded. For all the complaints about work-life balance, many Americans today engage in work even when they are nominally off duty, including on evenings and on weekends. Many fail to take sick days or exercise family leave opportunities even when these are available. Older workers cling to their jobs longer than in the recent past. Indeed, those who work the fewest hours wish they could work more. Adults now cling to their work lives not only for economic sustenance but for emotional and psychic security.[8]

Contemporary American adults are distinctive in the importance that they attach to work. Compared to adults in other postindustrial societies, American adults work longer hours and take shorter vacations. When asked to describe why they work, American adults are less likely to say that this is simply to support themselves and their family. Instead, adults emphasize work's importance as a source of identity, self-respect, and self-fulfillment. Work not only provides regularity and structure to adult lives; it is also a primary source of sociability. Given the significance attached to work, it is not surprising that the jobless and the retired frequently complain of boredom, loneliness, and their inability to make a meaningful contribution to their family and community.[9]

To be sure, the American compulsion to work is partly born of necessity, including the failure of incomes to keep up with inflation, the increase in competition in a global economy, and fear of unemployment. There are, of course, other factors that contribute to an intense engagement in work, including the constantly rising cost of a middle-class standard of living, an obsession with consumption, discontent with family life, and a desire to "get ahead." But adults do not simply work for money; along with love and childrearing, work is what gives most adults' lives meaning. Through work, adults achieve financial independence, provide for their families, and test and measure their self-worth. And yet, as Marx noted a century and a half ago, for most workers it is difficult to find genuine fulfillment in work. The characteristics of the modern workplace—the specialization of labor, the production of superfluous goods, the distance from the sources of what we consume, the detachment of meaning from work—have made self-fulfillment through work elusive.[10]

Americans highly value work even though a large proportion of the adult population, probably well over half, hold jobs that provide little in the way of autonomy or opportunities for self-expression. About half of Americans are paid by the hour, and about the same proportion work in jobs that involve physical labor or close supervision. A substantial proportion, especially among those who work in sales, hold jobs with unpredictable work schedules and few benefits. Compared to Western Europeans, working-class Americans are far more likely to be laid off and far less likely to be protected by union contracts.[11]

Despite frequent lamentations about a declining work ethic, work remains central to adults' identity. Certainly, some adults, mainly twentysomethings, regard their job as a "gig"—a casual diversion and transitory source of income until something better comes along. Still others, including many part-time, contingent, temporary, and hourly workers, can only wish for a full-time job with benefits. Many highly successful financiers, physicians, and corporate attorneys grumble about workplace stress and never-ending demands on their time. But amid the complaints, one hears a yearning for work invested with a sense of purpose and craft, for a job that is not simply a source of income, but a vehicle for meeting deeper needs for fulfillment, human connection, creativity, accomplishment, and personal satisfaction.[12]

The value that American adults attach to work today has deep historical roots, although the ways that Americans have defined work's value have shifted profoundly over time. The Puritan notion of work as a calling represented a shift away from earlier notions of work as a curse and a punishment. During the early and mid-nineteenth century, at the historical moment when the notion of the "self-made man" was formulated and the male breadwinner household arose, many male workers spoke of work as a source of "manly independence." During the later nineteenth century, at a time when a much higher proportion of the male workforce began to work for wages or a salary, new ways of defining work's value emerged. Some valued work for the goods that it could purchase. But large numbers emphasized the opportunities for advancement or a respected career. Toward the end of the twentieth century, a growing number of adults, female as well as male, looked to work as the preferred way to pursue their personal goals and fashion their identity, even to the detriment of their family life. At the same time, work commitment came to be equated with time on the job. Many feared that taking advantage of "family-friendly" policies, such as parental leave or flextime, would jeopardize their future career prospects.[13]

Today, sharp divides characterize adult engagement in the workforce, with distinct divisions between the overworked and underworked. Since 1970, a growing proportion of workers have been putting in either excessively long work weeks of fifty hours or more or relatively brief work weeks of thirty hours or less. Professionals and managers are especially likely to be overworked, even as less educated workers are more likely to be working less and struggling to find enough work. Meanwhile, dual-earner couples and single parents are especially likely to work long hours.[14]

From the colonial era onward, Americans have been of two minds about work. At some points in American history, a critical view has prevailed, associating work with drudgery, dependence, routine, and, beginning in the mid-nineteenth century, alienation and exploitation. At other times, the emphasis has been on work's positive elements. In recent years, an older language of complaint has given way to a view of work as a central element in a meaningful life. For some, apparently, work has become a compulsion. Many adults report feeling guilty when they are not working and being "productive."[15]

If Americans have long attached special significance to work, this has been accompanied by forceful indigenous critiques of work, bosses, and the workplace. Indeed, it can be argued that during the nineteenth century, stronger attacks on the emerging industrial order could be found in the United States than in Britain or continental Europe. Precisely because work was so laden with meaning, Americans, well before Marx, had already formulated criticisms of the realities of many jobs. This critique took a variety of forms. As early as the 1820s, as job specialization and labor regimentation increased, working-class protests against "wage slavery" mounted, with forceful denunciations of the exploitation of labor by heartless factory owners who threatened to undermine the foundations of republican liberty. Accompanying the wage slavery argument was a focus on the erosion of craft skills and worker autonomy. According to this line of argument, emerging patterns of work were repetitive and boring, mind-numbing and soul-robbing, stunting the development of individuals' higher faculties. During the twentieth century, the critique of work expanded to encompass nonphysical labor, culminating in Arthur Miller's howling lament in *Death of a Salesman* (1949), over the emptiness and purposelessness of much of the work that adults perform. As Miller's tragedy of the common man suggested, many jobs provide no intrinsic satisfaction or security, and employees produce no discernible products or measurable results, while basing their self-esteem solely on their earnings or upon the opinions of others.[16]

In the late 1960s and 1970s, a feminist-informed critique of work took hold. Unlike caring occupations, such as teaching, health care, or social work, sales and office work was said to lack any larger significance or genuinely useful purpose. Success in the competitive marketplace depended on guile and glibness, rather than ingenuity, initiative, imagination, and empathy. Work, from this perspective, came at the expense of family, community, and children. It was a source of stress and anxiety and motivated solely by monetary profit. In recent years, despite a few isolated calls to arms, like Matthew B. Crawford's best-selling *Shop Class as Soulcraft: An Inquiry into the Value of Work* (2009), with its forceful attack on pointless, enervating forms of labor, the language of alienation and exploitation has faded. The popular David Allan Coe song may have exclaimed "Take This Job and Shove It," but such examples of jukebox Marxist commentary have grown ever more rare in the years since 1974, when Johnny Paycheck turned the lyrics into a hit.[17]

Nearly two centuries ago, Henry David Thoreau asserted that "the mass of men lead lives of quiet desperation." Since the early nineteenth century, many adults have looked to work for more than the workplace can offer. Compared to Europeans, American adults, primarily men, but also some women, have been much more likely to look at work as a path to wealth, status, recognition, and personal worth, only to suffer acute disappointment. A commitment to work, much too often, came at the expense of other sources of engagement, including family, friendship, leisure, and well-rounded personal development. Today's heavy emphasis on work suggests that little has changed and that adults remain willing to subordinate other activities to the priority placed on work because its challenges are more clearly defined than are other aspects of adulthood.

Only in the last half century has work come to be viewed through a therapeutic lens, as a source of self-esteem and a pathway to personal fulfillment. The very words used to describe work serve as an index of shifting, and conflicting, attitudes. The earliest words, such as "labor," "drudgery," and "toil," equated work with exhausting physical exertion. Succeeding words in the mid- and late Middle Ages were less pejorative terms such as "livelihood," "craft," and "occupation," which, initially, referred to how people spent their time. The mid-sixteenth century saw the emergence of words that reflected a more positive valuation of work—such as "profession"—as well as a number of religiously derived terms, such as "calling" and "vocation," which spoke to work's inherent dignity and value. It was only in the eighteenth century that the word "job" appeared, referring to a paid position of employment, and only in the nineteenth century that the term "career" arose, describing the course of a person's employment and its opportunities for advancement.[18]

Classical antiquity tended to deprecate work in contrast to contemplation, a view that persisted into the Middle Ages. In Thomas Aquinas's influential view, work's value was indirect; it prevented idleness, ensured that families were provided for, and generated earnings that could be distributed as alms. The Protestant Reformation contributed to a radical revaluation of work's significance. Work became a calling invested with spiritual and moral value. As John Calvin put it, "All men were created to busy themselves with labor for the common good." In Martin Luther's eyes, every occupation had equal value in God's sight. Luther, however, retained a long-standing hostility toward ambition and aspiration, believing that individuals should not strive to rise above their appointed station in life. It was not until the late nineteenth century that work began to be regarded as a source of personal meaning and mobility. Work acquired subjective significance, as a way to clarify one's identity. As the novelist Joseph Conrad put it in *Heart of Darkness*, "I don't like work—no man does—but I like what is in the work, the case to find yourself."[19]

Perhaps the most important development in popular thinking about work is the equation of work with ambition. Today, there is a tendency to conceive of ambition positively, as an essential element in achievement, self-improvement, and advancement. Great accomplishments, we are told, are not simply the product of intelligence, looks, charm, talent, and luck, but of an unrelenting drive not found in other, less successful individuals. A synonym for "determination," "energy," and "passion," "ambition" denotes an insistent desire to climb the greasy pole, to excel and improve one's lot in life. To lack ambition is to be a slacker or drifter, aimless, complacent, and passive. Those who lack ambition lack the entrepreneurial instinct necessary for success. Thus it comes as a bit of a shock to discover that prior to the eighteenth century, ambition was universally disparaged as a sin or vice or form of mental illness. In societies that attach importance to social hierarchy and condemn social mobility and marriages among those who are unequal, ambition posed a threat to social stability. Ambition was associated with pride, presumption, and singularity, all of which were regarded negatively.[20]

A series of profound economic and ideological developments during the eighteenth century transformed ambition into a potential, if double-edged, virtue that could be harnessed for positive ends. By the early nineteenth century, aspirations for advancement and self-improvement came to be regarded as a force for progress. The Darwinian revolution, with its emphasis on the competitive struggle for survival, gave the concept of ambition a positive edge.

If the history of ambition up to the end of the nineteenth century is a story of the concept's ever higher valuation, the story in the twentieth century is more ambiguous. Ambition elicited a deepening ambivalence, carrying a penumbra of pushiness, naïve vulgarity, wishful thinking, and excessive go-getter optimism. It became, in short, déclassé. Today, the relentless self-promotion of Donald Trump and Kim Kardashian personifies ambition; earlier in the twentieth century, George F. Babbitt, Jay Gatsby, Flem Snopes, and Sammy Glick gave ambition a bad name. Ambition, in the early twenty-first century, is rarely viewed as an unmixed asset, as it was in the mid-nineteenth century. Rather, it needs to be tempered, balanced, and, above all, in a therapeutic culture, "healthy" rather than toxic to others.[21]

If, on the one hand, ambition is the opposite of laziness and sloth, it is often viewed as a noxious, pathological hunger for power, wealth, social standing, honor, and personal glory. Ambition can be the pursuit of one's dreams, but it can also involve the sacrifice of other values, especially love, family, and friendship. This is what is meant when one speaks critically of ambition as blind, flagrant, greedy, naked, raw, ruthless, and all-consuming. The word conjures images of selfish, self-absorbed, stressed, self-interested individuals who claw their way to the top, who step on others to get ahead, and who, we like to think, pay a high personal and psychological price for their success. Contemporary society, in short, tends to psychologize ambition, to treat it as a somewhat socially acceptable form of vanity and egotism. Indeed, contemporary psychologists frequently attribute neurosis and aggression to thwarted ambition.[22]

Even today, in a postfeminist age, ambition remains heavily gendered. There is a tendency to associate manliness with ambition, while linking female striving with egotism, selfishness, and self-aggrandizement. Ambition in women is still often considered unnatural, unwomanly, and unseemly. An ambitious woman, from this perspective, lacks a maternal instinct. Many men find it difficult to deal with ambitious women, and many assume that whenever women take time to care for their family, it is the "natural" thing to do as women are innately less ambitious than men.[23]

6.1. John Neagle, *Pat Lyon at the Forge*, 1826–1827. Oil on canvas. Accession number 1975.806. Courtesy of the Museum of Fine Arts, Boston. Photograph © 2015 Museum of Fine Arts, Boston.

It was in the early nineteenth century that work came to be defined in modern terms: as an activity performed over a specific period of the day for wages. A sharp division arose between modern work and the kinds of unpaid labor performed by women—namely, caring for children and maintaining a home. No longer was the latter considered to be work. In colonial America, women and girls had played a highly active role in economic production, engaging not only in spinning, weaving, and fabricating clothing, but tending gardens, making beer, and a host of other productive activities, while also selling goods at local markets. In the late eighteenth century, the growing desire for a cash income led many rural households to participate in various putting-out systems of production, producing boots, hats, shoes, and other commodities for merchant capitalists, who furnished raw materials and bought the products. Household industries provided work for thousands of women and children in rural areas. Shopkeepers or master craftspeople supplied farm families with raw materials, paid piece rates, and marketed the products. Among the goods produced were towels, sheets, table linens, coverlets, socks, gloves, carpets, thread, nails, and farm utensils. The quantity of goods generated was staggering. In New Hampshire, forty families produced 13,000 pounds of maple sugar annually. In 1809, farm families near Philadelphia produced more than 230,000 yards of cloth for sale, four times the amount of cloth produced by the area's textile factories. In Massachusetts, farm households produced more than 100,000 pairs of shoes a year—more than all the nation's professional shoemakers made. As early as 1791, Alexander Hamilton reported that the rural areas surrounding America's cities had become "a vast scene of household manufacturing . . . in many instances to an extent not only sufficient for the supply of the families in which they are made, but for sale, and even for export."[24]

But with the emergence of the factory system and the business office, household industries and family self-sufficiency declined. Increasingly, the household and the workplace separated. The culture gradually came to define the family as radically separate from the world of work. The early nineteenth century began to conceive of the family household as a "walled garden" and a "haven in a heartless world," separate and apart from the aggressive, self-serving forces of a market economy.[25]

The ideological division between home and work, and private and public, emerged despite the fact that tens of thousands of women and children worked outside the household. In the early stages of the industrial revolution, young native-born white women, generally between the ages of twelve and twenty-five, worked temporarily in mills, factories, and schools. Most, however, withdrew from the wage labor force after marriage; and increasingly, immigrant women supplanted unmarried native-born white women workers in factories and mills. The effect was to reinforce the notion that women and men occupied separate spheres, one characterized by sacrifice and selflessness, the other by competitive self-seeking. Accompanying the deepening ideological divide between private and public came the modern conception of work as time-oriented and wage-driven. Women's domestic roles, in stark contrast, were unpaid, task-oriented, and unending. Women's labors, in men's eyes, were stripped of the status of genuine work.[26]

In the first phase of industrialization, factories relied heavily on women and child labor. Textile and shoe manufacturing, in particular, had been associated with women in household production, and factories followed this earlier pattern. Yet even in the second half of the century, many labor-intensive industries—especially those dependent on piecework, such as electrical manufacturing—continued to employ large numbers of women. Other industries that employed women in high numbers were those of explosives, matches, and tobacco. The industries least likely to employ women were capital intensive, heavy industries, such as railroad, steel, and, later, automobile. Overall, the Industrial Revolution tended to physically separate men and women within and outside the workplace. Increasingly, men left home for the entire day, while women either worked at home or worked elsewhere in jobs segregated by sex.[27]

Gradually, a new form of family organization emerged in which the husband was expected to be the sole breadwinner. Originating among the urban middle class, the pattern spread gradually and unevenly to the working class. The male breadwinner ideal would form the basis for much of a man's sense of himself. During the eighteenth century, masculine identity was rooted in property ownership or possession of a craft skill. But as wage labor increased and the venue of work gradually shifted from the household to a work site, there was a tendency to sharpen the division between men's breadwinning role and women's homemaking and childrearing roles. Masculinity came to be identified with technical skills, authority, and especially with providing household funds. Male bread-winner families only briefly constituted a majority of households. During the nineteenth century, most immigrant and working-class men were part of a collective family economy, in which individual and group decisions, such as whether to migrate or to send a child to school or to work or to take in boarders and lodgers, were made in the interests of the family unit (as defined by the father).[28]

There can be no doubt that many families regarded the male bread-winner model as a way to best balance the family's wage-earning, home-making, and childrearing responsibilities. It is difficult today to appreciate the heavy demands of maintaining a nineteenth-century household, and it was not until housework and cooking became less time-consuming that married women in large numbers entered the paid work force. As recently as 1900, the typical housewife devoted fifty-eight hours a week to such tasks as cooking and laundering. In 1975, in contrast, the amount of time spent on various household tasks had fallen to eighteen hours per week.[29]

The extensive gap in women and men's earnings discouraged women from working outside the home. Generally, the pay available to a woman was a third to half of that of a man. As the availability of relatively well-paid service jobs for women increased during and after World War II, re-ducing the gap in male and female wages, many married women seized these opportunities. In addition, the frequency of unplanned pregnancies that had previously discouraged married women from the paid workforce was remedied by the release of the birth control pill in 1960, which en-couraged women to delay marriage and devote more time to higher edu-cation by enabling them to plan the timing of childbirths.[30]

Labor activism and government policy played a pivotal role in the growth and subsequent decline of the male breadwinner family. During the late nineteenth and early twentieth centuries, organized labor adopted a variety of strategies to sustain the male breadwinner, including enactment of so-called protective legislation, which restricted the hours and conditions of female labor, and pressure for a family wage, which would allow a single breadwinner to support a family. To encourage male breadwinner families, the state and federal governments used labor regulations (including hourly, minimum wage, and safety regulations, tax codes, and home financing) to secure the male position.[31]

The male breadwinner family had profound social implications. Work and school schedules presupposed a full-time mother available to care for children and deal with household repairs. By restricting women's work opportunities, the male breadwinner discouraged divorce and single motherhood, and, apparently, contributed to a sharp decline in rates of out-of-wedlock births. It also limited the prevalence of the double shift, in which women were expected to combine paid labor outside the home with unpaid domestic labor. One result of the erosion of this family model was a time deficit for women, who had less time for leisure and fewer opportunities to devote to themselves, and a crisis of caregiving, as single-parent and dual-earner families strived to organize childcare and balance work with other responsibilities.[32]

If, in the first half of the twentieth century, public policy sought to reinforce the male breadwinner family through policies that made hiring of women more expensive and less convenient, the second half of the century saw a reversal. A series of public policy actions opened the labor force to growing numbers of women. These included the Equal Pay Act of 1963 (mandating equal pay for identical work), Title VII of the 1964 Civil Rights Act (prohibiting discrimination in hiring, compensation, promotion, classification, and training), and the 1965 Executive Order 11246 (which required affirmative action plans by government contractors).[33]

The gender divide was only one among many divisions that have characterized the American way of work. In colonial America, the most obvious divide in the realm of work was between those who worked voluntarily and those whose work was coerced. Unfree labor was widespread, even before the sharp increase in chattel slavery in the late seventeenth century. About half of the roughly 500,000 European migrants to British North America during the seventeenth and eighteenth century arrived as indentured servants, while another 50,000 were convicts. Rates of unfree labor, of course, varied widely across region. Between 15 and 20 percent of New England's migrants were indentured servants, compared to perhaps half or more in the Chesapeake region of Maryland and Virginia. Over time, the proportion of indentured servants fell sharply, as servants completed their terms of service and as natural reproduction increased the native-born population. Meanwhile, compared to England, many artisans, mechanics, and other adult workers were far less likely to be subjected to the threat of corporal punishment by a master or to legal restrictions on quitting a job. Nevertheless, a majority of the population continued to occupy various states of dependency.[34]

Slavery was, of course, the most visible form of unfree labor. At the time of the American Revolution, enslaved Africans could be found from Quebec to the tip of Argentina, and in British America they made up 20 percent of the population and an even higher proportion of the workforce. But there were many other forms of dependent labor. Idle persons could be set to work, either in a workhouse or by being fostered out to a household. Bound service among whites continued to be found among immigrants and the young. Apprenticeship and domestic service were widespread among those in their teens and twenties. Menial day laborers, called "hirelings," were not uncommon, especially in seaports, and sailors, in particular, were vulnerable to harsh physical punishments.[35]

As for young women, apprenticeship opportunities were limited large to "housewifely" duties like cooking and sewing. In New England before 1685, there was only one occupation open to single women: domestic servitude under the supervision of a mistress or master, for which one received meals, clothing, and a place to sleep and wages of just three or four pounds a year, less than half that of a male servant. The responsibilities were largely the same as those of goodwives: cleaning house, spinning flax, dipping candles, canning preserves, roasting meat, caring for children, spinning, and fabricating clothes. Many married women sold poultry, butter, cheese, and garden produce in local markets. A much smaller number worked as wet nurses, midwives, and teachers in dame schools, where women cared for very young children and taught them to read and write, often in their own home. A very small number of New England women practiced medicine or operated millinery shops, sold beer, maintained cook shops, and kept inns.[36]

The grand narrative of American labor history is sometimes treated as a movement from status to contract, from the dependencies of slavery, patriarchal households, and other forms of hierarchy and coercion to free labor. There is a core of truth in this narrative. A significant shift in attitudes had begun to take place well before the Revolution, as a commitment to rigorous patriarchal authority started to erode, at least in New England and the Middle Atlantic colonies. By the early eighteenth century, journeymen artisans were free to leave a job without fear of arrest. By the 1740s, indentured servants could obtain part-time releases from service. Meanwhile, corporal punishment was increasingly seen as capricious and counterproductive in work relations. As reformers sought to promote a nonviolent, temperate society, profound changes occurred in popular attitudes in the North towards discipline, pain, violence, and aggressive displays of anger. By 1800, masters and mistresses could no longer legally punish adult servants physically, and by 1820, minors could no longer be subjected to corporal punishment. Around the same time, most states abolished imprisonment for debt (under the pragmatic principle that imprisoned debtors would be unable to repay their debts). One of the more striking changes following the Revolution involved the transformation of unpaid servants into hired "help."[37]

The Whiggish tale of a shift from status to contract, however, obscures as much as it reveals. It shrouds the deteriorating conditions of the so-called lower orders. Poverty and landlessness increased until, by the time of the American Revolution, there was a considerable population of vulnerable wage workers in urban areas (a number greatly augmented, during the course of the Revolution, by an influx of women displaced from farms after a husband or father's death, many of whom turned to prostitution to support themselves). It masks the growing power of employers to fire employees at will. Both workers and employers were now free to terminate labor contracts at any time without any threat of legal sanction (though workers who failed to give advance notice of quitting might forfeit any wages that they were owed). In addition, the right of workers to form unions and to bargain collectively with employers remained vague. Even after the landmark 1842 Massachusetts decision *Commonwealth v. Hunt,* which overturned an 1806 decision declaring unions illegal conspiracies in constraint of trade, unions remained subject to injunctions and anti-trust laws.[38]

Moreover, there were persistent limitations on the rights of women and African Americans and others. Despite enactment in the 1830s of the first married women's property rights laws (which were often deemed "cup and saucer" laws, since they allowed women to hold title to property owned prior to marriage), married women's control of their own wages remained ambiguous. Indeed, as late as 1887, married women had no legal right to their earnings in a third of the states. Meanwhile, statutes in the post–Civil War Southern states allowed African American workers to be imprisoned for breach of a labor contract, including unauthorized absence, desertion, neglect of duties, or lack of diligence. Not until 1908 would the Supreme Court strike down all use of penal sanctions for breaches in contracts. What we see is a shift from a system in which masters exercised control over a worker's labor to an arrangement in which labor became a commodity exchanged for a price.[39]

The Industrial Revolution deepened the divide between manual and mental labor. The quickening pace of trade and finance during the early nineteenth century not only increased the demand for middle-class clerks and shopkeepers, but also dramatically increased demand for unskilled workers, including street scrapers, seamstresses, mariners, ditch diggers, dockhands, street sweepers, carters, domestic servants, woodcutters, rag pickers, and day laborers who earned extremely low incomes and led difficult lives. An arrest in January 1850 underscores the plight of unskilled workers. Police in Newburyport, Massachusetts, arrested John McFeaing for stealing wood from the wharves. McFeaing pleaded necessity, and a public investigation was conducted. Investigators found McFeaing's wife and four children living "in the extremity of misery. The children were

6.2. Miners after work, c. 1915–1925.

all scantily supplied with clothing and not one had a shoe to his feet. There was not a stick of firewood or scarcely a morsel of food in the house, and everything betokened the most abject want and misery." McFeaing's predicament was not uncommon at that time. In 1851 Horace Greeley, editor of the *New York Tribune*, estimated the minimum weekly budget needed to support a family of five. Essential expenditures for rent, food, fuel, and clothing amounted to $10.37 a week. In that year, a shoemaker or a printer earned just $4 to $6 a week, a male textile operative $6.50 a week, and an unskilled laborer just $1 a week. The only manual laborers able to earn Greeley's minimum were blacksmiths and machinists.[40]

Frequent bouts of unemployment compounded the problems of the unskilled. In Massachusetts, upward of 40 percent of all workers were out of a job for part of a year, usually for four months or more. Fluctuations in demand, inclement weather, interruptions in transportation, technological displacement, fire, injury, and illness all could leave workers jobless.[41] Typically, a male laborer earned just two-thirds of his family's income. The other third was earned by wives and children. Many married women performed work in the home, such as embroidery and making artificial flowers, tailoring garments, or doing laundry. The wages of children were critical for a family's standard of living. Children under the age of fifteen contributed about 20 percent of the income of many working-class families. These children worked not because their parents were heartless, but because children's earnings were absolutely essential to the family's survival.[42]

Through the first six decades of the twentieth century, the central workplace divide was between blue-collar and white-collar workers, between those engaged in physical labor or who wore uniforms or worked in service jobs and were often paid by the hour, and salaried jobs in the professions, management, administration, or sales. In general, the blue-collar jobs were not only more physically demanding, but also more stressful and less stable. Hours were often erratic. There was a tendency to equate the blue- and white-collar divide with differences in character, motivation, and intelligence, treating blue-collar jobs as mindless, repetitive, and undemanding intellectually. In fact, such jobs as waitressing, hair styling, plumbing, and welding are cognitively demanding and involve a high level of interpersonal planning and problem-solving skills.[43]

In recent years, however, the significance of the divide between white- and blue-collar employment has blurred, with the rapid expansion of low wage, nonunionized service sector jobs—especially in the "pink collar" sector, a term coined during World War II to describe the low-paying service occupations held by women, who worked as secretaries, cashiers, and bank tellers. These jobs, which generally do not require a college diploma, do not readily fall into the white- or blue-collar sectors. Factors contributing to this blurring include the growth of economic sectors with large numbers of low-wage workers involved in services to others, such as food service workers, hospitality workers, flight attendants, security guards, child care workers, and home health aides; the outsourcing of certain jobs, such as repair, maintenance, and data processing, previously performed in-house; and the decline in employment in manufacturing, craft, transportation, construction, mechanical, mining, and farm occupations. Many of the service jobs require employees to maintain an upbeat, cheerful demeanor in their face-to-face interactions with clients, customers, and patients, to appear to be caring and responsive, and to mask negative emotions, despite the strains and stress of the work. For the first time, employers are not only regulating the pace and conditions of work, but managing workers' emotions, tone, deportment, and facial expression.[44]

Certain jobs have a symbolic significance far beyond the actual number of jobholders. These jobs become emblems of an era, embodying a time period's aspirations or anxieties. Some, like the bootlegger during Prohibition or the drug dealer from the 1980s onward, are not jobs in a normal sense, but rather part of an illegal economy. Others, like the so-called mill girl, sales girl, and office girl, signify broader transformations in the economy, such as the shift of women out of domestic employment and into public spaces. Such jobs acquire special meanings within the culture and deserve a closer look.

For example, the hobo is the classic example of the marginal male worker. The post–Civil War economy had a huge demand for seasonal manual workers, which was met by a vast floating labor force of migratory laborers. Seasonal transient labor played an indispensable role harvesting crops, logging, and mining in the Midwest and the West, and in urban areas, performing casual labor in rail yards, shipping depots, iron mines, and grain elevators. These "kings" or "knights" of the road picked and crated such crops as apples, beets, cotton, hops, oranges, and wheat, and left a lasting imprint on the language, adding such phrases as "hot shot" (a fast freight train), "glad rags" (dressy clothes), and "flop house" to the American vernacular. In the late 1880s, a new word, "hobo," arose to describe these men, replacing an earlier word "tramp," which had first appeared during the depression of the 1870s, and "bum," which was first used around 1864. In the early twentieth century, contemporaries distinguished hoboes, who migrated in search of work, from "tramps," or wanderers who worked extremely intermittently, and "bums," who neither worked nor wandered, and who lived by begging and scrounging. The Civil War itself helped give rise to the hobo, creating a large group of men whose ties to a particular town or city were disrupted by war and who had learned how to live outdoors and forage for food. The bulk of transient workers were native-born; only about 12 percent of wage workers on farms were foreign-born. Rapid railroad expansion transformed short-distance into long-distance migration, allowing men to travel hundreds of miles in pursuit of unskilled casual work. Itinerant train hoppers, hoboes rode the rails and congregated in skid row areas of cities in the late fall and winter. For many working-class young men well into the twentieth century, tramping was a rite of passage and a stage in the life cycle before settling down. Among the most famous transients were the future Supreme Court Justice William O. Douglas, the novelist Jack London, and the actor Clark Gable.[45]

At times, the hobo way of life has been romanticized as a life of wanderlust, mobility, and freedom from the rat race. Charlie Chaplin made his reputation as the "little tramp," dressed baggy pants, big boots, and bowler hat. In the classic 1936 screwball comedy, *My Man Godfrey,* William Powell plays an erudite hobo who lives in the city dump, unshaven, scruffy, and dressed in tattered clothes, but who is eventually revealed to be the scion of an elite Boston family. There can be no doubt that the hoboes elaborated an alternative or even oppositional subculture, a "prepolitical" response to the industrial economy, wage dependency, and Victorian domesticity. But hoboes' lives were also extremely dangerous. More than 47,000 freight hoppers died on the rails between 1898 and 1908 due to accidental falls.[46]

Hoboes evoked loathing and fear. Beginning with the tramp scare of the 1870s, migratory laborers came to be viewed widely as a moral, medical, and sexual menace, lacking a proper work ethic, drinking excessively, and engaging in sexual immorality and petty theft. Indeed, the language hoboes used to describe themselves was highly sexualized, speaking of "prushuns" (lads) and "jockers" (their protectors), "wolves" and "lambs," and even "husbands" and "wives." Fears of a tramp army, reinforced by the Great Railroad Strike of 1877, led states and municipalities to enact strict anti-vagrancy laws during the late nineteenth century. At the same time, proponents of "scientific charity," who thought charity should be rational and secular rather than sectarian and sentimental, called for an end to private almsgiving and government relief as a way to discourage vagrancy and idleness. Frequently hoboes were victimized by employment agencies, and harassed by local police, railroad "bulls," and vigilantes fearful of labor radicals. Although Progressive-era social investigators often stereotyped and demonized hoboes as deviants, criminals, pedophiles, and disease carriers, the period's reformers also opened soup kitchens, municipal lodging houses, and the first shelters for homeless men, including hoboes. The Salvation Army, founded in England in 1865 and introduced into the United States in 1880, also sought to minister and shelter the homeless.[47]

During the 1910s and 1920s mechanization and an influx of migratory labor from Mexico, the Philippines, and other foreign countries brought an end to the era of the hobo, but the Great Depression thrust transient casual labor back into the public consciousness as hobo jungles (camping sites for hoboes near railroad lines or freight yards) and Hoovervilles (shantytowns housing the dispossessed and destitute) sprouted up in many cities. In contrast to an earlier era, when most transients were in their thirties, growing numbers were then in their teens and early twenties as well as their forties and fifties. Most continued to be male, unmarried, white, and native-born. Between 1933 and 1935, the Federal Transient Program, the first federal program to address the needs of this group of people, established some 300 transient centers in cities and another 300 in rural areas. Meanwhile, a variety of other institutions emerged to serve the needs of transient men and women who could not find work, including missions, flophouses, and shelters.

Between the early 1940s and 1960s, the transients faded from public attention. These people were largely dismissed with pejoratives: as derelicts, panhandlers, vagrants, and winos. But during the 1970s, 1980s, and 1990s, the problem of homelessness became inescapable in larger cities, with mounting numbers of individuals losing jobs and homes and sleeping on sidewalks or heating grates and soliciting money on city streets and in subways. Unlike the older population that had congregated in skid rows, this population was younger, and more likely to include African Americans, Hispanics, and women and children, victims of a changing economy that no longer had a place for unskilled and uneducated workers. The swelling numbers of homeless also reflected the effects of urban renewal, which had demolished and displaced poorer residents, as well as growing numbers of young people "aging out" of the foster care system with nowhere to go other than the street or a shelter. The escalating numbers included victims of the crack "epidemic," the erosion of welfare recipients' purchasing power, and the release of the mentally ill from public institutions. Gentrification also made this population more visible through the elimination of flophouses and single-room-occupancy hotels, which had provided extremely low-cost apartments.[48]

In spite of an array of social programs, the problem of the homeless remains a pressing national issue. Its roots ultimately lie not in alcoholism, addiction, or untreated mental illness, but in displacement, high housing costs, an inadequate social welfare system, irregular employment, and low wages for unskilled or casual workers. For the most part, the homeless turn out not to be demonstrably different from other low-income Americans, with the dividing line between the homeless and others living in poverty becoming more blurred. In the early twenty-first century, homelessness is inextricably linked to an economy that has diminishing need for those who can provide heavy labor or for marginal workers who drift in and out of the labor force.

Alongside hobos, tramps, and vagabonds, another occupational group that has had a singularly important place in the American imagination is the traveling salesman. From early nineteenth-century peddlers to late-twentieth-century "detail men" and early twenty-first century road warriors, the salesman in popular culture has a notably negative image. He—and most salesmen in the past were indeed men—has been stereotyped as slick, glib, wily, a crafty manipulator of human desire, untrustworthy, and a peripatetic drifter. Well before the twentieth century, the traveling salesman joke became a staple of American popular humor. Double-edged, risqué, and often savagely misogynistic, these jokes at once laid bare the naiveté and credulity of customers (typically coded as farm housewives) and the assertiveness and amorality of the salesman.[49]

These disapproving images have a long history. As early as 1823, a former Yale College president, Timothy Dwight, warned that "Men who begin life with bargaining for small wares will almost invariably become sharpers." From the lightning-rod huckster in Herman Melville's *Moby-Dick* to Willy Loman in Arthur Miller's *Death of a Salesman,* the salesman in American literature has repeatedly been depicted as having certain quintessentially American traits: He is represented as striving, restless, rootless, and overly assertive, filled with go-getting optimism and a penchant for positive thinking. Perhaps more than any other occupation, sales is treated as anything but an honorable career. Today's salespeople are commonly represented as living a life on the road (or in the sky), schmoozing, and wining and dining customers.[50]

Though frequently reviled, the salesman was integral to the development of a modern economy, creating a market for consumer items, such as clocks and locks, and pioneering the development of installment purchasing. The peddlers who began to crisscross backwoods America in the wake of the Revolution opened up isolated rural communities, disrupted local markets, and fed a growing appetite for consumer goods, from hardware to tin ware, buttons and pins, brooms and books. Itinerancy was common before the 1850s; alongside peddlers, there were traveling preachers, singing and dancing masters, portraitists and daguerreotypists, charlatans, performers, and entertainers ranging from puppeteers and jugglers to traveling circuses showcasing a "Pig of Knowledge," a "sapient dog," and "philosophical fish."[51]

Salesmanship and haggling were defining characteristics of peddling. One foreign observer claimed in 1837 that "No nation in the world understands the science of puffing more profoundly than the American." Peddlers ranged from destitute itinerants to traveling merchants who distributed goods that they had produced. The techniques that these men employed, including promotional giveaways and testimonials and using credit to maintain ties with customers, would be adopted by later salesmen. Peddlers were often outsiders, generating particular hostility from established store owners. A disproportionate share were Jews, and in antebellum America the words "Jew" and "trader" were often used interchangeably.[52]

Antebellum itinerants' sales efforts were uncoordinated, unscripted, and unsystematic. But following the Civil War, sales began to be professionalized. Independent peddlers, who continued to flourish in immigrant neighborhoods, sometimes settled down and became retailers. More common were sales representatives, including "canvassers," traveling sales agents and middlemen who distributed goods for specific companies, and "drummers," who were responsible for "drumming up" orders for rapidly expanding manufacturing corporations. Mark Twain illustrated the effectiveness of the new approach. To market the personal memoirs of Ulysses Grant, he and his publishing partner hired veterans who wore their Grand Army of the Republic badges. A thirty-seven-page manual told them how to sell the book to customers, calling on canvassers to use flattery and maintain eye contact with prospective buyers. One piece of advice was to "Put the book right in his lap, but you turn the pages." Using these techniques, Twain succeeded in selling more than 300,000 copies of Grant's autobiography.[53]

A principal figure in the effort to systematize and professionalize sales was John H. Patterson, founder of the National Cash Register Company. Inspired by Frederic Winslow Taylor's notions of scientific management, he strove to transform sales into a science. To this end, he trained his own sales force, made use of commissions, held motivational meetings, and established sales quotas. NCR salesmen were also schooled in dropping sand in competitors' machines to disable them and bribing freight agents to hold up shipments.[54]

Other key figures in the emergence of the modern salesman were Asa Candler of Coca-Cola, who helped popularize the drink by distributing thousands of coupons for a complimentary glass; and Henry John Heinz, who systematized the sale and distribution of condiments like ketchup. Alfred Fuller, whose hard-driving sales force of "Fuller Brush Men" came to epitomize the door-to-door salesman, was so well known that in Walt Disney's *Three Little Pigs*, the big bad wolf was disguised as a Fuller Brush man. In fact, the Great Depression augmented the importance of the traveling salesman, when companies responded to hard times by emphasizing compensation based on commissions. With a few notable exceptions, mainly involving the sale of beauty products and books, door-to-door sales was an exclusively male occupation. Managers and salesmen themselves felt compelled to emphasize the "manliness" of selling, stressing the competitiveness and persuasive verbal skills that the job required.[55]

The middle of the twentieth century brought the "golden age" of the door-to-door salesman to an end, as telemarketing began to replace face-to-face sales. Today, remnants of the older forms of door-to-door salesmanship persist, notably the sellers of Avon beauty products, Tupperware, and Mary Kay cosmetics who are predominantly women. But the decline of a particular form of salesmanship has not at all reduced the significance of face-to-face marketing. If the traveling salesman is less socially visible than he once was, retail and wholesale sales currently represents the second largest employment sector (trailing only professional and managerial employment) and accounts for nearly one out of every four jobs, ranging from sales reps and canvassers to placement agents, real estate brokers, sales and marketing professionals, and drug company detail men. These peoples' financial rewards depend almost entirely on performance—on their ability to cajole, wheedle, persuade, and charm customers. In today's workplaces, however, even those who are not explicitly engaged in the sale of products spend much of their time engaging in sales-like activities. Job seekers sell themselves in interviews, executives and managers pitch ideas in meetings, litigators plead before juries, and entrepreneurs entice investors, recruit employees, negotiate with vendors, or turn prospects into clients. As bureaucratic specialization has declined and small businesses and start-ups have proliferated, employees have come to engage in an increasing number of roles, with sales, defined broadly to include selling ideas and oneself, being increasingly central to their job.[56]

Whereas the hobo and the traveling salesman are associated with transience and casual connection to the labor market, another iconic figure in American economic history, the organization man, was best known for his willingness to subordinate his personal life and desires for the good

6.3. Commuters playing bridge on train to New York City, 1941. Photograph by John Collier.

of a single large corporation. Known for his loyalty to his company and his willingness to "toe the line" and "play the game," the organization man sought security and a sense of belonging within the corporation. The organization man represented the culmination of a trend toward white-collar, salaried, managerial, and administrative employment, which greatly accelerated in the late nineteenth century in the face of the economic turbulence of the era. The consolidation of corporate enterprise and the development of bureaucratic administrative structures represented a way to impose order on a highly volatile economy.

The title of Sloan Wilson's 1955 bestseller, *The Man in the Gray Flannel Suit*, quickly became shorthand for the organization man and the conformity and deadening qualities of the corporate rat race. The man in the gray flannel suit was supposed to blend in, be a team player, and put the interests of the organization ahead of his individual desires. In exchange for giving his full loyalty to the organization, he was promised security and the prospect of moving up the ladder. In his 1956 study *The Organization Man*, William H. Whyte reserved his bitterest criticism for the personality tests that many postwar corporations administered to potential employees, decrying their spurious precision and assaults on privacy. He attached an appendix to his book, "How to Cheat on Personality Tests," advising test-takers to give conventional answers, to say that they love their wife and children but don't let them get in the way of company work, that they rarely worry, and that they don't care much for books or music. Conformity to conventional expectations was the route to success.[57]

Wilson's book, like other classic works of postwar suburban fiction, including Richard Yate's *Revolutionary Road* (1961), John Updike's *Rabbit, Run* (1960), and John Cheever's *Bullet Park* (1969) feature unfulfilled, self-loathing protagonists, bored, frustrated wives, dissatisfying, undemanding jobs, and loveless, emotionally detached marriages. These books dealt with a particular generation of men, born in the 1920s, who grew up during the Great Depression and fought in World War II, commuted to work from their suburban houses, and experienced ennui and a yearning for something that they can't identify. In these books, alcohol and adultery become tools for dealing with the spiritual emptiness, emotional malaise, and banal consumerism of their lives. Meanwhile, seminal works of nonfiction, such as David Reisman's *The Lonely Crowd* (1950) and Whyte's *The Organization Man*, offered blistering critiques of the bureaucratic offices in which the men in gray flannel suits worked. "Fitting in" and "getting along" had become the virtues most in demand. Conventionality, including a supportive family, was a job requirement. Far from places of entrepreneurial daring and dynamism, postwar corporations had become preserves of mediocrity, favoring an ethic of loyalty, security, and belonging.[58]

In recent television shows like *Mad Men*, the postwar organization man has become an object of nostalgia. No longer do employees assume that they will spend their careers with a single company; nor are employees as willing to accept corporate transfers. But today's corporate workplace represents both an extension of and a reaction against the world of the organization man. On the one hand, the emphasis on human relations, associated with the pioneering industrial psychologists and management theorists Hugo Münsterberg and Elton Mayo, with its stress on morale, group dynamics, workplace harmony, and communication, persists. On the other hand, the critique of organizational sclerosis has been strongly embraced, as corporations have come to accept the argument of analysts like Whyte, who claimed that conformism and groupism made it difficult to innovate, change institutional procedures, or encourage creative thinking. Today's corporations, with their flattened hierarchies and their emphasis on leanness, flexibility, and just-in-time management, encourage a fundamentally different set of values: an ethic of adaptability, entrepreneurship, and job hopping.[59]

In short, the organization man has become an anachronism and an artifact from an earlier era. Radical reductions in the ranks of middle management have been accompanied by a shift in values, with initiative, flexibility, risk-taking, and entrepreneurship the qualities looming largest. A social contract in which corporations promised secure, steady employment and promotions in exchange for employee loyalty and hard work has broken down, and today's high levels of productivity are motivated as much by fear of layoffs as by hopes of advancement.[60]

Even in the heyday of the male breadwinner family, significant numbers of women worked inside or outside a home. As recently as 1960s, however, working women were concentrated in an extremely limited range of jobs, as maids, store clerks, receptionists, bookkeepers, or, if professionals, as librarians, teachers, and nurses. Certain jobs became paradigmatic of women's work. Among the most notable was employment as secretaries. Until the late nineteenth century, the office was the preserve of men, who served as bookkeepers, copyists, clerks, and office boys. But as family-run companies and partnerships gave way to large enterprises with customers and suppliers spread over vast distances, there was a growing need for workers to manage files and letters. During the six-decade span from 1870 to 1930, clerical work was redefined as women's work. From just 2,000 female clerical workers in 1870, the figure rose to 214,000 in 1900, 1.4 million in 1920, and 2 million in 1930. Gender segregation became a defining feature of office work, as women were largely excluded from business schools and executive positions, and confined to secretarial jobs involving typing or personnel management.[61]

Rather than displacing men, women took jobs created by new forms of communication, accounting, and record keeping. For insurance companies, banks, mail-order businesses, and manufacturing firms, women entered payroll data, tracked records, kept accounts, and typed memos and reports. Department stores, like Macy's, depended on female workers to check inventories and price goods. Women clerical workers were indispensable to the operation and coordination of large-scale business organizations.[62]

Women began to be associated with office work during the Civil War. In the 1850s, when Clara Barton, founder of the American Red Cross, worked temporarily in the U.S. Patents Office, the U.S. government employed only a handful of women. Indeed, when the Civil War erupted, not a single woman worked in a government office. But in 1862, a labor shortage in the Treasury Department led U.S. Treasurer Francis Elias Spinner to seek female clerks to cut, sign, and count Treasury bills. Soon, this example was followed by the Bureau of Internal Revenue and the Bureau of Engraving and Printing. The women received $600 a year, compared to the $1,200 to $1,800 for the men they replaced. The war generated a substantial number of widows and orphans desperate for work. To secure a government job, a woman had to gain the support of a man of political power. Many applied directly to President Abraham Lincoln.[63]

Almost as soon as women entered public offices, allegations of sexual harassment arose. In 1864, twenty of the female Treasury employees sent affidavits to the House Committee in the District of Columbia testifying "that they could only get their places, or hold them, by yielding to the embraces of the said gentleman (a Mr. S. M. Clark)." In a letter to his wife, the Capitol's architect, Thomas Ustick Walter wrote, "The corruptions of this place are dreadful; I cannot understand how any body can like to live here; it is a perfect Sodom." As it was, the gentleman named Clark received no punishment.[64]

The invention of the typewriter served as a catalyst for the widespread entry of women into clerical positions. After more than thirty failed attempts, dating back to the 1820s, to devise a mechanical device capable of producing characters similar to printer's type, E. Remington and Sons, a manufacturer of sewing machines, began to sell the first commercially successful typewriter in 1874. Remington's sales rose from 1,200 in 1881 to half a million in 1900.

The invention of the typewriter coincided with a vast increase in the amount of paperwork companies generated. Because a skilled typist could type ninety to one hundred words a minute, compared to the fastest hand writer, who could produce only about sixty-five words a minute, because carbon paper made it easy to duplicate documents, and because female typists earned half to two-thirds of their male counterparts, female clerical workers quickly became a staple of business offices.[65]

The 1910s opened office work to women on a large scale. Women could be paid significantly less than men with equivalent educations, and since most worked only temporarily, there was little threat of unionization. For many young women, especially high school graduates from middle-class homes, clerical work, like teaching and, to a lesser extent, nursing, offered a respectable and relatively remunerative work option, with conditions far better than those available elsewhere. Meanwhile, advertisers and movie makers associated office work with glamour and romance, portraying the secretary as resourceful, youthful, and fun-loving. The $6 to $15 a week earned by clerical workers was far more than the $2 to $5 a week earned by domestic servants or the $1.50 to $8 earned by female factory operatives. Many young women regarded clerical work as a route to upward mobility and as a far more attractive way than domestic service or factory work to achieve financial independence from parents. The daughters of immigrants viewed office work as a symbol of Americanization.

Part of the appeal of clerical work was non-economic; it proved relatively easy for female clerical workers to change jobs. But for most, discouraged by low pay and limited opportunities for advancement, the work proved to be a temporary way station prior to marriage. In fact, many companies fired female employees who married.[66]

Office work was as heavily influenced by the efficiency movement known as Taylorism on the factory floor. Managers and executives developed elaborate office hierarchies that were supposedly based on skill, but were in fact stratified by age, marital status, and nationality. Immigrants were assigned to stenographer pools; women who stayed in office work past their twenties became personnel managers (since women were regarded as natural psychologists), accountants, private secretaries, or supervisors. During the early and mid-twentieth century, African American women found clerical employment only in civil service offices and black-owned businesses.[67]

Of all the jobs that have come to symbolize the growth in women's employment, one stands out: Rosie the Riveter, the archetype of women workers in wartime. World War II offered unprecedented opportunities for married women to work outside the home and the office. It provided an unmatched chance to redefine gender roles and relations. In 1940, about a quarter of all white women and almost 40 percent of all black women were in the paid labor force. But only 15 percent of married women were working for wages. By the end of the war, about two-thirds of adult women, and over half of married women, had worked outside the home. In contrast to World War I, in which most women workers in defense industries were immigrants or African Americans—operating drill presses and milling machines; assembling rifles, fuses, and detonators; loading powder into hand grenades; working in food processing plants; and stitching covers for airplane wings—World War II attracted a broader range of the female population. The "Rosie the Riveters" were not of a single type. Women workers included large numbers of African Americans, Latinas, former housewives, and older women. In such traditionally male-dominated industries as shipbuilding and automotive manufacturing, employers segregated women war workers into distinct job categories. Although the U.S.

government called on women to join the workforce, provisions for child care were extremely limited. There was no American counterpart to the British policies, which created food kitchens to cook meals for women workers and accommodated women workers' need for time to shop. During the war, government policy at once encouraged and restricted women's access to jobs. It also conveyed a powerful message that married women's participation in the workforce was meant to be temporary. With her penciled eyebrows and muscled forearms, Norman Rockwell's image of Rosie the Riveter underscores the dual-edged message that women received about wartime employment: Women were told that it was patriotic to work, but that this would not come at the expense of their femininity. Popular magazines, too, sought to reassure women that they need not choose between employment and traditional femininity. The dominant cultural definition of woman's place remained marriage and family-oriented. Stories in popular magazines targeted at working-class women, such as *True Romance*, often featured romances between young women workers and white-collar bosses, treating wartime labor as a step to upward mobility and marriage. Wartime films, in contrast, presented a more ambiguous picture. Alongside "maternal dramas" like *Mrs. Miniver* (1942), which portrayed female power and bonding in a positive light within the context of domesticity, there were "career women comedies," like *Woman of the Year* (1942) and *Adam's Rib* (1949), which dramatized the conflict between femininity and achievement and portrayed female independence and egalitarian marriages in a positive light, as well as "films of suspicion and mistrust," like *Gaslight* (1944) and *A Letter to Three Wives* (1949), which depicted gender antagonism.[68]

When the war was over, about 50 percent of the women in war production wanted to keep working, but were either replaced by men or demoted to lower-paying "women's" jobs. Messages from government and popular media encouraged women to step aside and reassume the roles of mother and housewife. In one characteristic story in the *Saturday Evening Post*, a woman gladly shifts from serving as an airplane pilot to working as a stewardess. If, on the one hand, women's World War II work experience altered women's self-image, providing a heightened sense of their own

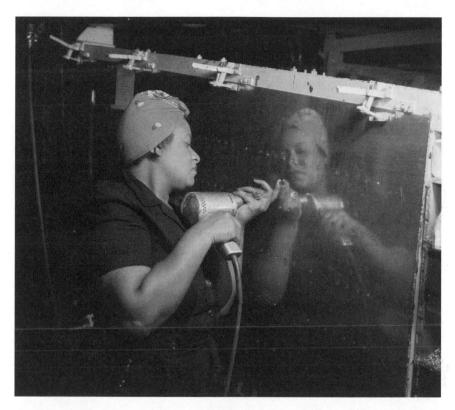

6.4. Woman working on a Vengeance dive bomber, 1942. Photograph by
Alfred T. Palmer.

worth that carried over into their later lives, it also did not lead to a fundamental redefinition of gender and family roles.[69]

Another obstruction to women's shift from full-time housewife to salaried worker has been the expectation that they should take responsibility
for most household chores, care of children, and maintaining emotional
relationships with relatives and family friends. Inflexible workplaces, which
expect well-paid employees to be on-call at all times and available to work
overtime and relocate if a job requires, often prove incompatible with cultural norms of childrearing and caregiving. Some women responded to
this expectation by pursuing the "mommy track," a career path in which
a woman sacrifices opportunities for promotion and raises in order to

devote more time to domestic responsibilities. Others resort to part-time jobs. Addressing work-family conflict not only requires men to assume greater responsibility for housework and childcare, but family-friendly workplace policies including flexible scheduling, job sharing, telecommuting, and paid family leaves. Workplace cultures still tend to link compensation and promotions to a particular definition of the ideal worker and in terms of gender roles, which still tend to privilege men as primary breadwinners whose work responsibilities take precedence over caregiving roles.[70]

Today, women are twice as likely as men to work part-time. More than one woman in four holds a part-time job, and a significant majority of working mothers report a preference for part-time work as the only way to balance their roles and responsibilities. In fact, women were at the forefront in the growth of part-time work, a development that has radically reshaped the employment landscape. Part-time and temporary employment and independent contracting have become hallmarks of the "new" economy. Temp workers, contract workers, contingent workers, adjuncts, interns, freelancers, and other independent contractors, who now constitute close to 10 percent of the workforce, allow businesses to reduce their fixed costs, quickly adjust the size of their workforce in response to shifts in economic conditions, and transfer the costs of unemployment insurance, workman's compensation, and employee benefits to staffing agencies or the workers themselves.[71]

The pioneers in the rise of temporary employment were staffing companies such as Kelly Girls, originally founded as Russell Kelly Office Service in 1947, and Manpower Inc., established in 1948. Prior to World War II, commercial employment agencies (which first appeared around 1890) and other labor recruiters and contractors had a reputation as highly abusive, charging excessive fees, misrepresenting job opportunities, and colluding with employers to keep wages low. To combat that image and forestall opposition from labor unions, the new staffing agencies exploited gender stereotypes, popularizing the image of the "Kelly Girl," a respectable housewife who worked part-time or temporarily to earn "pin money" or to lead a more fulfilling life. Even though the companies employed large numbers of men from the beginning, the temp agencies claimed to focus on providing temporary replacements for female clerical workers who were sick or on vacation.[72]

Temporary staffing agencies contributed to a shift in cultural values, helping to normalize and legitimate part-time and temporary work as an acceptable form of employment. Rejecting the view that was dominant between the 1920s and 1960s and held that part-time workers were inefficient and employee turnover should be discouraged, a new mindset stressed the disadvantages of permanent, full-time workers. One 1971 Kelly Girl ad underscored this mindset, holding up the temp worker as less expensive, easier to manage, and less difficult to terminate than a full-time employee.

> [She] never takes a vacation or holiday. Never asks for a raise. Never costs you a dime for slack time. (When the workload drops, you drop her.) Never has a cold, slipped disc or loose tooth. (Not on your time anyway!) Never costs you for unemployment taxes and social security payments. (None of the paperwork, either!) Never costs you for fringe benefits. (They add up to 30% of every payroll dollar.) Never fails to please. (If our Kelly Girl employee doesn't work out, you don't pay. We're that sure of all our girls.)

The staffing agency was responsible for hiring, firing, payroll, assigning, and compensating the employee, freeing companies from worries about employee health insurance or retirement plans, threats of unionization, unemployment taxes, workers' compensation claims, and responsibility for checking on workers' citizenship status. In a volatile, highly competitive economy, the pitch that full-time employees were a costly headache proved highly attractive to a growing number of companies.[73]

Gradually, temporary employment expanded beyond the steno pool. The world's largest retailer, Walmart, which was founded in 1962, initially relied heavily on part-time women workers who were largely from conservative Protestant religious backgrounds and were resistant to unionization campaigns. By the 1970s, the largest increases in temporary jobs was in factories and warehouses, although the temp industry also provided substantial numbers of substitute teachers and information technology specialists, including computer programmers, systems analysts, and network engineers. Today, roughly 90 percent of corporations supplement their full-time staff with temporary employees.[74]

Evaluating the shift to a "flexible" workforce raises difficult challenges. On the one hand, many contingent and part-time jobs do not provide adequate salaries, benefits, or employee protections. Such jobs also, to some degree, reduce the number of available full-time positions. On the other hand, an indeterminate number of temporary and independent workers prefer contingent, part-time, and contractual work to traditional full-time employment, and a significant number of temp employees are subsequently hired full time. Temporary employment may also stabilize volatile labor markets, especially during times of economic uncertainty when companies are wary of expanding permanent employment. What one can say for certain is that the shift from an industrial to a service and information economy and the increase in global competition require workers to be entrepreneurial, flexible, and able to live with uncertainty and unpredictability.[75]

The nature of people's jobs not only affects their income but other essential facets of their lives: their relationship with their family, the time available for leisure, and their level of life satisfaction and stress, as well as their sense of agency, security, control, entitlement, and self-efficacy. A landmark study begun in 1923 underscores that elemental fact. In that year, sociologists Helen and Robert Lynd set out to study the effects of new technologies and new consumer goods and services — ranging from furnaces, telephones, vacuum cleaners, and washing machines, to automobiles, cigarettes, installment credit, radio, and the movies — upon American life. With support from John D. Rockefeller's Institute of Social and Religious Research, the Lynds focused on Muncie, Indiana, a town of 38,000 about fifty miles northeast of Indianapolis, and spent fifteen months documenting how the city's residents earned a living, socialized their young, practiced religion, spent their leisure time, and engaged in community activities. The Lynds published their findings as *Middletown: A Study in American Culture* in 1929. It drew nationwide attention and went through six printings, selling over 30,000 copies — a remarkable number for a work of social science.[76]

The Lynds most important conclusion involved the salience of social class. Class divisions underlay differences in every sphere of life: family patterns, childrearing practices, leisure activities, religious affiliation, levels of political involvement, and even attitudes toward race and ethnicity. Over 70 percent of the city's adult men—largely factory and construction workers—were members of the working class with the remainder belonging to the business class. Nearly half of the working-class wives worked for wages full time, compared to scarcely any business-class wives, 90 percent of whom had paid help and 33 percent of whom had full-time servants. Lacking substantial savings or unemployment insurance, insecurity, transience, and family instability characterized working-class life. Yet this social cleavage did not produce class antagonism. Indeed, one of the Lynds' key themes involved the decline after 1890 of an organized, politically conscious working class.[77]

An unexpected and especially striking finding involved the extent of instability among working-class families. The divorce rate in Muncie—forty-seven per one hundred marriages in 1920, fifty per one hundred in 1925, and fifty-four per one hundred in 1928—was about six times the national average and higher than Hollywood's. Later research confirmed that the high divorce rate was not the product of statistical error. Rather, it suggested the published state and national divorce statistics of the 1920s might be far too low.[78]

In recent years, stark class divisions in marital patterns and childrearing methods have again attracted national attention. A particular source of concern involves differences in marriage rates and labor force participation. Among those aged thirty to forty-nine in the blue-collar community, 84 percent were married in 1960 and only 48 percent in 2010. In 1962, 96 percent of children were living with both biological parents; by 2004, the proportion was 37 percent. Meanwhile, the share of households with someone working at least forty hours a week dropped from 81 percent in 1960 to 60 percent in 2008.[79]

After a prolonged period, stretching from World War II to the early 1970s, when working-class and middle-class patterns appeared to be converging, differences have since widened. Initially, the driving force appeared to be economic; adjusted for inflation, entry-level wages of male high school graduates fell 23 percent after 1973. Pay in manufacturing, adjusted for inflation, also fell sharply. Meanwhile, access to benefits also fell. In 1980, 65 percent of recent high school graduates working in the private sector had health benefits, but by 2009, that was down to 29 percent. But if the divergence was originally rooted in economics, it began to take on a life of its own, as disparities in nonmarital births, labor force participation, and approaches to childrearing widened, abetted by increasing residential segregation by class.[80]

~~~

Compared to people in many other societies, Americans have been more prone to think of work as a positive good—not simply as a livelihood, but as a calling, a craft, a career, or a source of identity, personal fulfillment, and social connection. Yet decades before the Civil War, a stinging critique of modern work—as a form of wage slavery, as dehumanizing, and as a soulless, mindless, and ultimately meaningless source of alienation—had arisen. In recent years, however, the critique of work has declined, although a handful of books continue to betray a yearning for meaningful work that a person can take pride in. Matthew B. Crawford's 2009 bestseller, *Shop Class as Soulcraft*, is only the latest in an extensive series of books, including Alain de Botton's *The Pleasures and Sorrows of Work* (2009), Richard Sennett's *The Craftsman* (2008), and Robert Pirsig's 1974 philosophically informed road novel, *Zen and the Art of Motorcycle Maintenance*, which give vivid expression to the frustrations, emptiness, and dissatisfaction of the contemporary workplace. These books decry the devaluing of skilled manual labor, the mind-numbing, soul-draining pointlessness of paper pushing, the sense that much work has no tangible result, and a call for a return to the craftsman ideal, the notion that material objects should be judged by their beauty and by the way they were produced, with carefully acquired skill and close attention to detail.[81]

The hunger for fulfilling and rewarding work initially arose in response to the introduction of the factory system. It received added impetus in reaction to the turn-of-the-century movement for scientific management associated with Frederick Winslow Taylor, with its emphasis on increased efficiency and productivity. This craving for meaningful labor found tangible expression in the late-nineteenth-century arts and crafts movement. A reaction against the impersonality, abstraction, and fragmentary nature of modern work was also apparent in the post–World War II rage for hobbies, such as woodworking.[82]

As early as 1911, the "father of industrial psychology," Hugo Münsterberg, called on managers to pay greater attention to issues of fatigue, monotony, work satisfaction, and rewards. Especially influential was Elton Mayo, who, in 1933, urged employers to pay greater attention to human relations in the workplace and to treat employees not as commodities but as human capital. More recent managerial strategies, such as team-building and Total Quality Management, a set of practices advanced by the statistician W. Edwards Deming to involve all employees in a process of continuously improving quality, productivity, and customer satisfaction, can be understood, in part, as efforts to encourage workers to feel a sense of agency, integration, adjustment, and teamwork. Displays of anger, which had been common in seventeenth- and eighteenth-century workplaces as a way to enforce workplace hierarchies, were to be suppressed. By the 1960s, anger, which had been viewed as a sign of manliness, came to be regarded as inappropriate, especially as growing numbers of women entered the workforce. It also could be illegal if it contributed to a hostile workplace environment.[83]

As industrial psychologists have long understood, Americans seek something more from work than a paycheck. Work has long been regarded as the vehicle for pursuing the American dream. Few phrases hold greater allure for Americans than the "American dream." The phrase originated in a popular 1931 work of history entitled *The Epic of America*, in which the author, James Truslow Adams, insisted that across the span of American history, people's behavior had been motivated by the dream of a better, richer, happier life. "Ever since we became an independent nation," he wrote, "each generation has seen an uprising of Americans to save that dream from the forces which appear to be overwhelming it."[84]

Ambiguous, but highly evocative, the phrase quickly caught the popular imagination. At various times, the phrase has carried a diversity of meanings. It has referred to upward class mobility, as personified by Benjamin Franklin, Abraham Lincoln, and Frederick Douglass. It has also referred to the more modest, mundane aspirations for home ownership and achieving the good life. During the civil rights era, Martin Luther King invoked the concept in his appeal for full equality of opportunity. In today's celebrity culture, the phrase has become associated with overnight fame and fortune, acquired without substantial effort.[85]

At the heart of the American dream lies a belief in individual agency: that each person has the power to mold her or his destiny, to pursue a personal dream, and to rise as far as talent and hard work will allow. Yet precisely because the phrase suggests limitless possibility, it raises the specter of frustration and disappointment. In a 1906 letter to H. G. Wells, William James called "the exclusive worship of the bitch-goddess SUCCESS" "our national disease." Like many later critics of American materialism, James thought Americans had a tendency to confuse the pursuit of financial success with the pursuit of happiness, personal fulfillment, and social acceptance.[86]

Failure, downward mobility, and inequality of opportunity are the inverse side of the American dream. Failure, however, has been far more common than success. One late-nineteenth-century observer claimed that 97 percent of American businesses failed. A go-getter culture of incessant striving celebrates the self-made man and regards the effort to improve oneself as a moral obligation. But what of the losers, the wastrels, the failures, the good for nothings, the ne'er do wells, the feckless, the plodders? They are derided as idlers, loafers, lazybones, free loaders, and slackers. In a nation that lionizes financial success and deifies the entrepreneurial spirit, failure has long been a source of shame and stigma. As Ralph Waldo Emerson wrote in his journal in 1846: "nobody fails who ought not to fail. There is always a reason, in the man, for his good or bad fortune."[87]

In the nineteenth century, failure was frequently traced to character flaws, to an absence of habits of industry and a lack of manliness, virility, and the "potent spirits." Shopkeepers took a particular interest in morality, not necessarily for religious or ethical reasons but because it was catastrophic for them to be bilked. Trust, moral rectitude, punctuality, prudence, and self-control were viewed as essential. In the twentieth century, in contrast, failure was attributed to personality weaknesses, especially a lack of persistence and determination. "Men succeed or fail . . . not from accident or external surrounds," a newspaper claimed in 1856, but rather from "possessing or wanting the elements in themselves." The diagnoses of failure, once limited to extravagance and an excess of ambition, now encompassed under-reaching as well as overreaching: idleness, sloth, and deficits in masculine drive.[88]

The notion that failure is a moral inadequacy has a long history. During the seventeenth century, ministers such as Cotton Mather and Samuel Moody regarded debt, in and of itself, as immoral. Over the course of the eighteenth century, a growing swath of the free population acquired debt, often to purchase consumer goods from Britain. The 1780s was a decade of particular volatility as British merchants flooded the American market with cheap consumer goods, and growing numbers of free white male Americans speculated in bank shares, banknotes, federal and state currencies, and land. In the late eighteenth century, insolvent merchants described themselves as "wholly unmanned," their reputation tarnished, their masculinity imperiled. Even then, a highly volatile market economy threatened to transform a respectable merchant or master craftsman into a "vile," "debased" "rogue." In a patronage society, in which personal connections were a primary source of short-term credit, loss of reputation was far more significant than it is today. Credit ultimately depended on confidence in a debtor's ability to pay. Business failure was commonly blamed on deception, indiscretion, and dishonesty.[89]

At a time when legal notions of limited liability and bankruptcy were not yet well-developed, a shipwreck, a fire, or an unexpected economic downturn could thrust a trader, speculator, or artisan into a debtor's prison, force the sale of his family's property, and cause a host of associates to default on their loans. In this context, business failure was described in intensively personal, moral terms. To go bankrupt was not merely to suffer a financial reversal, it was to be regarded as a deceitful knave or a despicable villain, who had betrayed his "friends" (a word that was widely used the eighteenth century to refer to one's patrons, clients, and kin). In an economy that depended heavily on trust, a reputation for honesty and reliability was indispensable. Debtors' prisons institutionalized a highly negative attitude toward debt. Everyone from pickpockets to vicious murderers was incarcerated in these squalid prisons, but unlike lawbreakers, debtors had to pay for their own food, fuel, and clothing.[90]

In the wake of the American Revolution, a host of innovative legal procedures, financial instruments, credit bureaus, and insurance policies greatly expanded the availability of credit, and thereby encouraged investment and risk-taking. Meanwhile, land grants to revolutionary war veterans and the proliferation of country banks fueled speculation in land. A by-product was the involvement of a growing proportion of the free population in a web of credit and debt. Among the innovations designed to increase the availability of credit and promote commerce were bills of exchange, book credits, fiat money, promissory notes, and tobacco and cotton warehouse receipts. The central, state, and local governments further facilitated trade and investment by issuing various kinds of currencies, bonds, and land titles while private entities distributed literally millions of dollars' worth of banknotes, checks, stock certificates, savings receipts, and mortgages. Yet while these new financial instruments stimulated investment, they also carried considerable economic risk and contributed to increased economic volatility. The economic life of members of the nineteenth century middle class was extremely precarious. Economic failure for a single individual often meant woe for an extended family, especially when other family members had loaned the lost capital. In 1841, about 1 percent of the adult white male population filed for bankruptcy.[91]

In the nineteenth century, moralists urged debtors to face up to their financial problems "manfully." One scholar estimates that about 40 percent of bankrupts altogether lost their proprietary independence, while another 40 percent were able to bounce back successfully and join the growing ranks of the free-labor, wage-earning class or the white-collar, salaried middle class. Many debtors adopted creative strategies to deal with their debts, transferring assets to their wives, giving relatives illegal priority over other creditors, and engaging in forms of check fraud in which two failing businessmen would endorse each other's notes.[92]

As the pace of commerce accelerated, the opportunities for bankruptcy increased and prompted recurrent efforts to reduce the risk of business failure. Alexis de Tocqueville was struck by the extent to which the United States condoned bankruptcy. In stark contrast to the system that prevailed in Britain, it was far easier for American debtors to discharge their obligations to creditors. The United States became the land of the second chance. Prior to the Civil War, Congress twice passed short-lived national bankruptcy laws, in 1800 and 1841. State and federal legislation enabled debtors as well as creditors to initiate bankruptcy proceedings, which unlike those in Britain, applied to merchants, artisans, and agricultural enterprises. By the mid-nineteenth century, Americans were increasingly of two minds about failure. Even as the older notion of failure as a personal flaw or weakness persisted, so, too, did another idea arise: namely, that debt was an inevitable consequence of an economy stressing risk-taking and entrepreneurial striving. The abolition of imprisonment for debt epitomized a shift in attitudes toward debt, which became increasingly (though never fully) divorced from morality and more closely tied to conceptions of a liberal economy.[93]

To reduce the risks of a credit-based economy, the first credit rating agencies appeared by the 1840s to assess individuals' credit worthiness. A pioneer in this area, the reformer Lewis Tappan, asked associates in the antislavery movement to report on the moral character and financial prospects of men doing business in their communities. Tappan subsequently turned to more reliable sources of information, including lawyers and bank cashiers, who received an anonymous code number and earned a percentage of any debt collected from local bankrupts. The reports were pointed: "I understand he has no energy & will never make a dollar, I reckon," reads one entry on a merchant felled by the panic of 1857. Another entry reported on a "h[a]rd drinker" who would nonetheless "make money anywhere," but then cautioned that "you can't tell where 'Rum' will take a man"; "visionary in his ideas," lamented the report on a brilliant inventor, but "a poor bus[iness]man . . . all his undertakings so far have been failures." Financial risk also encouraged the rise of salaried white-collar employment, especially following the depressions that recurred roughly every twenty years during the nineteenth century.[94]

Today, bankruptcy remains common. In every year since 1990, business and personal bankruptcies have exceeded 500,000. In the early twenty-first century, more people filed for bankruptcy each year than either graduated from college, got divorced, or were diagnosed with cancer. In instances like these, the American dream has become a nightmare. Nor is bankruptcy confined to the poor or the lower middle class. In terms of income, education, and assets, those who declare bankruptcy resemble those who do not. In the overwhelming majority of instances, bankruptcy is not the result of excessive credit-card spending, irresponsible purchases of luxury items, dishonesty, or fraud. Instead, it arises when adults stretch themselves to buy a home in a desirable neighborhood; then, almost any setback, including a severe illness, an accident, divorce, or a layoff, can result in serious financial hardship. With most household income committed to housing, car payments, child care, insurance, and other fixed expenses, families are ill-equipped to cope financially when unforeseen events strike. Bankruptcy, far from providing an easy solution to economic difficulties, often results in a host of detrimental social and psychological effects, including family relocation, loss of family possessions, a more negative outlook on life, increased levels of marital discord, family conflict, and agonizing bouts of depression and self-blame.[95]

In a 1983 cover story, *Time* magazine announced the dawn of a new economy. In contrast to the old economy, which rested upon heavy industry, construction, mass communication, marketing, and distribution, the new economy was based on knowledge, services, and technology and was far more personalized. Disruptive innovation was a defining feature of the new economy. In industry after industry, new entrants and discounters threatened the dominance of established firms. Mounting pressures from foreign competitors and from investors seeking rising stock prices pushed companies to become more agile. The Internet allowed aggressive startups to devastate the business models of such established industries as journalism, publishing, recorded music, and retailing, while improvements in communication and shipping sharply increased competition in the manufacturing and financial sectors by facilitating the global flow of goods, services, and investment capital. Innovative applications, software, and procedures challenged incumbent technologies and business processes.[96]

Distinguishing features of the new economy include an increase in outsourcing of jobs to subcontractors, heightened reliance on consultants, and extensive use of contingent, contract, and part-time workers. To maximize productivity and efficiency, companies have hollowed out the ranks of middle management. These developments have had profound consequences for adults' lives. Those with college degrees and especially with postgraduate education receive a substantial wage premium, while those with less education see their earnings stagnate. For those with executive or creative responsibilities, work hours have lengthened, but for many in lower paid sectors of the service economy, hours have become less predictable, jobs less secure, and earnings more volatile Digital communications have also eroded the sharp division between work and "life," which had begun to emerge during the early nineteenth century.[97]

The shift to the new economy has left many adults feeling anxious and insecure. It has also put large numbers at risk, forcing them to depend on themselves as corporate supports have been removed. In a highly fluid economy, where fewer employees can expect to spend their adult lives in the same industry, let alone the same company, individuals are expected to act like entrepreneurs, acquiring new skills, identifying and pursuing opportunities, and navigating a rapidly evolving economic landscape. Households that depend on two incomes may do well when both partners are working, but are highly vulnerable when one is laid off. The drift away from defined benefit pension plans, which guaranteed a steady monthly retirement income, to individually managed 401(k) plans, has made pensions more portable and given employees greater control over their investments, but also exposed workers to greater risks. In health care, too, individuals have had to assume greater responsibility and to manage medical savings accounts, co-pays, deductibles, and multiple health plan options made individuals. Relatively few adults are insulated from the risks posed by the new economy. Although the official poverty rate stands in the mid teens, a far higher proportion of Americans moves in and out of poverty over time. Altogether, roughly four out of five American adults are unemployed, near or below the poverty line, or dependent on welfare at some point in their lives.[98]

Why is it, Arthur Miller asked in 1949, shortly after the debut of *Death of a Salesman,* that contemporary novelists and playwrights write so few tragedies? He attributed this dearth to a misplaced belief that tragedy requires a figure of renown, a character of high rank and inherent nobility, who is brought low by a tragic flaw or an error in judgment. Miller's argument was that the pedestrian pathos of everyday American life was as worthy a subject of tragedy as the travails of the eminent. This, he maintained, was the case even when an ordinary American, witless and insensitive, failed to achieve the depth of psychological understanding that was an essential element in an Aristotelian definition of tragedy.[99]

In a nation of hard-headed, ambitious, dollar-worshipping pragmatists and wistful, romantic dreamers, the most profound tragedies, Miller suggested, involved individuals' inability—whether due to overwhelming circumstances or personal weakness and faults—to attain their expansive dreams and ambitions. By the standards of high tragedy, their plight was pathetic rather than tragic. But in Miller's views, the democratic strivings of ordinary adults are as deserving of respect as the misfortunes of the high bred. Indeed, these everyday calamities are all the more tragic since in today's highly competitive, globalized economy no one is shielded from sudden or unexpected loss of a job or reversals of fortune. Making matters worse, Americans today, as in Miller's time, largely reject the idea that success and failure are determined by outside forces. Instead, adults are far more likely to blame their failures upon themselves and to experience failure as a matter of personal shame and humiliation. In a society in which adults think of themselves as the authors of their own success and possess the highest aspirations for achievement and upward mobility in any highly developed society, great expectations are especially likely to lead to the great disappointments.[100]

CHAPTER SEVEN

The Angst of Adulthood

In 1869, two American neurologists, George M. Beard and Edwin H. Van Duesen, identified a disorder that they claimed was uniquely prevalent in the United States. Termed "neurasthenia," the ailment consisted of an array of chronic symptoms ranging from lethargy and melancholia to male impotence and amenorrhea (the absence of menstruation). Beard and Van Duesen attributed neurasthenia to the anxiety, fatigue, and nervous exhaustion brought on by the fast pace and stresses of urban life and the instability and competitiveness of the American economy. It was also related, in Beard's view, to unsettling changes in the nature of work, notably the rise of "brain work," and radical shifts in gender roles, including a sharp increase in "the mental activity of women." "All of this is modern, and originally American," Beard declared, "and no age, no country, and no form of civilization, not Greece, nor Rome, nor Spain, nor the Netherlands, in the days of their glory, possessed such maladies."[1]

Beard and Van Duesen were not alone in seeing American adults as especially anxiety-ridden. A generation earlier the French aristocrat Alexis de Tocqueville described a grim restlessness and a morose compulsiveness as defining features of the American character. From Henry David Thoreau through Erik Erikson and beyond, adulthood in the United States has been associated with a gnawing sense of anxiety, disquietude, loss, and malaise. During the twentieth century, the word commonly used to describe this intense yet amorphous sense of anxiety and inner turmoil was "angst." The first known use of the word in English occurred in an 1849 letter by the novelist George Eliot, written just five years after the Danish philosopher Søren Kierkegaard had used the term to refer to the unease that he considered a defining feature of the modern condition. In twentieth-century American popular culture, angst was commonly associated with the intensely self-conscious, easily embarrassed teenager, suffering from a generalized anger and abrupt mood swings. *Rebel Without a Cause* (1955), *Splendor in the Grass* (1961), *Dazed and Confused* (1993), and *Rushmore* (1998) were only the most notable examples of the popular films that contrasted adolescent angst and emotional volatility with the staid maturity of adulthood. Yet depression, mood disorders, and a generalized sense of anxiety are far more common among adults than among those in their teens. There is the angst of young adulthood, the feelings of loneliness, confusion, and fretfulness brought on by the stresses of maturation, as twenty-somethings seek to define who they are and navigate their way to a stable adult identity. Then there is the angst of midlife, the fretfulness, brooding, and wide-ranging sense of distress associated with parental death, marital conflict, job setbacks, financial strains, children leaving home, severe illness, or the symptoms of physical aging and declining cognitive functioning.

To speak of the angst of adulthood raises the specter of the "midlife crisis," a phrase introduced in 1965 by the Canadian psychoanalyst Elliott Jacques and popularized by Gail Sheehy's 1976 bestseller, *Passages: The Predictable Crises of Adult Life*. A confrontation with life's finitude and a recognition of the irretrievable loss of youth prompt dissatisfaction, stocktaking, confusion, and despair as the fantasies of young adulthood give way a more mundane realities. According to common cultural stereotypes, the midlife crisis often provokes an adulterous love affair, a divorce, or the purchase of a sports car as an adult seeks to recapture the hopefulness of youth. The crisis is often depicted as a narcissistic flight from responsibility, or, in somewhat contradictory fashion, as a daring attempt to achieve personal growth, pursue new relationships and new opportunities, and refuse to accept a stagnant status quo. In fact, the notion that midlife is a time of emotional turmoil and acting out is not a new one. Although the word "midlife" entered the English language only around 1895, a recognizably modern understanding of what it meant to be middle aged appeared decades earlier. Instead of being regarded as life's prime and associated with maturity and gravitas, or, conversely, as the start of senescence, in the mid-nineteenth century midlife was perceived as an age of loss. Women and men, in growing numbers, worried about bodily decline, a lack of physical and mental vigor, and, especially for women, absence of sexual desire. In such literary works as Frances Trollope's *The Widow Barnaby* (1839–1855), Anthony Trollope's *An Old Man's Love* (1884), Charlotte Brontë's *Shirley* (1849), and George Eliot's *Middlemarch* (1874), graying hair and crow's feet became outward symbols of internal decay. But if recognition of one's diminishing energies at times encouraged despair or disgust, it also might encourage a redirection of one's life course.[2]

As critics of the midlife crisis concept have pointed out, for substantial numbers of adults, the middle years are far from a period of emotional upheaval. Rather, for many, it is the time when relationships are most fulfilled and satisfying, finances most secure, and psychological well-being greatest. Many middle-aged adults report a greater sense of control over their jobs, relationships, and finances than at any other stage of life. Indeed, by some measures, adults at middle age are calmer and less irritable than those who are younger. But it is also true that the potential for stressful life events peaks during life's middle years as adults are challenged to juggle an excessive number of responsibilities in the home and workplace. Rather than referring to a "midlife crisis," it is helpful to speak of "midlife transitions," as individuals respond to a series of stresses ranging from maintaining troubled relationships, marital estrangement, or job loss as well as menopause and other physical signs of aging, the loss of parents, and children leaving home.[3]

The paradox of contemporary adulthood is that while, in many measurable ways, the quality of life has improved, the stresses of adulthood have not declined. Despite falling death rates and a higher material standard of living, even among the poor, the angst of adulthood has in many respects intensified. A more demanding work environment, an unstable economy, less secure intimate relationships, and, above all, mounting uncertainty about gender roles and expectations, have transformed adulthood into a truly liminal phase of life, a time of momentous challenge and anxiety.

~᙮~

Loss is an inevitable part of adulthood. We lose our youth, our looks, and our health. Parents die, friendships fade, marriages end, and children grow up, forging separate identities and independent lives. Job loss, absence of loved ones, and a host of setbacks and disappointments, however wrenching or traumatic, are integral and inevitable parts of growing older. For most adults, even our most intimate and significant emotional attachments prove impermanent, with fully half of marriages ending in divorce.[4]

If we are fortunate, some of our losses will contribute to our maturation, self-awareness, and psychological growth. They may lead us to shed dependencies, unrealistic expectations, and illusions, and thus to more effectively manage our lives. But some losses offer no solace. They may be irreversible and irretrievable, and in these instances we rely heavily on certain cultural values, conventions, and rituals in our struggle to cope.[5]

In a diary entry written in 1822, Susan Mansfield Huntington, the widow of the minister of Boston's South Church, described her reaction to reexamining the letters she had exchanged with her late husband. "Reading these letters," she wrote three years after his death, "(a thing which I never trusted myself to do before) seems to have revived all the exclusiveness & intensiveness of my love for him I once called husband. I am so filled with a sense of fearfulness of my loss & the awful chasm in my heart & affection that all on earth seems a void without him. 'I sit alone as a swallow upon the house top.'"[6]

Grieving is universal, but historical eras differ in the openness and intensity with which individuals express their grief and in the rapidity with which mourners are expected to reintegrate into everyday life. Rituals that surround mourning differ as do the links the living retain with the dead. At no point was grief expressed more publicly or with greater intensity than in the mid-nineteenth century, when deaths were much more common and less predictable than today, and when Romanticism valorized the display of extreme emotion. The lamentations that Alfred F. Armstrong, a Union soldier, expressed after his mother's death in 1863 were not atypical. "*'I am motherless!'* Oh! What an affliction. I can hardly sit still thinking of her all day."[7]

Distinct approaches to loss may be discerned in specific eras of American history. One, which predominated in colonial America, involved a studied resignation to God's will. Calvinist in inspiration, this perspective viewed loss as a heaven-sent affliction that reminds us not to overinvest in personal relationships. Calvinists taught believers that earthly attachments are invariably transitory, unlike one's relationship with God. Thus, losses should be accepted stoically. The more orthodox Calvinists opposed expensive burial customs and elaborate mourning and embalming as forms of idolatry. Death, for many American colonists, was as much an event of religious significance as a physical phenomenon, involving the separation of body and soul, escape from the mortal world of sin and toil, and, most important of all, divine judgment. Upon death, each person's depraved soul would be judged with no assurance of divine grace. No rituals or prayers or acts of piety could affect an individual's predestined fate. Despite admonitions for patient acceptance, many colonists experienced bitter spiritual torment in the face of death, since no one could be sure of the deceased's eternal fate, whether this would involve everlasting life in Heaven or the torments of never-ending damnation.[8]

Another response to loss, characteristic of the Victorian era, was profoundly sentimental. A cult of mourning found pointed expression in an outpouring of consolation essays, mourning manuals, and anthologies of death poetry. In contrast to their colonial forebears, nineteenth-century Americans held that grief should be openly, indeed ardently, expressed. Beginning in the early part of the century, mourning became highly ritualized as young women sewed weeping willows into memorial embroideries and made keepsake rings and jewelry out of locks of hair, while men wore pictures of lost loved ones in lockets.[9]

A product of the rise of liberal and evangelical Protestantism, this view regarded death as liberation from life's trials and tribulations, holding out the promise of eternal salvation and reunion with deceased loved ones in Heaven. Accompanying this altered view of death was a new attitude toward mourning. Demonstrative displays of emotion were greatly valued as an outward expression of inner sentiments. Nineteenth-century

America's sentimental culture regarded grief as the most sacred and significant of emotions, and, unlike the colonial era, tolerated much more effusive displays of attachment to a lost loved one. Grieving became (in Freud's words) "the only way of perpetuating that love which we do not want to relinquish."[10]

But mourning not only maintained the memory of the deceased; it was also seen to elevate and refine the mourner's sensibilities. "The most sacred of our social feelings," grief gave tangible expression to piety, fidelity, and the unbroken bonds of love. It was also the wellspring of sympathy and benevolence. As one minister put it: "When a river of love is suddenly checked in the heart by the death of a friend, it needs various channels to drain off the waters that otherwise must drown it in the suffocating agonies of repression. . . . [It] may turn to immediate acts of benevolence to human beings who may not know the depths of pain such love is wrung [from]." Victorian mourning rituals helped adults to share their grief and thus manage it.[11]

In stark contrast to the twentieth-century notion that mourners should achieve closure as quickly as possible, grieving, for much of the nineteenth century, was something to be prolonged and even cultivated. The narrator of Washington Irving's *Sketch Book* (1819) emphasized the value of perpetual mourning: "Where is the mother who would willingly forget the infant that perished like a blossom from her arms, though every recollection is a pang? . . . Where is the child who would willingly forget the most tender of parents, though to remember be but to lament?"[12]

Over time, the practices of sentimental bereavement and mourning became highly stylized and commercialized. The Victorian middle class defined exacting rules of etiquette and attire, from long black veils to jewelry made of hair, black-edged handkerchiefs, and lockets containing the loved one's image. Emotions, too, became subject to increasingly detailed and prescribed conventions, with the failure to display tearful expressions of grief considered unnatural. In the twentieth century, the Victorian emphasis on exaggerated displays of sorrow helped to provoke a strong reaction against excessive sentimentality as lugubrious, inauthentic, and even unhealthy.[13]

7.1. Charles Willson Peale, *Rachel Weeping*, 1772.

Thus, another approach to loss gained ground in the twentieth century, one that treated mourning as a psychological phenomenon needing to be alleviated and cured. Achieving closure became the new ideal. According to the emerging view, the function of grieving was to help individuals detach psychologically from the loved one as rapidly as possible, to accept the loss, and to move forward with their lives. Prolonged grieving and a failure to disconnect from the loss were considered a psychopathology requiring counseling or therapy. Freud's view that mourning involved ex-cruciatingly difficult "decathections" of emotions that had been invested into a loved one proved to be especially influential. The notion that the resolution of grief required a mourner to resolve feelings of remorse, guilt, and anger gradually took hold in popular culture. By the end of the twentieth century, the discourse of grieving and loss increasingly embraced the language of therapy, as psychologists and counselors began to speak of "healing" or "surviving" or "overcoming trauma."[14]

In actuality, mourners, across time periods, tend to retain bonds with the deceased. Moments of intense grief may grow less frequent over time, but do not disappear, and are often reactivated by an anniversary, a holiday, or a reminder. When viewed from a cross-cultural perspective, contemporary mainstream American culture is distinctive in its lack of communal mourning customs (such as the Irish wake or the Jewish *shiva*), and in the brief expected duration of an individual's grief. Loss and the ensuing pain are viewed as private and largely psychological phenomena, generally considered incommunicable and not shareable. Mourning itself is rarely experienced as communal and collective, but rather is treated as essentially self-therapeutic. Its purpose is to help the mourner to let go of the deceased and move on. This contrasts markedly with earlier eras when there were many efforts to sustain the memory of the deceased, often through memento mori, commemorative objects (such as the gloves or rings distributed at colonial New England funerals) that were symbolic reminders of the deceased. Even more noteworthy was the custom of naming newborns after recently deceased siblings. The names of children provided a living link to and ever-present reminder of the dead.

During the grieving process, a mourner must find a language to speak of the loss and construct a narrative that gives meaning to the now severed relationship. Before the twentieth century, this language was inextricably connected to religion. Death of a loved one was widely regarded as a spiritual test and an opportunity to reaffirm one's faith. Especially in the nineteenth century, hopes were expressed about the possibility of heavenly reunion in an afterlife. Many mourners looked to God for strength, and wrote that the loss brought them closer to grace and educated them about the brevity and evanescence of earthly life. In a diary entry written in 1846, William Brisbande reflected on the death of his teenaged son: "And now shall I have a reprising thought? God forbid. I would say to my soul, Peace, be still — and know that the judge of all the earth must do right. I cannot, I dare not wish him back. . . . O my Jesus! May from this hour be always thine, entirely thine!"[15]

Extracts from the diary of Sophia Lovick, written in 1897, after her baby's death, were not atypical. "Tears blind my eyes as I write. Oh my how sick he was, but now he is at rest, my little darling Jacob. Hope to meet you in heaven. God help me bear my sorrow." Yet for all the intensity of emotion expressed in such laments, certain feelings that would become commonplace during the twentieth century were not expressed, such as a pervasive sense of guilt or of remorse over words said or unsaid and emotions shared or unexpressed.[16]

In a society as diverse as the United States, mourning today takes many contrasting forms. Many Hispanic cultures commemorate the Day of the Dead and build private altars called *ofrendas* to honor the deceased. The altar area is decorated with photographs of the deceased, images of the Virgin Mary, flowers, and skulls made of sugar, all making concrete the death of the loved one. Among African Americans, mourning tends to be more communal and more enveloped in religion than among non-Hispanic whites. The church, rather than the therapist's office, is a primary source of solace. Deaths among African Americans are more likely to occur prematurely, and at funerals, emotional expression tends to be more demonstrative and less restrained. The loss is described not simply as a loss to the family, but to the community as a whole, and the individual's life is often cast as a struggle against various forms of oppression. Rather than something to be feared, death is often described as a passing over, as preparation for a life after death, which is promised to be more benign.[17]

The contrasting approaches to loss, characteristic of the seventeenth, eighteenth, nineteenth, and twentieth centuries, partly reflect shifts in the prevalence of death. Death in colonial America was an ever-present reality for the very young as for the elderly. During the seventeenth century, three out of every ten children died before the age of twenty-one, and it is not surprising that parents repeatedly reminded the young of the precariousness of life. Even in the middle of the nineteenth century, death remained commonplace. The death rate ranged from 2 to 6 percent of the population each year, compared to just 0.8 percent today, and many adults spent years dressed in funeral attire. For all of the Civil War's horrific bloodletting, the conflict increased the death rate only by about 10 percent.[18]

Responses to loss signaled a long-term transition from a culture of chance to a culture of control. Colonial Americans inhabited the very opposite world than one of medical logic or predictability. Women and men had a religious and realistic obligation to accept God's inscrutable will with a posture of deliberate, considered resignation. By the early nineteenth century, there was a mounting faith, nurtured by theology, philosophy, and science, in human agency and intervention. Older structures of meaning involving God's will that had enveloped death began to lose their grip, while new psychological understandings began to emerge. By the mid-twentieth century, the successes of medical science and technology had encouraged a belief that the world could be managed, risk eliminated, and fate mastered. Sickness and death could be diminished by medical science. Society offered some means of control over what had previously been seen as God's will. However, the success of human intervention also implied its failure. Such failure would now elicit emotions of anger, guilt, or frustration.[19]

Certain themes cut across these historically situated responses to loss. One is the unwelcome injunction to the bereaved to face up to the inexorable, inevitable reality of death. Loss, the bereaved are repeatedly told in every era, cannot be evaded or denied, and the retreat into some form of "magical thinking" cannot alleviate its pain. Another common rationale for loss is that it strengthens the spirit. For many seventeenth- and eighteenth-century Americans, loss seemed to offer an opportunity for spiritual growth, by helping individuals to shed worldly attachments. Spiritual growth, from this perspective, necessarily entailed personal pain. Beginning in the nineteenth century and intensifying in the twentieth, a more secular understanding of the supposed benefits of loss arose. Rejecting the older notions of loss as a test of faith and part of a larger, if inscrutable, good, and of God as a protective father who controls every aspect of life, this view saw acts of nature as arbitrary and independent of whether individuals were good or loving or faithful. Individuals can control only their response to loss and their behavior in the wake of it. Loss, in this perspective, is an integral part of everyone's life, and its acceptance plays a necessary role in maturation. It is the price one pays for caring and being connected to others and growing up. Yet, in all times, the conventions, customs, and understandings surrounding loss will never be sufficient to console and comfort the bereaved fully; nor can they adequately acknowledge the sorrow, anguish, and misery that have been experienced.[20]

For many staunch Calvinists, it proved impossible to maintain the attitude of resignation that their religion demanded. Bereaved parents pleaded with ministers, asking them to deny the doctrine of infant depravity upon the death of their baby. Nor did Victorian sentimentality provide sufficient solace or aid to accept the finality and permanence of loss. Spiritualism, which grew in popularity from the 1840s through World War I, sought to communicate between the living and dead and sustain the tie with the lost loved one. Prescribed words, emotions, and behaviors proved with time to be too inadequate for many and the idea of an eventual family reunion in heaven not sufficiently compelling to address a mourner's sorrow and pain.[21]

No approach to mourning, however, proved as isolating as the twentieth century's. Although scenes of violent death permeated popular culture, critics spoke, quite accurately, of a widespread "denial of death." A growing number of people died in hospitals away from the intimacy of home and separated from the intense emotion of family and friends. With the medicalization of death, elaborate formal mourning and consolation rituals largely disappeared. Mourning for a lost one became largely a private matter, with few appropriate ways to comfort the bereaved.[22]

Grieving, in and of itself, is not an illness to be cured. Loss needs to be acknowledged. Time does not, nor should it, mend all wounds. Some losses are indeed irreparable, and truly great sorrow never wholly

7.2. Widow and brother of the deceased grieving, Breathitt County, near Jackson, Kentucky, 1940. Photograph by Marion Post Wolcott.

diminishes. All we can hope is that the pain we suffer will make us more sensitive to the pain in other people's lives and more aware of the losses that lie at the heart of adulthood. This tragic vision, so profoundly at odds with the spirit of American optimism, is necessary if we are to truly appreciate the meaning and magnitude of loss. As Herman Melville wrote: "Enjoy the bright, keep it turned up perpetually if you can, but be honest, and don't deny the black." Yet, even with this acceptance, the importance of the comfort of others in dark times is one of the critical lessons of adulthood. Empathy for those in pain is a crucial aspect of maturity.[23]

Apart from the death of loved ones, adults must cope with other forms of loss. Some are physical, as youthful appearance or health fades. Others are personal, as children reach their teens and young adulthood and lead increasingly separate lives or as friendships end as a result of abrupt rifts or gradual separation. Still others are emotional, as illusions about marriage or family life and fantasies of personal success confront trying and intractable realities. For many adults, the most wrenching losses are psychological, as youthful dreams, expectations, and a sense of adequacy and possibility diminish. The result, often, is a profound and pervasive sense of regret.

Few adults are able to look back at their choices, actions, and dithering without feelings of self-judgment or sorrow. In her haunting signature 1960 song, "Non, Je Ne Regrette Rien," the great French vocalist Edith Piaf brushed aside her missteps and the betrayals and losses she had suffered. She declared that she "will have no regrets" over "all the things that went wrong," "for at last I have learned to be strong." But in a society that gives individuals many opportunities to choose their course in life, self-recrimination and regret are common to most, and in extreme form can become a debilitating source of depression.

Many classic poems and novels of adulthood end with words of regret. The timeless, if trite, refrain in John Greenleaf Whittier's "Maud Muller," written in 1856 is often repeated: "For all sad words of tongue or pen, The saddest are these: 'It might have been!'" Robert Frost's 1916 poem, "The Road Not Taken," too, is tinged with melancholy. The wistful, sardonic final phrase in Henry James's *The Wings of the Dove* — "We shall never be again as we were!" — is a timeless statement of the notion that each choice closes off future options. Then there is the cynical, bitter last line of Hemingway's *The Sun Also Rises* — "Isn't it pretty to think so" — with its lament that past choices and experiences are irretrievable.

To be sure, we are often told to stoically and fatalistically brush aside regret and recognize that certain things were meant to be and that matters generally work out for the best. But many studies, from the 1980s onward, have found that most adults report very high levels of regret. Indeed, regret, like loss, is a penalty one pays to be an adult capable of choice and decision. Acts and inactions, errors of commission and omission, leave a lasting sense of disappointment and remorse.

There is reason to think that our current cultural and historical context, with its surfeit of choices and opportunities, accentuates adult regrets. The most common involve sacrificing family relationships and friendships for work, or marrying too early or choosing the wrong partner or allowing a marriage to break down. Many adult regrets stem from a failure to live up to one's potential or self-image either by failing to take a risk or being passive when one should have acted straightforwardly. Social science surveys suggest that the deepest regrets stem from inaction, such as failing to achieve one's educational or career goals or to adequately fulfill the role of parent or spouse. In our contemporary culture of control, where each person is supposed to exercise dominion over her or his fate, regret is a vehicle for maintaining a sense of mastery. If one had made other choices and followed a different path, one's present life, presumably, would be happier and more fulfilled, but choices were made, and they have come to determine the present.[24]

If loss and regret are inevitable, and even necessary, parts of adulthood, so too is physical pain. Over half of adults suffer from one or more chronic health conditions, such as hypertension, coronary heart disease, diabetes, cancer, arthritis, hepatitis, weak or failing kidneys, pulmonary disease, or a serious respiratory problem. A third of adults aged forty-four to sixty-five have two or more chronic conditions. From the pangs of childbirth to the ravages of cancer, from migraine headaches to insomnia to arthritis, few, by late adulthood, escape the pains of aging and of disease.[25]

As with loss, society's approaches to pain have shifted profoundly over time. The American colonists viewed pain through a variety of lenses—as an inevitability, as punishment or curse, as a test or trial, as a reminder of the folly of investing too heavily in the worldly life, and as a pathway to redemption. By the mid-nineteenth century, new structures of meaning surrounded pain. Increasingly regarded as essentially physiological, pain was something to be treated and eased with an anesthetic or opiate or alcohol. In the twentieth century, pain, like loss, was psychologized and construed in scientific terms. Chronic pain, in rare instances, could be a spur to achievement, but more often it was viewed as devoid of broader cultural meaning or significance.[26]

Today, an estimated 20 percent of American adults suffer from chronic pain, and, according to some estimates, spend $100 billion annually to alleviate acute pain, from migraines to unbearable backaches. Alongside the excruciating aching, piercing, and burning sensation—the "terror that surpasses all description," as the English novelist, diarist, and playwright Fanny Burney wrote in 1812 following the removal of a breast abscess — is a sufferer's inability to accurately communicate pain's agonizing nature or to invest it with meaning. Even worse, suffering that lacks an obvious physical cause is often regarded as suspicious or psychosomatic.[27]

Prior to the mid-nineteenth century, pain was imbued with metaphysical meaning. There was the view of pain as merited retribution, evident in the Latin roots of the word, *poena,* which is generally translated as punishment. Then there was the spiritual view of pain as uplifting or transfiguring, the Romantic view of pain as something intense and even sublime, and the view of pain as transformative. A metaphysical conception of pain, that it is redemptive or merited, only slowly gave way to other views. Pain as redemptive or deserved helps explain why it took nearly a century before anesthesia was widely used to address the pangs of childbirth or to address other physical pains.[28]

Toward the middle of the nineteenth century, pain began to be desacralized and treated in secular and biological terms. Beginning with the use of ether in surgery in 1842, medicine sought various ways to relieve or manage pain. The discovery of anesthesia led an English periodical to announce: "We Have Conquered Pain." Pain, from this perspective, was best understood as the body's reaction to tissue damage. If the pain could be repressed and the tissue healed, pain would go away. This view gave rise to various palliatives that temporarily alleviated pain without dealing with an underlying cause; painkillers to prevent the pain from reaching consciousness; and sedatives to offer a soothing, calming, or tranquilizing effect.[29]

Especially influential were mind cures, which taught that right thinking contained healing powers. Originally popularized by a Maine philosopher, physician, and mesmerist named Phineas Parkhurst Quimby (1802–1866), mental healing profoundly influenced Mary Baker Eddy, the founder of Christian Science, and later faith healers. In the early twentieth-century United States, where the psychiatric profession was far weaker than in Europe, mind cures tapped into a widespread popular "can do" faith in willpower. This belief that mental powers and determination could triumph over any pain or obstacle is evident in the commitment to positive thinking espoused by the Reverend Norman Vincent Peale or, more recently, by positive psychology with its emphasis on grit as a key to success in life.[30]

Not simply a symptom of some readily identifiable physical damage, pain has a psychological and emotional dimension, which mind cure recognizes, but mistakenly believes can be addressed with healthy optimism and denial. In recent years, a neuropathic view of pain has arisen, which links chronic pain to profound changes in the functioning of the brain, the central nervous system, and sensory nerves, which must be addressed by changing patterns of perception and brain function, sometimes by using neuroimaging to help a patient alter the processing of neurons and nerve signaling.[31]

The association of adulthood with physical pains is longstanding. Much more recent is the linkage between adulthood and stress and anxiety, whether rooted in finances, work, interpersonal relationships, or responsibilities that seem overwhelming. Over the course of a lifetime, over a quarter of adults are diagnosed with an anxiety disorder, including obsessive-compulsive disorders, panic disorders, generalized anxiety disorders, phobias, or post-traumatic stress disorders. To cope with stress and anxiety, a third of adults take anxiety medications or sleeping pills. The most obvious sources of anxiety and stress are traumatic life events or crises: a divorce, a death in the family, job loss, or severe illness. Role changes, such as a marriage, a new job, or a new child, also contribute to anxiety and stress. Much more common, however, are the chronic or mundane hassles of life arising from the smaller pressures, irritations, and frustrations that build up day to day: health complaints, financial anxieties, negative interactions with spouses or children, job-related worries, care-giving responsibilities for aging parents, and traffic congestion.[32]

The word "anxiety" has Latin roots in the word *anxietas*, which refers to a mental and emotional restlessness that is associated with religious terror arising out of guilt, sinfulness, and eternal judgment and that can be relieved only by confession. It was not until the seventeenth century that "anxiety" acquired its modern secular connotations of worry, nervousness, and fretfulness. Robert Burton's 1621 treatise on *The Anatomy of Melancholia*, dealt not only with the burdens of the soul, but with more commonplace forms of distress, worry, trepidation, and depression. It was in the nineteenth century — when the Germans introduced the term *angst* to describe profound distress, the English introduced the word "panic," and the French adopted the word *angoisse* to refer to the spasms, sweating, shortness of breath, rapid heartbeat, and dizziness associated with acute anxiety — that "anxiety" acquired its associations with psychological distress.[33]

The word "stress" has even more recent origins. During the 1930s, the Austrian-Canadian endocrinologist Hans Selye, who was interested in the way that living organisms respond to environmental and psychological pressures, borrowed the term from physics and engineering and to physical strains placed on an object as it is bent or twisted. But it was not until the 1940s that the "stress," along with synonyms and antonyms such as "pressure," "strain," "fatigue," "tension," and "resilience," began to be used outside the field of metallurgy. Soon, other terms such as "snapping" and "breaking point" were adapted from the physical sciences, reflecting a view of the human self as potentially delicate and breakable, if an individual proved to be inelastic. Selye made the crucial observation that both positive experiences as well as traumas and negative pressures can cause stress.[34]

Why did the language of stress arise at a particular point in time? World War II played a crucial role, awakening researchers and the general public to "war nerves," "nervous tensions," and other psychological stresses induced by combat. Without a doubt, this new vocabulary also reflected the novel kinds of stresses and anxieties that individuals encountered in modern society, such as role overload, conflicts, and ambiguities that were emotional or psychological rather than physiological in origin. There were status anxieties, about one's standing in the social hierarchy; social anxieties rooted in fears of inadequacy and of how one is perceived by others; performance anxieties resting on fear of embarrassment or failure. And there were the anxieties rooted in a surfeit of choices, the "dizziness of freedom," to use Kierkegaard's evocative phrase. The language of stress and anxiety offered a way to explain otherwise inexplicable suffering or reprehensible behavior, such as emotional outbursts, writer's block, or an inability to concentrate, and to displace responsibility onto external forces acting upon an individual.[35]

The 1950s saw the emergence of the idea that certain kinds of personalities—notably the intensely ambitious, competitive, hard-driving Type A personality and those individuals prone to negativism—were especially vulnerable to stress-related diseases. Aggressive Type A personalities, who experience a constant sense of urgency, have a propensity to overreact to pressure, and are easily aroused to anger, were particularly susceptible to heart disease and strokes. Especially influential in developing the importance of individual differences in response to stress was the psychologist Richard S. Lazarus, who focused attention on the personal meanings that individuals gave to a stressful situation. It was Lazarus who popularized the notion of Teflon and Velcro personalities who responded to stresses either as "challenges" to be overcome or, alternatively, as "threats" to be vanquished.[36]

But this emphasis on individual personality difference obscured the fact that the incidence and nature of the stresses that individuals encounter vary according to such socioeconomic variables as income, education, marital status, ethnicity, race, gender, and immigrant status. Women, in general, report higher levels of stress than men, and the nature of the stresses encountered—involving work-family conflicts, excessive demands on their time, issues involving children, and tensions in relationships with relatives and friends—differ from those reported by men, which more often involve conflicts with coworkers. Lower-income adults report higher levels of stress than the more affluent. These individuals tend to receive less support from family, neighbors, or coworkers, and experience more financial, work, transportation, and health related stresses. For many individuals of color, encounters with discrimination are a common source of stress.[37]

Of course, it is how individuals handle stress, rather than stress itself, that affects adult health, and individual responses vary widely. Yet these variations are not simply idiosyncratic, but are generally related to socioeconomic and cultural factors that shift over time. At the same time, buffers against the effects of stress, such as perceptions of individual ability to take action, one's sense of control, and religious faith, matter a great deal and also differ across historical eras. Among the most obvious shifts in how adult have coped with stress are apparent in evolving attitudes toward displays of anger and in the consumption of alcohol.

Over the past two centuries, American society has sought, with some success, to restrain, channel, and defuse the overt expression of anger and the violence that often ensues. The American colonies showed few concerns about displays of anger. Masters within households, schools, and workplaces freely expressed anger and used corporal punishment as a way to enforce social hierarchy. There was, to be sure, concern about excessive anger, and to a limited extent, communal supervision and a culture of deference (and among elites, an emphasis on formal, stylized behavior) imposed some limits on aggressive displays of anger. But in contrast to later periods of American history, rage and violent fury were not deemed inappropriate in interpersonal relationships.[38]

By the middle of the eighteenth century, however, anger became increasingly problematic, as new religious and philosophical ideas stressed the value of emotional control. Advice manuals included the first specific injunctions against displays of temper, while diaries revealed a growing sense that anger should be struggled with and conquered. In the Age of Reason, bouts of rage and wrath came to be viewed as senseless, animalistic, and antithetical to an emerging ideal of rationality and gentility. Experts on childrearing rejected physical discipline and substituted a new ideal of instilling a capacity for self-control within children through the manipulation of guilt and shame. Writers on marriage warned that displays of anger, particularly by women, would ruin a marriage. Domestic harmony, rather than forceful assertions of hierarchy, became a new cultural ideal.[39]

By the middle of the nineteenth century, a growing number of parents sought to channel and harness aggressiveness in their sons, while urging their daughters to suppress any expressions of willfulness. Apparent in a rise in athletic activities, the notion of channeling aggressive impulses into sport reflected a belief that combativeness, when properly directed, was desirable. Similarly, it was seen as essential in a highly competitive economy in which success hinged on struggle and a willingness to take risks. Righteous anger was also deemed legitimate in the service of a larger cause, manifest in the campaign to abolish slavery or wage war against Spain or Germany. During the 1920s, the effort to suppress anger in personal relations extended into the workplace, as industrial psychologists, scientific managers, and human relations experts sought to promote harmonious interpersonal relations in office and retail settings. In increasingly bureaucratic settings and in the expanding service industries, anger was deemed detrimental to efficient business operations. Meanwhile, experts on childrearing encouraged parents to tolerate their children's mild temper tantrums, partly out of a fear that frustrating a child served only to intensify anger. But they also counseled parents to reason with their offspring, avoid overt conflicts, and teach their daughters and sons that anger was toxic and that exhibiting it could be harmful to their image. Then, too, marriage counselors, for the first time, declared that wives had a right to express controlled anger toward their husband, while advising them to restrain from yelling or nagging, and instead share their feelings calmly and talk out their concerns. The fear that anger could get out of control became a growing source of cultural anxiety.[40]

Toward the end of the twentieth century, efforts to curb expressions of anger and aggression within workplaces, schools, and homes intensified, partly in reaction to the argument, popular during the 1960s, that unexpressed, unconscious anger inevitably turns inward, producing frustration, depression, and other psychological disorders and allowing inequities and injustices to flourish, or that it turns outward into violence. According to a popular "let it all hang out" catchphrase of the time, it was dangerous to keep anger bottled up. During the 1970s, however, attention shifted away from pent-up anger to other forms of hostility such as bullying, harassment, intimidation, and various forms of "out-of-control" behavior, such as road rage and profanity in workplaces. Anger was something to be managed and repressed, and adult men and women were increasingly held to common standards of emotional restraint in public. Personnel and management experts deemed any screaming and shouting in the workplace unacceptable, while within the domestic sphere, family therapists came to view conflict-ridden relationships as being much more damaging than divorce. Contributing to the heightened concern with anger and its accompanying hostility and intolerance was the increasing diversity of workplaces as well as a growing emphasis on collaboration and teamwork; at the same time, Title VII of the Civil Rights Act of 1964 made it illegal to create a hostile workplace environment. Open displays of aggressive anger were viewed as legitimate only in specific realms, such as competitive team sports, politics, and warfare, and in the correction of injustice.[41]

Specialists in anger management, itself a new therapeutic field in the 1970s, devised a variety of techniques to defuse anger. Convinced that venting, rather than inducing cathartic release, too often inflamed angry emotions, these therapists recommended anger management strategies that emphasized problem solving, sharing feelings on an ongoing basis, relaxation techniques such as meditation and exercise, role playing to allow one to better understand other peoples' perspectives, and talking out problems with supportive listeners. Heightened value was attached to emotional and social intelligence — the ability to manage one's emotions and sense other people's feelings — and a growing number of companies responded by instituting sensitivity sessions, modeled on the "T-group," the sensitivity training workshops (or encounter groups) first held for managers at MIT during the 1940s and at the National Training Center for Group Development in Bethel, Maine, which sought to foster awareness of group dynamics and improve interpersonal skills through the uninhibited expression of feelings. Though certainly well-intentioned, these anger management strategies placed the burden of dealing with anger and frustrations on the individual and paid little attention to the societal and organizational arrangements, norms, and expectations that bred angry feelings.[42]

Over the course of American history, drinking alcohol has been the most common way that Americans adults have coped with stress. Today, roughly 70 percent of the adult population drinks regularly. About 5 percent, or over 11 million adults, are problem drinkers, and 17 percent, or over 39 million Americans, engage in binge drinking. Even a superficial familiarity with American literature reveals a litany of heavy drinkers, including Truman Capote, John Cheever, William Faulkner, F. Scott Fitzgerald, Ernest Hemingway, Jack Kerouac, Sinclair Lewis, Jack London, Edgar Allan Poe, and Tennessee Williams. For many, drinking provides a way to relax, release inhibitions, relieve stress, reduce self-consciousness, become more sociable, and obtain the high or buzz associated with ine-briation or intoxication. Because alcohol's physiological and psycholog-ical effects involve altering neuropsychological processes responsible for motor functioning, cognitive processing, emotional states, and impulse regulation, alcohol provides a temporary escape from stresses and pres-sures that are intrinsic to adult life.[43]

The cocktail party, the three-martini lunch, the celebratory toast, the ritualistic after work glass of wine, beer-quenched sports spectatorship—alcohol is, for most adults, an integral part of life. It also pervades popular culture. In film and literature, drink serves as a soporific, a social lubri-cant, a test of character, a release from everyday stresses and frustrations, a trigger for violence, and an emblem of masculinity. In the movies and in plays, adults often use drink as an analgesic, to dull pain or to cope with a loss that they cannot bear, as in *Who's Afraid of Virginia Woolf?* (1962), for example, though in other cases, such as W. C. Fields's *The Bank Dick* (1940) or *Arthur* (1981), inebriety is treated humorously. Meanwhile, heavy drinking is sometimes associated with particular ethnic groups or treated as a cause or symptom of social isolation, a symbol of over-indulgence or a lack of self-control, a response to feelings of emasculation, or a desperate attempt shore up a flagging sense of masculinity. Sometimes, drinking is glamorized as elegant and sophisticated (as in *The Thin Man* series) or as ritual of male camaraderie, and, at other times, pathologized as a disease, a social problem, a moral failing, or as a symptom of some deeper problem, often repressed homosexual impulses. Many of the best known cinematic treatments of drinking, such as *Lost Weekend* (1945) and *Best Years of Our Lives* (1946), focus on returning veterans and their attempt to deal with the traumatic ordeal that they have experienced. Others treat drinking as a cause or consequence of an unhappy marriage, as in *A Star is Born* (1937, 1954), *Come Back, Little Sheba* (1952), or *Days of Wine and Roses* (1962).

Still other, such as *I'll Cry Tomorrow* (1954), *Jim Thorpe All American* (1951), and *28 Days* (2000), focus on a protagonist's recovery.[44]

Over time, alcohol has been treated as a "good creature" created by God for man's pleasure by American colonists, as a "demon," a sin, and a threat to the family by nineteenth-century temperance advocates, and as a crime by Prohibitionists. Today, it is regarded with profound ambivalence. Drinking has deep roots in American culture. The *Arabella*, the ship that brought the first Puritans to Massachusetts Bay Colony, carried 10,000 gallons of beer and 120 hogsheads of malt so that the colonists could brew more. With the water supply often unhealthy and alternative beverages, such as tea or coffee, much more expensive, colonial Americans drank a great deal of alcohol. Generally this took the form of beer, ale, or hard cider. Over time, the amount and kinds of alcohol shifted markedly, as did the context in which adults drank. During the eighteenth century, rum, which was far more intoxicating than beer or ale, gained popularity. A 1737 "Drinker's Dictionary" printed in the *Pennsylvania Gazette* listed 228 terms for drunkenness. Rum was often consumed in taverns, which served as sites where men discussed politics, conducted business, gambled, and, in some instances, had assignations with prostitutes. Philadelphia had one tavern for every thirty-two male taxpayers in 1756 and one for every twenty-five adult males in 1790.[45]

Toward the end of the eighteenth century, whiskey supplanted rum, and both solitary drinking and boisterous, communal forms of binge drinking mushroomed. By 1820, the typical adult American consumed more than seven gallons of absolute alcohol a year (compared to 2.3 gallons today). Consumption had risen markedly over the preceding half century, fueled by the growing amounts of corn that farmers distilled into cheap whiskey, which could be transported more easily than bulk corn. In the 1820s, a gallon of whiskey cost just a quarter, and heavy drinking was an integral part of American life. Many people believed that downing a glass of whiskey before breakfast was conducive to good health. Instead of taking coffee breaks, people took a dram of liquor at eleven and again at four o'clock, as well as drinks after meals "to aid digestion" and a nightcap before going to sleep. Campaigning politicians offered voters generous amounts of liquor during campaigns and as rewards for "right voting" on election day. On the frontier, one evangelist noted, "a house could not be raised, a field of wheat cut down, nor could there be a log rolling, a husking, a quilting, a wedding, or a funeral without the aid of alcohol."[46]

Alcohol consumption, then as now, varied sharply along lines of gender, class, occupation, and ethnicity. The men who drank most heavily came disproportionately from the ranks of those with lowly paid, demanding manual jobs—canal workers, carters, farm laborers, fishermen, isolated frontiersmen, lumberjacks, sailors, and soldiers—while those arrested for public drunkenness were primarily the transient poor. Meanwhile, women, professionals, and upwardly aspiring artisans and clerks tended to drink less.

During the 1820s and 1830s, drinking became a potent cultural symbol, which, in the eyes of temperance reformers (who increasingly favored total abstinence), distinguished the vicious from the virtuous, much as smoking, in the late twentieth century, came, to its critics, to symbolize a divide between the health-conscious and those lacking impulse control and respect for the well-being of others. A growing number of clergymen declared that drinking distilled liquor was ungodly. Physicians linked alcohol to a variety of physical ailments. Many middle-class women blamed alcohol for the abuse of wives and children and the squandering of family resources. Societies for the prevention of pauperism blamed drink for crime and poverty. Many businesspeople identified drinking with inefficient and unproductive employees. To a rising middle class of professionals, small businesspeople, and manufacturers, temperance became a critical symbol of self-improvement, self-respect, progress, respectability, and upward mobility. It is not surprising to learn that Abraham Lincoln, an upwardly aspiring product of the hard-drinking Midwestern frontier, resolved early in life to abstain from alcohol.

More than in other Western societies, alcohol was a source of social division and contention in the United States. As early as 1712, a Massachusetts "Act against Intemperance, Immorality, and Profaneness, and for Reformation of Manners" had attempted to suppress drinking by restricting the issuance of liquor licenses, forbidding the sale of distilled spirits, prohibiting taverns from playing music, and posting the names of habitual drunkards. Today, the United States remains a society divided by drink. Roughly 30 percent of American adults abstain from alcohol, roughly triple the rate in Italy, Britain, or Germany. During the 1840s, partly in response to mass immigration from "heavy drinking cultures" (which, in fact, drank no more than most Americans in 1820), temperance advocates abandoned the tactic of moral suasion in favor of laws prohibiting the sale or manufacture of distilled spirits. Said one minister: "You might almost as well persuade the chained maniac to leave off howling, as to persuade him to leave off drinking."[47]

Even before the Eighteenth Amendment prohibiting the manufacture and sale of alcoholic beverages was ratified in 1919, about 65 percent of the country already banned alcohol. Initially, Prohibition was strongly supported by Progressive reformers, who viewed it as a tool for purifying American society and curbing poverty. America's entry into World War I made Prohibition seem patriotic, since many breweries were owned by German Americans. Meanwhile, proponents argued that grain should be made into bread for fighting men and not into liquor. Prohibition did briefly pay some public health dividends. By 1921, the death rate from alcoholism was cut by 80 percent from prewar levels, while alcohol-related crime dropped markedly. But seven years after Prohibition went into effect, the total deaths from adulterated liquor reached approximately 50,000, and many more cases of blindness and paralysis also arose. In the end, Prohibition made drinking more popular among the young, spawned organized crime, encouraged disrespect for law, sexually integrated male-dominated saloons and bars, encouraged solitary drinking, and led beer drinkers to hard liquor and cocktails. (One wit joked that "Prohibition succeeded in replacing good beer with bad gin.")[48]

Yet even though Prohibition has become the textbook example of misguided government efforts to shape morality, alcohol remains a serious cause of death, disability, and domestic abuse. Excessive drinking is the third leading lifestyle related cause of deaths among adults, following smoking, poor diet, and physical inactivity. Drunk driving is blamed for a third of the traffic deaths, and is a leading factor in cases of homicide, child abuse and neglect, domestic violence, and birth defects. Yet the principal reason adults drink so much alcohol is because it remains the chief way to relieve stress in a hectic, demanding society.[49]

In the years following Prohibition's repeal, rates of drinking remained relatively stable, with a few notable surges. Heavy drinking has historically been associated with unsettling societal upheavals, and so it is not surprising that rates of drinking jumped upward during and immediately after World War II and again in the 1970s, when the economy underwent far-reaching disruptions as a result of a sharp rise in oil prices and foreign imports, soaring rates of inflation, and abrupt transformations in gender roles and family relationships. Once again, we find that even though stress is experienced on a personal level, its roots are profoundly social. Yet, coping with the angst of adulthood on the individual level can explain the common resort to alcohol in the United States.[50]

~✵~

The current generation of adults has lived through historical transformations in private life as radical as any in the past century and a half. In stark contrast to the 1950s and 1960s, when the young achieved the markers of full adult identity in their early twenties, the transition to adulthood today generally extends into the late twenties or early thirties. Nor does this passage follow a pattern that an earlier generation had considered normal and that involved completing an education, getting a steady job, marrying, buying a house, and bearing children. Instead, the transition to adulthood has become circuitous and prolonged, often involving setbacks, reversals, and recurring dependence upon parents. Assumptions that earlier generations took for granted—about a lasting marriage, a steady career, and lifelong relationships with a group of friends—have eroded.

Adulthood today lacks a well-defined roadmap. Over the past half century, the life course lost its predictability and certainties, and adulthood became much more erratic, episodic, and capricious. Older assumptions about permanence, continuity, and steadiness faded as abrupt changes in careers and intimate relationships became the norm. Roles and expectations that had been formed a century and a half earlier eroded. No longer would anyone automatically assume that a man was his family's sole or primary breadwinner or that a married woman would subordinate her ambitions to her children and husband's well-being or that children would be born and raised solely within wedlock or that marriage would consist exclusively of a woman and a man. Today, individuals must define or negotiate their roles and relationships without clear rules or precedents to follow. Not surprisingly, this has bred insecurity, anger, and anxiety. At the same time, older structures of meaning that made sense of life's ups and downs crumbled. Neither traditional religion, with its implicit assumption that everything, good or bad, occurs for a reason, nor its secular middle-class counterpart, that virtue, healthy living, and hard work are rewarded, seems adequate to give meaning to the vicissitudes of contemporary life. Despite higher standards of living and dramatic improvements in health and life expectancy, uncertainty and instability are hallmarks of the adult condition.

Whether an adult reacts to the stresses, anxieties, and uncertainties of contemporary adulthood with equanimity or frustration, with defiance or anger, or with resignation or forbearance, or copes through smoking or exercise, by passively watching television, or by consuming alcohol, prescription medications, or illicit drugs, these responses are not merely idiosyncratic, but are generally related to socioeconomic and cultural factors that are determinative and that shift over time. A recurrent message in today's therapeutic culture is that it is through heartbreak, disappointment, and frustration that adults are challenged to cope, adapt, and grow up. A challenge that adults face is to embrace and integrate loss and change into their lives and learn from them. The inevitable losses and separations from loved ones, friends, and parents are, unsettlingly, primary vehicles through which adults can become more self-reflective, self-sufficient, and empathetic. It is through the realities of living and gaining and losing that adults mature.

Growing up, of course, is not simply a matter of growing older. It is ultimately about maturation, the ability to control impulses, assess risks, resist peer pressure, cope with conflict and frustration, and fully appreciate the significance of key life decisions. Reflection, self-assessment, and psychological self-understanding—these are attributes of an emotionally mature self. Unlike physical maturation, psychological maturity does not occur naturally, but if it emerges, it grows out of hard won experience and our confrontations with life's unexpected, inexplicable occurrences, as well as through our intimate encounters with loved ones, friends, and other acquaintances. As Shakespeare wrote in Sonnet 60:

> Like as the waves make towards the pebbled shore,
> So do our minutes hasten to their end;
> Each changing place with that which goes before,
> In sequent toil all forwards do contend.
> Nativity, once in the main of light,
> Crawls to maturity, wherewith being crown'd,
> Crooked eclipses'gainst his glory fight.

Only through the deeply challenging experiences of adulthood—the anxieties and fears that come with intimate relations with partners, family, and friends and with work that engages our minds and skills—are we able to let go of our insecurities, dependencies, defenses, and fairy-tale fantasies, and learn to be adult in the best sense: self-reliant but vulnerable, independent but not self-absorbed. Maturation requires an adult to learn to respect him- or herself and others, to tolerate others and to forgive them, to acknowledge the dignity of each individual, and to become an engaged, active citizen.

Adulthood can be bittersweet. As George Eliot so touchingly observed in *Middlemarch*, "Promises may not be kept, and an ardent outset may be followed by declension; latent powers may find their long-waited opportunity; a past error may urge a grand retrieval." But adulthood can also be the richest time of life, with greater possibilities for contentment than at any other age, as one lives in the present, not confronting an endless future.[51]

Epilogue: Reclaiming Adulthood

In Henry James's 1893 short story, "The Middle Years," the protagonist, a writer, regrets the fact that he had devoted his entire life to learning how to write. If only he had a second life, he laments, he could now apply the lessons. But, he reflects, we do not get a second chance. "We work in the dark," James wrote, " — we do what we can — we give what we have. Our doubt is our passion and our passion is our task." James made a similar point in his 1903 masterpiece, *The Ambassadors*. In that novel's most famous passage, the fifty-five-year-old protagonist, who has led a circumscribed, unfulfilled life, tells a young acquaintance: "Live all you can; it's a mistake not to. It doesn't so much matter what you do in particular, so long as you have your life." But as for himself, James's character is convinced, "It's too late."[1]

In *Middle Age*, a darkly comic novel written a century later, Joyce Carol Oates offers a subtle twist on James's message. A character's death, in the novel's opening pages, prompts myriad reactions among his friends and neighbors — idealism, grief, divorce, flight. Although the book is subtitled "a romance," it shares James's association of middle age with futility and despair. Set, like so many classic novels of adulthood, in an affluent suburb, it presents a bleak portrait of parent-child and spousal estrangement. And yet its overarching theme is that life, even in middle age, can still be transformed, for better or worse, and that the passions and desires of youth remain unextinguished. In stark contrast to James's portrait of a world bereft of second chances, Oates describes a society where the middle aged face choices about whether they should continue along the path that they have paved, with grace and dignity, or chuck this aside and try to start anew, if that is truly possible.

It is in literature that one finds the most nuanced and insightful depictions of American adulthood. Many classic mid-twentieth-century novels and plays paint adulthood as a rather dull and dismal stage of life. There is Eugene O'Neill's 1939 drama, *The Iceman Cometh,* with its portrait of drunks, clinging to their pipe dreams while numbing themselves with alcohol. Or Arthur Miller's 1949 play *Death of a Salesman,* with its indelible image of a man tortured by his failure to live up to his daydreams of financial success. Or Edward Albee's 1962 play *Who's Afraid of Virginia Woolf?,* with its wrenching portrait of a marriage that consists of a grim stream of pointless, excoriating arguments and emotional and physical abuse, psychological warfare and venomous mind games, vicious verbal insults and brutal barbs and bickering. Or Mary McCarthy's 1963 novel *The Group,* which follows eight graduates of the Vassar class of 1933, who had vowed to lead different lives than their mothers. The novel chronicles their struggles with the norms of their time as these young women wrestle with sexuality (both heterosexual and lesbian), infidelity, spousal abuse, motherhood, mental illness, and sexual discrimination in the workplace. Adulthood, in many mid-century novels and dramas, is a time of discontent, delusion, and despair.

In the works of John Cheever, John Updike, and many lesser writers, disillusionment has overtaken youthful hopes and dreams, marriages have descended into boredom or guerilla warfare, and children have separated emotionally from their parents. The characters, having lost their youthful energy and self-confidence, feel impelled to reflect on their lives and relationships. Characters wax philosophical about their marriages, their work, and their relationships with children, relatives, and friends. Do they feel fulfilled, or, instead, do they simply go through the motions? Do they still feel connected to their spouses, or do they simply coexist on parallel, nonintersecting, planes? Has their life been meaningful or worthless? Melancholy and haunting yearnings pervade the fiction of midlife individuals in their familial and interpersonal relations. Beset by feelings of shame and guilt, characters fret privately about doubt, regret, and remorse, yet feel unable to express and share their emotions openly. The fiction of middle age explores the existential dimensions of everyday life: the petty deceptions, cruelties, and nagging dissatisfactions that beset even the privileged at midlife. A literature of melancholia, these works of fiction tend to view adult lives as self-absorbed, materialistic, and vapid, and to focus on the superficially commonplace tragedies of mid-life: divorce, infidelity, and job loss.

Middle age begins when one looks into a mirror only to see a stranger. Hair grays and thins, waistlines thicken, gums recede, skin sags, lines and wrinkles grow more pronounced. The body's inevitable decline has begun, the metabolism slows, women's biological clock runs out, and male anxieties about their sexual prowess intensify. Often holding stressful jobs and managing costly mortgages, many of the middle aged find themselves members of the sandwich generation, responsible for both children and aging parents.

To be sure, a relentlessly upbeat popular culture offers a counternarrative. Rather than a time of doubt and conflict, middle age, from this perspective, is the most fruitful time of life, when income is highest, authority greatest, and relationships most stable. At midlife, an individual's cognitive powers are at their sharpest and emotions most balanced. After years of striving, middle age provides opportunities for renewal, reassessment, and reordering of priorities. The midlife crisis, with its sordid images of affairs, dumped spouses, and newly purchased sports cars and motorcycles, we are told, is a myth: Only about 10 to 15 percent of adults experience aging in terms of psychological turmoil and personal upheaval. In fact, it is true: For all its obligations, demands, stresses, and losses, adulthood truly is the time when an individual's capacities, competence, and resources are greatest. For many Americans, adulthood is the prime of life.

But for a substantial portion of the adult population today, adulthood is anything but prime time. Some suffer serious health problems. About 4 percent of men and 6 percent of women struggle with cancer during midlife and many more suffer from chronic ailments, including arthritis, back aches, diabetes, high blood pressure, migraine headaches, and insomnia. Despite dramatic increases in life expectancy, many die prematurely during midlife, at rates far higher than most adults estimate.

Between 1900 and 2000, the share of the United States population that lived to age sixty-five jumped from 41 percent to 82 percent. Nevertheless, there is a greater than one-in-six chance for a man and a one-in-nine chance for a woman to die between the ages of twenty-five and sixty-five.[2]

But even many of those who remain healthy experience midlife as a time of personal stress, financial hardship, and loneliness, and turn to alcohol, tobacco, or legal or illicit drugs to cope. Some 20 percent of adults report a serious drinking problem and nearly a third use tranquilizers and other drugs to handle anxiety. Depression and other stress-related mental health problems abound. In a society with unusually high rates of geographic mobility, social disconnection, relationship and job turnover, a limited social safety net, an unstable job market, and relatively weak extended kinship ties, it is easy for adult lives to fall off the tracks. An accident, an illness, a divorce, or a company's downsizing is often all that separates a stable life from one that is overwhelming. And this society does little to aid or insulate individuals from a fickle and capricious fate.[3]

The challenges are not merely economic. The dark side of the American dream is unfulfilled aspirations and quixotic illusions of making it big. A consumerist culture that regards life as a smorgasbord of endless options accentuates the possibility for frustration and regret. In a society with high expectations of material success and personal fulfillment, accompanied by Gatsby-esque fantasies of self-reinvention and self-advancement, it is not surprising that many adults feel disappointment and dissatisfaction.

We have traced the rise and fall of a particular conception of adulthood. This is an adulthood defined by certain culturally prescribed roles and responsibilities: by marriage, a full-time job, home ownership, and childrearing, as well as by distinctive dress and hair styles and even recreational activities. This conception has, in recent years, evolved into something quite different: a notion of adulthood as an outlook and self-image, defined by financial independence, a distinctive state of mind, and particular symbols of psychological maturity, including a rejection of the impulsivity and recklessness of youth.[4]

This outlook arises out of certain social as well as individual experiences that inevitably entail a certain loss of innocence and naiveté and the acquisition of certain enduring obligations that arise out of personal, familial, and work relations. Maturation is not simply a matter of frontal lobe development, which popular neuroscience associates with judgment, foresight, and impulse control. Rather, it is life experience, sometimes bitter, often sweet, that drives the journey to maturity. Adulthood is demanding in ways that childhood and adolescence are not. Adults bear responsibilities for themselves and others and face setbacks and calamities that those who are younger are generally spared. Choices made in adulthood more often stick and carry lasting costs. In a youth-oriented society, which prizes vigor, health, novelty, and a youthful appearance, it is easy to dismiss adulthood as life's anticlimax. Yet few adults would turn back the clock even if they could. Most who have fashioned an adult identity and a path for themselves have managed to forge meaningful bonds of connection and caring with partners and friends, with children whom they nurture, and with work that provides a degree of stimulation and satisfaction.[5]

F. Scott Fitzgerald considered a mild depression the attitude most appropriate to middle age, and it is certainly true that adulthood entails numerous incidents of loss, unrealized dreams, unfulfilled fantasies, and frustrated ambitions. But it is more productive to think of adulthood as Friedrich Nietzsche did: as a work of art that we ourselves create. Many of the stresses, anxieties, and work-family conflicts that contemporary adults experience are, in large measure, a product of the collapse of the norms that defined adulthood for a century and a half. But the breakdown of those norms has also liberated adults from rigid, restrictive role definitions that resulted in the lives of quiet desperation that Thoreau so memorably described in *Walden*.[6]

After a prolonged period in which adulthood was disparaged, it is time to reimagine this period of life in its bittersweet plentitude. After World War II, adulthood became associated with conformity to certain societal norms and expectations. It entailed embracing certain gender-specific social roles, dressing and behaving in a serious manner, and settling down. That definition of adulthood has been dismissed as overly rigid, inflexible, and confining. But there is another way to think about adulthood: as the polar opposite of the immaturity, naiveté, and inexperience of childhood or the recklessness and carelessness of adolescence and the early and mid-twenties. There are wonders to a life that is grappled with; it brings one closer to emotional intimacy. It offers the joys of laughter, tears, companionship, and, above all, self-knowledge. Ours is a society profoundly ambivalent about growing up. In a society in constant flux, adaptability, resilience, and go-getter ambition are the virtues most in demand, and these attributes are generally associated with youth. But there is another set of virtues deserving of appreciation. If immaturity connotes irresponsibility and abandon, then maturity implies responsibility, reliability, sensible judgment, and the wisdom that can be acquired only through experience and reflection. It is this definition of adulthood that deserves to be reclaimed.

Notes

Credits

Index

Notes

PROLOGUE

1 The historian Thomas R. Cole offers an alternate reading of the paintings in *The Journey of Life: A Cultural History of Aging in America* (New York: Cambridge University Press, 1992), 120–127.

2 The quotations can be found in the National Gallery of Art's overview of Thomas Cole, *The Voyage of Life: Childhood*, 1842, at http://www.nga.gov /content/ngaweb/Collection/highlights/highlight52450.html. Also see Matthew Baigell, *Thomas Cole* (New York: Watson-Guptill Publications, 1981); Edward H. Dwight and Richard J. Boyle, "Rediscovery: Thomas Cole's 'Voyage of Life,'" *L'Art et les Artistes* 55 (May 1967): 60–63; Ellwood C. Parry, III, *The Art of Thomas Cole: Ambition and Imagination* (Newark: University of Delaware Press, 1988; Earl A. Powell, *Thomas Cole* (New York: Harry N. Abrams, 2000); Paul D. Schweizer, "Another Possible Literary Source for Thomas Cole's *Voyage of Life*," in "New Discoveries in American Art," ed. Jayne A. Kuchina, special issue, *American Art Journal* 15 (1983): 74–75; William H. Truettner and Alan Wallach, *Thomas Cole: Landscape into History* (New Haven, Conn.: Yale University Press, 1994); Alan Wallach, "The Voyage of Life as Popular Art," *Art Bulletin* 59 (1957): 234.

3 Thomas Cole quoted in National Gallery of Art, *The Voyage of Life: Childhood*, 1842, http://www.nga.gov/content/ngaweb/Collection/highlights/high light52450.html.

4 J. A. Burrow, *The Ages of Man: A Study in Medieval Writing and Thought* (Oxford: Clarendon Press, 1988), 2, 5, 55; Elizabeth Sears, *The Ages of Man: Medieval Interpretations of the Life Cycle* (Princeton, N.J.: Princeton University Press, 1986), 54–79, 82–90.

5 Burrow, *The Ages of Man*, 2, 5, 55; Sears, *The Ages of Man*, 3–4, 9–79.

6 Burrow, *The Ages of Man*, 2, 5, 55; Sears, *The Ages of Man*, 3–4, 9–79.

7 For artistic representations of the ages of man and woman, see Sears, *The Ages of Man*, 131–155.

8 For Aristotle's view of midlife as life's pinnacle, see his *Rhetoric*, book II, chapter 14. On the uses of Aristotle's viewpoint by later writers, see Joshua

Scodel, "Dryden the Critic's Historicist and Cosmopolitan Mean," in *Au-delà de la Póetique: Aristote et la littérature de la Renaissance,* ed. Ulrich Langer (Geneva: Librairie Droz, 2002), 87.

9   On Milton Bradley's Checkered Game of Life, see Jill Lepore, "The Meaning of Life," *New Yorker,* May 21, 2007, http://www.newyorker.com/reporting /2007/05/21/070521fa_fact_lepore.

10 Gwen Sharp, "Changing Biology: Age at First Menstruation," *Sociological Images,* September 19, 2008, http://thesocietypages.org/socimages/2008 /09/19/changing-biology-age-at-first-menstruation/; Elizabeth Weil, "Puberty before Age 10: A New 'Normal'?" *New York Times,* March 30, 2012, MM30.

11 Steven Mintz, "Life Stages," in *Encyclopedia of American Social History,* ed. Mary Kupiec Cayton, Elliott J. Gorn, and Peter W. Williams, (New York: Charles Scribner's Sons, 1993), 3:2011–2022.

12 Steven Mintz, *Huck's Raft: A History of American Childhood* (Cambridge, Mass.: Belknap Press of Harvard University Press, 2004).

13 W. Andrew Achenbaum, *Old Age in the New Land: The American Experience since 1790* (Baltimore: Johns Hopkins University Press, 1980); Carole Haber, *Beyond Sixty-Five: The Dilemma of Old Age in America's Past* (Cambridge: Cambridge University Press, 1985).

14 Howard P. Chudacoff, *How Old Are You? Age Consciousness in American Culture* (Princeton, N.J.: Princeton University Press, 1990).

15 On shifting conceptions of adulthood and midlife, see David Bainbridge, *Middle Age: A Natural History* (London: Portobello Books, 2013); Patricia Cohen, *In Our Prime: The Fascinating History and Promising Future of Middle Age* (New York: Scribner, 2013); Margaret Morganroth Gullette, *Aged by Culture* (Chicago: University of Chicago Press, 2004), *Declining to Decline: Cultural Combat and the Politics of the Midlife* (Charlottesville, Va.: University Press of Virginia, 1997), and *Safe at Last in the Middle Years: The Invention of the Midlife Progress Novel* (Berkeley: University of California Press, 1988); and Kay Heath, *Aging by the Book: The Emergence of Midlife in Victorian Britain* (Albany: State University of New York Press, 2009).

16 On shifting legal definitions of the age of maturity and responsibility, see Ross W. Beales Jr., "In Search of the Historical Child: Miniature Adulthood and Youth in Colonial New England," *American Quarterly* 27, no. 4 (October 1975): 379–398.

17 On the rise of developmentalist thinking, see Winthrop D. Jordan, "Searching for Adulthood in America," *Daedalus* 105, no. 4 (Fall 1976): 1–11.

18 Henri Bergson, *Creative Evolution* [1907] (New York: Henry Holt & Co., 1911), 8.

19 Howard P. Chudacoff, *Age Consciousness in American Culture* (Princeton, N.J.: Princeton University Press, 1989). Also see Christopher Aceto and Holly Epstein Ojalvo, "Acting Your Age: Considering the Age of Responsibility," *New York Times*, November 17, 2009, http://learning.blogs.nytimes. com/2009/11/17/acting-your-age-considering-the-age-of-responsibility /?_r=o.

I. THE TANGLED TRANSITION TO ADULTHOOD

1 Gordon Berlin, Frank F. Furstenberg Jr., and Mary C. Waters, "Introducing the Issue: Transition to Adulthood," *Future of Children* 20, no. 1 (Spring 2010): 4.

2 Jeffrey Jensen Arnett, *Emerging Adulthood: The Winding Road from the Late Teens through the Twenties* (New York. Oxford University Press, 2004).

3 Berlin, Furstenberg, and Waters, "Introducing the Issue," 4.

4 On immigration, see Rubén G. Rumbaut and Golnaz Komaie, "Immigration and Adult Transitions," *Future of Children* 20, no. 1 (Spring 2010): 43–66. On the impact of independent living, see Michael J. Rosenfeld, *The Age of Independence: Interracial Unions, Same-Sex Unions, and the Changing American Family* (Cambridge, Mass.: Harvard University Press, 2009).

5 Barbara Hofer and Abigail Sullivan Moore, *The iConnected Parent: Staying Close to Your Kids in College (and beyond) while Letting Them Grow Up* (New York: Free Press, 2010).

6 Steven Mintz, *Huck's Raft: A History of American Childhood* (Cambridge, Mass.: Belknap Press of Harvard University Press, 2004), 19; James Gilbert, *A Cycle of Outrage: America's Reaction to the Juvenile Delinquent in the 1950s* (New York: Oxford University Press, 1988).

7 Kenneth Keniston, *The Uncommitted: Alienated Youth in American Society* (New York: Harcourt, Brace & World, 1965; Jon Grinspan, "Anxious Youth, Then and Now," *New York Times*, December 31, 2013, A19, http://www .nytimes.com/2014/01/01/opinion/anxious-youth-then-and-now.html; Randolph Silliman Bourne, *Youth and Life* (Boston: Houghton, Mifflin Company, 1913), 20.

8 Katherine S. Newman, *The Accordion Family: Boomerang Kids, Anxious Parents, and the Private Toll of Global Competition* (Boston: Beacon Press, 2012).

9 On Thoreau's youth, see Michael Sims, *The Adventures of Henry Thoreau: A Young Man's Unlikely Path to Walden Pond* (New York: Bloomsbury USA, 2014). On youth as a stage of life characterized by abrupt shifts between independent and dependent status, see Joseph F. Kett, *Rites of Passage: Adolescence in America, 1790 to the Present* (New York: Basic Books, 1977).

10 Steven Mintz, "The Kids Are Moving Back in After College? Smart Career Move," *Washington Post*, June 1, 2012, http://www.washingtonpost.com /opinions/the-kids-are-moving-back-in-after-college-smart-career -move/2012/06/01/gJQAMWla7U_story.html.

11 Ibid.

12 Sharon Jayson, "Tightrope 20s: Risky Behavior Doesn't End with Teen Years," *USA Today,* August 14, 2007, http://www.usatoday.com/life /lifestyle/2007-08-14-risky-20s_N.htm.

13 Capt. Marryatt, C. B., *A Diary in America, with Remarks on Its Institutions* (Philadelphia: Carey & Hart, 1839), 2:218.

14 Mintz, *Huck's Raft*, 7–31. On the breakdown of the apprenticeship system, see W. J. Rorabaugh, *Craft Apprentice: From Franklin to the Machine Age in America* (New York: Oxford University Press, 1986).

15 John Dane, "A Declaration of Remarkable Providences in the Course of My Life," *New England Historical and Genealogical Register* 8 (April 1854): 149–156.

16 On Melville, see Andrew Delbanco, *Melville: His World and Work* (New York: Random House, 2005), 17–36. On Mark Twain, see Ron Powers, *Dangerous Waters: A Biography of the Boy Who Became Mark Twain* (Cambridge, Mass.: Da Capo Press, 1999). On Lucy Larcom, see her autobiography, *A New England Girlhood: Outlined from Memory* (Boston: Houghton Mifflin, 1889).

17 Carol F. Karlsen, *The Journal of Esther Edwards Burr, 1754–1757* (New Haven, Conn.: Yale University Press, 1984).

18 Ibid., 95, 156, 175, 216.

19 On Lucy Larcom, see her autobiography, *A New England Girlhood*, 183.

20 Drawing on hundreds of autobiographical accounts, Harvey J. Graff, *Conflicting Paths: Growing Up in America* (Cambridge, Mass.: Harvard University Press, 1995), identifies a series of trajectories to adulthood.

21 John Van Der Zee, *Bound Over: Indentured Servitude and American Conscience* (New York: Simon and Schuster, 1985), 210. Lincoln quoted in Allan Guelzo, *Abraham Lincoln: Redeemer President* (Grand Rapids: William B. Eerdmans Publishing, 1999), 121.

22 Colman quoted in Ross W. Beales, Jr., "In Search of the Historical Child: Miniature Adulthood and Youth in Colonial New England," *American Quarterly* 27, no. 4 (1975): 20.

23 N. Ray Hiner, "Adolescence in Eighteenth-Century America," *History of Childhood Quarterly* 3 (Fall 1975): 253–280.

24 Nancy F. Cott, *The Bonds of Womanhood: "Woman's Sphere" in New England, 1780–1835*, 2nd ed. (New Haven, Conn.: Yale University Press, 1997).

25 Stephanie Coontz, *The Social Origins of Private Life: A History of American Families, 1600–1900* (London: Verso, 1988); Mintz, *Huck's Raft*, 75–93.

26 Mintz, *Huck's Raft*, 75–93.

27 Ibid., 133–153.

28 Joseph F. Kett, *Rites of Passage: Adolescence in America, 1790 to the Present* (New York: Basic Books, 1977), 111–172.

29 On the diversity of today's young adults, see Mary C. Waters, Patrick J. Carr, Maria J. Kefalas, and Jennifer Holdaway, *Coming of Age in America: The Transition to Adulthood in the Twenty-First Century* (Berkeley: University of California Press, 2011); Jennifer M. Silva, *Coming Up Short: Working-Class Adulthood in an Age of Uncertainty* (New York: Oxford University Press, 2013); Richard D. Alba and Mary C. Waters, eds., *The Next Generation: Immigrant Youth in a Comparative Perspective* (New York: New York University Press, 2011); Philip Kasinitz, John H. Mollenkopf, Mary C. Waters, and Jennifer Holdaway, *Inheriting the City: The Children of Immigrants Come of Age* (New York: Russell Sage, 2010); and Carola Suárez-Orozco and Marcelo M. Suárez-Orozco, *Children of Immigration* (Cambridge, Mass.: Harvard University Press, 2002). On the failure of colleges to help students define realistic career objectives and pathways, see Barbara Schneider and David Stevenson, *The Ambitious Generation: America's Teenagers, Motivated but Directionless* (New Haven, Conn.: Yale University Press, 2000).

30 On the role of institutions in the transition to adulthood, see Joann S. Lee, "An Institutional Framework for the Study of the Transition to Adulthood," *Youth & Society* 20 (2012): 1–25.

31 On the impact of participation in the Vietnam War on development during young adulthood, see Timothy J. Owens, *From Adolescence to Adulthood in the Vietnam Era* (New York: Springer, 2005).

32 Ryan Kelty, Meredith Kleykamp, and David R. Segal, "The Military and the Transition to Adulthood," *Future of Children* 20, no. 1 (Spring 2010): 181–207; Giuseppe Caforio, ed., *Handbook of the Sociology of the Military* (New York: Springer, 2006).

33 Kelty, Kleykamp, and Segal, "The Military and the Transition to Adulthood," 194–196.

34 G. Stanley Hall, *Adolescence: Its Psychology and Its Relations to Physiology, Anthropology, Sociology, Sex, Crime, Religion, and Education* (New York: D. Appleton & Co., 1905); Jeffrey Jensen Arnett, *Emerging Adulthood: The Winding Road from the Late Teens through the Twenties* (New York: Oxford University Press, 2006).

35 "The Racial Gap in College Participation Rates," *Journal of Blacks in Higher Education,* September 23, 2013, http://www.jbhe.com/2013/09/the-racial-gap-in-college-participation-rates/.

36 "Percentage of Students Entering and Completing College, and College Persistence, by Income Quartile," Russell Sage Foundation, http://www.russellsage.org/node/4032.

37 Carla Rivera, "Study Finds Low Graduation Rates among Part-Time College Students," *Los Angeles Times,* September 27, 2011, http://articles.latimes.com/2011/sep/27/local/la-me-college-report-20110928.

38 Jeffry H. Morrison, *John Witherspoon and the Foundation of the American Republic* (Notre Dame, Ind.: University of Notre Dame Press, 2005).

39 Colin B. Burke, *American Collegiate Populations: A Test of the Traditional View* (New York: New York University Press, 1982); Donald G. Tewksbury, *The Founding of American Colleges and Universities before the Civil War* (New York: Archon Books, 1965).

40 Burke, *American Collegiate Populations.*

41 Arthur M. Cohen and Carrie B. Kisker, *The Shaping of American Higher Education: Emergence and Growth of the Contemporary System,* 2nd ed. (San Francisco: Jossey-Bass, 2009).

42 Jenna Johnson, "Today's Typical College Students Often Juggle Work, Children and Bills with Coursework," *Washington Post,* September 14, 2013, http://articles.washingtonpost.com/2013-09-14/local/42057980_1

_college-students-hispanic-students-international-students; Ben Castleman, "'Non-Traditional' Students Are Majority on College Campuses," *Wall Street Journal*, July 6, 2013, http://blogs.wsj.com/economics/2013/07/06/number-of-the-week-non-traditional-students-are-majority-on-college-campuses/.

43 Steven Brint and Jerome Karabel, *The Diverted Dream: Community Colleges and the Promise of Educational Opportunity in America, 1900–1985* (New York: Oxford University Press, 1991). For statistics on persistence and graduation, see Community College FAQs, Community College Research Center, http://ccrc.tc.columbia.edu/Community-College-FAQs.html.

44 On the late nineteenth-century college as "playworld," see Laurence R. Veysey, *The Emergence of the American University* (Chicago: University of Chicago Press, 1970), 277, and, more generally, 268–301. On college as a coming-of-age experience, see Michael Moffatt, *Coming of Age in New Jersey: College and American Culture* (New Brunswick, N.J.: Rutgers University Press, 1989); John E. Conklin, *Campus Life in the Movies: A Critical Survey from the Silent Era to the Present* (Jefferson, N.C.: Mcfarland & Co., 2008); David B. Hinton, *Celluloid Ivy: Higher Education in the Movies 1960–1990* (n.p: n.p., 1994); Wiley Lee Umphlett, *The Movies Go to College: Hollywood and the World of the College-Life Film* (Cranbury, N.J.: Associated University Presses, 1984).

45 Veysey, *Emergence of the American University*, 268–301; Steven J. Novak, *The Rights of Youth: American Colleges and Student Revolt, 1798–1815* (Cambridge, Mass.: Harvard University, 1977).

46 Novak, *The Rights of Youth*, 2, 4; Kett, *Rites of Passage*, 51–59; Rex Bowman and Carlos Santos, *Rot, Riot, and Rebellion: Mr. Jefferson's Struggle to Save the University that Changed America* (Charlottesville: University Press of Virginia, 2013).

47 The quotations can be found in Novak, *The Rights of Youth*, 9, 76.

48 Veysey, *The Emergence of the American University*, 268–301. On fraternities, see Nicholas L. Syrett, *The Company He Keeps: A History of White College Fraternities* (Chapel Hill: University of North Carolina Press, 2009). On "co-eds," see Lynn Peril, *College Girls: Bluestockings, Sex Kittens, and Co-eds, Then and Now* (New York: W. W. Norton & Company, 2006).

49 Michael Moffatt, "College Life: Undergraduate Culture and Higher Education," *Journal of Higher Education* 62, no. 1 (January–February 1991): 50–52.

50 Mary Grigsby, *College Life through the Eyes of Students* (Albany: State University of New York Press, 2009).

51 Anthony P. Carnevale, "For a Middle-Class Life, College Is Crucial," *New York Times*, March 1, 2012, http://www.nytimes.com/roomforde bate/2012/03/01/should-college-be-for-everyone/for-a-middle-class -life-college-is-crucial; Anthony P. Carnevale, "College Is Still Worth It," *Inside Higher Ed*, January 14, 2011, http://www.insidehighered.com /views/2011/01/14/carnevale_college_is_still_worth_it_for_americans; Anthony P. Carnevale, Jeff Strohl, and Michelle Melton, *What's It Worth: The Economic Value of College Majors* (Washington, D.C.: Georgetown Center on Education and the Workforce, n.d.), http://www9.georgetown .edu/grad/gppi/hpi/cew/pdfs/whatsitworth-complete.pdf. On the diversity of today's young adults, see Waters et al., *Coming of Age in America;* Silva, *Coming Up Short;* Alba and Waters, *The Next Generation;* Kasinitz et al., *Inheriting the City;* and Suárez-Orozco and Suárez-Orozco, *Children of Immigration*. On the failure of colleges to help students define realistic career objectives and pathways, see Schneider and Stevenson, *The Ambitious Generation*.

52 On the European bildungsroman, see Gregory Castle, *Reading the Modernist Bildungsroman* (Gainesville: University Press of Florida, 2006); Thomas L. Jeffers, *Apprenticeships: The Bildungsroman from Goethe to Santayana* (New York: Palgrave Macmillan, 2005); Todd Curtis Kontje, *The German Bildungsroman: History of a National Genre* (Columbia, S.C.: Camden House, 1993); Franco Moretti, *The Way of the World: The Bildungsroman in European Culture* (London: Verso, 1987); Giovanna Summerfield, *New Perspectives on the European Bildungsroman* (New York: Continuum, 2010); Martin Swales, *The German Bildungsroman from Wieland to Hesse* (Princeton, N.J.: Princeton University Press, 1978).

53 Moretti, *The Way of the World*.

54 On the problematizing of the passage to adulthood, see Rorabaugh, *The Craft Apprentice;* Kett, *Rites of Passage*.

55 On the American female coming-of-age narrative, see Christy Rishoi, *From Girl to Woman: American Women's Coming-of-Age Narratives* (Albany: State University of New York Press, 2003). On ethnic bildungsromane, see Maria

Mazziotti Gillan and Jennifer Gillan, *Growing Up Ethnic in America* (New York: Penguin Books, 1999). On African American coming-of-age narratives more generally, see W. Lawrence Hogue, *The African American Male* (Albany: State University of New York Press, 2003); and Geta J. Leseur, *Ten Is the Age of Darkness: The Black Bildungsroman* (Columbia: University of Missouri Press, 1995). On Asian American bildungsromane, see Jennifer Ho, *Consumption and Identity in Asian American Coming-of-Age Novels* (New York: Routledge, 2012).

56 Mary Frosch, *Coming of Age in America: A Multicultural Anthology* (New York: New Press, 2007).

57 John R. Gillis, *Youth and History: Tradition and Change in European Age Relations* (New York: Academic Press, 1974).

58 On the nineteenth-century male culture of adaptation to adulthood, see Glenn Wallach, *Obedient Sons: The Discourse of Youth and Generations in American Culture, 1630–1860* (Amherst: University of Massachusetts Press, 2007). On young women's coming of age, see Cott, *The Bonds of Womanhood;* and Jane Hunter, *How Young Ladies Became Girls: The Victorian Origins of American Girlhood* (New Haven, Conn.: Yale University Press, 2003).

59 Quoted in Christine Stansell, *City of Women: Sex and Class in New York, 1789–1860* (New York: Alfred A. Knopf, 1982), 90.

60 Quotations on g'hal culture can be found in Stansell, *City of Women,* 93. On the b'hoy sporting culture, see Tyler Anbinder, *Five Points: The Nineteenth-Century New York City Neighborhood* (New York: Free Press, 2001), esp. 52, and Richard B. Stott, *Workers in the Metropolis: Class, Ethnicity, and Youth in Antebellum New York City* (Ithaca, N.Y.: Cornell University Press, 1990).

61 Quoted in Eric C. Schneider, *Vampires, Dragons and Egyptian Kings: Youth Gangs in Postwar New York* (Princeton, N.J.: Princeton University Press, 1999), 52.

62 Kathy Peiss, *Cheap Amusements: Working Women and Leisure in Turn-of-the-Century New York* (Philadelphia: Temple University Press, 1986), 43.

63 The quotations can be found in William Graebner, *Coming of Age in Buffalo: Youth and Authority in the Postwar Era* (Philadelphia: Temple University Press, 1989), 17–18.

64 Claudia Goldin, "America's Graduation from High School: The Evolution and Spread of Secondary Schooling in the Twentieth Century," *Journal of Economic History* 58, no. 2 (1998): 345–374.

65 Edgar Z. Friedenberg, *The Vanishing Adolescent* (Boston: Beacon Press, 1959); Bennett M. Berger, "Adolescence and Beyond," *Social Problems* 10, no. 4 (Spring 1963): 394–408.

66 The quotations can be found in Paul Goodman, *Growing Up Absurd: Problems of Youth in the Organized System* (New York: Random House, 1960), 21, and Bennett M. Berger, "Adolescence and Beyond," *Social Problems* 10, no. 4 (1963): 401. Also see John J. Enck, "Review of *Growing Up Absurd* by Paul Goodman and *Our Visit to Niagara* by Paul Goodman," *Wisconsin Studies in Contemporary Literature* 1, no. 3 (Autumn 1960): 89–103.

67 James Coleman, *The Adolescent Society: The Social Life of the Teenager and Its Impact on Education* (Glencoe, Ill.: Free Press, 1961); August B. Hollingshead, *Elmtown's Youth: The Impact of Social Class on Adolescents* (New York: John Wiley & Sons, 1949).

68 Keniston, *The Uncommitted*.

69 Braceland quoted in Mintz, *Huck's Raft*, 301.

70 On the generation gap, see Richard A. Settersten Jr., Frank F. Furstenberg Jr., and Rubén G. Rumbaut, eds., *On the Frontier of Adulthood: Theory, Research, and Public Policy* (Chicago: University of Chicago Press, 2008), 192.

71 Rebecca de Schweinitz, *If We Could Change the World: Young People and America's Long Struggle for Racial Equality* (Chapel Hill: University of North Carolina Press, 2009).

72 Anne Moody, *Coming of Age in Mississippi* (New York: Doubleday, 1968).

73 Anne Koedt, the source of the reference to women's status within the civil rights and New Left movements, is quoted in Dawn Keetley and John Pettegrew, eds., *Public Women, Public Words: A Documentary History of American Feminism* (Oxford: Rowman and Littlefield, 2002), 3:18–19. Also see Peter G. Filene, *Him/Her/Self: Gender Identities in Modern America* (Baltimore: Johns Hopkins University Press, 1974, 1998), 212.

74 Jonathan S. Epstein, ed., *Youth Culture: Identity in a Postmodern World* (Malden, Mass.: Blackwell Publishers, 1998), 1–23.

75 On Seijin no Hi, see Katherine S. Newman, *The Accordion Family: Boomerang Kids, Anxious Parents, and the Private Toll of Global Competition* (Boston: Beacon Press, 2012), 1. Also see Merry White, *The Material Child: Coming of Age in Japan and America* (New York: Free Press, 1994), viii.

76 On *rumspringa,* see Tom Shachtman, *Rumspringa: To Be or Not to Be Amish* (New York: North Point Press, 2006). On the *quinceañera,* see Julia Alvarez, *Once upon a Quinceañera: Coming of Age in the USA* (New York: Viking, 2007). On Jewish American coming-of-age rituals, see Melissa R. Klapper, *Jewish Girls Coming of Age in America, 1860–1920* (New York: New York University Press, 2005). On coming of age in the recent United States more generally, see Graebner, *Coming of Age in Buffalo;* and Annette B. Hemmings, *Coming of Age in U.S. High Schools: Economic, Kinship, Religious, and Political Crosscurrents* (Mahwah, N.J.: Lawrence Erlbaum, 2008). In 1992, in the case of *Lee v. Weisman,* the U.S. Supreme Court ruled that public schools cannot sponsor prayer at graduation ceremonies.

77 Harry Blatterer, *Coming of Age in Times of Uncertainty* (New York: Berghahn Books, 2009).

78 Arnold van Gennep, *Rites of Passage* (Chicago: University of Chicago Press, 1961); Victor Turner, *The Ritual Process* (Chicago: Aldine Transaction, 1995).

79 Carol A. Markstrom, *Empowerment of North American Indian Girls: Ritual Expressions at Puberty* (Lincoln: University of Nebraska Press, 2008); Steven Mintz, *Native American Voices: A History & Anthology* (Malden, Mass.: Wiley-Blackwell, 2000), 60–74.

80 Margaret Mead, *Coming of Age in Samoa: A Psychological Study of Primitive Youth for Western Civilisation* (New York: William Morrow and Company, 1928).

81 Ibid. Frequently Asked Questions to the Kinsey Institute, http://www.iub.edu/~kinsey/resources/FAQ.html#Age; W. D. Mosher, A. Chandra, and J. Jones, "Sexual Behavior and Selected Health Measures: Men and Women 15–44 Years of Age, United States, 2002," *Advance Data from Vital and Health Statistics,* no. 362 (Hyattsville, Md.: National Center for Health Statistics, 2005).

82 Laura Carpenter, *Virginity Lost: An Intimate Portrait of First Sexual Experiences* (New York: New York University Press, 2005); Sharon Thompson, *Going All the Way: Teenage Girls' Tales of Sex, Romance, and Pregnancy* (New York: Hill & Wang, 1996).

83 Carpenter, *Virginity Lost;* Thompson, *Going All the Way.*

84 Carpenter, *Virginity Lost;* Thompson, *Going All the Way.*

85 Centers for Disease Control and Prevention, *Teenagers in the United States: Sexual Activity, Contraceptive Use, and Childbearing, 2006–2010,* National

Survey of Family Growth, Vital Health Statistics, Series 23, no. 31 (October 2011), http://www.cdc.gov/nchs/data/series/sr_23/sr23_031.pdf; Mark D. Regenerus, *Sex and Religion in the Lives of American Teenagers* (New York: Oxford University Press, 2011); Mark Regenerus and Jeremy Uecker, *Premarital Sex in America: How Young Americans Meet, Mate, and Think about Marrying* (New York: Oxford University Press, 2011).

86 Kathleen A. Bogle, *Hooking Up: Sex, Dating, and Relationships on Campus* (New York: New York University Press, 2008); Donna Freitas, *The End of Sex: How Hookup Culture is Leaving a Generation Unhappy, Sexually Unfulfilled, and Confused about Intimacy* (New York: Basic Books, 2013); and Laura Sessions Stepp, *Unhooked: How Young Women Pursue Sex, Delay Love and Lose at Both* (New York: Riverhead Trade, 2008).

87 Regenerus, *Sex and Religion in the Lives of American Teenagers;* Regenerus and Uecker, *Premarital Sex in America.*

88 Anjani Chandra, William D. Mosher, Casey Copen, and Catlainn Sionean, "Sexual Behavior, Sexual Attraction, and Sexual Identity in the United States: Data from the 2006–2008 National Survey of Family Growth," *National Health Statistics Reports,* no. 36 (March 3, 2011), http://www.cdc.gov/nchs/data/nhsr/nhsr036.pdf. According to this study, some 18 percent of the young women reported same-sex attraction, compared to 7 percent of the young men; 14 percent of the women and 5 percent of the men said they had engaged in same-sex behavior.

89 Maxcy is quoted in Richard Godbeer, *The Overflowing of Friendship: Love between Men and the Creation of the American Republic* (Baltimore: Johns Hopkins University Press, 2009), 58. On male same-sex activity in rural areas, see Alfred C. Kinsey, Wardell B. Pomery, and Clyde E. Martin, *Sexual Behavior in the Human Male* (Philadelphia: W. B. Saunders, 1948); John Howard, *Men Like That: A Southern Queer History* (Chicago: University of Chicago Press, 1999) and Peter Boag, *Same-Sex Affairs: Constructing and Controlling Homosexuality in the Pacific Northwest* (Berkeley: University of California Press, 2003). On same-sex identity formation, see Steven Seidman, *Beyond the Closet: The Transformation of Gay and Lesbian Life* (New York: Routledge, 2003), and Chandra et al., "Sexual Behavior, Sexual Attraction, and Sexual Identity in the United States."

90 Seidman, *Beyond the Closet;* Susan Driver, ed., *Queer Youth Cultures* (Albany: SUNY Press, 2008), 1–25.

91 Meg Jay, *The Defining Decade: Why Your Twenties Matter—And How to Make the Most of Them Now* (New York: Twelve Publishing, 2012). Also see, Sharon Jayson, "Walking the Tightrope of the 20s," *USA Today*, August 15, 2007, 1D, http://usatoday30.usatoday.com/printedition/life/20070815/d _cover15.art.htm.

92 Eliot quoted in *Charles W. Eliot: President of Harvard University, 1869–1901* (Boston: Houghton Mifflin, 1930), 1:57. William Watts Folwell quoted in *William Watts Folwell: The Autobiography and Letters of a Pioneer of Culture*, ed. Solon J. Buck (Minneapolis: University of Minnesota Press, 1933), 120. Also see Burton J. Bledstein, *Culture of Professionalism: The Middle Class and the Development of Higher Education in America* (New York: Norton, 1976), 159.

93 Jane Addams, *Twenty Years at Hull-House* (New York: Macmillan Co., 1911), 118.

94 On the emergence of the notion of a career, see Bledstein, *Culture of Professionalism*.

95 Henry Adams, *The Education of Henry Adams: An Autobiography* (Boston: Houghton, Mifflin Co., 1918).

96 Quoted in Lukman Harees, *The Mirage of Dignity on the Highways of Human 'Progress': The Bystanders Perspective* (Bloomington, Ind.: AuthorHouse, 2012), 405. The quotation originally appeared as a comment to an article by Robin Marantz Henig, "What Is It About 20-Somethings?," *New York Times Magazine*, Aug. 22, 2010, MM 28ff., http://www.nytimes.com/2010 /08/22/magazine/22Adulthood-t.html?_r=1.

2. ACHIEVING INTIMACY

1 Daniel Goleman, "Worries about Intimacy Are Rising, Therapists Find," *New York Times*, November 3, 1987, C1; Dan P. McAdams, *Intimacy* (Garden City, N.Y.: Doubleday, 1989); Dan P. McAdams, "Intimacy Motivation and Subjective Mental Health in a Nationwide Sample," *Journal of Personality* 55 (1987): 395–413.

2 Martin E. P. Seligman and Mihaly Csikszentmihalyi, "Positive Psychology: An Introduction," *American Psychologist* 55 (January 2000): 5–14.

3 The quotation is from Kate Taylor, "Timeless Tokens of Affection," *New York Sun*, February 15, 2007, http://www.nysun.com/arts/timeless-tokens -of-affection/48758/. For examples of nineteenth-century tokens of affection,

see Jane Katcher, David A. Schorsch, and Ruth Wolfe, *Expressions of Innocence and Eloquence: Selections from the Jane Katcher Collection of Americana* (Seattle: Marquand Books, 2006). Also see Leigh Eric Schmidt, "The Fashioning of a Modern Holiday: St. Valentine's Day, 1840–1870," *Winterthur Portfolio* 28, no. 4 (Winter 1993): 209–245.

4 Katcher, Schorsch, and Wolfe, *Expressions of Innocence and Eloquence.*

5 Ann Douglas, *The Feminization of American Culture* (New York: Alfred A. Knopf, Inc., 1977).

6 The most extreme version of this thesis can be found in Edward Shorter, *The Making of the Modern Family* (New York: Basic Books, 1977). Also see Stephanie Coontz, *Marriage, a History: How Love Conquered Marriage* (New York: Penguin, 2006).

7 *Othello*, 1.3.334–335. Stanley Wells, *Shakespeare, Sex, and Love* (New York: Oxford University Press, 2010); Allan Bloom, *Shakespeare on Love and Friendship* (Chicago: University of Chicago Press, 2000); Bernard J. Dobski and Dustin A. Gish, eds., *Souls with Longing: Representations of Honor and Love in Shakespeare* (New York: Lexington Books, 2011).

8 Robert C. Solomon, *Love: Emotion, Myth, and Metaphor* (Amherst, N.Y.: Prometheus Books, 1990), xx–xxxv, 3–65.

9 Ann Swidler, *Talk of Love: How Culture Matters* (Chicago: University of Chicago Press, 2003).

10 Jean-Claude Kaufmann, *The Curious History of Love* (Malden, Mass.: Polity Press, 2011); Alan Soble, *Philosophy of Sex and Love*, 2nd ed. (St. Paul, Minn.: Paragon House, 2008); Robert C. Solomon, *About Love: Reinventing Romance for Our Times* (Indianapolis: Hackett, 2006); Simon May, *Love: A History* (New Haven, Conn.: Yale University Press, 2013).

11 Edward Taylor quoted in John Hoyt Lockwood, *Westfield and Its Historic Influences, 1669–1919* (Westfield, Mass.: Printed by the author, 1922), 1:157. Also see Sally K. Gallagher, *Evangelical Identity and Gendered Family Life* (Piscataway, N.J.: Rutgers University Press, 2003), 22; Richard Godbeer, *Sexual Revolution in Early America* (Baltimore: Johns Hopkins University Press, 2002), 52; Jay Fliegelman, *Prodigals and Pilgrims: The American Revolution against Patriarchal Authority, 1750–1800* (Cambridge: Cambridge University Press, 1985), 137.

12 Alexander Rice quoted in Ellen K. Rothman, *Hands and Hearts: A History of Courtship in America* (New York: Basic Books, 1984), 338.

13 Henry Poor quoted in ibid., 338.

14 Karen Lystra, *Searching the Heart: Women, Men, and Romantic Love in Nineteenth-Century America* (New York: Oxford University Press, 1989).

15 Gilbert H. Barnes and Dwight L. Dumond, eds., *Letters of Theodore Dwight Weld, Angelina Grimké Weld and Sarah Grimké, 1822–1844* (New York: D. Appleton-Century Co., 1934), 2:533.

16 Ibid.

17 Ibid. Also see Chris Dixon, *Perfecting the Family: Antislavery Marriages in Nineteenth-century America* (Amherst: University of Massachusetts Press, 1997).

18 Rothman, *Hands and Hearts.*

19 Carroll Smith-Rosenberg, "The Female World of Love and Ritual: Relations between Women in Nineteenth-Century America," in *Disorderly Conduct: Visions of Gender in Victorian America* (New York: Oxford University Press, 1985), 53–76.

20 Solomon, *About Love,* 42–48, 54–62.

21 Freud quoted in Robert C. Solomon, *In Defense of Sentimentality* (New York: Oxford University Press, 2004), 178. T. S. Eliot quoted in Donald J. Childs, *T. S. Eliot: Mystic, Son and Lover* (London: Bloomsbury Academic, 1997). Gloria Steinem quoted in Myron Magnet, ed., *Modern Sex: Liberation and Its Discontents* (Chicago: Ivan Dee, 2001), 36. Also see Solomon, *Love,* 192; Solomon, *About Love,* 36.

22 Helen Fisher, *Why We Love: The Nature and Chemistry of Romantic Love* (New York: Holt Paperbacks, 2004); Eva Illouz, *Why Love Hurts: A Sociological Explanation* (Malden, Mass.: Polity Press, 2012); Dan Slater, *Love in the Time of Algorithms: What Technology Does to Meeting and Mating* (New York: Current, 2013); Andrew Trees, *Decoding Love* (New York: Avery Trade, 2010).

23 George Bernard Shaw, "Overruled: A Comedy of Matrimonial Holidays," *Hearst's Magazine* 23 (1913): 687.

24 Jennifer Sue Hirsch and Holly Wardlow, *Modern Loves: The Anthropology of Romantic Courtship and Companionate Marriage* (Ann Arbor: University of Michigan Press, 2006); Eva Illouz, *Consuming the Romantic Utopia: Love and the Cultural Contradictions of Capitalism* (Berkeley: University of California Press, 1997); David Shumway, *Modern Love: Romance, Intimacy, and the Marriage Crisis* (New York: New York University Press, 2003).

25 Allan Bloom, *Love and Friendship* (New York: Simon & Schuster, 1993).

26 Aristotle quoted in Richard Godbeer, *The Overflowing of Friendship: Love between Men and the Creation of the American Republic* (Baltimore: Johns Hopkins University Press, 2009), 157. Also see Lorraine Smith Pangle, *Aristotle and the Philosophy of Friendship* (Cambridge: Cambridge University Press, 2003), 221; Albrecht Classen and Marilyn Sandidge, *Friendship in the Middle Ages and Early Modern Age* (Berlin: Walter de Gruyter, 2010), 551; Peter Brown, *Augustine of Hippo: A Biography* (Berkeley: University of California Press, 1967), 16.

27 Mark Vernon, "Is True Friendship Dying Away?" *USA Today,* July 26, 2010, http://usatoday30.usatoday.com/news/opinion/forum/2010–07–27 -column27_ST_N.htm.

28 John Gillies, ed., *Aristotle's Ethics and Politics* (London: A. Strahan and T. Cadell, 1797), 1:33. Cicero quoted in Caleb Crain, *American Sympathy: Men, Friendship, and Literature in the New Nation* (New Haven, Conn.: Yale University Press, 2001), 147.

29 On whether Americans have grown more isolated socially, see Miller McPherson and Lynn Smith-Lovin, "Social Isolation in America: Changes in Core Discussion Networks over Two Decades," *American Sociological Review* 71 (June 2006): 353–375; Hua Wang and Barry Wellman, "Social Connectivity in America: Changes in Adult Friendship Network Size From 2002 to 2007," *American Behavioral Scientist* 53, no. 8 (April 2010): 1148–1169. On friendship during adulthood, see Rosemary M. Blieszner and Rebecca G. Adams, *Adult Friendship* (Newbury Park, Calif.: Sage Publications, 1992); Robert Brain, *Friends and Lovers* (London: Hart-Davis MacGibbon, 1976); Heather Devere and Preston King, eds., *The Challenge to Friendship in Modernity* (Portland, Or.: F. Cass, 2000); Beverley Fehr, *Friendship Processes* (Thousand Oaks, Calif.: Sage Publications, 1996); Liz Spencer and Ray Pahl, *Rethinking Friendship: Hidden Solidarities Today* (Princeton, N.J.: Princeton University Press, 2006).

30 Barbara Caine, *Friendship: A History* (Oakville, Conn.: Equinox Publishers, 2008); Joseph Epstein, *Friendship: An Exposé* (Boston: Houghton Mifflin, 2006). For a vivid example of the dangers of social isolation, see Eric Klinenberg, *Heat Wave: A Social Autopsy of Disaster in Chicago* (Chicago: University of Chicago Press, 2003). Also see Robert D. Putnam, *Bowling Alone: The Collapse and Revival of American Community* (New York: Touchstone Books, 2001).

31 Spencer and Pahl, *Rethinking Friendship;* Epstein, *Friendship.*

32 Baron George Gordon Byron Byron, ed., *The Poetical Works of Lord Byron* (London: Frederick Warne and Co., 1891), 29.

33 Philips quoted in Penelope Anderson, *Friendship's Shadows: Women's Friendship and the Politics of Betrayal in England, 1640–1705* (Edinburgh: Edinburgh University Press, 2012), 106n28. Also see Sarah H. Matthews, *Friendships through the Life Course* (Beverly Hills, Calif.: Sage, 1986).

34 On face-to-face and side-by-side friendships, see Robyn Ryle, *Questioning Gender: A Sociological Exploration* (Thousand Oaks, Calif.: Sage, 2015), 215. Michael S. Kimmel, *The Gendered Society* (New York: Oxford University Press, 2000), 211, critically examines the supposed gendered differences in friendship styles.

35 David Konstan, *Friendship in the Classical World* (Cambridge: Cambridge University Press, 1997). Also see Caine, *Friendship.*

36 Daniel Mendelsohn, "The Man behind the Curtain," *Arion: A Journal of Humanities and the Classics,* third series 3, no. 2–3 (Fall 1995–Winter 1996): 241–273.

37 Wells, *Shakespeare, Sex, and Love;* John S. Garrison, *Friendship and Queer Theory in the Renaissance: Gender and Sexuality in Early Modern England* (New York: Routledge, 2013); Thomas MacFaul, *Male Friendship in Shakespeare and His Contemporaries* (Cambridge: Cambridge University Press, 2009).

38 Keith Thomas, *The Ends of Life: Roads to Fulfillment in Early Modern England* (New York: Oxford University Press, 2009).

39 Francis Bacon, *The Major Works,* ed. Brian Vickers (New York: Oxford University Press, 1996), 301; Lisa Hill and Peter McCarthy, "Hume, Smith, and Ferguson: Friendship in Commercial Society," in *Challenge to Friendship in Modernity,* ed. Devere and King, 33–49.

40 James Gibson quoted in Godbeer, *The Overflowing of Friendship,* 32. Charles Brockden Brown quoted in Crain, *American Sympathy,* 66. Also see Mark C. Carnes, *Secret Ritual and Manhood in Victorian America* (New Haven, Conn.: Yale University Press, 1991), 32; Peter B. Messent, *Mark Twain and Male Friendship* (New York: Oxford University Press, 2009); Linda W. Rosenzweig, *Another Self: Middle Class American Women and Their Friends in the Twentieth Century* (New York: New York University Press, 1999).

41 On same-sex friendships, see E. Anthony Rotundo, *American Manhood: Transformations in Masculinity from the Revolution to the Modern Era* (New

York: Basic Books, 1994); Smith-Rosenberg, "The Female World of Love and Ritual."

42 On fraternity and sorority in abolitionist circles, see Jean Fagan Yellin and John C. Van Horne, *The Abolitionist Sisterhood: Women's Political Culture in Antebellum America* (Ithaca, N.Y.: Cornell University Press, 1994); John Stauffer, *The Black Hearts of Men: Radical Abolitionists and the Transformation of Race* (Cambridge, Mass.: Harvard University Press, 2004).

43 On recent male friendships, see Peter M. Nardi, *Men's Friendships* (Newbury Park, Calif.: Sage Publications, 1992) and Peter M. Nardi, *Gay Men's Friendships: Invincible Communities* (Chicago: University of Chicago Press, 1999). For historical perspectives, see Carnes, *Secret Ritual and Manhood in Victorian America;* Craine, *American Sympathy;* Godbeer, *The Overflowing of Friendship;* Messent, *Mark Twain and Male Friendship.*

44 Burr quoted in Philip Greven, *The Protestant Temperament: Patterns of Child-Rearing, Religious Experience, and the Self in Early America* (New York: Alfred A. Knopf, 1977), 135. Also see Carol F. Karlsen and Laurie Crumpacker, *The Journal of Esther Edwards Burr, 1754–1757* (New Haven, Conn.: Yale University Press, 1986).

45 On the history of women's friendships, see Sharon Marcus, *Between Women: Friendship, Desire, and Marriage in Victorian England* (Princeton, N.J.: Princeton University Press, 2007); Melanie Tebbutt, *Women's Talk: A Social History of "Gossip" in Working Class Neighbourhoods, 1880–1960* (Brookfield, Vt.: Scolar Press, Ashgate, 1995); Kelly Valen, *Twisted Sisterhood: Unraveling the Dark Legacy of Female Friendship* (New York: Ballentine, 2010); Martha Vicinus, *Intimate Friends: Women Who Loved Women, 1778–1928* (Chicago: University of Chicago Press, 2006). On women's friendships in film, see Karen Hollinger, *In the Company of Women: Contemporary Female Friendship Films* (Minneapolis: University of Minnesota Press, 1998). On friendships in literary texts, see Patricia Ann Meyer Spacks, *Gossip* (Chicago: University of Chicago Press, 1986); Ronald Sharp, *Friendship and Literature: Spirit and Form* (Durham, N.C.: Duke University Press, 1986); Ronald A. Sharp and Eudora Welty, eds., *Norton Book of Friendship* (New York: Norton, 1991).

46 Stacey J. Oliker, *Best Friends and Marriage: Exchange among Women Best Friends* (Berkeley: University of California Press, 1989); Sandy Sheehy,

Connecting: The Enduring Power of Female Friendship (New York: Morrow, 2000).

47 On Platonic friendships, see Victor Luftig, *Seeing Together: Friendship between the Sexes in English Writing* (Stanford, Calif.: Stanford University Press, 1993); Juliet Lapidos, "What's Plato Got to Do with It?," *Slate*, September 27, 2010, http://www.slate.com/articles/life/strictly_platonic/2010/09/whats _plato_got_to_do_with_it.html.

48 Derek Attridge, ed., *The Cambridge Companion to James Joyce*, 2nd ed. (Cambridge: Cambridge University Press, 2004), 101; "Platonic Friends Gain Popularity as Women Move into Marketplace," *Sarasota Herald-Tribune*, April 19, 1982, http://news.google.com/newspapers?nid=1755&dat=1982 0419&id=dkk1AAAAIBAJ&sjid=JWgEAAAAIBAJ&pg=6406, 2796839.

49 Richard Dellamora, *Friendship's Bonds: Democracy and the Novel in Victorian England* (Philadelphia: University of Pennsylvania Press, 2004), 189; George Santayana, *The Life of Reason* (Amherst, N.Y.: Prometheus Books, 1998), 156.

50 "Platonic Friends Gain Popularity."

51 Alfred Riggs Ferguson and Jean Ferguson Carr, eds., *The Essays of Ralph Waldo Emerson*, (Cambridge, Mass.: Harvard University Press, 1987), 116.

52 Nardi, *Men's Friendships*, 1–14,132–152; Stephanie Coontz, "Too Close for Comfort," *New York Times*, November 7, 2006, http://www.nytimes .com/2006/11/07/opinion/07coontz.html?pagewanted=all&_r=0.

53 Caine, *Friendship*, 317–356; Epstein, *Friendship*, 56–68, 180–204.

54 Catherine Donovan, Brian Heaphy, and Jeffrey Weeks, *Same-Sex Intimacies: Families of Choice and Other Life Experiments* (New York: Routledge, 2013); Ewan Fergus, "Facebook: Destroying Friendship or Bringing Us Together?," *Herald* (Glasgow), August 3, 2009, 8; Tim Soutphommasane, "True Friends Lost in the Social Whirlwind," *Weekend Australian*, November 13, 2010, 12. The quotation from Aristotle can be found in James Boswell, *The Life of Samuel Johnson* (London: George Bell and Sons, 1884), 3:8. Keith Hampton, Lauren Sessions Goulet, Eun Ja Her, and Lee Rainie, "Social Isolation and New Technology," Report from the Pew Internet and American Life Project, November 4, 2009, http://www.pewinternet.org/~/ media//Files/Reports/2009/PIP_Tech_and_Social_Isolation.pdf, concluded

that those with mobile phones and Internet access had larger, more diverse social networks than those who did not, and that time spent on the Internet did not come at the expense of close, interpersonal relationships.

3. I DO

1 Nathaniel Hawthorne quoted in Patricia Dunlavy Valenti, *Sophia Peabody Hawthorne: A Life,* vol. 1, *1809–1847* (Columbia: University of Missouri Press, 2004), 184, and "Passages from Hawthorne's Notebooks," *The Atlantic* 18 (1866): 189. Sophia Peabody Hawthorne quoted in Ronald A. Bosco and Jillmarie Murphy, *Hawthorne in His Own Time* (Iowa City: University of Iowa Press 2007), 42. Also see T. Walter Herbert, *Dearest Beloved: The Hawthornes and the Making of the Middle-Class Family* (Berkeley: University of California Press, 1993).

2 Margaret Fuller quoted in Herbert, *Dearest Beloved,* xvi. Hawthorne quoted in Herbert, *Dearest Beloved,* 75. Sophia Peabody Hawthorne quoted in Randall Stewart, *Nathaniel Hawthorne, A Biography* (New Haven, Conn.: Yale University Press, 1948), 166. Also see, James R. Mellow, *Nathaniel Hawthorne in His Times* (Boston: Houghton Mifflin Harcourt Publishing Co., 1980), 459.

3 Eliot quoted in George Eliot, *Middlemarch: A Study of Provincial Life*, in *The Works of George Eliot,* ed. John Walter Cross (Edinburgh: William Blackwood and Sons, 1878), 3:455. Shakespeare quoted in *Othello,* act 3, scene 3, line 309, in *The Works of William Shakespeare,* ed. Sir Henry Irving and Frank A. Marshall (London: Gresham Publishing Co., 1906), 9:49.

4 For the Whiggish view, see Edward Shorter, *The Making of the Modern Family* (New York: Basic Books, 1976). For an example of the declensionist view, see Barbara Dafoe Whitehead, *The Divorce Culture* (New York: Knopf, 1997).

   For the history of marriage, see Elizabeth Abbott, *A History of Marriage* (New York: Seven Story Press, 2007); George Chauncey, *Why Marriage: The History Shaping Today's Debate over Gay Equality* (New York: Basic Books, 2005); Stephanie Coontz, *Marriage, a History: How Love Conquered Marriage* (New York: Penguin, 2006); Nancy F. Cott, *Public Vows: A History of Marriage and the Nation* (Cambridge, Mass.: Harvard University Press, 2002); John Gillis, *For Better, For Worse: British Marriages, 1600 to the Present* (New York: Oxford University Press, 1985); E. J. Graff, *What Is*

Marriage For? (Boston: Beacon Press, 2004). On interfaith marriages in the past, see Anne C. Rose, *Beloved Strangers: Interfaith Families in Nineteenth-Century America* (Cambridge, Mass.: Harvard University Press, 2001).

5 On homogamy in marriage, see Marco H. D. van Leeuwen and Ineke Maas, "Endogamy and Social Class in History: An Overview," supplement, *International Review of Social History* 50 (2005): 1–23; Zoe Williams, "Across the Barricades: Love over the Class Divide," *Guardian*, October 19, 2012, http://www.theguardian.com/lifeandstyle/2012/oct/19/class-divide-relationships-posh-rough; Tamar Lewin, "When Richer Weds Poorer, Money Isn't the Only Difference," *New York Times*, May 19, 2005, http://www.nytimes.com/2005/05/19/national/class/MARRIAGE-FINAL.html?pagewanted=all. Linda A. Pollock, *Forgotten Children: Parent-Child Relations from 1500 to 1900* (Cambridge: Cambridge University Press, 1984); Stephen Ozment, *When Father Ruled: Family Life in Reformation Europe* (Cambridge, Mass.: Harvard University Press, 1984); Gillis, *For Better, For Worse*.

6 Coontz, *Marriage, a History*.

7 Robert L. Griswold, *Fatherhood in America: A History* (New York: Basic Books, 1993).

8 Carl N. Degler, *At Odds: Women and the Family in America from the Revolution to the Present* (New York: Oxford University Press, 1980); Hendrik Hartog, *Man and Wife in America: A History* (Cambridge, Mass.: Harvard University Press, 2002); Jane Sullivan, "The Gap between Men and Women," *Age*, August 16, 2003, http://www.theage.com.au/articles/2003/08/15/1060871755569.html.

9 Andrew J. Cherlin, *The Marriage-Go-Round: The State of Marriage and the Family in America Today* (New York: Vintage, 2010).

10 *A Portrait of Stepfamilies*, Pew Research Social & Demographic Trends, January 13, 2011, http://www.pewsocialtrends.org/2011/01/13/a-portrait-of-stepfamilies/.

11 In its 1968 ruling in *Levy v. Louisiana* (391 U.S. 68), the Supreme Court held that the Fourteenth Amendment's guarantee of equal protection granted inheritance rights to "illegitimate" children. A 1973 ruling in *Gomez v. Perez* (409 U.S. 535) overturned state laws that freed men from financial responsibility for children born outside of wedlock.

12 Coontz, *Marriage, a History*, 263–314.

13 Frank F. Furstenberg Jr., "Fifty Years of Family Change: From Consensus to Complexity," *Annals of the American Academy of Political and Social Science* 654 (2014): 15.

14 Mintz and Kellogg, *Domestic Revolutions*, 203–238.

15 Robert Barnes, "On High Court, a Diversity of Marriages," *Washington Post*, March 18, 2013, A1.

16 Cherlin, *The Marriage-Go-Round;* Elizabeth Fox-Genovese, *Marriage: The Dream that Refuses to Die* (Wilmington, Del.: ISI Books, 2008); Arland Thornton, *Marriage and Cohabitation* (Chicago: University of Chicago Press, 2007).

17 Lewis Henry Morgan, *The League of the Ho-de-no-sau-nee or Iroquois*, ed. Herbert M. Lloyd (New York: Dodd, Mead and Company, 1922).

18 Lewis Henry Morgan, *Systems of Consanguinity and Affinity of the Human Family* (Washington, D.C.: Smithsonian Institution, 1871).

19 On the anthropology of marriage, see Robin Fox, *Kinship and Marriage: An Anthropological Perspective* (Cambridge: Cambridge University Press, 1984); Janice E. Stockard, *Marriage in Culture: Practice and Meaning across Diverse Societies* (Stamford, Conn.: Cengage Learning, 2001).

20 John Witte Jr., *From Sacrament to Contract: Marriage, Religion, and Law in the Western Tradition*, 2nd ed. (Louisville, Ky.: Westminster John Knox Press, 1997).

21 Luther quoted in Frances E. Dolan, "Shakespeare and Marriage: An Open Question," *Literature Compass* 8, no. 9 (2011): 620. William Gouge, *Of Domesticall Duties* (Norwood, N.J.: Theatrum Orbis Terrarum, 1976), 17.

22 Gataker quoted in Bruce Wilson Young, *Family Life in the Age of Shakespeare* (Westport, Conn.: Greenwood, 2009), 45. Milton quoted in Witte, *From Sacrament to Contract*, ix.

23 B. J. Sokol and Mary Sokol, *Shakespeare, Law, and Marriage* (Cambridge: Cambridge University Press, 2003); Sid Ray, *Holy Estates: Marriage and Monarchy in Shakespeare and His Contemporaries* (Selinsgrove, Penn.: Susquehanna University Press, 2004); Amy Kenny, "Domestic Relations in Shakespeare" (Ph.D. dissertation, University of Sussex, 2011), http://sro.sussex.ac.uk/42121/1/Kenny,_Amy.pdf; Dolan, "Shakespeare and Marriage"; Lisa Hopkins, *The Shakespearean Marriage* (New York: Palgrave Macmillan, 1998); Carol Thomas Neely, *Broken Nuptials in Shakespeare's Plays* (New Haven, Conn.: Yale University Press, 1985); Loreen L. Giese,

Courtships, Marriage Customs, and Shakespeare's Comedies (New York: Palgrave Macmillan, 2006); Ann Jennalie Cook, *Making a Match: Courtship in Shakespeare and His Society* (Princeton, N.J.: Princeton University Press, 1991).

24 The parody of the Elizabethan Book of Common Prayer's reasons for marriage can be found in *All's Well that Ends Well*, act 1, scene 3, in *The Works of William Shakespeare*, ed. Sir Henry Irving and Frank A. Marshall (London: Gresham Publishing Co., 1906), 8:100–103. Katherine's concluding speech in *The Taming of the Shrew* is in act 5, scene 2, lines 140–183, in *The Works of William Shakespeare*, 3:190. Within the Shakespearean canon, one sees a wide range of marriages: arranged marriages, strategic marital alliances, and mercenary marriages, but also love matches and playful conjugal sparring. One encounters examples of domestic patriarchy, aristocratic unions that are instruments for consolidating property and forging political alliances, as well as an emerging bourgeois view, which regarded intense conjugal unions as an essential source of social stability and the production of legitimate offspring.

In his generally hostile treatment of romantic love and of marriages freely chosen, Shakespeare echoed a dominant cultural consensus, which was skeptical of the capacity of unbridled passion, romantic attraction, or unions contracted across boundaries of race or social standing to generate enduring bonds. But what is especially striking is the diversity in his portrayals of marriage. Certain generalizations about Shakespearean marriages seem justified. Few marriages in the plays are truly happy, and the tragedies, in particular, raise doubts about marriage's ability to provide lasting personal satisfaction or ensure social stability. In *Othello*, two wives, Desdemona and Emilia, are unfairly accused of infidelity and murdered. In *Macbeth*, the title character's love for his "dearest partner of greatness" and "dearest love" gives way to estrangement and mutual contempt. In *Hamlet*, the Prince regards his mother's remarriage as incestuous, unnatural, and overly hasty. The tragedy also contrasts Gertrude's steadfast devotion to her husband with Claudius's shallow attachment to her.

25 The reference to "clog" can be found in *All's Well that Ends Well*, act 2, scene 5. The references to marriage can be found in can be found in act 5, scene 5, in *Henry VI, Part I*, in *Shakespeare's Works* (Chicago: Belford Clarke & Co., 1884), 5:88–92.

26 Steven Mintz and Susan Kellogg, *Domestic Revolutions: A History of American Family Life* (New York: Free Press, 1988), 1–24.

27 Ibid.

28 Lyle Koehler, *A Search for Power: The "Weaker Sex" in Seventeenth-Century New England* (Urbana: University of Illinois Press, 1980); Laurel Thatcher Ulrich, *Good Wives: Image and Reality in the Lives of Women in Northern New England, 1650–1750* (New York: Vintage, 1991); Marilyn Yalom, *A History of the Wife* (New York: Harper, 2002).

29 Mintz and Kellogg, *Domestic Revolutions*, 1–42.

30 Nancy F. Cott, *The Bonds of Womanhood: "Woman's Sphere" in New England, 1780–1835*, 2nd ed. (New Haven, Conn.: Yale University Press, 1997); Karen Lystra, *Searching the Heart: Women, Men, and Romantic Love in Nineteenth-Century America* (New York: Oxford University Press, 1989); Ellen K. Rothman, *Hands and Hearts: A History of Courtship in America* (New York: Basic Books, 1984).

31 Steven Mintz, *Huck's Raft: A History of American Childhood* (Cambridge, Mass.: Belknap Press of Harvard University Press, 2004), 75–93.

32 The quotations can be found in Rothman, *Hands and Hearts*, 72. On Mary Fish's "Portrait of a Good Husband," see Joy Day Buel and Richard Buel, *The Way of Duty: A Woman and Her Family in Revolutionary America* (New York: W. W. Norton, 1995), 79–83.

33 Cott, *The Bonds of Womanhood*, 80; Rothman, *Hands and Hearts*, 63, 68.

34 Elizabeth Freeman, *The Wedding Complex: Forms of Belonging in Modern American Culture* (Durham, N.C.: Duke University Press, 2002); Jaclyn Geller, *Here Comes the Bride: Women, Weddings, and the Marriage Mystique* (New York: Four Walls Eight Windows, 2001); Vicki Howard, *Brides, Inc.: American Weddings and the Business of Tradition* (Philadelphia: University of Pennsylvania Press, 2008); Chrys Ingraham, *White Weddings: Romancing Heterosexuality in Popular Culture* (New York: Routledge, 1999); Katherine Jellison, *It's Our Day: America's Love Affair with the White Wedding, 1945–2005* (Lawrence: University Press of Kansas, 2008); Rebecca Mead, *One Perfect Day: The Selling of the American Wedding* (New York: Penguin Books, 2007); Cele C. Otnes and Elizabeth Pleck, *Cinderella Dreams: The Allure of the Lavish Wedding* (Berkeley: University of California Press, 2003); Carol Wallace, *All Dressed in White:*

The Irresistible Rise of the American Wedding (New York: Penguin Books, 2004).

35 Rothman, *Hands and Hearts*, 63, 68, 76–80, 165–172.

36 Arnold van Gennep, *Rites of Passage* (Chicago: University of Chicago Press, 1961); Victor Turner, *The Ritual Process* (Chicago: Aldine Transaction, 1995). On young women's increasingly wrenching transition to marriage, see Cott, *The Bonds of Womanhood;* Rothman, *Hands and Hearts*, 160–166, 269–271, 274–276; and Lystra, *Searching the Heart.*

37 Mintz and Kellogg, *Domestic Revolutions*, 43–66.

38 Ibid. On Harriet Beecher Stowe, see Kathryn Kish Sklar, *Catharine Beecher* (New Haven, Conn.: Yale University Press, 1973), 320n2.

39 Mark C. Carnes, *Secret Ritual and Manhood in Victorian America* (New Haven, Conn.: Yale University Press, 1991).

40 Mintz and Kellogg, *Domestic Revolutions*, 107–132.

41 Ibid., 133–150.

42 Stephanie Coontz, *A Strange Stirring: The Feminine Mystique and American Women at the Dawn of the 1960s* (Philadelphia: Basic Books, 2011).

43 Glenda Riley, *Divorce: An American Tradition* (New York: Oxford University Press, 1991).

44 Jessie Bernard, *The Future of Marriage* (New York: World Publishing Co., 1972).

45 Coontz, *Marriage: A History;* Judith S. Wallerstein and Sandra Blakeslee, *The Good Marriage: How and Why Love Lasts* (New York: Grand Central Publishing, 1996).

46 Andrew J. Cherlin, "The Deinstitutionalization of Marriage," *Journal of Marriage and Family* 66, no. 4 (November 2004): 848–861.

47 The quotation can be found in Alice Morse Earle, *Customs and Fashions in Old New England* (New York: Charles Scribner's Sons, 1894), 290.

48 In a 1931 speech entitled "Professions for Women," Woolf wrote: "Killing the Angel in the House was part of the occupation of a woman writer." See Virginia Woolf, The *Death of the Moth and Other Essays* (New York: Harcourt, Brace & Co., 1942), 235–242.

49 Barbara Ehrenreich, *The Hearts of Men: American Dreams and the Flight from Commitment* (Garden City, N.Y.: Anchor Press/Doubleday, 1983); Griswold, *Fatherhood in America;* Michael S. Kimmel, *Manhood in America: A Cultural History* (New York: Oxford University Press, 2012); Ralph LaRossa, *The*

Modernization of Fatherhood: A Social and Political History (Chicago: University of Chicago Press, 1997).

50 Frank F. Furstenberg Jr., "Good Dads–Bad Dads: Two Faces of Fatherhood," in *The Changing American Family and Public Policy*, ed. Andrew J. Cherlin (Washington, D.C.: Urban Institute, 1988), 193–218.

51 Anne S. Lombard, *Making Manhood: Growing Up Male in Colonial New England* (Cambridge, Mass.: Harvard University Press, 2003); Lisa Wilson, *Ye Heart of a Man: The Domestic Life of Men in Colonial New England* (New Haven, Conn.: Yale University Press, 1999).

52 Stephen M. Frank, *Life with Father: Parenthood and Masculinity in the Nineteenth-Century American North* (Baltimore: Johns Hopkins University Press, 1998); Shawn Johansen, *Family Men: Middle-Class Fatherhood in Industrializing America* (New York: Routledge, 2001); David Leverenz, *Manhood and the American Renaissance* (Ithaca, N.Y.: Cornell University Press, 1989); David Leverenz, *Paternalism Incorporated: Fables of American Fatherhood, 1865–1940* (Ithaca, N.Y.: Cornell University Press, 2003).

53 Griswold, *Fatherhood in America*, 43–80; LaRossa, *The Modernization of Fatherhood*, 1–40.

54 Kimmel, *Manhood in America*, 1–9; Mintz and Kellogg, *Domestic Revolutions*, 133–150, 177–202.

55 Steven Mintz, "From Patriarchy to Androgyny and Other Myths: Placing Men's Family Roles in Historical Perspective," in *Men in Families: When Do They Get Involved? What Difference Does it Make?*, ed. Alan Booth and Ann C. Crouter (Mahwah, N.J.: Lawrence Erlbaum Associates Publishers, 1998), 3–30; Ralph LaRossa, *Of War and Men: World War II in the Lives of Fathers and Their Families* (Chicago: University of Chicago Press, 2011).

56 Kimmel, *Manhood in America*, 261–328.

57 Jeanine Basinger, *I Do and I Don't: A History of Marriage in the Movies* (New York: Alfred A. Knopf, 2012), xiii.

58 Stanley Cavell, *Pursuits of Happiness: The Hollywood Comedy of Remarriage* (Cambridge, Mass.: Harvard Film Studies, 1981), 161–188; Wexman, *Creating the Couple: Love, Marriage, and Hollywood Performance* (Princeton, N.J.: Princeton University Press, 1993); Marjorie Garber, *Vested Interests: Cross-dressing and Cultural Anxiety* (New York: Routledge, 1997), 1–20; Basinger, *I Do and I Don't*, 109.

59 Basinger, *I Do and I Don't*, 131–253, 309–364; Tom O'Brien, *The Screening of America: Movies and Values from Rocky to Rain Man* (New York: Continuum, 1990).

60 Basinger, *I Do and I Don't*, 184.

61 Michael Medved, *Hollywood vs. America: Popular Culture and the War on Traditional Values* (New York: HarperCollins, 1992), 95–160, argues that popular films waged an assault on the family, promoting promiscuity, maligning marriage, encouraging illegitimacy, and undercutting parental authority. It is indeed the case that only a handful of movies, like *The Thin Man* series, presented an appealing vision of marriage, wherein partners trade clever remarks and share adventures, and thereby illustrated what a companionate marriage might look like. Many movies have cast marriage in less flattering terms, featuring impulsive or shotgun marriages, long-suffering wives, and searing conflict. It would be a gross exaggeration, however, to conclude that Hollywood films are largely anti-marriage. Romantic comedies consistently portray marriage as love's ultimate affirmation and any intimate relationship's ultimate endpoint.

62 Kristin Celello, *Making Marriage Work: A History of Marriage and Divorce in the Twentieth-Century United States* (Chapel Hill: University of North Carolina Press, 2012); Rebecca Davis, *More Perfect Unions: The American Search for Marital Bliss* (Cambridge, Mass.: Harvard University Press, 2010); Deborah Weinstein, *The Pathological Family: Postwar America and the Rise of Family Therapy* (Ithaca, N.Y.: Cornell University Press, 2013).

63 On eugenics, social and mental hygiene, and marriage counseling, see Wendy Kline, *Building a Better Race: Gender, Sexuality, and Eugenics from the Turn of the Century to the Baby Boom* (Berkeley: University of California Press, 2001), 124–156; Morris Siegel, *Constructive Eugenics and Rational Marriage* (Toronto: McClelland & Stewart, 1934).

64 Davis, *More Perfect Unions*, 136–175; Celello, *Making Marriage Work*, 13–102.

65 Paul Popenoe's criticism of "mixed marriages" is quoted in Davis, *More Perfect Unions*, 111.

66 Dorothy Carnegie, *How to Help Your Husband Get Ahead in His Social and Business Life* (New York: Greystone Press, 1953). Also see Celello, *Making Marriage Work*, 72–102; Davis, *More Perfect Unions*, 136–175.

67 Emily Mudd, *The Practice of Marriage Counseling; An Experience Study and Guide for Teachers, Leaders and Counselors* (New York: Association Press, 1959); Morgan, *The Total Woman* (New York: Pocket, 1990).

68 Celello, *Making Marriage Work*, 119.

69 June Carbone and Naomi Cahn, "Inequality and Marriage," *Chronicle of Higher Education*, May 12, 2014, http://chronicle.com/article/Is-Wedlock-for-the-Wealthy-/146429/?cid=cr&utm_source=cr&utm_medium=en; Betsey Stevenson and Justin Wolfers, "Marriage and Divorce: Changes and Their Driving Forces," *Journal of Economic Perspectives* 21 (2007): 27–52; "Marriage and Divorce: Patterns by Gender, Race, and Educational Attainment," *Monthly Labor Review*, Bureau of Labor Statistics, U.S. Department of Labor, October 2013, http://www.bls.gov/opub/mlr/2013/article/marriage-and-divorce-patterns-by-gender-race-and-educational-attainment.htm.

70 Celello, *Making Marriage Work*, 129.

71 Ibid., 125.

72 The quotations can be found in Robert S. Lynd and Helen Merrell Lynd, *Middletown: A Study in American Culture* (New York: Harcourt Brace & World, 1929), 120, 125. Also see Celello, *Making Marriage Work*, 125; Betsey Stevenson and Justin Wolfers, "Bargaining in the Shadow of the Law: Divorce Laws and Family Distress," *Quarterly Journal of Economics* 121 (2006): 267–288. Demie Kurz, *For Richer, For Poorer: Mothers Confront Divorce* (New York: Routledge, 1995); Theodore Caplow, Howard M. Bahr, Bruce A. Chadwick, Reuben Hill, and Margaret Holmes Williamson, *Middletown Families: Fifty Years of Change and Continuity* (Minneapolis: University of Minnesota Press, 1982), 48.

73 See, for example, Mirra Komarovsky, *Blue Collar Marriage* (New York: Random House, 1964), 28–32, 50–72, 140, 148–150, 180–184.

74 Lee Rainwater, *Family Design: Marital Sexuality, Family Size, and Contraception* (Chicago: Aldine. 1965).

75 Ibid.; Lee Rainwater, *And the Poor Get Children: Sex, Contraception, and Family Planning in the Working Class* (Chicago: Quadrangle, 1960); Herbert J. Gans, *The Urban Villagers* (Glencoe, Ill.: The Free Press, 1962); David Halle, *America's Working Man: Work, Home, and Politics among Blue-Collar Property Owners* (Chicago: University of Chicago Press, 1984); E. E. LeMasters, *Blue Collar Aristocrats: Lifestyles at a Working-Class Tavern* (Madison: University of Wisconsin Press, 1975).

76 Lillian Rubin, *Worlds of Pain: Life in the Working-Class Family* (New York: Basic Books, 1976).

77 *The Negro Family: The Case for National Action*, Office of Policy Planning and Research, United States Department of Labor, March 1965, 5.

78 Mintz and Kellogg, *Domestic Revolutions*, 67–82.

79 Ibid. Family patterns that emerged under slavery differed in significant respects from those found among white Southerners. In contrast to the endogamy widely practiced among the planter elites, enslaved African Americans eschewed first-cousin marriages.

80 Elizabeth Pleck, *Black Migration and Poverty: Boston, 1870–1900* (New York: Academic Press, 1979).

81 Frank F. Furstenberg Jr., "The Making of the Black Family: Race and Class in Qualitative Studies in the Twentieth Century," *Annual Review of Sociology* 33 (2007): 429–448; Kathryn Edin and Maria Kefalas, *Promises I Can Keep: Why Poor Women Put Motherhood before Marriage* (Berkeley: University of California Press, 2005), 104–137.

82 Kathryn Edin and Timothy J. Nelson, *Doing the Best I Can: Fatherhood in the Inner City* (Berkeley: University of California Press, 2013); Elliott Leibow, *Tally's Corner: A Study of Negro Streetcorner Men*, 2nd ed. (Lanham: Rowman & Littlefield, 2003); Katherine S. Newman, *No Shame in My Game: The Working Poor in the Inner City* (New York: Vintage, 2000); Carol B. Stack, *All Our Kin: Strategies for Survival in the Black Community* (New York: Basic Books, 1997).

83 Frank F. Furstenberg Jr., "Diverging Development: The Not-So-Invisible Hand of Social Class in the United States," Network on Transitions to Adulthood Research Network Working Paper, 2006, http://transitions.s410 .sureserver.com/wp-content/uploads/2011/08/invisiblehand_final.rev _.pdf; Frank F. Furstenberg Jr., "The Intersections of Social Class and the Transition to Adulthood," *New Directions for Child and Adolescent Development*, 119 (2008): 1–10; "Births to Unmarried Women," *Child Trends Databank*, July 2014, 3–4, http://www.childtrends.org/wp-content /uploads/2012/11/75_Births_to_Unmarried_Women.pdf.

84 Marcia Carlson and Paula England, *Social Class and Changing Families in an Unequal America* (Stanford, Calif.: Stanford University Press, 2011); Charles A. Murray, *Coming Apart: The State of White America, 1960–2010* (New York: Crown Forum, 2012).

85 Steven L. Nock, James D. Wright, and Laura Ann Sanchez, *Covenant Marriage: The Movement to Reclaim Tradition in America* (New Brunswick, N.J.: Rutgers University Press, 2008).

86 Melanie Heath, *One Marriage under God: The Campaign to Promote Marriage in America* (New York: New York University Press, 2012).

87 Jason Pierceson, *Same-Sex Marriage in the United States: The Road to the Supreme Court* (Lanham, Md.: Rowman & Littlefield, 2013), 32; Karen M. Dunak, *As Long as We Both Shall Love: The White Wedding in Postwar America* (New York: New York University Press, 2013), 145.

88 Chauncey, *Why Marriage*, 59–136.

89 Lee Walzer, *Marriage on Trial: A Handbook with Cases, Laws, and Documents* (Santa Barbara, Calif.: ABC Clio, 2005), 51; General Accounting Office, Table of Statutory Provisions Involving Marital Status, January 23, 2004, http://www.gao.gov/new.items/d04353r.pdf.

90 Lucy Stone quoted in *Friends and Sisters: Letters between Lucy Stone and Antoinette Brown, 1846–93*, ed. Carol Lasser and Marlene Deahl Merrill (Urbana: University of Illinois Press, 1987), 56. Also see Hartog, *Man and Wife*, 122; Marylynn Salmon, *Women and the Law of Property in Early America* (Chapel Hill: University of North Carolina Press, 1986).

91 Quoted in *Report of the Debates and Proceedings of the Convention for the Revision of the Constitution of the State of New-York*, reported by William G. Bishop and William H. Attree (Albany: Evening Atlas, 1846), 1057. Also see Hartog, *Man and* Wife, 113, 117.

92 Nancy F. Cott, *Public Vows: A History of Marriage and the Nation* (Cambridge, Mass.: Harvard University Press, 2002). On miscegenation, see Peggy Pascoe, *What Comes Naturally: Miscegenation Law and the Making of Race in America* (New York: Oxford University Press, 2010); Martha Hodes, *White Women, Black Men: Illicit Sex in the Nineteenth-Century South* (New Haven, Conn.: Yale University Press, 1999); Cherlin, "The Deinstitutionalization of Marriage"; Stephanie Coontz, "Taking Marriage Private," *New York Times*, November 26, 2007, http://www.nytimes.com/2007/11/26/opinion/26coontz.html?_r=0.

93 United States v. Windsor, 570 U.S 25–26 (2013).

94 Pierceson, *Same-Sex Marriage in the United States*, 23–118; Michael J. Klarman, *From the Closet to the Altar: Courts, Backlash, and the Struggle for Same-Sex Marriage* (New York: Oxford University Press, 2013), 3–74;

Tiziana Nazio, *Cohabitation, Family & Society* (New York: Routledge, 2008).

95 Furstenberg, "Fifty Years of Family Change," 12–30; Isabel V. Sawhill, *Generation Unbound: Drifting into Sex and Parenthood without Marriage* (Washington, D.C.: Brookings Institution, 2014), 65–82.

4. I DON'T

1 Linda V. Carlisle, *Elizabeth Packard: A Noble Fight* (Urbana: University of Illinois Press, 2010), 1–15, 68–77.

On Mary Todd Lincoln's confinement, see Jean H. Baker, *Mary Todd Lincoln: A Biography* (New York: W. W. Norton & Company, 1987); Mark E. Neely Jr. and R. Gerald McMurtry, *The Insanity File: The Case of Mary Todd Lincoln* (Carbondale, Ill.: Southern Illinois University Press, 1986). Debate still rages about whether her confinement was appropriate or whether she was, rather, the eccentric victim of an unsympathetic patriarchal society. Symptoms that motivated her son to involuntarily commit her included paranoia, erratic finances (shifting between extravagant expenditures and exaggerated fears of penury), extreme interminable mourning, and physiological problems including debilitating headaches.

2 Carlisle, *Elizabeth Packard*, 57–117.

3 Ibid.

4 Kathryn Burns-Howard, "Slaves of the Marriage Union," Opinionator blog, *New York Times*, June 19, 2013, http://opinionator.blogs.nytimes.com/2013 /06/19/slaves-of-the-marriage-union/?_php=true&_type=blogs& _r=0.

5 Arthur Murray, ed., *The Works of Samuel Johnson, LL. D.* (New York: George Dearborn, 1836), 1:474.

6 Rachel Ablow, *The Marriage of Minds: Reading Sympathy in the Victorian Marriage Plot* (Stanford: Stanford University Press, 2007); Joseph Allen Boone, *Tradition Counter Tradition: Love and the Form of Fiction* (Chicago: University of Chicago. Press, 1987); Kelly Hager, *Dickens and the Rise of Divorce: The Failed-Marriage Plot and the Novel Tradition* (Burlington, Vt.: Ashgate, 2010)

7 Knox quoted in David Brion Davis and Steven Mintz, *Boisterous Sea of Liberty* (New York: Oxford University Press, 1998), 195. Declaration of Sentiments quoted in Elizabeth Cady Stanton, Susan Brownell Anthony, Matilda Joslyn

Gage, and Ida Husted Harper, *History of Woman Suffrage* (Rochester, N.Y.: Charles Mann, 1889), 1:70–71.

8 Queen Victoria quoted in Hager, *Dickens and the Rise of Divorce*, 1.

9 Dickens, *Little Dorrit*, in *The Works of Charles Dickens* (New York: Books Inc., 1868), 582.

10 Anne Bradstreet, *To My Husband and Other Poems*, ed. Robert Hutchinson (Mineola, N.Y.: Dover Publications, 2000), 1. Also see Francis J. Bremer, *First Founders: American Puritans and Puritanism in an Atlantic World* (Lebanon: University of New Hampshire Press, 2012), 6.

11 Lyle Koehler, *A Search for Power: The "Weaker Sex" in Seventeenth-Century New England* (Urbana: University of Illinois Press, 1980), 136–160, esp. 139 and 155–156; Steven Mintz and Susan Kellogg, *Domestic Revolutions: A Social History of American Family Life* (New York: Free Press, 1988), 11.

12 Koehler, *A Search for Power,* 144–145.

13 Mintz and Kellogg, *Domestic Revolutions,* 11–12.

14 Roderick Phillips, *Putting Asunder: A History of Divorce in Western Society* (Cambridge: Cambridge University Press, 1988).

15 Mary Beth Sievens, *Stray Wives: Marital Conflict in Early National New England* (New York: New York University Press, 2005), 4.

16 Sheila L. Skemp, *First Lady of Letters: Judith Sargent Murray and the Struggle for Female Independence* (Philadelphia: University of Pennsylvania Press, 2013); Carolyn L. Karcher, *The First Woman in the Republic: A Cultural Biography of Lydia Maria Child* (Durham, N.C.: Duke University Press, 1998).

17 Hendrik Hartog, *Man and Wife in America: A History* (Cambridge, Mass.: Harvard University Press, 2002).

18 Phillips, *Putting Asunder.*

19 Glenda Riley, *Divorce: An American Tradition* (New York: Oxford University Press, 1991), 10.

20 Mintz and Kellogg, *Domestic Revolutions,* 61.

21 Frank L. Dewey, "Thomas Jefferson's Notes on Divorce," *William and Mary Quarterly,* 3rd ser., 39, no. 1 (January 1982): 212–223.

22 Ann Lauer Estin, "Family Law Federalism: Divorce and the Constitution," *William and Mary Bill of Rights Journal* 16 (2007): 381–432.

23 David Brion Davis, *Antebellum American Culture* (Lexington, Mass.: D. C. Heath, 1979), 7–8, 93–97.

24 Norma Basch, *Framing American Divorce: From the Revolutionary Generation to the Victorians* (Berkeley: University of California Press, 1999).

25 Ibid.

26 Robert L. Griswold, "The Evolution of the Doctrine of Mental Cruelty in Victorian American Divorce, 1790–1900," *Journal of Social History* 20, no. 1 (1986): 127–148.

27 Riley, *Divorce: An American Tradition.*

28 Steven Ruggles, "The Rise of Divorce and Separation in the United States, 1880–1990," *Demography* 34 (1997): 455.

29 Lynne Carol Halem, *Divorce Reform: Changing Legal and Social Perspectives* (New York: The Free Press, 1980), 116–157.

30 Ibid., 127.

31 Lenore J. Weitzman and Ruth B. Dixon, "The Transformation of Marriage through No-Fault Divorce: The Case of the United States," in *Marriage and Cohabitation in Contemporary Society,* ed. John M. Eekelaar and Sanford Katz (Toronto: Buttersworth, 1980), 143–153; Herbert Jacob, *Silent Revolution: The Transformation of Divorce Law in the United States* (Chicago: University of Chicago Press, 1988); Halem, *Divorce Reform.*

32 Lenore J. Weitzman, *The Unexpected Social and Economic Consequences for Women and Children in America* (New York: Free Press, 1985), 339.

33 Ibid.; Richard R. Peterson, "A Re-Evaluation of the Economic Consequences of Divorce," *American Sociological Review* 61 (1996): 528–536.

34 *The Novels and Tales of Henry James* (London: Macmillan and Co., 1908), 10:36.

35 Paul R. Amato, "Children of Divorce in the 1990s: An Update of the Amato and Keith (1991) Meta-Analysis," *Journal of Family Psychology* 15 (2001): 355–370; Amato and J. M. Sobolewski, "The Effects of Divorce and Marital Discord on Adult Children's Psychological Well-Being," *American Sociological Review* 66 (2001): 900–921; Paul R. Amato, "Research on Divorce: Continuing Trends and New Developments," *Journal of Marriage and Family* 72 (2010): 650–666; Paula Fomby and Andrew J. Cherlin, "Family Instability and Child Well-Being," *American Sociological Review* 72, (2007): 181–204; Hal Arkowitz and Scott O. Lilienfeld, "Is Divorce Bad for Children?," *Scientific American,* February 14, 2013, http://www.scientificamerican.com/article/is-divorce-bad-for-children/.

36 Leonard Falkner, *Painted Lady: Eliza Jumel: Her Life and Times* [1962] (New York: Literary Licensing, 2011).

37 Donald J. Greiner, *Adultery in the American Novel: Updike, James and Hawthorne* (Columbia: University of South Carolina Press, 1985); Tony Tanner, *Adultery in the Novel: Contract and Transgression* (Baltimore: Johns Hopkins University Press, 1981).

38 Jeanine Basinger, *I Do and I Don't: A History of Marriage in the Movies* (New York: Knopf, 2013); Stanley Cavell, *Pursuits of Happiness: The Hollywood Comedy of Remarriage* (Cambridge, Mass.: Harvard University Press, 1984); Virginia Wright Wexman, *Creating the Couple: Love, Marriage, and Hollywood Performance* (Princeton, N.J.: Princeton University Press, 1993).

39 Brenda Cossman, *Sexual Citizens: The Legal and Cultural Regulation of Sex and Belonging* (Stanford: Stanford University Press, 2007), 86.

40 Alfred Charles Kinsey, *Sexual Behavior in the Human Female* (Bloomington: Indiana University Press, 1998), 429; Angus McLaren, *Sexual Blackmail: A Modern History* (Cambridge, Mass.: Harvard University Press, 2002), 258–260. Also see Sarah E. Igo, *The Average American: Surveys, Citizens, and the Making of a Mass Public* (Cambridge, Mass.: Harvard University Press, 2007), 252; K. A. Cuordileone, *Manhood and American Political Culture in the Cold War* (New York: Routledge, 2005).

41 Judith Treas and Deirdre Giesen, "Sexual Infidelity among Married and Cohabiting Americans," *Journal of Marriage and Family* 62, no. 1 (February 2000): 48–60.

42 Philip Cohen, "How to Live in a World Where Marriage Is in Decline," *Atlantic,* June 4, 2013, http://www.theatlantic.com/sexes/archive/2013/06/how-to-live-in-a-world-where-marriage-is-in-decline/276476/; Stephanie Coontz, "The Disestablishment of Marriage," *New York Times,* June 22, 2013, http://www.nytimes.com/2013/06/23/opinion/sunday/coontz-the-disestablishment-of-marriage.html.

43 Judith Stacey, *Brave New Families: Stories of Domestic Upheaval in Late Twentieth-Century America* (New York: Basic Books, 1990).

44 "Speech of Miss Polly Baker," *The Covent Garden Magazine Or the Amorous Repository* (1774), 3:225–227; Max Hall, *Benjamin Franklin & Polly Baker: The History of a Literary Deception* (Chapel Hill: Published for the Institute of Early American History and Culture by the University of North Carolina Press [1960]).

45 Linda Gordon and Sara McLanahan, "Single Parenthood in 1900," *Journal of Family History* 16 (1991): 97–116; Kristen Anderson, "The Number of U.S. Children Living in Single-Parent Homes Has Nearly Doubled in 50 Years: Census Data," LifeSiteNews.com, January 4, 2013, http://www.lifesite news.com/news/the-number-of-children-living-in-single-parent-homes -has-nearly-doubled-in/; Luke Rosiak, "Fathers Disappear from House- holds across America," *Washington Times*, December 25, 2012, http://www .washingtontimes.com/news/2012/dec/25/fathers-disappear-from-house holds-across-america/?page=all.

46 Gordon and McLanahan, "Single Parenthood in 1900"; Anderson, "Number of U.S. Children Living in Single-Parent Homes"; Rosiak, "Fathers Disappear from Households across America."

47 Gordon and McLanahan, "Single Parenthood in 1900."

48 Ibid.

49 Linda Gordon, *Single Mothers and the History of Welfare, 1890–1935* (New York: The Free Press, 1994).

50 Ibid.

51 Frank Furstenberg Jr., "The Recent Transformation of the American Family: Witnessing and Exploring Social Change," in *Social Class and Changing Families in an Unequal America*, ed. Marcia J. Carlson and Paula England (Stanford, Calif.: Stanford University Press, 2011), 192–220.

52 Jared Bernstein, "The Limits of Marriage as a Path out of Poverty," Economix blog, *New York Times*, January 20, 2014, http://economix.blogs.nytimes. com/2014/01/20/the-limits-of-marriage-as-a-path-out-of-poverty/.

53 Ibid.; Aparna Mathur, Hao Fu, and Peter Hansen, "The Mysterious and Alarming Rise of Single Motherhood in America," *Atlantic*, September 3, 2013, http://www.theatlantic.com/business/archive/2013/09/the-mysterious -and-alarming-rise-of-single-parenthood-in-america/279203/.

54 Alan Booth and Ann C. Crouter, *Just Living Together: Implications of Cohabitation on Families, Children, and Social Policy* (Mahwah, N.J.: Lawrence Erlbaum Associates, 2002); Ginger S. Frost, *Living in Sin: Cohabiting as Husband and Wife in Nineteenth-Century England* (New York: Manchester University Press, 2008); Elizabeth Pleck, *Not Just Roommates: Cohabitation after the Sexual Revolution* (Chicago: University of Chicago Press, 2012); Frank D. Fincham and Ming Cui, eds., *Romantic Relationships in Emerging Adulthood* (Cambridge: Cambridge University Press, 2011), 236.

55 Maureen Dabbagh, *Parental Kidnapping in America: An Historical and Cultural Analysis* (Jefferson, N.C.: McFarland and Co., 2012), 9; Julius E. Thompson, James L. Conyers Jr., and Nancy J. Dawson, eds., *The Frederick Douglass Encyclopedia* (Westport, Conn.: Greenwood, 2009), 124; Maria Diedrich, *Love across Color Lines: Ottilie Assing and Frederick Douglass* (New York: Hill & Wang, 2000), 186; Göran Lind, *Common Law Marriage: A Legal Institution for Cohabitation* (New York: Oxford University Press, 2008); Otto E. Koegel, *Common Law Marriage and Its Development in the United States* (Washington, D.C.: J. Byrne & Co., 1922); Ariela R. Dubler, *In the Shadow of Marriage: Widows, Common Law Wives, and the Legal Construction of Marriage* (Ph.D. dissertation, Yale University, 2003).

56 Pleck, *Not Just Roommates*, chap. 7.

57 *McLaughlin v. Florida*, Florida 379 U.S. 184 (1964); *King v. Smith*, 392 U.S. 309 (1968).

58 Pleck, *Not Just Roommates*.

59 Bella DePaulo, *Singled Out: How Singles Are Stereotyped, Stigmatized, and Ignored, and Still Live Happily Ever After* (New York: St. Martin's Griffin, 2007); Eric Klinenberg, *Going Solo: The Extraordinary Rise and Surprising Appeal of Living Alone* (New York: Penguin, 2013); E. Kay Trimberger, *The New Single Woman* (Boston: Beacon Press, 2005).

60 Stephen S. Mills, *A History of the Unmarried* (Little Rock, Ark.: Sibling Rivalry Press, 2014).

61 Howard P. Chudacoff, *Age of the Bachelor: Creating an American Subculture* (Princeton, N.J.: Princeton University Press, 2000), 21–44.

62 Ibid., 45–74

63 Ibid., 251–282; Barbara Ehrenreich, *The Hearts of Men: American Dreams and the Flight from Commitment* (Garden City, N.Y.: Anchor. Press/ Doubleday, 1984), 29–87.

64 Greg quoted in Blanche Wiesen Cook, "Incomplete Lives," *Women's Review of Books* 3, no. 1 (October 1985): 5.

65 Mitchell quoted in Phebe Mitchell Kendall, ed., *Maria Mitchell, Life, Letters, and Journals*, (Boston: Lee and Shepard, 1896), 26; Cary quoted in Edmund Hudson, *An American Woman's Life and Work: A Memorial of Mary Clemmer* (Boston: Ticknor and Company, 1886), 56; Howland's words are inscribed on her gravestone. Also see Gerda Lerner, "Single Women in Nineteenth-Century Society," *Reviews in American History* no. 1 (March 1987): 94–100;

Lee Virginia Chambers-Schiller, *Liberty, A Better Husband: Single Women in America: The Generations of 1780–1840* (New Haven, Conn.: Yale University Press, 1984), 54; Martha Vicinus, *Independent Women: Work and Community for Single Women, 1850–1920* (Chicago: University of Chicago Press, 1985).

66 Clare Taylor, *Women of the Anti-Slavery Movement: The Weston Sisters* (New York: St. Martin's, 1995); Jean Fagan Yellin and John C. Van Horne, *The Abolitionist Sisterhood: Women's Political Culture in Antebellum America* (Ithaca, N.Y.: Cornell University Press, 1994).

67 Rachel Hope Cleves, "A Field of Possibilities: Erotic Variations in Early America," *William and Mary Quarterly* 70, no. 3 (July 2013): 581–590; Cleves, *Charity and Sylvia: A Same-Sex Marriage in Early America* (New York: Oxford University Press, 2014), 92–141; Mark Bushnell, "The Diary (and Secrets?) of Sylvia Drake," *Barre Montpellier Times Argus*, April 5, 2009, http://www.timesargus.com/article/20090405/1016/FEATURE07.

68 Felicia Kornbluh, "Welfare Mothers," *Women's Review of Books* 12, no. 2 (November 1994): 17.

69 Regina G. Kunzel, *Fallen Women, Problem Girls: Unmarried Mothers and the Professionalization of Social Work, 1890–1945* (New Haven, Conn.: Yale University Press, 1993); Christine Jacobson Carter, *Southern Single Blessedness: Unmarried Women in the Urban South, 1800–1865* (Urbana: University of Illinois Press, 2006); Bridgit Hill, *Women Alone: Spinsters in England, 1660–1850* (New Haven, Conn.: Yale University Press, 2001).

70 Carter, *Southern Single Blessedness*.

71 In 1900, 31.2 percent of adult women were unmarried, compared to 23.6 percent in 2010. Marital Status of the Population by Sex, 1900–2010, Infoplease.com, http://www.infoplease.com/ipa/A0193922.html#ixzz2rn1dxIXr.

72 Linda Gordon, "Work and the Single Girl," *Women's Review of Books* 6, no. 2 (November 1988): 7–8. Also see Joanne J. Meyerowitz, *Women Adrift: Independent Wage Earners in Chicago, 1880–1930* (Chicago: University of Chicago Press, 1988).

73 Margaret Marsh and Wanda Ronner, *Empty Cradle: Infertility in America* (Baltimore: Johns Hopkins University Press, 1996); Elaine Tyler May, *Barren in the Promised Land: Childless Americans and the Pursuit of Happiness* (New York: Basic Books, 1995).

74 Steven Mintz, *Huck's Raft: A History of American Childhood* (Cambridge, Mass.: Harvard University Press, 2004), 77.

75 Marsh and Ronner, *Empty Cradle*, 9–40; May, *Barren in the Promised Land*, 21–60.

76 For an example of child placement practices during the Great Depression, see Russell Baker, *Growing Up* (New York: Signet, 1992).

77 Kate Harper, *The Childfree Alternative* (Brattleboro, Vt.: Stephen Greene Press, 1980); Irene Reti, ed., *Childless by Choice: A Feminist Anthology* (Santa Cruz, Calif.: Herbooks, 1992).

78 Joan Rothschild, *The Dream of the Perfect Child* (Bloomington: Indiana University Press, 2005).

79 DePaulo, *Singled Out;* Klinenberg, *Going Solo*.

80 Andrew J. Cherlin, *Marriage-Go-Round: The State of Marriage and the Family in America Today* (New York: Alfred A. Knopf, 2009).

81 Margot Canaday, *The Straight State: Sexuality and Citizenship in Twentieth-Century America* (Princeton, N.J.: Princeton University Press, 2011); Steven Nock, James Wright, and Laura Sanchez, *Covenant Marriage: The Movement to Reclaim Tradition in America* (New Brunswick, N.J.: Rutgers University Press, 2008).

5. THE TRIALS OF PARENTING

1 Peter N. Stearns, *Anxious Parents: A History of Modern Childrearing in America* (New York: New York University Press, 2004); Frank Furedi, *Paranoid Parenting* (London: Allen Lane, 2001).

2 Howard Chudacoff, *Children at Play: An American History* (New York: New York University Press, 2008); Gary Cross, *Kids' Stuff: Toys and the Changing World of American Childhood* (Cambridge, Mass.: Harvard University Press, 1997).

3 Richard Louv, *Last Child in the Woods: Saving Our Children from Nature-Deficit Disorder* (Chapel Hill, N.C.: Algonquin Books, 2008); Lenore Skenazy, *Free-Range Kids* (San Francisco: Jossey-Bass, 2010); David F. Lancy, "Talking Trash or Taking It Out?," *Psychology Today*, February 15, 2011, http://www.psychologytoday.com/blog/benign-neglect/201102/talking-trash-or-taking-it-out; David F. Lancy, "Toys or Tools," *Psychology Today*, December 2, 2010, http://www.psychologytoday.com/blog/benign-neglect/201012/toys-or-tools; David F. Lancy, "Gamesmanship," *Psychology Today*, November 8, 2010, http://www.psychologytoday.com/blog/benign-neglect/201011/gamesmanship.

4 Garey Ramey and Valerie A. Ramey, "The Rug Rat Race," *National Bureau of Economic Research*, NBER Working Paper No. 15284 (August 2009); "Married Parents' Use of Time Summary," Bureau of Labor Statistics, U.S. Department of Labor, May 8, 2008, http://www.bls.gov/news.release/atus2 .nro.htm.

5 Stearns, *Anxious Parents*.

6 Eliana Garces, Duncan Thomas, and Janet Currie, "Longer Term Effects of Head Start" (2000), http://www.princeton.edu/~jcurrie/publications /Longer_Term_Effects_HeadSt.pdf; "Head Start Research: Third Grade Follow-Up to the Head Start Impact Study," Office of Planning, Research and Evaluation, Administration for Children and Families, U.S. Department of Health and Human Services, October 2012, http://www.acf.hhs.gov /sites/default/files/opre/head_start_report.pdf.

7 John Stuart Mill, *Autobiography of John Stuart Mill* (New York: Columbia University Press, 1924).

8 David C. Ward, *Charles Willson Peale: Art and Selfhood in the Early Republic* (Berkeley: University of California Press, 2004); Charles C. Sellers, *Charles Willson Peale* (New York: Scribner, 1969).

9 Edgeworth quoted in Beatrix L. Tollemache, ed., *Richard Lovell Edgeworth, A Selection From His Memoirs* (London: Rivington, Perceval, and Co., 1896), 39; Also see Tony Lyons, *The Education Work of Richard Lovell Edgeworth, Irish Educator and Inventor, 1744–1817* (Lewiston, N.Y.: Edwin Mellen Press, 2003).

10 Wendy Moore, *How to Create the Perfect Wife: Britain's Most Ineligible Bachelor and His Enlightened Quest to Train the Ideal Mate* (New York: Basic, 2013).

11 Erasmus quoted in Hugh Cunningham, *Children and Childhood in Western Society since 1500* (New York: Routledge, 2005), 43. Also see Blaine Greteman, *The Poetics and Politics of Youth in Milton's England* (Cambridge: Cambridge University Press, 2013); Michael Witmore, *Pretty Creatures: Children and Fiction in the English Renaissance* (Ithaca, N.Y.: Cornell University Press, 2007).

12 Steven Mintz, *Huck's Raft: A History of American Childhood* (Cambridge: Mass.: Belknap Press of Harvard University Press, 2004) 58; Mary Beth Norton, *Founding Mothers and Fathers: Gendered Power and the Forming of American Society* (New York: Alfred A. Knopf, 1996), 98; Anthony Krupp,

Reason's Children: Childhood in Early Modern Philosophy (Cranbury, N.J.: Associated Universities Press, 2009).

13 Henry Fielding, *The History of Tom Jones: A Foundling* (New York: White, Stopes, and Allen, 1885), 1:105.

14 William Cadogan quoted in Christina Hardyment, *Dream Babies: Childcare Advice from John Locke to Gina Ford* (New York: Oxford University Press, 1984), 10.

15 Lord Chesterfield quoted in Hugh Cunningham, *The Invention of Childhood* (London: BBC Books, 2006), 116. Also see Anthony Fletcher, *Gender, Sex and Subordination in England, 1500–1800* (New Haven, Conn.: Yale University Press, 1995), 303.

16 Mintz, *Huck's Raft*, 32–52.

17 Steven Mintz, *Native American Voices: A History and Anthology* (Hoboken, N.J.: Wiley-Blackwell, 2000), 60–74.

18 Ibid., 7–31.

19 Mather quoted in David E. Stannard, *The Puritan Way of Death: A Study in Religion, Culture, and Social Change* (New York: Oxford University Press, 1977), 50. Also see Mintz, *Huck's Raft*, 11.

20 Barry Levy, *Quakers and the American Family* (New York: Oxford University Press, 1988), 123–230. Also see Mintz, *Huck's Raft*, 32–52.

21 Mintz, *Huck's Raft*, 25–42.

22 Ibid., 75–93.

23 Ibid., 53–93.

24 Vivian C. Fox and Martin H. Quitt, *Loving, Parenting, and Dying: The Family Cycle in England* (New York: Psychohistory Press, 1980), 302; *The Works of John Locke: Some Thoughts Concerning Education* (London: C. and J. Rivington, 1824), 8:41; Andrew O'Malley, *Making of the Modern Child: Children's Literature and Childhood in the Late Eighteenth Century* (New York: Routledge, 2003).

25 Mintz, *Huck's Raft*, 53–72.

26 Ibid.

27 Sarah Randolph, *The Domestic Life of Thomas Jefferson* (Scituate, Mass.: Digital Scanning, 2001), 70; Charles Francis Adams, ed., *Familiar Letters of John Adams and His Wife, Abigail Adams* (New York: Hurd and Houghton, 1875), 335.

28 Linda K. Kerber, *Women of the Republic: Intellect and Ideology in Revolutionary America* (Chapel Hill: University of North Carolina Press, 1997); Lindal

Buchanan, *Rhetorics of Motherhood* (Carbondale: Southern Illinois University Press, 2013).

29 Mintz, *Huck's Raft*, 75–93.

30 Bushnell quoted in Philip Greven, *The Protestant Temperament: Patterns of Child-Rearing, Religious Experience, and the Self in Early America* (Chicago: University of Chicago Press, 1977), 173. Child quoted in James E. Block, *The Crucible of Consent: American Child Rearing and the Forging of Liberal Society* (Cambridge, Mass.: Harvard University Press, 2012), 177.

31 Mintz, *Huck's Raft*, 133–153.

32 Ibid., 94–117.

33 Ibid.; Marie Jenkins Schwartz, *Born in Bondage: Growing Up Enslaved in the Antebellum South* (Cambridge, Mass.: Harvard University Press, 2001).

34 Mintz, *Huck's Raft*, 133–153.

35 Ibid.

36 Annette K. Vance Dorey, *Better Baby Contests: The Scientific Quest for Perfect Childhood Health in the Early Twentieth Century* (Jefferson, N.C.: Mcfarland & Co., 1999).

37 Mintz, *Huck's Raft*, 185–199.

38 Molly Ladd-Taylor, *Raising a Baby the Government Way: Mothers' Letters to the Children's Bureau, 1915–1932* (New Brunswick, N.J.: Rutgers University Press, 1986). Also see Kriste Lindenmeyer, *"A Right to Childhood": The U.S. Children's Bureau and Child Welfare, 1912–46* (Urbana: University of Illinois Press, 1997).

39 Louise Bates Ames, *Arnold Gesell: Themes of His Work* (New York: Human Sciences Press, 1989). Also see Kathleen W. Jones, *Taming the Troublesome Child: American Families, Child Guidance, and the Limits of Psychiatric Authority* (Cambridge, Mass.: Harvard University Press, 1999).

40 For historical perspectives on sibling relations, see Annette Atkins, *We Grew Up Together: Brothers and Sisters in Nineteenth-Century America* (Urbana: University of Illinois Press, 2000); George Howe Colt, *Brothers: On His Brothers and Brothers in History* (New York: Scribner, 2012); C. Dallett Hemphill, *Siblings: Brothers and Sisters in American History* (New York: Oxford University Press, 2011). For a social science perspective, see Frank J. Sulloway, *Born to Rebel: Birth Order, Family Dynamics, and Creative Lives* (New York: Vintage, 1997).

41 Mintz, *Huck's Raft*, 213–232.

42 Jones, *Taming the Troublesome Child.*

43 Mintz, *Huck's Raft*, 233–253.

44 Ibid., 254–274; Ralph LaRossa, *Of War and Men: World War II in the Lives of Fathers and their Families* (Chicago: University of Chicago Press, 2011).

45 Jeremy Holmes, *John Bowlby and Attachment Theory* (New York: Routledge, 1993); Frank C. P. Van der Horst, *John Bowlby — From Psychoanalysis to Ethology: Unravelling the Roots of Attachment Theory* (Malden, Mass.: Wiley-Blackwell, 2011).

46 Mintz, *Huck's Raft*, 254–274.

47 Ibid., 275–309. On Benjamin Spock, see Grant, *Raising Baby by the Book: The Education of American Mothers* (New Haven, Conn.: Yale University Press, 1998); Thomas Maier, *Dr. Spock: An American Life* (New York: Harcourt Brace, 1998).

48 Allison Davis and Robert J. Havighurst, "Social Class and Color Differences in Child Rearing," *American Sociological Review* 11 (December 1946): 698–710.

49 Mintz, *Huck's Raft*, 275–309.

50 Ibid., 310–371.

51 Ibid.

52 Joan Rothschild, *The Dream of the Perfect Child* (Bloomington: Indiana University Press, 2005).

53 Nathaniel Branden, *The Psychology of Self-Esteem: A New Concept of Man's Psychological Nature* (New York: Bantam Books, 1971); Stearns, *Anxious Parents*.

54 Mintz, *Huck's Raft*, 335–371.

55 Ibid.

56 Ibid., 372–386; E. Mavis Hetherington, *For Better or For Worse: Divorce Reconsidered* (New York: W. W. Norton, 2002).

57 James A. Schultz, *The Knowledge of Childhood in the German Middle Ages, 1100–1350* (Philadelphia: University of Pennsylvania Press, 1995).

58 Diana Baumrind, "Current Patterns of Parental Authority," *Developmental Psychology* 4 no. 1, pt. 2 (January 1971): 1–103.

59 William Sears and Martha Sears, *The Attachment Parenting Book: A Commonsense Guide to Understanding and Nurturing Your Baby* (Boston: Little, Brown, 2001).

60 Annette Lareau, *Unequal Childhoods: Class, Race, and Family Life*, 2nd ed. (Berkeley: University of California Press, 2011); Amy Chua, *Battle Hymn of the Tiger Mother* (New York: Penguin, 2011).

61 Judith Rich Harris, *The Nurture Assumption: Why Children Turn Out the Way They Do, Parents Matter Less Than You Think and Peers Matter More* (New York: Free Press, 1998).

62 Hardyment, *Dream Babies*.

63 Joyce Antler, *You Never Call! You Never Write! A History of the Jewish Mother* (New York: Oxford University Press, 2007).

64 Ibid., 72–99.

65 Diane Eyer, *Motherguilt* (New York: Times Books/Random House, 1996); Molly Ladd-Taylor, *Bad Mothers: The Politics of Blame in Twentieth-Century America* (New York: New York University Press, 1998); Rebecca Jo Plant, *Mom: The Transformation of Motherhood in Modern America* (Chicago: University of Chicago Press, 2010).

66 Sarah Arnold, *Maternal Horror Film: Melodrama and Motherhood* (New York: Palgrave Macmillan, 2013); Donna Bassin, Margaret Honey, and Meryle Mahrer Kaplan, eds., *Representations of Motherhood* (New Haven, Conn.: Yale University Press, 1996); David Greven, *Representations of Femininity in American Genre Cinema* (New York: Palgrave Macmillan, 2013); Alena Amato Ruggerio, ed., *Media Depictions of Brides, Wives, and Mothers* (Lanham, Md.: Lexington Books, 2012); Loren King, "Femme Fertiles," *Boston Globe*, May 9, 2010, http://www.boston.com/ae/movies/articles/2010/05/09/through_the_years_movies_have_embraced_motherhood__both_the_good_and_the_bad/.

67 Richard Corliss, *Mom in the Movies* (New York: Simon & Schuster, 2014), 21–34, 119–151.

68 The quotation, by Burton Rascoe, the editor and literary critic of the *New York Herald Tribune*, can be found in Ladd-Taylor, *Bad Mothers*, 266; Plant, *Mom*, 90.

69 Plant, *Mom*, 19–54.

70 Myra C. Glenn, *Campaigns against Corporal Punishment: Prisoners, Sailors, Women, and Children in Antebellum America* (Albany: State University of New York Press, 1984); Philip J. Greven, *Spare the Child: The Religious Roots of Punishment and the Psychological Impact of Physical Abuse* (New York: Knopf, 1990).

71 Elizabeth Hatkin Pleck, *Domestic Tyranny: The Making of Social Policy against Family Violence from Colonial Times to the Present* (New York: Oxford University Press, 1987).

72 Greven, *Spare the Child.*

73 Glenn, *Campaigns against Corporal Punishment;* Mintz, *Huck's Raft,* 75–93.

74 Glenn, *Campaigns Against Corporal Punishment.*

75 On therapeutic approaches to childrearing, see T. K. Taylor and A. Biglan, "Behavioral Family Interventions for Improving Child-Rearing: A Review of the Literature for Clinicians and Policy Makers," *Clinical Child and Family Psychology Review* 1 (March 1998): 41–60.

76 Joan E. Durrant and Anne B. Smith, eds., *Global Pathways to Abolishing Physical Punishment: Realizing Children's Rights* (New York: Routledge, 2011).

77 Pleck, *Domestic Tyranny.*

78 Lela B. Costin, Howard Jacob Karger, and David Stoesz, *The Politics of Child Abuse in America* (New York: Oxford University Press, 1996), 23–45, 51–66.

79 Ibid., 57; Mintz, *Huck's Raft,* 168.

80 Steven Mintz, "Placing Children's Rights in Historical Perspective," *Criminal Law Bulletin* 44 (May–June 2008), http://www.law.uh.edu /center4clp/events/gault-at-40/papers/44N03CrimLawBulletin2 -Gault-Mintz.pdf.

81 The quotation about the decline of the grosser forms of abuse can be found in Pleck, *Domestic Tyranny,* 40. Also see Pleck, *Domestic Tyranny,* 87; *Linda* Gordon, *Heroes in their Own Lives: The Politics and History of Family Violence* (New York: Viking, 1988), 1–26.

82 Child Trends Data Bank, 2014, http://www.childtrends.org/?indicators =child-maltreatment; U.S. Department of Health and Human Services, Administration for Children and Families, Administration on Children, Youth and Families, Children's Bureau, http://www.acf.hhs.gov/programs /cb, http://www.acf.hhs.gov/sites/default/files/cb/afcarsreport20.pdf; *Child Maltreatment 2011,* U.S. Department of Health and Human Services, Administration for Children and Families, Administration on Children, Youth and Families, Children's Bureau (Washington, D.C., 2012), http:// www.acf.hhs.gov/sites/default/files/cb/cm11.pdf.

83 Ray E. Helfer and C. Henry Kempe, eds., *The Battered Child* (Chicago: University of Chicago Press, 1968); Judith Sealander, *The Failed Century of the Child* (Cambridge: Cambridge University Press, 2003); Lynn Sacco, *Unspeakable: Father-Daughter Incest in American History* (Baltimore: Johns

Hopkins University Press, 2009); L. E. Behl, J. L. Crouch, P. F. May, A. L. Valente, and H. A. Conyngham, "Ethnicity in Child Maltreatment Research: A Content Analysis," *Child Maltreatment* 6, no. 2 (May 2001): 143–147.

Currently, there are about 700,000 substantiated cases of child abuse or neglect a year, down sharply from over a million in 1994, at the peak of the crack epidemic. Typically children in foster care spend a year or two with a foster family or in an institution or group home, though nearly 10 percent spend five years or more apart from their birth family. Child Trends Data Bank, 2014; *Child Maltreatment 2011.*

84 *Child Maltreatment 2011;* J. Briere and D. M. Eliot, "Prevalence and Psychological Sequence of Self-Reported Childhood Physical and Sexual Abuse in General Population," *Child Abuse and Neglect* 27, no. 10 (2003): 1205–1222.

Emily Douglas and D. Finkelhor, Childhood Sexual Abuse Fact Sheet, Crimes Against Children Research Center, May 2005, http://www.unh.edu/ccrc/factsheet/pdf/CSA-FS20.pdf. D. Finkelhor, "The Prevention of Childhood Sexual Abuse," *Future of Children* 19, no. 2 (2009): 169–194. D. Kilpatrick, R. Acierno, B. Saunders, H. Resnick, C. Best, and P. Schnurr, *National Survey of Adolescents* (Charleston, S.C.: Medical University of South Carolina, National Crime Victims Research and Treatment Center, 1998)."Sexual Assault of Young Children as Reported to Law Enforcement: Victim, Incident, and Offender Characteristics." U.S. Department of Justice, Bureau of Justice Statistics, 2000.

85 Matthew Waites, *The Age of Consent: Young People, Sexuality, and Citizenship* (New York: Palgrave Macmillan, 2005); Stephen Robertson, *Crimes against Children: Sexual Violence and Legal Culture in New York City, 1880–1960* (Chapel Hill: University of North Carolina Press, 2005).

86 Robertson, *Crimes against Children;* Steven Mintz, "Placing Childhood Sexual Abuse in Historical Perspective," *Immanent Frame* (2012), http://blogs.ssrc.org/tif/2012/07/13/placing-childhood-sexual-abuse-in-historical-perspective/.

87 Mintz, "Placing Childhood Sexual Abuse in Historical Perspective."

88 "Mandatory Reporters of Child Abuse and Neglect," Administration for Children and Families, U.S. Department of Health and Human Services (2012), https://www.childwelfare.gov/systemwide/laws_policies/statutes/manda.cfm.

89 Ray E. Helfer, "The Etiology of Child Abuse," *Pediatrics* 51 (1973): 777–779; J. Belsky and J. Vondra, "Lessons from Child Abuse: The Determinants of Parenting," in *Child Maltreatment*, ed. Dante Cicchetti and Vicki Carlson (Cambridge: Cambridge University Press, 1989), 168; J. M. Gaudin Jr., "Child Neglect: A Guide for Intervention," U.S. Department of Health and Human Services, 1993, https://www.childwelfare.gov/pubs/usermanuals/neglect_93/neglectc.cfm; Stanley M. Sturt, ed., *Child Abuse: New Research* (New York: Nova Science Publishers, 2006). On the "ecology of poverty," in which many children often grow up in unstable households with a caregiver subject to depression, see David K. Shipler, *The Working Poor: Invisible in America* (New York: Random House, 2005).

90 Daniel T. Kline identified these forms of abuse in an online posting, "Holding Therapy," March 7, 1998, History-child-family listserv, history-child-family@mailbase.ac.uk.

91 Christopher Ingraham, "Start Saving Now: Day Care Costs More than College in 31 States," *Washington Post*, April 9, 2014, http://www.washingtonpost.com/blogs/wonkblog/wp/2014/04/09/start-saving-now-day-care-costs-more-than-college-in-31-states/; "Who's Minding the Kids? Child Care Arrangements: Spring 2011" (Washington, D.C.: U.S. Bureau of the Census, 2011), http://www.census.gov/prod/2013pubs/p70-135.pdf.

92 Elizabeth Rose, *A Mother's Job: The History of Day Care, 1890–1960* (New York: Oxford University Press, 2003).

93 Ibid.; Jean Bethke Elshtain, *Jane Addams and the Dream of American Democracy* (New York: Basic Books, 2002), 106.

94 Mintz, *Huck's Raft*, 179–180, 244.

95 Ibid., 173, 179.

96 Ibid.; Steven Mintz and Susan Kellogg, *Domestic Revolutions: A Social History of American Family Life* (New York: Free Press, 1988), 129, 163–164, 218.

97 Mintz, *Huck's Raft*, 273.

98 Ibid.

99 Mintz and Kellogg, *Domestic Revolutions*, 223–225.

100 President Nixon quoted in Sonya Michel, *Children's Interests /Mothers' Rights: The Shaping of America's Child Care Policy* (New Haven, Conn.: Yale University Press, 1999), 250.

101 Edward Zigler, Katherine W. Marsland, and Heather Lord, *The Tragedy of Child Care in America* (New Haven, Conn.: Yale University Press, 2009).

102 "Who's Minding the Kids?"

103 Michel, *Children's Interests/Mothers' Rights;* V. Celia Lascarides and Blythe F. Hinitz, *History of Early Childhood Education* (New York: Falmer Press, 2000); Elizabeth Rose, *The Promise of Preschool: From Head Start to Universal Pre-Kindergarten* (New York: Oxford University Press, 2010).

104 Eunice Kennedy Shriver, "Hope for Retarded Children," *Saturday Evening Post,* September 22, 1962, http://www.eunicekennedyshriver.org/articles /article/148.

105 Philip L. Safford, *A History of Childhood and Disability* (New York: Teachers College Press, 1996).

106 Mintz, *Huck's Raft,* 324.

107 Ibid.; *Pennsylvania Association for Retarded Children v. Commonwealth of Pennsylvania* (334 F. Supp. 1257 E. D. Pa. 1971); *Mills v. Board of Education of the District of Columbia,* 348 F. Supp 866 (D. DC 1972).

108 For parental accounts of raising children with disabilities, see Rachel Adams, *Disregarding Henry: A Memoir of Motherhood, Disability, and Discovery* (New Haven, Conn.: Yale University Press, 2013); Martha Beck, *Expecting Adam: A True Story of Birth, Rebirth, and Everyday Magic* (New York: Times Books, 1999); Michael Bérubé, *Life as We Know It: A Father, a Family, and an Exceptional Child* (New York: Random House, 1996); Helen Featherstone, *A Difference in the Family: Living with a Disabled Child* (New York: Penguin, 1981); Marianne Leone, *Jesse: A Mother's Story* (New York: Simon & Schuster, 2011).

109 The quotation can be found in Michael Winerip, "They'll Do It Themselves, Thanks," *New York Times,* March 11, 2007, 14NJ, 1. Also see Jason Kingsley and Mitchell Levitz, *Count Us In: Growing Up with Down Syndrome* (New York: Harcourt, Brace, 1994); Jacques Steinberg, "Opening a Window Despite a Disability," *New York Times,* March 20, 1994, sec. 1, 38.

110 David J. Rothman and Sheila M. Rothman, *The Willowbrook Wars: Bringing the Mentally Disabled into the Community* (Piscataway, N.J.: Aldine Transaction, 2005).

111 Kingsley quoted in Steinberg, "Opening a Window Despite a Disability," sec. 1, 38.

112 Judy S. DeLoache and Alma Gottlieb, *A World of Babies: Imagined Childcare Guides for Seven Societies* (Cambridge: Cambridge University Press, 2000); David F. Lancy, *The Anthropology of Childhood: Cherubs, Chattel, Changelings* (Cambridge: Cambridge University Press, 2008); Meredith F. Small, *Kids: How Biology and Culture Shape the Way We Raise Young Children* (New York: Anchor Books, 2002); Meredith F. Small, *Our Babies, Ourselves: How Biology and Culture Shape the Way We Parent* (New York: Anchor Press, 1999).

113 Nicholas Day, *Baby Meets World: Suck, Smile, Touch, Toddle* (New York: St. Martin's Press, 2013); Annette Lareau, *Unequal Childhoods: Class, Race, and Family Life*, 2nd ed. (Berkeley: University of California Press, 2011), 1–13, 165–233, 259–262.

114 Sara Harkness and Charles M. Super, "Themes and Variations: Parental Ethnotheories in Western Cultures," in *Parental Beliefs, Parenting, and Child Development in Cross-Cultural Perspective*, ed. K. Rubin (New York: Psychology Press, n.d.), http://brown.edu/Departments/Human_Development_Center/Roundtable/Harkness.pdf; Pamela Druckerman, *Bringing Up Bébé: One American Mother Discovers the Wisdom of French Parenting* (New York: Penguin, 2012).

115 Zena Smith Blau, "Class Structure, Mobility, and Change in Child Rearing," *Sociometry* 28, no. 2 (June, 1965): 210–219.

116 Stanley Lieberson, *A Matter of Taste: How Names, Fashions, and Culture Change* (New Haven, Conn.: Yale University Press, 2010).

117 Lyle Koehler, *A Search for Power: The "Weaker Sex" in Seventeenth-Century* (Urbana: University of Illinois Press, 1980), 29.

118 Lieberson, *A Matter of Taste;* David Brooks, "Goodbye, George and John," *New York Times,* August 7, 2007, http://www.nytimes.com/2007/08/07/opinion/07brooks.html.

119 Lieberson, *A Matter of Taste.*

120 Ibid.

121 Steven Mintz, "Why the History of Childhood Matters," *Journal of the History of Childhood and Youth* 5, no. 1 (Winter 2012): 16–28.

122 Chudacoff, *Children at Play;* Mark Hyman, "Keep Sports Fun," Room for Debate, *New York Times,* October 10, 2013, http://www.nytimes.com/roomfordebate/2013/10/10/childrens-sportslife-balance/keep-sports-fun-3. On children's health and disabilities, see Janet Golden, Richard

Meckel, and Heather Munro Prescott, *Children and Youth in Sickness and in Health: A Historical Handbook and Guide* (Westport, Conn.: Greenwood, 2004).

123 Mintz, "Why the History of Childhood Matters."

124 Ibid.

6. FINDING FULFILLMENT IN WORK

1 Studs Terkel, *Working: People Talk about What They Do All Day and How They Feel about What They Do* (New York: Pantheon, 1974), xi–xxiv. For Elmer Ruiz, the gravedigger, see ibid., 507–512; for Donna Murray, the bookbinder, see ibid., 309–312; for Dolores Dante, the waitress, see ibid., 293–298. Also see Adam Cohen, "What Studs Terkel's 'Working' Says about Worker Malaise Today," *New York Times*, May 31, 2004, A16.

2 Terkel, *Working*, 105.

3 Ibid., xxiv.

4 John Bowe, Marisa Bowe, and Sabin C. Streeter, *Gig: Americans Talk about Their Jobs* (New York: Three Rivers Press, 2001).

5 Marjorie A. Ford, ed., *The Changing World of Work* (New York: Pearson/Longman, 2005).

6 Charles B. Camp, "Paradise Lost: Utopian GM Plant in Ohio Falls from Grace under Strain of Balky Machinery, Workers," *Wall Street Journal*, January 31, 1972, 28; Ken Weller, "1970–1972: The Lordstown Struggle and the Real Crisis in Production," http://libcom.org/library/lordstown-struggle-ken-weller; Ken Weller, "Sabotage at Lordstown?," *Time*, February 7, 1972), 82; Betsy Carter, "Lordstown Today," *Newsweek*, March 17, 1975, 14.

7 Warren Brown, "Growing Mellow in Lordstown; Realities of the'80s Dampen Fires of the'70s at GM Plant; 'Craziness Is Gone' at Lordstown," *Washington Post*, March 21, 1982, F1; James B. Treece, "The Mood at Lordstown Changed from Confrontation to Cooperation," *Automotive News*, October 31, 2011, NaN.

8 Jerry A. Jacobs and Kathleen Gerson, *The Time Bind: Work, Family, and Gender Inequality* (Cambridge, Mass.: Harvard University Press, 2005).

9 Joanne B. Ciulla, *The Working Life: The Promise and Betrayal of Modern Work* (New York: Random House, 1999); Peter N. Stearns, *From Alienation to*

Addiction: Modern American Work in Global Historical Perspective (Boulder, Col.: Paradigm Publishers, 2008).

10 Ciulla, *The Working Life*, 3–72.

11 Alain De Botton, *The Pleasures and Sorrows of Work* (New York: Pantheon Books, 2009); Al Gini, *My Job, My Self: Work and the Creation of the Modern Individual* (New York: Routledge, 2000); Tom Juravich, *At the Altar of the Bottom Line: The Degradation of Work in the 21st Century* (Amherst: University of Massachusetts Press, 2009); Arne L. Kalleberg, *Good Jobs, Bad Jobs: The Rise of Polarized and Precarious Employment Systems in the United States, 1970s–2000s* (New York: Russell Sage, 2011); Daniel H. Pink, *Free Agent Nation: How America's New Independent Workers Are Transforming the Way We Live* (New York: Warner Books, 2001).

12 John W. Budd, *The Thought of Work* (Ithaca, N.Y.: ILR Press, 2011).

13 Ibid.

14 Jacobs and Gerson, *The Time Bind*.

15 Budd, *The Thought of Work;* Arlie Russell Hochschild, *The Time Bind: When Work Becomes Home and Home Becomes Work* (New York: Metropolitan/ Holt, 2001).

16 On pre-Marxian critiques of workplace exploitation, see Sean Wilentz, *Chants Democratic: New York City and the Rise of the American Working Class, 1788–1850* (New York: Oxford University Press, 2004). Arthur Miller explicates his argument about the soul-numbing impact of modern work in "Tragedy and the Common Man," *New York Times*, February 27, 1949, http://www.nytimes.com/books/00/11/12/specials/miller-common .html. For an overview of recent feminist approaches to the subject of workplace exploitation, see Ann Ferguson and Rosemary Henessey, "Feminist Perspectives on Class and Work," *Stanford Encyclopedia of Philosophy*, ed. Edward N. Zalta, Winter 2010 ed., http://plato.stanford.edu/entries /feminism-class/.

17 Matthew B. Crawford, *Shop Class as Soulcraft: An Inquiry into the Value of Work* (New York: Penguin, 2010). Also see Richard Sennett, *The Craftsman* (New Haven, Conn.: Yale University Press, 2008).

18 Budd, *The Thought of Work*.

19 Keith Thomas, *The Ends of Life: Roads to Fulfillment in Early Modern England* (New York: Oxford University Press, 2009), 78–109; Joseph Conrad, *Heart of Darkness* (New York: Vintage, 2007), 77; T. H. L. Parker, ed.,

John Calvin's New Testament Commentaries: A Harmony of the Gospels, Matthew, Mark, & Luke (Grand Rapids, Mich.: Wm. B. Eerdmans Publishing Co., 1972), 2:89.

20 Joseph Epstein, *Ambition: The Secret Passion* (Chicago: Ivan R. Dee, 1989); William Casey King, *Ambition, a History: From Vice to Virtue* (New Haven, Conn.: Yale University Press, 2013).

21 Peter Gay, *The Cultivation of Hatred*, vol. 4 of *The Bourgeois Experience: Victoria to Freud* (New York: W. W. Norton, 1993).

22 Peter N. Stearns, *Satisfaction Not Guaranteed: Dilemmas of Progress in Modern Society* (New York: New York University Press, 2012).

23 Sheryl Sandberg, *Lean In: Women, Work, and the Will to Lead* (New York: Knopf, 2013); Debora L. Spar, *Wonder Women: Sex, Power, and the Quest for Perfection* (New York: Sarah Crichton Books, 2013).

24 On the distinction between preindustrial and industrial conceptions of work and their connections to gender, see Nancy F. Cott, *The Bonds of Womanhood: "Woman's Sphere" in New England* (New Haven, Conn.: Yale University Press, 1977), 19–62. Harold C. Syrett, ed., *Papers of Alexander Hamilton* (New York: Columbia University Press, 1979), 26:638; Christopher Clark, *The Roots of Rural Capitalism: Western Massachusetts, 1780–1860* (Ithaca, N.Y.: Cornell University Press, 1992); James A. Henretta, *The Evolution of American Society, 1700–1815* (Lexington, Mass.: D. C. Heath and Co., 1973).

25 Cott, *Bonds of Womanhood.* For a British comparison, see Leonore Davidoff and Catherine Hall, *Family Fortunes: Men and Women of the English Middle Class, 1780–1850* (New York: Routledge, 2003).

26 On women faculty workers, see Alice Kessler-Harris, *Out to Work: A History of Wage-Earning Women in the United States* (New York: Oxford University Press, 2003); Thomas Louis Dublin, *Women at Work: The Transformation of Work and Community in Lowell, Massachusetts, 1826–1860* (New York: Columbia University Press, 1981). On shifting conceptions of time, see E. P. Thompson, "Time, Work-Discipline and Industrial Capitalism," *Past & Present* 38, no. 1 (1967): 56–97.

27 Thomas Dublin, *Farm to Factory* (New York: Columbia University Press, 1993).

28 Michael S. Kimmel, *Manhood in America: A Cultural History* (New York: Oxford University Press, 2012); E. Anthony Rotundo, *American Manhood: Transformations in Masculinity from the Revolution to the Modern Era* (New

York: Basic Books, 1994). In France, the male breadwinner model never achieved the dominance that it did in Britain or the United States. Colin Creighton, "The Rise and Decline of the 'Male Breadwinner Family' in Britain," *Cambridge Journal of Economics* 23 (1999): 519–541; C. Creighton, "The Rise of the Male Breadwinner Family: A Reappraisal," *Comparative Studies in Society and History* 38 (1996): 310–337; Jessie Bernard, "The Good-Provider Role: Its Rise and Fall," *American Psychologist* 36 (1981): 1–12.

29 Joann Vanek, "Time Spent in Housework," *Scientific American* 5 (November 1974): 116–120.

30 Kristie M. Engemann and Michael T. Owyang, "Social Changes Lead Married Women into Labor Force," *Regional Economist*, April 2006, http://www.stlouisfed.org/publications/re/articles/?id=336; Raquel Fernández, Alessandra Fogli, and Claudia Olivetti, "Mothers and Sons: Preference Formation and Female Labor Force Dynamics," *Quarterly Journal of Economics* 119, no. 4 (November 2004): 1249–1299; Claudia Goldin, *Understanding the Gender Gap* (New York: Oxford University Press, 1990).

31 Angelique Janssens, ed., *The Rise and Decline of the Male Breadwinner Family? Studies in Gendered Patterns of Labour Division and Household Organisation* (Cambridge: Cambridge University Press, 1998); Jeremy Greenwood, Ananth Seshadri, and Mehmet Yorukoglu, "Engines of Liberation," *Review of Economic Studies* 72 (January 2005): 109–133; Elaine Tyler May, *America and the Pill: A History of Promise, Peril, and Liberation* (New York: Basic Books, 2010); Claudia Goldin and Lawrence F. Katz, "The Power of the Pill: Oral Contraceptives and Women's Career and Marriage Decisions," *Journal of Political Economy* 110, no. 4 (August 2002): 730–770.

32 Stephanie Coontz, "The Family in Upheaval," *Philadelphia Inquirer*, June 19, 2005, http://www.stephaniecoontz.com/articles/article17.htm.

33 Angélique Janssens, "The Rise and Decline of the Male Breadwinner Family?: Studies in Gendered Patterns of Labour Division and Household Organisation," *International Review of Social History* 42, suppl. S5 (September 1997): 1–23.

34 Christopher Tomlins, *Freedom Bound: Law, Labor, and Civic Identity in Colonizing English America, 1580–1865* (New York: Cambridge University Press, 2010), 247, 249, 265, 272.

35 David Brion Davis, *Inhuman Bondage: The Rise and Fall of Slavery in the New World* (New York: Oxford University Press, 2008); John Van Der Zee, *Bound Over: Indentured Servitude and American Conscience* (New York: Holiday House, 1986).

36 Lyle Koehler, *A Search for Power: The "Weaker Sex" in Seventeenth-Century New England* (Urbana: University of Illinois Press, 1980), 111.

37 Van Der Zee, *Bound Over;* Gordon S. Wood, *The Radicalism of the American Revolution* (New York: Vintage, 1993); Myra Glenn, *Campaigns against Corporal Punishment: Prisoners, Sailors, Women, and Children in Antebellum America* (Albany: State University of New York Press, 1984).

38 Tomlins, *Freedom Bound;* Christopher Tomlins, *Law, Labor, and Ideology in the Early American Republic* (Cambridge: Cambridge University Press, 1993).

39 On married women's right to their own earnings, see Joyce W. Warren, *Women, Money, and the Law: Nineteenth-Century Fiction, Gender, and the Courts* (Iowa City: University of Iowa Press. 2005), 51–53. On penal sanctions for contract violations, see *Bailey v. Alabama,* 219 U.S. 219 (1911).

40 Wilentz, *Chants Democratic;* Stephan Thernstrom, *Poverty and Progress: Social Mobility in a Nineteenth-Century City* (Cambridge, Mass.: Harvard University Press, 1964), 21.

41 Alexander Keyssar, *Out of Work: The First Century of Unemployment in Massachusetts* (Cambridge: Cambridge University Press, 1986).

42 Thernstrom, *Poverty and Progress,* 22.

43 "Carpenters have an eye for length, line, and angle; mechanics troubleshoot by listening; hair stylists are attuned to shape, texture, and motion. Sensory data merge with concept, as when an auto mechanic relies on sound, vibration, and even smell to understand what cannot be observed." Mike Rose, "Blue-Collar Brilliance: Questioning Assumptions about Intelligence, Work, and Social Class," *American Scholar,* Summer 2009, http://theamerican scholar.org/blue-collar-brilliance/.

44 David H. Autor and David Dorn, "The Growth of Low Skill Service Jobs and the Polarization of the U.S. Labor Market," *American Economic Review* 103, no. 5 (2011): 1553–1597, http://scii.mit.edu/wp content/uploads/2011/11/Autor-Dorn-Spec-Svcs-Rev-June21-20112.pdf.

45 Mark Wyman, *Hoboes: Bindlestiffs, Fruit Tramps, and the Harvesting of the West* (New York: Hill & Wang, 2010).

46 Ibid.

47 Ibid.

48 Kenneth L. Kusmer, *Down and Out, On the Road: The Homeless in American History* (New York: Oxford University Press, 2002), 211.

49 Timothy B. Spears, *100 Years on the Road: The Traveling Salesman in American Culture* (New Haven, Conn.: Yale University Press, 1997).

50 Timothy Dwight, *Travels in New England and New York* (London: W. Baynes and Ogle, Duncan, 1823), 1:233.

51 Alice Morse Earle, *Customs and Fashions in Old New England* (New York: Charles Scribner's Sons, 1894), 244.

52 Peter Benes and Jane Montague Benes, eds., *Itinerancy in New England and New York* (Boston: Boston University, 1984), 243. In 1862, in one despicable incident during the Civil War, Ulysses S. Grant issued his infamous General Order No. 11, which expelled all Jews from Kentucky, Tennessee, and Mississippi. Early in 1863, Abraham Lincoln had the order revoked.

53 Walter A Friedman, *Birth of a Salesman: The Transformation of Selling in America* (Cambridge, Mass.: Harvard University Press, 2004), 46.

54 Ibid., 118–148.

55 Ibid., 207.

56 Ibid.; Daniel H. Pink, *To Sell Is Human* (New York: Riverhead, 2012).

57 Rosabeth Moss Kanter, *Men and Women of the Corporation*, new ed. (New York: Basic Books, 1993); Jeanette N. Cleveland, Margaret Stockdale, Kevin R. Murphy, and Barbara A. Gutek, *Women and Men in Organizations: Sex and Gender Issues at Work* (New York: Psychology Press, 2000); Leon Lipson, "Review of *The Organization Man* by William H. Whyte," *Yale Law Journal* 66, no. 8 (July 1957): 1267–1276.

58 Benjamin Christopher Stroud, "Perilous Landscapes: The Postwar Suburb in Twentieth-Century American Fiction" (Ph.D. dissertation, University of Michigan, 2009), 1–14.

59 Clayton M. Christensen, *The Innovator's Dilemma* (New York: Harpers Business, 2011).

60 Sharon Beder, "Conformity Not Conducive to Creativity," *Engineers Australia*, April 1999, 60, http://www.uow.edu.au/~sharonb/columns/engcol13.html.

61 Cindy Aron, *Ladies and Gentlemen of the Civil Service* (New York: Oxford University Press, 1987), 3–10; M. Christine Anderson, "Gender, Class,

and Culture: Women Secretarial and Clerical Workers in the United States, 1925–1955" (Ph.D. dissertation, Ohio State University, 1986); Ilene DeVault, *Sons and Daughters of Labor: Class and Clerical Work in Turn-of-the-Century Pittsburgh* (Ithaca, N.Y.: Cornell University Press, 1990); Angel Kwolek-Folland, "The Business of Gender: The Redefinition of Male and Female and the Modern Business Office in the United States, 1880–1930" (Ph.D. dissertation, University of Minnesota, 1987); Ava Baron, ed., *Work Engendered: Toward a New History of American Labor* (Ithaca, N.Y.: Cornell University Press, 1991); Lisa M. Fine, *The Souls of the Skyscraper: Female Clerical Workers in Chicago, 1870–1930* (Philadelphia: Temple University Press,1990).

62 Aron, *Ladies and Gentlemen of the Civil Service*, 63–95; DeVault, *Sons and Daughters of Labor*, 9–23.

63 Aron, *Ladies and Gentlemen of the Civil Service*, 3–10.

64 Sarah Booth Conroy, "Hints of Historic Harassment: At the Kiplinger, a Show of Old Federal Power Plays," *Washington Post*, December 1, 1991, F1; Julie Berebitsky, *Sex and the Office: A History of Gender, Power, and Desire* (New Haven, Conn.: Yale University Press, 2012), 25–116, 141–176, 251–286; DeVault, *Sons and Daughters of Labor*, 162–183.

65 Donald Hoke, "The Woman and the Typewriter: Case Study in Technological Innovation and Social Change," *Business and Economic History* 8 (1979): 76–88, available at: http://www.h-net.org/~business/bhcweb/publica tions/BEHprint/v008/p0076-p0088.pdf.

66 Aron, *Ladies and Gentlemen of the Civil Service*, 63–95.

67 Ibid.; DeVault, *Sons and Daughters of Labor*, 9–23, 105–171.

68 Maureen Honey, *Creating Rosie the Riveter: Class, Gender, and Propaganda during World War II* (Amherst: University of Massachusetts Press, 1984); Sherna Berger Gluck, *Rosie the Riveter Revisited: Women, the War, and Social Change* (New York: Meridian, 1988).

69 Stephanie Coontz, *A Strange Stirring: The Feminine Mystique and American Women at the Dawn of the 1960s* (New York: Basic Books, 2011), 35–58.

70 Joan C. Williams, *Reshaping the Work-Family Debate: Why Men and Class Matter* (Cambridge, Mass.: Harvard University Press, 2012); Joan C. Williams, *Unbending Gender: Why Family and Work Conflict and What to Do about It* (New York: Oxford University Press, 2001); Arlie Hochschild, *The Second Shift* (New York: Penguin, 2003); Brigid Schulte, *Overwhelmed:*

Work, Love, and Play When No One Has the Time (New York: Farrar, Strauss, Giroux, 2014).

71 U.S. Department of Labor, "Women's Employment during the Recovery," May 3, 2011, available at http://www.dol.gov/_sec/media/reports /FemaleLaborForce/FemaleLaborForce.pdf. On the impact of part-time employment on women's well-being and ability to balance conflicting responsibilities, see Cheryl Buehler and Marion O'Brien, "Mothers' Part-Time Employment: Associations with Mother and Family Well-Being," *Journal of Family Psychology* 25, no. 6 (2011): 895–906. On the issue of whether working mothers would prefer to work full or part-time, see "The Harried Life of the Working Mother," Pew Research (2009), http://www.pewso cialtrends.org/2009/10/01/the-harried-life-of-the-working-mother/; Erika Christakis, "Let's Not Forget, Many Working Moms Want to Work Less," *Time*, June 12, 2013, http://ideas.time.com/2013/06/12/lets-not-forget -many-working-moms-want-to-work-less/#ixzz2qDZ76T4q; K. J. Dell'Antonia, "Do Working Mothers Really Prefer Part-Time Jobs?," *New York Times*, December 16, 2011, http://parenting.blogs.nytimes.com /2011/12/16/do-working-moms-really-prefer-part-time-jobs/; Jeffrey A. Eisenach, "The Role of Independent Contractors in the U.S. Economy" (working paper, Navigant Economics, December 2010), http://www .aei.org/files/2012/08/22/-the-role-of-independent-contractors-in-the -us-economy_123302207143.pdf.

72 Erin Hatton, *The Temp Economy: From Kelly Girls to Permatemps in Postwar America* (Philadelphia: Temple University Press, 2011); Erin Hatton, "The Rise of the Permanent Temp Economy," *New York Times*, January 28, 2013, SR, 3; Harris Freeman and George Gonos, "Regulating the Employment Sharks: Reconceptualizing the Legal Status of the Commercial Temp Agency," *WorkingUSA: The Journal of Labor and Society* 8 (March 2005): 297–298, http://www2.potsdam.edu/gonosgc/Regulating.pdf.

73 The ad is quoted in Hatton, *The Temp Economy*, 50. Also see *Michael* Grabell, "The Expendables," Propublica, June 27, 2013, http://www.propublica.org /article/the-expendables-how-the-temps-who-power-corporate-giants -are-getting-crushe.

74 Bethany Moreton, *To Serve God and Walmart: The Making of Christian Free Enterprise* (Cambridge, Mass.: Harvard University Press, 2010); Nelson Lichtenstein, *Wal-Mart: The Face of Twenty-First-Century Capitalism* (New York: New Press, 2006); Hatton, *The Temp Economy*, 1.

75 Charles Wilbanks, "Temp Work Raises Long-Term Questions for Economy," *CBS Moneywatch*, March 7, 2013, http://www.cbsnews.com/news/temp-work-raises-long-term-questions-for-economy/; Steve King, "The Two Sides of the Temp Economy," *Small Business Labs*, February 7, 2013, http://www.smallbizlabs.com/2013/02/the-two-sides-of-the-temp-economy.html; Stephanie Coontz, "How Can We Help Men? By Helping Women," *New York Times*, January 11, 2013, http://www.nytimes.com/2014/01/12/opinion/sunday/how-can-we-help-men-by-helping-women.html.

76 Robert Lynd and Helen Lynd, *Middletown: A Study in American Culture* (New York: Harcourt, Brace and World, 1929).

77 Ibid.

78 Theodore Caplow, Bruce A. Chadwick, Howard M. Bahr, and Reuben Hill, *Middletown Families* (Minneapolis: University of Minnesota Press, 1982); Ellen Kay Trimberger, "Middletown Revisited: From Class Politics to Politics of the Family," *Theory and Society* 13, no. 2 (March 1984): 239–247.

79 Robert J. Samuelson, "Murray's 'Coming Apart' Misses Our History," *Washington Post*, February 24, 2012, http://www.washingtonpost.com/opinions/the-real-class-warfare/2012/02/24/gIQALdFdcR_story.html.

80 Even in the most advanced factories, pay in manufacturing currently ranges from $15 to 19 an hour, or just $30,000 to $38,000 a year. Harold Meyerson, "A New Vision for America: Restoring a Country That Makes Things," *Washington Post*, February 9, 2012, http://www.washingtonpost.com/opinions/a-new-vision-for-america-restoring-a-country-that-makes-things/2012/01/25/gIQAETCRRQ_story.html. Paul Krugman, "Money and Morals," *New York Times*, February 9, 2012, http://www.nytimes.com/2012/02/10/opinion/krugman-money-and-morals.html. It is important to note, however, that nonmarital births among whites have been rising since 1925, suggesting that economics alone are not driving this development. Paula England, Lawrence L. Wu, and Emily Fitzgibbons Shafer, "Cohort Trends in Premarital First Births: What Roles for the Retreat from Marriage?," *Demography* 50 (2013): 2075–2104.

81 Jackson Lears, "The 20th-Century Fate of the Craft Ideal," audio lecture, Art Institute of Chicago, January 14, 2010, http://www.artic.edu/aic/resources/resource/993?search_id=1&index=0; Robert Pirsi, *Zen and the Art of Motorcycle Maintenance* (New York: William Morrow, 1974).

82 Robert Kanigel, *The One Best Way: Frederick Winslow Taylor and the Enigma of Efficiency* (New York: Viking, 1997).

83 Hugo Münsterberg, *Psychology and Industrial Efficiency* (Boston: Houghton Mifflin, 1913); Richard Bendix, *Work and Authority in Industry* (New Brunswick: Transaction Publishers, 2001).

84 James Truslow Adams, *The Epic of America* (Boston: Little, Brown, 1931), xx.

85 Jim Cullen, *The American Dream: A Short History of an Idea That Shaped a Nation* (New York: Oxford University Press, 2003); Andrew Delbanco, *The Real American Dream: A Meditation on Hope* (Cambridge, Mass.: Harvard University Press, 1999); Kathryn Hume, *American Dream, American Nightmare: Fiction Since 1960* (Urbana: University of Illinois Press, 2000); Elizabeth Long, *The American Dream and the Popular Novel* (Boston: Routledge & K. Paul, 1985).

   A preoccupation with upward mobility remains intense. A recent source of concern can be seen in research findings that suggest that Americans enjoy less economic mobility than their peers in Canada and much of Western Europe. See Jason DeParle, "Harder for Americans to Rise from Lower Rungs," *New York Times*, January 4, 2012, A1, http://www.nytimes.com/2012/01/05/us/harder-for-americans-to-rise-from-lower-rungs.html.

86 Henry James, ed., *The Letters of William James* (New York: Cosimo, 2008), 260.

87 Emerson quoted in Scott A. Sandage, *Born Losers: A History of Failure in America* (Cambridge, Mass.: Harvard University Press, 2005), 46. Also see Judith Hilkey, *Character Is Capital: Success Manuals and Manhood in Gilded Age America* (Chapel Hill: University of North Carolina Press, 1997), 78.

88 Edward J. Balleisen, *Navigating Failure: Bankruptcy and Commercial Society in Antebellum America* (Chapel Hill: University of North Carolina Press, 2001); Bruce H. Mann, *Republic of Debtors: Bankruptcy in the Age of American Independence* (Cambridge, Mass.: Harvard University Press, 2002); Sandage, *Born Losers*, 92.

89 Sandage, *Born Losers*, 46.

90 Ibid., 92.

91 Toby Ditz, "Shipwrecked; or, Masculinity Imperiled: Mercantile Representations of Failure and the Gendered Self in Eighteenth-Century Philadelphia," *Journal of American History* 81, no.1 (June 1994): 51–80; Andrew M. Schocket, "Revolution #10?: IOUs and Debts No Honest Man Could Pay in the Early Republic," *Reviews in American History* 34 (2006): 315–323.

92 Balleisen, *Navigating Failure*.

93 Ibid., 77, 117, 118, 184.

94 Sandage, *Born Losers,* 142, 146, 151.

95 Michelle J. White, "Bankruptcy: Past Puzzles, Recent Reforms, and the Mortgage Crisis" (Working Paper 14549, National Bureau of Economic Research, Cambridge, Mass., December 2008), http://www.nber.org /papers/w14549.pdf; Elizabeth Warren and Amelia Warren Tyazi, *The Two-Income Trap: Why Middle-Class Mothers and Fathers Are Going Bro*ke (New York: Basic Books, 2003); Katherine Newman, *Falling from Grace: Downward Mobility in the Age of Affluence* (Cambridge, Mass.: Harvard University Press 1997); Roland Gary Jones, Esq., *They Went Broke?! Bankruptcies and Money Disasters of the Rich & Famous* (New York: Gramercy Books, 1999.); Les B. Whitbeck, Ronald L. Simons Conger, Rand D. Conger, Frederick O. Lorenz, Shirley Huck, and Glenn H. Elder, "Family Economic Hardship, Parental Support, and Adolescent Self-Esteem," *Social Psychology Quarterly* 54 (December 1991): 353–363; Christopher G. Davis and Janet Mantler, "The Consequences of Financial Stress for Individuals, Families, and Society," Ottawa. Centre for Research on Stress, Coping, and Well-being, Carleton University, March 31, 2004, http://http-server .carleton.ca/~jmantler/pdfs/financial%20distress%20DSI.pdf.

96 Charles P. Alexander, "The New Economy," *Time,* May 30, 1983; Clayton M. Christensen, *The Innovator's Dilemma: The Revolutionary Book That Will Change the Way You Do Business* (Cambridge, Mass.: Harvard Business School Press, 1997).

97 Jacob Hacker, *The Great Risk Shift* (New York: Oxford University Press, 2006); Jill Lepore, "Away from My Desk: The Office from Beginning to End," *New Yorker,* May 12, 2014, http://www.newyorker.com/arts/critics /books/2014/05/12/140512crbo_books_lepore?currentPage=all.

98 Hacker, *Great Risk Shift;* Hope Yen, "4 in 5 in USA Face Near-Poverty, No Work," *USAToday,* July 28, 2013, http://www.usatoday.com/story/money /business/2013/07/28/americans-poverty-no-work/2594203/; Mark R. Rank, "Poverty in America is Mainstream," *New York Times,* SR 12, http://opinion ator.blogs.nytimes.com/2013/11/02/poverty-in-america-is-mainstream/? _php=true&_type=blogs&_r=0; Lepore, "Away from My Desk."

99 Arthur Miller, "Tragedy and the Common Man," in *The Theater Essays of Arthur Miller,* ed. Robert A. Martin and Steven R. Centola (New York: Viking Press, 1978), 3–7. Also see Bert Cardullo, "*Death of a Salesman* and Death of a Salesman: The Swollen Legacy of Arthur Miller," *Columbia Journal of*

American Studies, n.d., accessed October 10, 2014, http://www.columbia
.edu/cu/cjas/june_miller.html.

100 In 2011, only 36 percent of Americans believed that "success in life is determined by outside forces," reports the Pew Global Attitudes survey. In
France and Germany, the responses were 57 and 72 percent, respectively.
Samuelson, "Murray's 'Coming Apart' Misses Our History."

7. THE ANGST OF ADULTHOOD

1 George M. Beard quoted in his *American Nervousness: Its Causes and
Consequences* (New York: Putnam, 1881), vii–viii. Also see David Burnham,
"American Exceptionalism in a Perhaps Unexpected Arena," *Reviews in
American History* 40, no, 4 (December 2012): 646–650; Tom Lutz,
American Nervousness 1903: An Anecdotal History (Ithaca, N.Y.: Cornell
University Press. 1991); David G. Schuster, *Neurasthenic Nation: America's
Search for Health, Happiness, and Comfort, 1869–1920* (New Brunswick,
N.J.: Rutgers University Press, 2011); Elaine Showalter, "Our Age of
Anxiety," *Chronicle of Higher Education*, April 8, 2013, https://chronicle
.com/article/Our-Age-of-Anxiety/138255/.

2 Kay Heath, *Aging by the Book: The Emergence of Midlife in Victorian
Britain* (Albany: State University of New York Press, 2009); Stanley
Brandes, *Forty: The Age and the Symbol* (Knoxville: University of Tennessee
Press, 1985); Linda A. Westervelt, *Beyond Innocence, or the Altersroman in
Modern Fiction* (Columbia: University of Missouri Press, 1997); Jan
Freeman, "Don't Be Afraid of Angst," *Pittsburgh Post-Gazette*, July 13,
2008, G–5.

3 Elliott Jaques, "Death and the Midlife Crisis," *International Journal of
Psychoanalysis* 46 (1965): 502–513; Gail Sheehy, *Passages: Predictable
Crises of Adult Life* (New York: EP Dutton, 1976); Margie Lachman, ed.,
Handbook of Midlife Development (New York: John Wiley & Sons, 2001);
Sally Squires, "Midlife without a Crisis," *Washington Post*, April 19, 1999,
Z20; A. Kruger, The Mid-Life Transition: Crisis or Chimera? *Psychological
Reports* 75 (1994): 1299–1305; Margie Lachman, "Development in
Midlife," *Annual Review of Psychology* 55 (2004): 305–331; Elaine
Wethington, "Expecting Stress: Americans and the Midlife Crisis"
Motivation and Emotion 24 (2000): 85–103; Susan Krauss Whitbourne,
J. R. Sneed, and A. Sayer, "Psychosocial Development from College

through Midlife: A 34-Year Sequential Study," *Developmental Psychology* 45 (2009): 1328–1340.

4 Judith Viorst, *Necessary Losses: The Loves, Illusions, Dependencies, and Impossible Expectations That All of Us Have to Give Up in Order to Grow* (New York: Simon & Schuster, 1986).

5 Ibid., 15–33.

6 Paul C. Rosenblatt. *Bitter, Bitter Tears: Nineteenth-Century Diarists and Twentieth-Century Grief Theories* (Minneapolis: University of Minnesota Press, 1983), 21.

7 Ibid., 18.

8 Peter Balaam, *Misery's Mathematics: Mourning, Compensation, and Reality in Antebellum American Literature* (New York: Routledge, 2009); Peter Gregg Slater, *Children in the New England Mind in Death and in Life* (Hamden, Conn.: Archon Books. 1977); David E. Stannard, *The Puritan Way of Death* (Oxford: Oxford University Press, 1977).

9 Ann Douglas, *The Feminization of American Culture* (New York: Alfred A. Knopf, 1977), 200–226.

10 Freud to Ludwig Binswanger, quoted in John Bowlby, *Loss: Sadness and Depression* (New York: Basic Books, 1980), 23.

11 The quotations are from Karen Haltunnen, *Confidence Men and Painted Women: A Study of Middle-Class Culture in America, 1830–1870* (New Haven, Conn.: Yale University Press, 1982), 130, 131.

12 Quoted in Balaam, *Misery's Mathematics*, 4.

13 Haltunnen, *Confidence Men and Painted Women*, 124–152.

14 Sigmund Freud, "Mourning and Melancholia" (1917), *The Standard Edition of the Complete Psychological Works of Sigmund Freud*, ed. James Strachey, Anna Freud, Carrie Lee Rothgeb, and Angela Richards (London: Hogarth Press, [1953–1974]), 14:243–258.

15 William Brisbande quoted in Rosenblatt, *Bitter, Bitter Tears*, 115.

16 Ibid., 41–42.

17 Paul C. Rosenblatt and Beverly R. Wallace, *African American Grief* (New York: Taylor & Francis, 2005).

18 Stannard, *The Puritan Way of Death;* Nicholas Marshall, "The Great Exaggeration: Death and the Civil War," *Journal of the Civil War Era* 4 (March 2014), 3–27; and Nicholas Marshall, "The Civil War Death Toll, Reconsidered," *New York Times,* Opinionator blog, April 15, 2014, http://

opinionator.blogs.nytimes.com/2014/04/15/the-civil-war-death-toll
-reconsidered/.

19 Carroll Smith-Rosenberg, *Disorderly Conduct: Visions of Gender in Victorian America* (New York: A.A. Knopf, 1985), 197–216.

20 Viorst, *Necessary Losses*. Challenging Elisabeth Kubler-Ross's five stages of grieving model, George A. Bonanno, *The Other Side of Sadness: What the New Science of Bereavement Tells Us about Life after Loss* (New York: Basic Books, 2009), examines contrasting ways that various cultures find meaning in loss and cope with the bereavement process.

21 David Cannadine, "War and Death, Grief and Mourning in Modern Britain," in *Mirrors of Mortality: Studies in the Social History of Death*, ed. Joachim Whaley (New York: St. Martin's Press, 1981), 187–242. On spiritualism, see Robert S. Cox, *Body and Soul: A Sympathetic History of American Spiritualism* (Charlottesville: University Press of Virginia, 2003).

22 On twentieth-century attitudes toward death, see Ernest Becker, *The Denial of Death* (New York: The Free Press, 1974).

23 Herman Melville, *The Complete Stories of Herman Melville*, ed. Jay Leyda (New York: Random House, 1949), 56.

24 Thomas Giloviqh and Victoria Husted Medvec, "The Experience of Regret: What, When, and Why," *Psychological Review* 102, no. 2 (1995): 379–395, esp. 392, http://psych.cornell.edu/sites/default/files/Gilo_%26_Medvec_95.pdf.

25 Brian W. Ward and Jeannine S. Schiller, "Prevalence of Multiple Chronic Conditions among US Adults: Estimates from the National Health Interview Survey, 2010," *Preventing Chronic Disease*, 10 (2013), available at http://dx.doi.org/10.5888/pcd10.120203; Ward and Schiller, "Multiple Chronic Conditions among US Adults: A 2012 Update," *Preventing Chronic Disease*, 11 (2014), available at: http://www.cdc.gov/pcd/issues/2014/13_0389.htm.

26 Melanie Thernstrom, *The Pain Chronicles: Cures, Myths, Mysteries, Prayers, Diaries, Brain Scans, Healing and the Science of Suffering* (New York: Farrar, Strauss, 2010).

27 Ibid., 96.

28 Ibid., 72.

29 Ibid., 87.

30 Eric Caplan, *Mind Games: American Culture and the Birth of Psychotherapy* (Berkeley: University of California Press, 2001).

31 Thernstrom, *The Pain Chronicles*.

32 Rick Nauert, "Multiple Origins for Adult Anxiety," *PsychCentral*, February 12, 2007, available at http://psychcentral.com/news/page/6?Match= 1&s=social+phobia.

33 Cary L. Cooper and Philip J. Dewe, *Stress: A Brief History* (Malden, Mass.: Wiley-Blackwell, 2004).

34 Ibid.

35 Susan McGinley, "Daily Stress in Midlife: Charting the Ebb and Flow of People's Lives," 1997, available at http://ag.arizona.edu/pubs/general /resrpt1997/stress_in_midlife.html.

36 M. Friedman and R. H. Rosenman, "Association of Specific Overt Behavior Pattern with Blood and Cardiovascular Findings: Blood Cholesterol Level, Blood Clotting Time, Incidence of Arcus Senilis, and Clinical Coronary Artery Disease," *Journal of the American Medical Association* 169 (1959): 1286– 1296. Richard S. Lazarus, *Psychological Stress and the Coping Process* (New York: McGraw-Hill, 1966).

37 Orville Gilbert Brim, Carol D. Ryff, and Ronald C. Kessler, *How Healthy Are We? A National Study of Well-Being at Midlife* (Chicago: University of Chicago Press, 2005).

38 Carl Zisowitz Stearns and Peter N. Stearns, *Anger: The Struggle of Emotional Control in America's History* (Chicago: University of Chicago Press, 1986), 1–17. Somewhat similar arguments, on a more expansive historical canvas, can be found in Norbert Elias, *The Civilizing Process: The History of Manners* (New York: Urizen. 1978), and Steven Pinker, *The Better Angels of Our Nature: Why Violence Has Declined* (New York: Penguin, 2011).

39 Stearns and Stearns, *Anger*, 18–68.

40 Ibid., 69–109, 109–210.

41 Ibid., 211–240; Carol Tavris, *Anger: The Misunderstood Emotion*, rev. ed. (New York: Touchstone, 1989), 17–26, 286–319.

42 Tavris, *Anger*, 27–285; Sandra P. Thomas, "Anger: The Mismanaged Emotion," *Dermatology Nursing* 15 (2003): 51–57, available at http://www .medscape.com/viewarticle/460619_9; Daniel Goleman, *Emotional Intelligence: Why It Can Matter More Than IQ* (New York: Bantam, 2005); Daniel Goleman, *Social Intelligence: The New Science of Human Relationships* (New York: Bantam, 2007). On T-groups and sensitivity training, see Daniel

Engber, "Sensitivity Training 101," *Slate,* June 27, 2006, http://www.slate.com/articles/news_and_politics/explainer/2006/06/sensitivity_training_101.html.

43 On the incidence of drinking, see "Alcohol and Public Health: Data, Trends, and Maps," Centers for Disease Control and Prevention, March 24, 2014, available at http://www.cdc.gov/alcohol/data-stats.htm; David J. Hanson, "Alcoholic Beverage Consumption in the U.S.: Patterns and Trends," available at http://www2.potsdam.edu/alcohol/Controversies/1116895242.html#.U2zzpoGK9ow; "Apparent Per Capita Alcohol Consumption: National, State, and Regional Trends, 1977–2012," National Institute on Alcohol Abuse and Alcoholism, Division of Epidemiology and Prevention Research, Surveillance Report No. 98, available at http://pubs.niaaa.nih.gov/publications/surveillance98/CONS12.htm.

For American writers and drinking, see O.M. Dardis, *The Thirsty Muse: Alcohol and the American Writer* (New York: Ticknor & Fields, 1989); Donald W. Goodwin, *Alcohol and the Writer* (Kansas City: Andrews and McMeel, 1988); Olivia Laing, *The Trip to Echo Spring: On Writers and Drinking* (New York: Picador, 2014).

On drinking's physiological and psychological effects, see Amitava Dasgupta, *The Science of Drinking* (Plymouth, Eng.: Rowman & Littlefield Publishers, 2012); Joshua Gowin, "Your Brain on Alcohol," *Psychology Today,* June 18, 2010, http://www.psychologytoday.com/blog/you-illuminated/201006/your-brain-alcohol; Kevin Kampworth, "Why Do We Get Emotional When We Drink?," *Mentalfloss.com,* April 10, 2013, http://mentalfloss.com/article/49963/why-do-we-get-emotional-when-we-drink.

44 Lori Rotskoff, *Love on the Rocks: Men, Women, and Alcohol in Postwar America* (Chapel Hill: University of North Carolina Press, 2002); Michael C. Gerald, "Drugs and Alcohol Go to Hollywood," *Pharmacy in History* 48, no. 3 (2006): 116–138.

45 Dean Albertson, "Puritan Liquor in the Planting of New England," *New England Quarterly* 23, no. 4 (December 1950): 477–490, esp. 479; Daniel Okrent, *Last Call: The Rise and Fall of Prohibition* (New York: Scribner, 2010), 7–8.

46 *Autobiography of Rev. James B. Finley* (Bedford, Mass.: Applewood Books, 2009), 248. This book was originally published in 1853.

47 Peter C. Mancall, "The Art of Getting Drunk in Massachusetts," *Reviews in American History* 24, no. 3 (September 1996): 383–388; David J. Hanson, "Abstaining from Alcohol: Abstainers, Teetotalers, or Non-Drinkers," Alcohol Problems & Solutions, 2014, available at http://www2.potsdam .edu/alcohol/Controversies/1110387548.html#.VDe7ffldVRY. http:// www2.potsdam.edu/alcohol/Controversies/1110387548.html#. U21SBYGK_Po; U. S. Department of Health and Human Services, Substance Abuse and Mental Health Administration, National Household Survey on Drug Abuse, 1997 (Washington, D.C.: DHHS, 1998); J. W. Wright, ed., *The New York Times 2000 Almanac* (New York: Penguin, 1999), 398. For men, binge drinking means consuming five or more drinks at a time, and for women, four or more drinks. "Problem drinkers" are those men who partake of fifteen or more drinks a week and women who have eight or more. Reverend Leonard Bacon, quoted in Mark Edward Lender and James Kirby Martin, *Drinking in America: A History*, rev. ed. (New York: Free Press, 1987), 73.

48 Lender and Martin, *Drinking in America;* Okrent, *Last Call.*

49 "Alcohol Use and Health," Centers for Disease Control and Prevention, August 19, 2014, available at, http://www.cdc.gov/alcohol/fact-sheets /alcohol-use.htm.

50 "Alcohol and Public Health: Data, Trends, and Maps"; Hanson, "Alcoholic Beverage Consumption in the U.S."

51 George Eliot, *Middlemarch: A Study of Provincial Life,* in *Works of George Eliot,* ed. John Walter Cross (Edinburgh: William Blackwood and Sons, 1901), 7:602.

EPILOGUE

1 Henry James, "The Middle Years," *Scribner's Magazine* 13, no. 5 (May 1893): 620; James, *The Ambassadors* (New York: Harper & Brothers, 1903), 149.

2 Only about 5 percent of contemporary adults believe that they will die prior to the age of sixty-five. However, altogether, about a quarter of deaths occur among those younger than the age of sixty-five. For those under the age of forty-five, the most likely cause of death are accidents and homi- cides; for those older, cancer and heart disease. Between 1979 and 2004, the proportion of those living to age seventy-five rose from 23 percent to 64 percent; and to age eighty-five, from 6 percent to 35 percent. See "Amid

Improving Life Expectancy Rates, Risk of Premature Death is Still Significant for Americans," 2007, http://us.milliman.com/insight/re search/insurance/pdfs/The-changing-face-of-mortality-risk-in-the -United-States/; *The Burden of Cancer in American Adults*, 2005, http:// www.pfizer.com/files/products/The_Burden_of_Cancer_in _American_Adults.pdf, 2–3, 6.

3 A late 2013 Gallup poll reported that 51 percent of adults were thriving, 45 percent said they were struggling, and 4 percent were suffering. See http:// www.gallup.com/poll/wellbeing.aspx.

    According to a 2006 Pew study, 34 percent of adults said they were very happy, half said pretty happy, and 15 percent not too happy. Nearly half of those with a family income over $100,000 were very happy compared to 24 percent of those with family income less than $30,000. See http://www.pew socialtrends.org/2006/02/13/are-we-happy-yet/.

    For statistics on drinking, see National Institute on Alcohol Abuse and Alcoholism, "Alcohol Facts and Statistics," July 2014, http://www.niaaa .nih.gov/alcohol-health/overview-alcohol-consumption/alcohol -facts-and-statistics. For statistics on illicit drug use, see Results from the 2011 National Survey on Drug Use and Health: Summary of National Findings, http://www.samhsa.gov/data/nsduh/2k11results/nsduhresults2011.pdf.

4 In the post–World War II era, these age-related leisure activities included bridge, canasta, and mahjong, and for men, golf and various hobbies.

5 Arthur C. Brooks, "A Formula for Happiness," *New York Times*, December 15, 2013, SR1, http://www.nytimes.com/2013/12/15/opinion/sunday/a-formula -for-happiness.html.

6 F. Scott Fitzgerald, *The Crack-Up*, ed. Edmund Wilson (New York: New Directions Books, 1993), 84.

P.1. Thomas Cole, *The Voyage of Life: Manhood,* 1842. Oil on canvas. Ailsa Mellon Bruce Fund. Accession number 1971.16.3. Courtesy of the National Gallery of Art.

P.2. *The Life and age of woman, stages of woman's life from the cradle to the grave.* New York: James Baillie, c. 1848. Library of Congress Prints and Photographs Division [LC-DIG-ppmsca-12817].

P.3. *The Life and age of man, stages of man's life from the cradle to the grave.* New York: James Baillie, c. 1848. Library of Congress Prints and Photographs Division [LC-DIG-ppmsca-12818].

1.1. Georgetown University graduation, June 9, 1924. Library of Congress Prints and Photographs Division [LC-DIG-npcc-11628].

1.2. Doing the twist in the baggage car, 1962. Herman Hiller, photographer. New York World-Telegram and the Sun Newspaper Photograph Collection, Library of Congress Prints and Photographs Division [LC-USZ62–126079].

1.3. Photograph taken near the Woodstock music festival, August 18, 1969. Ric Manning, photographer. With permission of the photographer under a Creative Commons attribution license.

2.1. Anne Pitts, "Valentine," 1806. From the Collection of Nancy Rosin. Hoag Levins, photographer. With permission of Nancy Rosin and Hoag Levins.

2.2. "Love's Reward," c. 1908. Library of Congress Prints and Photographs Division [LC-USZ62–59208].

2.3. Teenage couple embrace on the bank of the Frio Canyon River, 1973. Records of the Environmental Protection Agency, 1944–2006, National Archives and Records Administration [ARC identifier: 708].

3.1. John Lewis Krimmel, *Country Wedding, Bishop White Officiating,* 1814. Oil on canvas. Accession number 1842.2.1. Courtesy of the Pennsylvania Academy of the Fine Arts

3.2. "The Wedding March," c. 1897. Library of Congress Prints and Photographs Division [LC-USZ62–73408].

3.3. "She Was Led to the Altar," c. 1908. Library of Congress Prints and Photographs Division [LC-USZ62–50397].

3.4. A couple leaving the altar, 2004. David Ball, photographer. With permission of the photographer under a GNU Free Documentation License.

3.5. Recently married couples leaving City Hall in Seattle on the first day of same-sex marriage in Washington State, 2012. Dennis Bratland, photographer. With permission of the photographer under a Creative Commons attribution license.

4.1. "Divorce, the Lesser Evil," February 7, 1900. Udo J. Keppler, artist. Library of Congress Prints and Photographs Division [LC-DIG-ppmsca-25393].

4.2. Cover of sheet music for "Divorced," 1893. Library of Congress Music Division [LC Classification 56/3783].

5.1. Portrait of the Smith Family, c. 1807. Attributed to Captain James Smith (Scottish-born American artist, 1762–1818). Accession No. 2011.100.1, image # R2011–2621. Abby Aldrich Rockefeller Folk Art Museum, the Colonial Williamsburg Foundation. Museum Purchase.

5.2. Family of slaves at the Gaines' house, 1861 or 1862. G. H. (George Harper) Houghton, photographer. Library of Congress Prints and Photographs Division [LC-USZC4–4575].

5.3. Employed miner's family, Scott's Run, West Virginia, 1937. Lewis Hine, photographer. Still Picture Records Section, Special Media Services Division, National Archives and Records Administration [Local Identifier: 69-RP-107].

5.4. Homecoming, 2006. Cassandra Locke, photographer. Air Force News [ID 123030973].

6.1. John Neagle, *Pat Lyon at the Forge*, 1826–1827. Oil on canvas. Accession number 1975.806. Courtesy of the Museum of Fine Arts, Boston. Photograph © 2015 Museum of Fine Arts, Boston.

6.2. Miners after work, c. 1915–1925. Detroit Publishing Company Photograph Collection, Library of Congress Prints and Photographs Division, [LC-D420–2352].

6.3. Commuters playing bridge on train to New York City, 1941. John Collier, photographer. Courtesy of the Library of Congress Prints and Photographs Division [LC-USF34–080917-E].

6.4. Woman working on a Vengeance dive bomber, 1942. Alfred T. Palmer, photographer. Library of Congress Prints and Photographs Division [LC-DIG-fsac-1a35371].

7.1. Charles Willson Peale, *Rachel Weeping*, 1772, enlarged 1776; retouched 1818. Oil on canvas. Gift of the Barra Foundation, Inc. Courtesy of the Philadelphia Museum of Art.

7.2. Widow and brother of the deceased grieving, Breathitt County, near Jackson, Kentucky, 1940. Marion Post Wolcott, photographer. Library of Congress Prints and Photographs Division [LC-USF33- 031073-M5].

Index